Constructions of Disorder

Constructions of Disorder

Meaning-Making Frameworks for Psychotherapy

Edited by
Robert A. Neimeyer and
Jonathan D. Raskin

American Psychological Association • Washington, DC

Published by
American Psychological Association
750 First Street, NE
Washington, DC 20002

Copies may be ordered from
APA Order Department
P.O. Box 92984
Washington, DC 20090-2984

In the U.K., Europe, Africa, and the Middle East, copies may be ordered from
American Psychological Association
3 Henrietta Street
Covent Garden, London
WC2E 8LU England

Typeset in Goudy by World Composition Services, Inc., Sterling, VA

Printer: Hamilton Printing Co., Rensselaer, NY
Dust jacket designer: Naylor Design, Upper Marlboro, MD
Technical/Production Editor: Amy J. Clarke

Library of Congress Cataloging-in-Publication Data
Constructions of disorder : meaning-making frameworks for psychotherapy / edited by
    Robert A. Neimeyer and Jonathan D. Raskin.
        p.   cm.
    Includes bibliographical references and index.
    ISBN 1-55798-629-0 (hardcover : acid-free paper).
    1. Psychotherapy—Philosophy.   2. Postmodernism—Psychological aspects.
3. Constructivism (Psychology).   4. Personal construct therapy.   5. Storytelling—
Therapeutic use.   I. Neimeyer, Robert A., 1954–   .   II. Raskin, Jonathan D.
RC437.5.C647   2000
616.89'14'01—dc21   99-41598
                                                                                  CIP

British Library Cataloguing-in-Publication Data
A CIP record is available from the British Library.

Printed in the United States of America
First Edition

*To Vittorio Guidano (August 4, 1944–August 31, 1999),
whose untimely death deprives us
of an inspired mentor, trusted colleague, and irreplaceable friend.*

CONTENTS

CONTRIBUTORS

Lynne Angus, PhD, Department of Psychology, York University, North York, Toronto, Ontario, Canada

Giampiero Arciero, MD, Director of Research, Institute of Post-Rational Cognitive Therapy, Rome, Italy

Laura S. Brown, PhD, independent practice, Seattle, WA

Mark A. Celentana, MA, Department of Psychology, Miami University, Oxford, OH

Paul F. Cook, PhD, Department of Psychiatry, University of Colorado Health Sciences Center, Denver

Wendy Drewery, PhD, Department of Education Studies, University of Waikato, Hamilton, New Zealand

Bruce Ecker, MA, independent practice, Oakland, CA

Jay S. Efran, PhD, Department of Psychology, Temple University, Philadelphia, PA

April J. Faidley, PhD, Meridian Psychological Associates, Indianapolis, IN

Kenneth J. Gergen, PhD, Department of Psychology, Swarthmore College, Swarthmore, PA

Óscar F. Gonçalves, PhD, Department of Psychology, University of Minho, Braga, Portugal

Vittorio F. Guidano, MD, deceased, former Director, Institute of Post-Rational Cognitive Therapy, Rome, Italy

Laurel Hulley, MA, independent practice, Oakland, CA

Thomas J. Johnson, PhD, Department of Psychology, Indiana State University, Terre Haute

Reid E. Klion, PhD, Indiana University School of Medicine, and Roudebush Veterans Administration Medical Center, Indianapolis

Yifaht Korman, MA, Department of Psychology, York University, North York, Toronto, Ontario, Canada

Larry M. Leitner, PhD, Department of Psychology, Miami University, Oxford, OH

Adam M. Lewandowski, MA, Department of Psychology, State University of New York at New Paltz

Michael J. Mahoney, PhD, Department of Psychology, University of North Texas, Denton

Sheila McNamee, PhD, Department of Communication, University of New Hampshire, Durham

Gerald Monk, DipT, Department of Education Studies, University of Waikato, Hamilton, New Zealand

Robert A. Neimeyer, PhD, Department of Psychology, University of Memphis, Memphis, TN

David T. Pfenninger, PhD, Praxis, Indianapolis, IN

Jonathan D. Raskin, PhD, Department of Psychology, State University of New York at New Paltz

Sandra A. Rigazio-DiGilio, PhD, Marriage & Family Therapy Program, School of Family Studies, University of Connecticut, Storrs

John Winslade, DipT, Department of Education Studies, University of Waikato, Hamilton, New Zealand

PREFACE

With a new millennium come new possibilities, new directions, and—in the academic world—new projects! We are pleased to present you with the fruits of one such project that has intrigued the two of us for some time and that we trust will fascinate you as well. The object of our fascination is psychological disorder, more specifically psychological disorder in light of the burgeoning postmodern worldview. What we aimed for in the pages that follow is a different kind of book, one that challenges postmodern psychologists (i.e., all those calling themselves constructivists, constructionists, or narrative therapists) to address a thorny issue, namely, their conception of *psychological disorder* and its "treatment." Because most of us—as constructivists and constructionists—adopt a nonpathologizing orientation toward our clients, we typically avoid standard diagnostic nosology in our attempt to join in problem-dissolving conversations with our clients. We help clients reauthor their life narratives or experiment with new constructions of self and relationship that afford more hopeful possibilities for the future.

Recently, however, constructivists and constructionists have come under criticism for their failure to specify in what way their clients experience difficulties inviting psychotherapeutic attention and how this "read" of clients' positions gives form or direction to their interventions. Some critics, for example, take issue with the tendency of postmodern therapists to revel in their clients' individuality, to an extent that makes the therapy itself unsystematic, unresearchable, and ultimately unteachable. As constructivist therapists, we feel this charge is unfair. We suspect that constructivist and constructionist therapists make use of a variety of sophisticated but often implicit "theories" of disorder, whether applied at the level of the individual's meaning system or the broader social narratives in which these are embedded. Thus, we invite you to join us on a journey into the clinical theory and practice of a select group of constructivist and constructionist therapists. In this volume, these scholar–practitioners articulate how the major traditions of constructivist psychotherapy are used to conceptualize client difficulties and illustrate how some of these difficulties might be dealt with in the clinical context.

In organizing this volume, we asked contributors to provide (a) their view of psychological disorder, distress, or problems and (b) their typical ways of assessing and addressing these in therapy. Because constructivism is sometimes charged with being "long on theory and short on practice," we asked contributors to illustrate their work with various case examples. We recognize that many models of constructivist–constructionist–narrative therapy operate with a highly differentiated set of diagnostic dimensions or descriptive categories (e.g., concerning clients' affective style, core organizing principles, tasks, patterns of attachment, dominant narratives). Furthermore, we acknowledge that no brief chapter can do justice to the subtlety of a therapy in use. But we believe that a serious discussion of the concept of *disorder* as it implicitly or explicitly guides constructivist and constructionist practice will help advance the postmodern conversation and sharpen its practical implications for clinicians, students, other professionals, and perhaps even insurance companies.

Regardless of who you are or why you have picked up this book, we hope that you will find what follows helpful in explicating constructionist and constructivist perspectives on disorder and psychotherapy. It is our hope that this volume will usefully perturb traditional thinking about disorder and prompt further creative conceptualizations of diagnosis and psychotherapy as psychology moves into the dawn of a new postmodern millennium.

ACKNOWLEDGMENTS

In a sense, this book began as a series of oral conversations about the concept of disorder in constructivist psychotherapy and has ended up as something similar—only in written form! In the course of this transformation from talk to text, we have benefited from our discussions with innumerable friends, colleagues, students, and—most importantly—clients, many of whose contributions can be read between the lines of this volume. In particular, our ideas have been sharpened in conversations prior to and during our work on this project with Mike Acree, Adam Anderson, Tim Anderson, Luis Botella, Sara Bridges, Mark Burrell, Franz Epting, David Epston, Chuck Lawe, Heidi Levitt, Kenneth Sewell, Alan Stewart, Stanton Wortham, and Kayoko Yokoyama. Of course, our work has also been greatly influenced by many of the authors of the chapters to follow. In addition, we appreciate the understanding of our spouses, Kathy and Shay, and our children, Eric, Michael, and Ari, as we have spent more hours than we anticipated interacting with the computer rather than with them. Without their patience (and willingness to forego their own access to email and electronic games!), this project could never have been realized. Furthermore, Jon would like to acknowledge his parents, Paula and Sherman, and his brother, Daniel. Finally, we are indebted to Margaret Schlegel at the American Psychological Association Books Department for sharing our vision of psychotherapy as a deep engagement with the personal and social meanings that shape human life. Her delicate touch was critical to orchestrating the sort of developmental feedback regarding the manuscript that prompted each chapter toward greater clarity and coherence. We hope that the resulting volume offers clinical readers several novel constructions of disorder and illustrates some useful meaning-making frameworks for psychotherapy.

I

(DE)CONSTRUCTING DISORDER

1

ON PRACTICING POSTMODERN THERAPY IN MODERN TIMES

ROBERT A. NEIMEYER AND JONATHAN D. RASKIN

In a sense, this book is an exercise in paradox. On the one hand, constructivist, social constructionist, and narrative approaches to psychotherapy—with their emphasis on the inevitably personal and social processes of meaning making—characteristically avoid the stigmatizing implications of psychological "diagnosis" and the unequal power relationships between therapist and client that sustain this practice. On the other hand, all therapists, those from these "postmodern" perspectives included, regulate their engagement with clients on the basis of *some* conceptualization of human distress, whether implicit or explicit. We therefore decided to invite prominent theorists associated with this increasingly influential tradition to articulate the implicit order in their approach to clinical "disorder" and its implications for psychotherapeutic strategy and technique. The chapters that constitute this volume represent the creative responses of 24 leading constructivist, narrative, and social constructionist scholars and therapists to this invitation.

Our decision as editors to undertake this project stemmed from both personal and professional factors. On a personal level, we, like the other contributors to this book, live in two worlds: the world of constructivist theory and that of clinical and counseling practice. This uncomfortable dual membership in two rather different systems of discourse challenges us daily with such questions as "How can we conceptualize this client's struggles in a way that is therapeutically useful and still communicate intelligibly with colleagues and case managers?" and "How might postmodern principles be used to critique, and perhaps transform, a system of managed care that seems more responsive to economic than human values?" Although the implicit answers to such urgent questions vary from one author to another, an engagement with these issues pervades the remarks and chapters that follow.

On a professional level, a move toward greater specification of concepts and procedures seems especially appropriate at this time, when constructivists are being criticized for being "long on theory and short on practice" and postmodern approaches generally stand accused of "unspecifiability." Although along with most adherents to these traditions, we would resist the push toward simplistic manualization of method, we nonetheless believe that it is both possible and desirable to reflect on our own psychotherapeutic discourse and tease out its connection to our work with clients. The contributors to this volume share this perspective and, in varying degrees, in their respective chapters have attempted to "clear a space" for postmodern alternatives through critiquing traditional discourses of disorder and fleshing out alternatives that they view as more personally viable, contextually sensitive, and ethically defensible.

THE POSTMODERN FAMILY OF THERAPIES

Because not all readers feel equally "at home" with the elusive terminology of postmodern psychology, a few definitional remarks might be in order to set the stage for the chapters that follow. As we use it, the term *postmodern psychotherapy* encompasses a family of therapeutic approaches, including avowedly constructivist, social constructionist, and narrative theories. *Postmodernism* itself represents a much broader cultural trend, one with expressions in the fields of art, architecture, cultural anthropology, historical research, legal studies, literary criticism, linguistics, mass communication, semiotics, and contemporary philosophy, to name just a few. Needless to say, offering an adequate definition of this trend that would do justice to the transformations in each of these domains of intellectual life would be a daunting task.[1] But in general, postmodern participants in each of these

---

[1] Readers interested in gaining a foothold in this slippery terrain might wish to consult Anderson (1990) for a readable introduction to postmodern thought as well as the text by Appignanesi and Garratt (1995), which is postmodern in both its formatting and its content. For a more scholarly analysis of postmodernism and its relation to constructivist psychology, see Botella (1995).

areas radically question the assumptions that undergird the "establishment" positions they critique and often audaciously attempt to supplant.

Within the more delimited domain of psychotherapy, postmodern approaches constitute a "fuzzy set" of principles and practices that dissent in important ways from dominant trends in modern psychology, both theoretical and applied. What unites them is a shared "negative identity" deriving from their repudiation of traditional ontological assumptions (bearing on the nature of "reality") and epistemological frameworks (bearing on the nature of knowledge).[2] For modernists, reality is single, stable, and in principle knowable—qualities that modern psychologists attribute to the "self" as part of this same natural order. Accordingly, various modern psychotherapies have been viewed in terms of improving the client's "reality contact" by minimizing nonconscious cognitive distortions, training clients to work more efficiently toward their goals using approved methods, and encouraging them to express and actualize their "true" selves in the accepting medium of the therapeutic relationship. Much of this effort is legitimized through the discourse of scientific research, which is seen as measuring essential structures of the "healthy" personality, reliably diagnosing deviations from the norm, and empirically establishing the efficacy of preferred interventions designed to correct such disorders. For most of the 20th century, this objectivist orientation has held sway in the allied fields of psychotherapy and psychotherapy research, forming a common program endorsed by many proponents of psychodynamic, cognitive–behavioral, and humanistic psychology, despite their manifest differences.[3]

In contrast, postmodern approaches turn nearly every feature of this modern, objectivist orientation on its head. The fundamental faith in a single reality that provides a common point of orientation across people, cultures, and historical periods has been eroded and replaced by a recognition, or even a celebration, of the multiple realities conditioned by individual, social, and temporal factors. In this view, language—broadly defined to include all symbolic acts—represents a matrix of meaning that actually constitutes, rather than merely reflects, the reality in which one positions oneself. For psychologists adopting this perspective, the self also loses its standing as an essential, stable, and knowable point of departure or destination, becoming instead an elusive process, a contingent construction of persons-in-contexts that is amenable to reflexive deconstruction and reconstruction in the ever-changing relational medium of psychotherapy.

---

[2] A more extended discussion of the negative and positive identities of constructivist and social constructionist thought can be found in Neimeyer (1998), along with an argument for the complementarity of these two postmodern variations in providing a frame for counseling and psychotherapy.
[3] For a detailed consideration of the epistemological and strategic preferences of objectivist and constructivist psychotherapists, see Neimeyer and Mahoney (1995).

Although some psychotherapy theorists within this family of approaches find inspiration in recent research in cognitive science, developmental psychology, and psychopathology, others have drawn more heavily on literary and philosophical models and methods to generate fresh perspectives for a given client or for the field of psychotherapy as a whole.

As in most families, communication among the different constructivist, social constructionist, and narrative perspectives is marked by occasional dissent as well as agreement, with each cluster developing its own distinctive positive identity beyond its common negative identity established by a critique of modernist assumptions. In some cases, this contributes to disagreement about exactly what perspectives fit the general contours of postmodern thinking and which do not.[4] Even among self-identified postmodern perspectives, there are a diversity of emphases. Thus, *constructivists* tend to focus on experiential exploration of the tacit processes of self-construction, especially in the crucible of intimate attachment relationships. Constructivists emphasize how each individual creates personal representations of self and world as well as the ability of persons to transcend problematic constructions and construe things in wholly new ways.[5] As a consequence of this emphasis on individuality, broader systemic factors recede somewhat into the background, and deeply personal meanings and metaphors are given priority in psychotherapeutic approaches that share a constructivist vision. In contrast, *social constructionists*—who themselves constitute a complex and even contradictory camp[6]—differ from constructivists in their emphasis on the social as opposed to individual origins of meaning and in their concentration on discursive practices as opposed to individual cognitions as the objects of study, critique, and transformation. In social constructionism, what it means to be a person is determined by cultural ways of talking about and conceptualizing personhood. The account of personhood produced by this cultural

---

[4]For example, some readers might question our inclusion of feminist perspectives in a book on postmodern psychotherapies, arguing that feminists make recourse to an unreconstructed view of such terms as *power* as essential, immutable descriptions of (oppressive) social orders rather than alternative ways of "languaging" about an ambiguous reality. However, in keeping with our constructivist epistemology, we are more concerned with the viability of our classification (i.e., with its practical utility) than its validity in some absolute sense. Thus, it seems useful to stretch the fuzzy set of postmodern perspectives to include feminist approaches that critically deconstruct traditional (and often highly "gendered") conceptions of psychological health and disorder. In our view, this inclusion is further justified by the common tendency of feminist and (other) postmodern scholars to promote a relational view of self and an appreciation of the constitutive role of language in configuring social realities. For an accessible introduction to these issues, see Goldberger (1996).
[5]The idea that there are an infinite number of ways to construe events is the crux of *constructive alternativism*, the backbone of personal construct psychology (Kelly, 1955), the original clinical constructivist theory. Fransella (1996) offered a readable introduction to personal construct theory, and Mahoney (1991) provided a wider ranging summary of contemporary, post-Kellian constructivist thought.
[6]Burr (1995) provided an accessible and comprehensive overview of social constructionism in psychology, differentiating among the various theories and theorists in a clear and thorough way.

negotiation becomes the lived experience of members of that culture; thus, identity and disorder are socially constructed, and there are as many disorder constructions as there are cultures. It is of no surprise, then, that therapists allied with this perspective concentrate as much on cultural critique as individual change and are drawn toward systemic and collaborative models of therapy that attempt to "level the playing field" between client and counselor. Finally, *narrative theorists* combine features of both of these perspectives, positing that people are inveterate storytellers who attempt to organize their experience into coherent accounts. From this perspective, the story of one's life can become incoherent, oppressive, or circular in a way that requires a deconstructive reading of its limiting assumptions. Therapy, in this view, becomes a form of literary liberation, encouraging clients to resist the oppressive narratives that they have been offered by dominant forms of discourse and instead become the authors of more hopeful life stories.[7] In summary, each of these approaches develops its own variation on a postmodern theme, and each—constructivism, narrative psychology, and social constructionism—is exemplified by the chapters constituting the successive parts of this volume.[8]

POSTMODERNISM IN PRACTICE

The past 10 to 15 years have witnessed dramatic changes in the "behavioral health delivery system," especially in the United States but also increasingly abroad. Ironically, this has been the very period during which postmodern approaches to psychotherapy have come of age, many of which clearly dissent from the trends toward rationing of treatment, criteria of "medical necessity," and the documentation of simple observable and symptomatic improvement as criteria of therapeutic accountability. This tension between the demands of a belt-tightening system of managed care and its apparent resistance by many constructivist, social constructionist, and narrative therapists may lead some readers to question the practicality of a postmodern therapy in light of the economic realities imposed by living in a modern world.

It is not surprising that our own view of the viability of postmodern approaches in the current cultural context is more optimistic. On the one

---

[7]Comparative overviews of these three postmodern variations are provided by Cox and Lyddon (1997) and Neimeyer (1998).
[8]Constructivist work is best illustrated by the chapters in Parts II and III, narrative work in Part IV, and social constructionist perspectives in Part V. However, in keeping with the spirit of cross-fertilization that animates this field and to which we hope this volume contributes, authors in each of these sections draw on the integrative insights of the others to critique existing diagnostic practices and to reach toward more constructive alternatives.

hand, constructivist, social constructionist, and narrative therapies have frequently been on the cutting edge in the development of brief therapies that refuse to sacrifice subtlety of discourse for speed of delivery. As the chapters that follow amply demonstrate, postmodern perspectives are replete with practical strategies for fostering deep reflection on the part of both clients and therapists, techniques for experimenting with new solutions to old problems, and helpful heuristics for addressing contextual constraints on personal change. On the other hand, a number of the contributors to this volume provide a basis for ongoing criticism of managed care practices that diminish the prospects for meaningful long-term transformation in personal and social structures. Common to all of the authors in this volume is the conviction that change-producing psychotherapy, defined as the art of having profound and transformative conversations, is determined less by its length than by the skill and willingness of its practitioners to deeply engage the (inter)personal matrices of meaning by which their clients are constrained as a precondition to extending them.

In terms of the conceptualization of disorder—the primary focus of this volume—postmodern critics would argue that existing psychiatric nosologies radically underspecify how a practicing professional would actually intervene in a client's problems on the basis of a given diagnosis. In response, many of the authors of the chapters that follow attempt to close the gap between theory and practice by advancing various conceptualizations of distress that carry concrete implications for therapeutic strategies. For example, if critical emotional experiences are viewed as "underreferenced" in one's explicit account of life-shaping events, then this leads logically to the use of experientially engaging methods for "reentering" these incidents to extract new meaning from them. Alternatively, if one's life is dominated by a narrative of self that diminishes rather than enhances a sense of agency (construing oneself as "anorexic," "depressed," etc.), this suggests the utility of various forms of "protest" against the dominant account and means of publicizing an alternative story with relevant audiences. Thus, in spite of their diversity, postmodern therapists subscribe to the shared belief that constructing a more clinically useful account of psychological disorder requires a creative practice that respects, rather than neglects, the ambiguities and paradoxes of human existence.

Finally, postmodern practitioners must contend with the calls for accountability that have spawned a push for empirically validated treatments (EVTs). Although constructivist, narrative, and social constructionist therapists are as concerned as any with the quality of services they provide, they generally rest uneasily with the EVT trend. These misgivings are anchored in numerous concerns, among which are (a) the common preference of constructivists for more individualized criteria of change that focus on personal meanings as much as observable actions,[9] (b) an interest in qualitative research on processes of change more than "horse race" comparisons of preferred and nonpreferred theories,[10] (c) a distrust of reified clinical diagnostic categories as a basis for demonstrating treatment specificity,[11] and (d) suspicions about the political agenda of powerful groups attempting to marginalize other approaches in a bid to consolidate their hegemony over funding for both research and clinical practice.[12] Nonetheless, a number of constructivist and narrative therapies have been evaluated by controlled outcome studies, with promising results.[13] Several of the authors of the chapters that follow allude to supportive research and like these authors, we trust that the greater specification of practice principles contained in this volume will contribute to more clinically useful research in the future. We hope, however, that the richness of a postmodern perspective will not be lost in a push to manualize and operationalize these therapies in an effort to legitimize them.

In summary and in keeping with a spirit of postmodern pluralism, the authors of these chapters offer no single, authoritative solution to the problems of practicing in a modern milieu. In some respects, contributors to this volume position themselves as the "loyal opposition" to mainstream trends in the discipline: oppositional, because they contend against its more dehumanizing aspects, but loyal, because they generally strive to work within the system to secure services for their clients and an audience for their efforts. At times, this may require postmodern practitioners to be "multilingual," speaking first a language of medical necessity and measurable outcomes with managed care representatives, second a conceptually richer discourse with fellow psychotherapy theorists, and third a more metaphoric and personal

---

[9] Winter (1992) provided an extensive review of research on individualized assessment of change in personal constructs over the course of several theoretically distinctive therapies.

[10] Toukmanian and Rennie (1992) offered a trenchant analysis of the respective strengths of process and outcome research, with exemplary studies in each tradition.

[11] As a single example of the problems engendered by the preemptive focus on psychiatric diagnosis as a precondition to determining treatment efficacy, consider the case of constructivist therapy for sexual abuse, which meets rigorous criteria of efficacy in controlled outcome research. Despite the demonstrated effectiveness of such therapies in improving clients' symptomatic and social functioning (Alexander, Neimeyer, & Follette, 1991; Alexander, Neimeyer, Follette, Moore, & Harter, 1989; Harter & Neimeyer, 1995), such research fails to constitute evidence of an EVT simply because incestuously abused women do not constitute a defined diagnostic category within the *Diagnostic and Statistical Manual of Mental Disorders* (American Psychiatric Association, 1994). Constructivists would respond that assessments of efficacy might well be based on nonpsychiatric groupings of clients, such as those self-referred for help with a significant life problem, such as childhood sexual abuse.

[12] For an extended discussion of the disenfranchisement of many therapies by the EVT movement, see Bohart, O'Hara, and Leitner (1998).

[13] Greenberg, Elliott, and Lietaer (1994) offered the most authoritative review of studies on humanistic, experiential, and constructivist therapies, considering the substantial evidence for their efficacy, as well as additional research on their processes and mechanisms of change.

idiom with clients whose worlds of meaning they seek to enter. Although this use of apparently conflicting languages may seem disingenuous to some, from a postmodern worldview each of these languages is just that: a "local" and potentially useful mode of discourse that has both affordances and limitations. Thus, the drive toward a single, universally valid language of psychotherapy and psychopathology may be as self-defeating and hegemonic as attempting to coerce people of all nationalities and subcultures to speak only English.[14] From the more pluralistic perspective advocated here, psychotherapists are neither required nor forbidden to use any particular languages of disorder, singly or combined. That is, psychotherapy theorists and practitioners are not beholden to any particular discourse of disorder, even those that seem permanently embedded within clinical practice. Should any or all of the current languages of disorder and therapy be deemed outmoded, their meanings and uses can be renegotiated or, if preferred, can even be discarded wholesale.

ORGANIZATION OF THIS VOLUME

The chapters that follow represent the responses of 24 prominent postmodern psychotherapists to our editorial challenge, which asked them to explicate and, when appropriate, illustrate their conceptualization of psychological distress and its implications for psychotherapy. The resulting essays are as stylistically varied as their contributors, but generally they cluster into two groups. The first set explores various *constructions of disorder*, both traditional and nontraditional, in an attempt to carve out a space for more clinically fertile views of human problems. The second, although also concerned with conceptual issues, focuses more specifically on *disorders of construction* and offers concrete examples of how these are addressed in the counseling context. Thus, the reader can expect to find a smorgasbord of possibilities in the pages that follow, varying in their balance of scholarly reflection and direct practice relevance but all providing food for thought.

Jon Raskin and Adam Lewandowski begin this effort by discussing the shortcomings of relying on any singular, all-encompassing scheme for understanding disorder, such as the *DSM*. In particular, they focus on the importance of human involvement in developing systems for conceptualizing pathology. People devising any system of disorder are inevitably personally and socially embedded in the process as well as engaged in the cultural milieu that sets the process into motion. By revealing the sociopolitical underpinnings of the dominant *DSM* framework for psychological diagnosis,

---

[14]For an analysis of the limitations of "common language" proposals from a constructivist standpoint, see Neimeyer (1993).

these authors open up the possibility that quite different frameworks might be devised that could carry more useful and liberating possibilities for psychotherapy.

The next major section of the book comprises three chapters, each of which focuses on the dynamics of the construction of self and their possible disruption. Mike Mahoney establishes the theme for this section by exploring core ordering processes and their role in comprehending people's psychological struggles; in his view, disorder is a psychological *happening* more than an ontological *thing* because human beings are always attempting to order and organize their psychological experience. Psychotherapy, therefore, revolves around efforts to assist clients in establishing, or constructing, ordered understandings of self and experience. Bruce Ecker and Laurel Hulley extend this frame while moving in a somewhat different direction. They offer a novel synthesis of constructivist and psychodynamic theory that elucidates both the (conscious) "anti-symptom" and (unconscious) "pro-symptom" positions that characterize clinical disorder and describe a procedure of radical questioning that articulates and deconstructs the premises that lead the client to seek but simultaneously resist change. Illustrating their rapid, experientially vivid procedures with actual session transcripts, they demonstrate how exploring the deeper meaning of the symptom promotes prompt resolution of many presenting problems. Finally, Giampiero Arciero and Vittorio Guidano conceptualize the dialectical interplay between experience and explanation and explore the way in which these are woven together in personal self-narratives to achieve a sustainable sense of self. They then exemplify this theoretical perspective using an extended case study, featuring the use of a "moviola" method for reviewing and reframing critical episodes from the client's life so as to foster a more coherent identity. Together, these authors in this section argue for the importance of grasping the hidden rationality or personal logic of a client's self-construction and of prompting its development through exploration of emotionally vivid experiences that may be "underreferenced" in his or her explicit self-understanding.

The second section of the book offers three different perspectives on the assessment of personal meanings and their elaboration in psychotherapy. Jay Efran and Paul Cook begin by envisioning psychotherapy as an essentially linguistic endeavor, considering language as a fundamental form of social action. From this perspective, the therapist's task is to use language incisively to clarify patterns of self-deception and hypocrisy arising from a client's competing loyalties to different social groups. Thomas Johnson, David Pfenninger, and Reid Klion then discuss transitive diagnosis, a forward-looking approach to the assessment of personal structures of meaning anchored in Kelly's (1955) personal construct theory. Unlike more classificatory systems of diagnosis, their model emphasizes the personal and social processes of meaning construction; assessment and therapy entail working with clients in a process of elaborating the ever-evolving dimensions of meaning that clients use to comprehend their experiences. They discuss many of Kelly's early ideas on transitive diagnosis, integrating work from a variety of constructivist approaches that have developed since Kelly's day. Finally, Larry Leitner, April Faidley, and Mark Celentana describe the essentials of an experiential personal construct psychotherapy, which explains human disorder in terms of the attempt to protect oneself in various ways from the terror of permitting others to contact, and potentially invalidate, one's core sense of self. Therapy thereby becomes a moment-to-moment process of identifying and respectfully questioning clients' attempts to distance or defend themselves from risky but life-sustaining closeness to other people, including their therapists. A common feature of these three approaches is their view of the therapist as a figure who both elicits and gently perturbs the client's limiting assumptive frames through active participation in the therapeutic process.

The third section extends a theme hinted at in earlier chapters in the volume: life as a process of narrative construction. Bob Neimeyer opens this section by emphasizing the rather different, and in some respects conflicting, ways in which "the self" is constructed (or deconstructed) in constructivist and social constructionist discourse and the implications this carries for an understanding of problematic self-narratives. Drawing extensively on literary theory, he then offers numerous clinical illustrations of strategies for elaborating the form of client stories as well as helping clients reposition themselves as authors over the course of therapy. Wendy Drewery, John Winslade, and Gerald Monk further develop this view by situating narratives in a cultural context and criticizing the Western tendency toward "individualizing discourses" that attribute problems to people. As an alternative, they present a form of narrative therapy in which the goal is to free people from texts of identity that have become dominant and oppressive. Oscar Gonçalves, Yifaht Korman, and Lynne Angus conclude the section by describing the key concepts of a cognitive–narrative conceptualization of distress and by illustrating their potential contributions to psychotherapy research and practice. In combination, these three chapters provide a deep exploration of the narrative metaphor and help bridge the gap between an abstract understanding of life-as-story and the concrete implementation of this analogy in psychotherapy.

The book concludes with a section that places the discussion of disorder in a broader social setting. Laura Brown begins by setting forth a feminist critique of diagnostic discourse, especially as it has been used to rationalize or justify androcentric biases and the relegation of women to more marginal positions in Western culture. Sandra Rigazio-DiGilio then outlines and illustrates a systemic developmental framework for the diagnosis of client processing styles and the boundaries these place on problem conceptualization and resolution. A feature of both authors is their sensitivity to variations in meaning making as a function of gender and culture and their suspicion about privileging any one way of construing distress and the circumstances in which it is anchored. Finally, Ken Gergen and Sheila McNamee bring the book full circle with a multifaceted critique of disordering discourses and hint at the evolution of more relationally based and liberating forms of problem conceptualization in the future.

CONCLUSION

We hope the diverse attempts of contributors to this volume to interrogate existing practices and formulate a range of therapeutic alternatives will help psychotherapists of many orientations reach toward fresh understandings of human distress and envision fresh forms of intervention coherent with these novel approaches. Ultimately, being a constructivist, constructionist, or narrative therapist does not imply theoretically abstracting oneself from the concrete world of human suffering. We trust that this book conveys some of the practical and conceptual vigor of this perspective.

REFERENCES

Alexander, P. C., Neimeyer, R. A., & Follette, V. M. (1991). Group therapy for women sexually abused as children: A controlled study and investigation of individual differences. *Journal of Interpersonal Violence, 6,* 219–231.

Alexander, P. C., Neimeyer, R. A., Follette, V. M., Moore, M. K., & Harter, S. L. (1989). A comparison of group treatments of women sexually abused as children. *Journal of Consulting and Clinical Psychology, 57,* 479–483.

American Psychiatric Association. (1994). *Diagnostic and statistical manual of mental disorders* (4th ed.). Washington, DC: Author.

Anderson, W. T. (1990). *Reality isn't what it used to be.* New York: Harper & Row.

Appignanesi, R., & Garratt, C. (1995). *Postmodernism for beginners.* Cambridge, UK: Icon/Penguin.

Bohart, A. C., O'Hara, M., & Leitner, L. M. (1998). Emprically violated treatments: Disenfranchisement of humanistic and other psychotherapies. *Psychotherapy Research, 8,* 141–157.

Botella, L. (1995). Personal construct theory, constructivism, and postmodern thought. In R. A. Neimeyer & G. J. Neimeyer (Eds.), *Advances in personal construct psychology* (Vol. 3, pp. 3–35). Greenwich, CT: JAI Press.

Burr, V. (1995). *An introduction to social constructionism.* London: Routledge.

Cox, L. M., & Lyddon, W. J. (1997). Constructivist conceptions of the self. *Journal of Constructivist Psychology, 10,* 201–220.

Fransella, F. (1996). *George Kelly*. London: Sage.

Goldberger, N. R. (1996). Women's constructions of truth, self, authority, and power. In H. Rosen & K. T. Kuehlwein (Eds.), *Constructing realities* (pp. 167–193). San Francisco: Jossey Bass.

Greenberg, L., Elliott, R., & Lietaer, G. (1994). Research on experiential psychotherapies. In A. E. Bergin & S. L. Garfield (Eds.), *Handbook of psychotherapy and behavior change* (4th ed., pp. 509–539). New York: Wiley.

Harter, S. L., & Neimeyer, R. A. (1995). Long term effects of child sexual abuse: Toward a constructivist theory of trauma and its treatment. In R. A. Neimeyer & G. J. Neimeyer (Eds.), *Advances in personal construct theory* (Vol. 3, pp. 229–269). Greenwich, CT: JAI Press.

Kelly, G. A. (1955). *The psychology of personal constructs*. New York: Norton.

Mahoney, M. J. (1991). *Human change processes*. New York: Basic Books.

Neimeyer, R. A. (1993). Constructivism and the problem of psychotherapy integration. *Journal of Psychotherapy Integration, 3,* 133–157.

Neimeyer, R. A. (1998). Social constructionism in the counselling context. *Counselling Psychology Quarterly, 11,* 135–149.

Neimeyer, R. A., & Mahoney, M. J. (Eds.). (1995). *Constructivism in psychotherapy*. Washington, DC: American Psychological Association.

Toukmanian, S. G., & Rennie, D. L. (1992). *Psychotherapy process research: Paradigmatic and narrative approaches*. Newbury Park, CA: Sage.

Winter, D. A. (1992). *Personal construct psychology in clinical practice*. London: Routledge.

2

THE CONSTRUCTION OF DISORDER AS HUMAN ENTERPRISE

JONATHAN D. RASKIN AND ADAM M. LEWANDOWSKI

Currently, most clinicians and researchers, regardless of theoretical orientation, use the *Diagnostic and Statistical Manual of Mental Disorders* (currently in its fifth version [*DSM-IV*[1]]; American Psychiatric Association [APA], 1994) as a primary tool in delineating psychological abnormality from other, apparently normal modes of experience. In fact, because of its phenomenal success in three consecutive versions over the last 20 years, the *DSM* has been hailed for triumphantly ushering in a revolution in scientific diagnosis of mental disorders. In each version of the *DSM* published since 1980, APA has applied a theoretical model of abnormality that views mental disorders as naturally occurring, objective entities that are readily amenable to empirical investigation (APA, 1980, 1987, 1994). Critics of the various versions of *DSM* have often argued that *DSM* categories lack

An earlier version of this chapter was presented at the 8th Biennial Conference of the North American Personal Construct Network, Denton, Texas, in July 1998. We thank Larry Leitner for feedback on several drafts of this chapter.

[1]For further clarification, each of the three versions of the *Diagnostic and Statistical Manual* published since 1980 (*DSM-III*, *DSM-III-R*, and *DSM-IV*) share a close family resemblance, and each has enjoyed tremendous success. For simplicity's sake, henceforward we generally refer to only the *DSM-IV* because it is the manual in use as of this writing. However, our ideas apply to *DSM-IV*'s two older siblings and will likely apply to forthcoming *DSM*s so long as these manuals continue to closely resemble the manuals published since *DSM-III*.

objective, scientific data to support them (Caplan, 1995; Coleman, 1984; Kirk & Kutchins, 1992; Kutchins & Kirk, 1997; Szasz, 1987). Often these critics have focused their attention on changes to the manual attributable to political maneuverings rather than scientific advances. They commonly claim that a diagnostic manual cannot be based on objective scientific data if disorder categories can be negotiated (sometimes even voted) in and out. Because scientifically inclined people are generally appalled by the idea that naturally occurring phenomena can be dismissed by a vote, each successive DSM has been criticized for not being scientific or objective enough.

Applying a constructivist perspective, we have difficulty accepting the DSM-IV as an impartial instrument that describes naturally occurring phenomena. This is because constructivists often doubt the human ability to know the world "as it is" in an objective sense that is independent of personal and social constructions (Anderson, 1995; Burr, 1995; Gergen, 1991, 1994; Hayes & Oppenheim, 1997; Lyddon, 1995; Neimeyer, 1997; Rosen, 1996; Sexton, 1997). We want to clarify that the terms constructivist and constructivism are used throughout this chapter to represent the diverse group of perspectives labeled variously as "personal constructivism," "cognitive constructivism," "social constructionism," "the constructive psychologies," "narrative psychology," and "postmodern psychology." These perspectives differ somewhat from one another, but all emphasize that ways of understanding are perpetually changing human inventions; that is, human knowledge is actively constructed within the personal and social domains. Constructivism, as broadly demarcated herein, emphasizes the personal, social, and cultural meanings that influence human understanding. People perceive the world from a point of view, and differences between subjective points of view need to be resolved through interpersonal communication and negotiation. In constructivist psychology, individuals and the societies they form create representations of disorder as part of the human effort to draw meaning from experience.

Following a constructivist model, the reality of disorder is subjectively experienced; although every individual experientially knows what a disorder is, this knowledge is constructed within the interpersonal context. The concepts of normality and abnormality, even those offered in the DSM-IV, are inventions more than discoveries. Accenting invention over discovery leads us to diverge from many of the critics of psychiatric diagnosis because we do not condemn the DSM-IV for its use of social negotiation (yes, sometimes even votes) when it comes to constructing definitions of disorder. In other words, we do not fault APA for failing to write the DSM-IV objectively or scientifically enough. Instead, we reject the very contention that the DSM-IV can ever be objective *at all* if objectivity means ignoring the centrality of subjective human involvement in constructing definitions of psychological disorder. Critics who pit scientific procedure against interpersonal negotiation in the production of the *DSM-IV* remain within a framework that upholds the neutrality of empirical investigation while downplaying the human components of science in the creation of knowledge schemes. For constructivists, stressing the importance, even the necessity, of human dialogue and negotiation is central to the creation of scientific models of disorder.

In this chapter, we pay special attention to ways in which constructions of disorder are often applied in a preemptive manner. In George Kelly's (1955/1991a, 1955/1991b) personal construct theory of constructivism, "preemption is a way of ruling out *other constructs*" (1955/1991a, p. 382, emphasis in original). Preemption occurs when mental health professionals choose a particular construction of disorder while dismissing all other alternatives. Preemption often is encouraged because traditional science seeks the most valid, versus most viable, constructions of reality. Because of the *DSM-IV's* tremendous success and its traditional science foundation, it is often used in a preemptive manner. As a result, alternative constructions of disorder are sometimes not entertained, leaving new possibilities overlooked. In applied practice, singular reliance on one construction of disorder creates narrowly limited clinical realities for clients, therapists, and laypeople.

Throughout this chapter, we explicitly analyze diagnostic constructions as acts of meaning. We examine ways in which dominant *DSM-IV* constructions of disorder often create therapeutic "realities," and we propose that seeing diagnostic nosologies as meaningful, humanly created constructions to which we do not owe allegiance allows the clinician and client to entertain an infinite array of potential constructions of client concerns. The consequences of such a radical openness are examined in relation to several clinical examples. We alter the names of the clients and therapists discussed to conceal their identities. Clinical information has been disguised as well.

PREEMPTION AND THE NONCANONICAL: THE CASE OF MARK

Concerns about *DSM*-style diagnosis have been put forward from a variety of constructivist perspectives, including personal construct psychology (Faidley & Leitner, 1993; Honos-Webb & Leitner, 1997; Raskin & Epting, 1993, 1995), social constructionism (Drewery, Winslade, & Monk, chap. 10, this volume; Gergen, 1994, Gergen & McNamee, chap. 14, this volume; Parker, Georgaca, Harper, McLaughlin, & Stowell-Smith, 1995), and cultural constructivism (Gaines, 1992a, 1992b). Like most critics of *DSM-IV*, constructivists sometimes question the use of dividing people into categories of "abnormal" and "normal." Still there does seem to be an overwhelming tendency to distinguish "deviance" from normality. Many constructivists examine this from the standpoint of personal meanings devised to explain and predict. For example, personal constructivism (Kelly, 1955/1991a, 1955/1991b) proposes that people construe the world by using bipolar dimensions of understanding. Most simply, people need to define what something is not to also understand what it is. *Abnormal* and *normal* are constructs people invented as a way to understand and explain certain forms of human experience. Along similar lines, Bruner (1990) proposed that the uncommon, or noncanonical, ignites explanatory efforts. Customary and expected behaviors are usually taken for granted. Unexpected and uncommon behaviors set off a search for meanings and causes, which is why most research examines noncanonical, or aberrant, modes of behaving and experiencing. Take homosexuality, for example. Its contemporary location on the cusp between abnormal and normal potentially explains why there is so much research and discussion about its causes and meanings, whereas consideration of the causes and meanings of heterosexuality is rare (Epting, Raskin, & Burke, 1994).

When it comes to psychopathology, preemption and the noncanonical often occur together, as evident in the following case example about schizophrenia.

> Mark is a former hospital inpatient diagnosed with schizophrenia. He is having difficulty obtaining a job, despite spending much time with his psychologist working on interviewing skills. Although Mark is doing quite well in simulated role-plays of job interviews, he avoids real interviews at every turn. When asked directly about this by his therapist, Mark bluntly replies, "I can't hold down a job. After all, I'm schizophrenic!"

Mark's odd and disturbing behavior requires explanation, and an effective explanation is found in a dominant social construction of abnormality, namely schizophrenia. Construing Mark as "schizophrenic" is not inherently a good or bad thing per se, but it contributes to certain clinical realities. One possible outcome in this case is construing Mark as ill and prescribing him drugs. Indeed, Mark may experience this positively, especially given mental health professionals' current tendency to conceptualize a large percentage of problems brought to them as medical dilemmas requiring chemical treatment (Breggin, 1991; Valenstein, 1998). Even if Mark experiences taking prescription drugs positively, he incorporates the schizophrenic construction into his sense of self. Thus, to Mark, holding down a job seems impossible in light of his illness. An illness-based construction (like any construction) can be seen both positively and negatively. When used in a clinical scenario, the positive and negative elements of this kind of construction are reflected in a client's experienced reality. Constructivism argues that illness-based social constructions of disorder may be useful but are not obligatory.

We are not implying that efforts to explain the atypical should be eliminated. On the contrary, efforts to explain the unexpected are an important and seemingly adaptive component of human existence. Such efforts help allay anxiety, which occurs within Kelly's (1955/1991a) personal construct psychology when events cannot be accounted for by one's present constructions. To alleviate anxiety, a person may revise his or her current ways of understanding or create wholly new understandings. We see the development of new constructions of disorder as a way to reduce anxiety among clinicians and clients who may find current constructions of disorder lacking in their ability to explain the noncanonical. Developing new constructions of disorder can be a way to better account for the many diagnostic exceptions that occur in clinical practice when one tries to apply traditional nosological categories to clients. That is, fairly often clients do not fit nicely into the preordained categories laid out for them in the same way that clients in textbook examples do. Perhaps clinicians tend to overlook this because to attend to it would mean that their nosological system is not as predictive and meaningful as they might like. This realization, in turn, unleashes Kellian anxiety, which then results in preempting current constructions of disorder over alternatives simply as a way to avoid the aforementioned anxiety.

Constructivism encourages people to "play" with various constructions of the noncanonical by encouraging resistance of the anxiety that leads to the preemptive application of familar constructions of disorder. It suggests other possibilities made available when one's initial constructions of the noncanonical are complemented by simultaneously encouraging multiple alternative constructions of the same experience. Preemption, by its very definition, involves foreclosure of meaning making. When preemption occurs, the client and therapist are likely to cease searching for ways to explain the noncanonical. Once Mark construes himself as a schizophrenic, other meaningful ways of construing his circumstances are eliminated. Constructivism discourages foreclosing meaning making through preemptive adoption of only one construction of disorder.

Constructivists tend to believe that underscoring the meaning and viability of a construction of disorder, versus simply its validity, allows greater latitude for researchers and clinicians because it encourages entertaining a multiplicity of perspectives. Before discussing psychopathology in the context of constructivism and multiplicity of meaning, however, it is necessary to grapple with the *DSM-IV*. We lay the groundwork for our argument by providing a brief history of the *DSM-IV* and its critics. Then we expand on the work of these critics by supplementing their criticisms with some distinctly constructivist ideas. Finally, we argue for a constructivist approach to disorder by highlighting the central role of human involvement and meaning making in inventing viable notions of psychopathology. Human involvement occurs regardless of whether the construction of disorder at hand is rooted in the ideology of *DSM-IV*, constructivism, or some other theoretical orientation. Because personal realities are constituted by one's constructions of events, fostering multiplicity in applying constructions of disorder expands the number of possibilities open to therapists and clients and keeps an emphasis on the constructed aspects of knowledge about disorder.

DSM-IV AND THE CRITICS OF MENTAL DISORDER

The last 20 years have seen each successive version of the *DSM* riding high. Having developed a categorical system much like that of traditional medicine, the manual has enjoyed tremendous success. The *DSM-IV* provides descriptions of mental disorders, explicitly disavowing any attempt at etiological explanation (APA, 1994). By implementing a multiaxial approach, wherein diagnoses are made along five distinct axes, and by using diagnostic criteria to enhance consensus regarding the specific behavioral manifestations of symptoms, the *DSM-IV* has overcome its past reputation for poor reliability and validity. In addition to its clinical success and great import with regard to insurance reimbursements, the *DSM-IV* has been a boon to researchers, who more readily can operationalize variables using the manual's multiaxial, diagnostic criteria approach.

Although not central to our argument, we question both the atheoretical claims of the *DSM-IV* and the notion that it has universal benefit for researchers. In using behavioral diagnostic criteria to diagnose problems, we argue that the *DSM-IV* implicitly advantages certain types of explanations over others. It advantages approaches that attend to symptom reduction rather than psychological meaning. As constructivists, this concerns us because even though we often attend to the former, we are equally (if not more) concerned with the latter. Furthermore, with regard to the *DSM-IV*'s being a boon to researchers, it seems to us that researchers who like *DSM-IV* categories are the ones most inclined to find *DSM-IV*'s operational definitions of benefit. Those who wish to develop research programs using non-*DSM-IV* operational definitions may actually find the preemptive influence of such categories a hindrance.

Although each version of *DSM* published since 1980 has been very successful in terms of its influence and its claims to scientific respectability, various critics have been quite vocal about perceived problems in the manual. Constructivists often criticize the *DSM-IV* for the reasons just discussed, but most other critics of the *DSM-IV* have actually attacked the manual for what it claims to do best: function as a scientific instrument. Kirk and Kutchins (1992; Kutchins & Kirk, 1997) and Paula Caplan (1995) were some of the more visible faultfinders of the various *DSMs*. However, the likes of Thomas Szasz (1987), Lee Coleman (1984), Stanton Peele (1989), Elliot Valenstein (1998), and Jeffrey Masson (1988) have, as part of theses that go well beyond the *DSMs*, contributed their criticisms too.

We are sympathetic to these authors' attempts to demystify the awesome influence of the *DSM-IV*, but we are disappointed that their focus of attack is so often on the *DSM-IV*'s failures as a science project. In so doing, these authors, like those of the *DSM-IV*, subscribe to a view of science that minimizes the role of interpersonally constructed meanings in devising models of psychological disorder. This brings to mind the seminal work of Thomas Kuhn (1962), with his attention to the importance of scientific paradigms (i.e., "meaningful constructions" in constructivist parlance) on the practice of scientific research and the form of scientific knowledge. Constructivism sees interpersonally negotiated meanings as an integral part of the endeavor to construct definitions of disorder and an overlooked aspect of science in general.

DSM-IV critics generally do not offer a consistent vision of neutral science as the answer to effectively constructing categories of disorder. Many critics, when not espousing the "scientism" criticism of the *DSM-IV*, have argued that human involvement is as important as empirical investigation for conceptualizing psychopathology. Szasz (1987) and Coleman (1984), for example, asserted that the scientific precision aimed for by *DSM* authors is unnecessary in the realm of psychological problems; psychotherapists are better conceptualized as modern-day shamans or priests than scientific medical practitioners (Szasz, 1974, 1987, 1994). Masson (1988) went so far as to argue for abolishing psychotherapy altogether because he believes that personal biases about psychological normality necessarily lead to therapeutic corruption. Even Szasz (1974, 1987), whose work we see as reflecting constructivist themes (Raskin, 1997; Raskin & Epting, 1993, 1995), distinguished mental disorder from physical disorder, using the argument that physical disorders are real diseases whereas mental disorders are metaphorical inventions. By comparison, constructivists push the issue further, contending that all categories of disorder, even physical disorder categories convincingly explored scientifically, are the product of human beings constructing meaningful systems for understanding their world. Several issues germane to *DSM-IV*'s history provide examples of how the various incarnations of the *DSM* have been criticized for their reliance on rhetoric and negotiation rather than science. Briefly discussing these issues affords an opportunity to begin elaborating the idea that human involvement, often in the form of interpersonal negotiation, is part of the meaning-making process inherent to generating any diagnostic scheme, even such diagnostic schemes as the *DSM-IV*, which are devised through scientific method.

DSM AS POLITICS, NOT SCIENCE

Voting Out Homosexuality: Morality or Science?

Although the *DSM-III* (APA, 1980) seemed to mark a new day in psychiatric diagnosis, critics have highlighted the controversial and embarrassing politics that surrounded the removal of homosexuality from the manual. Kutchins and Kirk (1997; Kirk & Kutchins, 1992) provided an indepth, step-by-step analysis of the myriad maneuvers that occurred during the days leading up to homosexuality's declassification as a mental disorder. The narrative history of homosexuality as a mental disorder is fascinating: from full inclusion in *DSM-II* (APA, 1968), to partial inclusion as ego-dystonic homosexuality in *DSM-III* (APA, 1980), to full expulsion in *DSM-III-R* (APA, 1987) and *DSM-IV* (APA, 1994), to concerns about recent biological explanations possibly producing efforts to reincorporate homosexuality into future *DSMs* (Kutchins & Kirk, 1997). In reflecting on their historical account of homosexuality's rise and fall as a mental disorder, Kutchins and Kirk (1997) observed that when it comes to classifying mental disorders, "political considerations, personal interests, and economic pressures are major factors. Throughout the entire struggle over the inclusion or exclusion of homosexuality from [the] DSM, the minor role played by scientific research has been striking" (p. 99). In telling the history of the *DSM-IV*, politics, not science, was the unfortunate means by which homosexuality was included or excluded. Kutchins and Kirk (1997) lamented that in the future the "decision to return the homosexuality diagnosis to the manual may be justified on the basis of new genetic research data, but it, too, will be based on political considerations far more than on the validity of scientific findings" (p. 99).

Kutchins and Kirk (1997) were not alone in using homosexuality to make clear that the political overshadows the scientific in the *DSM-IV*. Caplan (1995) complained that homosexuality's continued inclusion in some form through the *DSM-III* was the result of the *DSM* authors' sexist and homophobic biases. Coleman (1984) even presented the vote count for the exclusion of homosexuality from the *DSM-III*: "5,854 called for elimination, 3,180 for retention, and 367 abstained" (p. 18). These authors' arguments imply, more or less subtly, that rhetoric is a bane to efforts to diagnose psychopathology and that the *DSM-IV* is a product of politics rather than science. Of course, to constructivists, rhetoric and argument give way to negotiated meanings and are thus a central part of any science of disorder. Were rhetoric and argument not a part of science, then scientific papers would not require discussion sections because the truth of the matter would be revealed simply by perusing the data. Constructivism emphasizes rhetoric and argument as unavoidable components of scientific knowledge construction.

A significant aspect of the controversy regarding homosexuality-as-mental-disorder surrounds whether the decision to classify homosexuality as a disorder is primarily a scientific or moral decision. In many respects, we challenge the problematic construct dimension of scientific versus moral. This dimension creates much confusion for the *DSM-IV* critics. Sometimes, the *DSM-IV* critics want to expand the scientific end of the dimension to better incorporate the concept of mental disorder. From this vantage point, clients' personal constructions either produce mental disorder or are the products of mental disorder. The moral side of the dimension is minimized to maintain scientific status. In contrast, at other times critics want to expand the moral end of the dimension, shrinking or eliminating the concept of mental disorder. When this occurs, the social aspects of human interactions are placed in the forefront and psychological problems become ethical, rather than scientific, dilemmas. Science becomes all but irrelevant to understanding psychological difficulties, although it is often still valued in the realm of physical disorders. Cartesian mind–body dualism results, with science espousing body and morality championing mind.

Mind–body dualism is generally considered a hallmark of "half-baked" theorizing. However, we are reminded of Polanyi's (1958; Polanyi & Prosch, 1975) contention that all knowledge is personal knowledge rooted in one's passions and commitments. From Polanyi's perspective, when people choose science or morality as a focal point for understanding, they make a commitment to both what is focused on and its subsidiary assumptions and see things according to the dictates implied. Of course, people can always step back from their commitments and choose new focal points because science and morality are merely two possible focal points for tacitly understanding experience. No focal point can ultimately justify itself as an original point-of-departure because no system can prove its underlying premises without resorting to additional underlying premises. Furthermore, once one steps away from one's commitments to study them as one's focal points, the experience of living those commitments is fundamentally altered, in the same way that studying the phonetics of a word prevents one from simultaneously comprehending the meaning of the word (Polanyi & Prosch, 1975). In their tendency to dwell within a primarily scientific or moral scheme, people tell others as much about their personal commitments as they do about the nature of science and morality. Science and morality, like mind and body, simply become different starting points in one's active and passionate quest for constructing a coherent knowledge scheme.

Going from Polanyi (1958; Polanyi & Prosch, 1975) to Kelly (1955/1991a, 1955/1991b), we suggest that scientific versus moral can also be viewed as a construct dimension that may have outlived its usefulness. Even if this construct dimension is not completely abandoned as an either–or dichotomy, at the very least its boundaries might be blurred. From our point of view, scientists are enmeshed in an enterprise that encompasses the moral, on the levels of both personal and social construction. Science and morality need not be construed as opposing and incompatible ends of the same dimension. The implications for constructing definitions of disorder are immense and quite relevant to the *DSM-IV*. It is unfortunate that the *DSM-IV*'s proponents and critics often seem ensnared by the scientific versus moral dimension, arguing one side, the other, or alternating inconsistently between both sides.

Sexism and Racism in Diagnosis: Bias

Issues of sexism and racism in the *DSM-IV* definitions of disorder have also generated a great deal of attention. Caplan (1995) eloquently described her hard-fought battles to keep controversial categories such as premenstrual syndrome, self-defeating personality disorder, and paraphilic rapism out of the *DSM-IV*. She contended that these categories are biased against women in that they pathologize unique aspects of a woman's experience. Premenstrual syndrome pathologizes the biological and psychological components of menstruation, self-defeating personality disorder blames women who are victims of abuse, and paraphilic rapism excuses the sexual aggression of men who assault women (Caplan, 1995). Inclusion of these disorders in either the main body or appendices of each successive *DSM* has long been the center of heated political debates.

In considering the inclusion or exclusion of discriminatory categories from the *DSM-IV*, Kutchins and Kirk (1997) told the story behind the political demise of self-defeating personality disorder (also known as "masochistic personality disorder") and cited recent research on racism and the *DSM-IV* (Kutchins & Kirk, 1997). Once again, the problem of racism and sexism is considered mainly a scientific one.

> Too little science goes into producing the handbook. Far more than being based on careful research, the handbook's contents are determined by the powerful *DSM* leaders' gatekeeping—unscientific decisions about which diagnoses will be allowed through and which will be kept out of the handbook. (Caplan, 1995, p. 185)

Kutchins and Kirk (1997) observed that "there has been no significant correction of the biases incorporated into DSM diagnoses" (p. 237). This primary focus on biased science implies that better science might indeed produce better definitions of disorder. Although sympathetic to this point, as constructivists we are skeptical about the implication that one can correct biases, especially if doing so is equated with being neutral in a way that wholly avoids partiality. The idea that one can eliminate bias leads to a common dead end, in that it denies a point of view and a place of standing to those who construct definitions of disorder. It omits the human component of disorder construction. Infusing doubt over the plausibility of an unbiased diagnostic scheme encourages openness to a plethora of disorder conceptualizations; it allows for open dialogue, something that unflagging allegiance to the DSM-IV discourages. Upholding the impossibility of neutrality does not mean people should stop complaining about perceived biases in the DSM-IV. It is worthwhile for people to discuss what they believe to be the underlying constructions of any knowledge system, even if because of human embeddedness within social and personal meanings, biases in diagnosis or any other knowledge system will never be eliminated. Rather than presume that bias can be eliminated, constructivists, in the spirit of Foucault's philosophy (Rabinow, 1984), focus instead on issues of power and influence in imposing diagnostic ideologies on people. That is, what is the perspective of the system at hand, and how do people come to internalize and adhere to a system's rendering of psychopathology?

Reliability, Validity, and Definition of Mental Disorder: Negotiation

Scientific criticisms of the DSM-IV occur most directly in analyses of diagnostic reliability and validity. Kirk and Kutchins (1992) argued that the DSM-III's developers purposely manipulated ways in which reliability data were interpreted to establish the DSM-III and its successors as scientifically respectable representatives of diagnostic nosology. They questioned the DSM-IV's validity, noting its failure to use a consistent and clear definition of mental disorder, as well as its inability to "*adequately distinguish mental disorders from other problems that manifest in the same behaviors*" (Kutchins & Kirk, 1997, p. 251, emphasis in original). This is their ultimate suggestion: "DSM should narrow its definition of mental disorders and the accompanying diagnostic criteria to those conditions where there is substantial scientific consensus that there is evidence of an internal mental dysfunction" (p. 264). Of interest is that in choosing the phrase *scientific consensus*, Kutchins and Kirk suggested that there is a role for human negotiation within a scientific approach to psychopathology. The nature and context of such negotiation is something to examine as we highlight areas where the DSM-IV's critics seem to be moving in a constructivist direction.

Expertise

Common to all the critics of mental disorder is a skepticism regarding the ability of mental health professionals to effectively function as experts capable of distinguishing psychological health from illness. Kutchins and Kirk (1997; Kirk & Kutchins, 1992) and Caplan (1995) based their doubts about psychiatric diagnostic expertise on the scientific shortcomings of research on mental disorders. Dawes (1994) and Valenstein (1998) also addressed scientific deficiencies. However, they did so more broadly than just about the *DSM-IV*, with Dawes focusing on scientific shortcomings of various clinical and diagnostic approaches and Valenstein focusing on weak science behind both *DSM-IV* categories and predominant biological models of mental disorder. However, despite their somewhat different areas of attention, all these authors raised concerns about the scientific standing of systems for conceptualizing, diagnosing, and treating psychopathology.

Refocusing specifically on the *DSM-IV*, Kutchins and Kirk (1997) suggested that "DSM and its sponsors should be much more modest in their proclamations about the scientific foundations of the manual" (p. 264). Caplan (1995) echoed this sentiment in stating that "the *DSM* authors *unjustifiably claim* that through scientific research they have found the Truth about normality and abnormality" (p. 57, italics in original). Valenstein (1998) made a similar point, observing that "scientific considerations do not play a significant role in the manual. Instead, the psychiatric tradition and sociopolitical considerations seem to have played the major roles in shaping this document" (p. 161). Szasz (1974, 1987) was perhaps the most outspoken about the issue, speaking of "putative" rather than "proven" illnesses and arguing that psychiatry oversteps its bounds by redefining moral problems as scientific.

Constructivists do not cleave such a firm line between science and the extraneous factors that most *DSM-IV* critics contend contaminate the *DSM-IV* as a scientific document. Although they often sympathize with critics who point out scientific limitations of the *DSM-IV*, constructivists generally are skeptical that better science will eliminate things such as the "psychiatric tradition" and "sociopolitical considerations." These factors cannot be eliminated because any system of disorder must be devised within some kind of intellectual tradition and sociopolitical order. Of course, if people cannot reach the objective truth about what disorder really is, then viable constructions of disorder must compete with one another on the basis of their use and meaningfulness in particular clinical situations.

Meaning and Intentions

When not critiquing the *DSM-IV* from a scientific standpoint, the critics of mental disorder often emphasize the importance of *meaning* and *intentions* in understanding psychological functioning. For example, although they wished to retain the concept of mental disorder, Kutchins and Kirk (1997) considered the *DSM-IV*'s range of convenience, or applicability, too expansive: "Far too often, the psychiatric bible has been making us crazy—when we are just human" (p. 265). Caplan (1995) was even more explicit about preferring meaning and intentions to categorical distinctions: "I cannot say that I have found it either personally or professionally useful to classify anyone as normal or abnormal" (p. 44). She elaborated that

> when I want to help people, the kinds of questions I have found useful are those such as "Can they think logically and clearly about what is happening to them?" or "Does their behavior seem to be motivated by love, fear, need for power, or hatred?" (p. 44)

This is similar to Szasz's (1974, 1987) contention that mental disorders are better conceived of as "problems in living." Rather than pathologize common forms of human experience, Szasz (1974) emphasized the political and personal aspects of these experiences. He used the metaphor of game playing in arguing that behavior patterns classified as mental illnesses are more suitably viewed as meaningful actions "made to happen by sentient, intelligent human beings" (p. 201). In fact, for Szasz, only meaningful games are psychologically beneficial: "To live meaningfully, man must be interested in and invested in more than just objects. He must have games he finds worth playing" (p. 254). Similar to Szasz and the other critics of the *DSM-IV*'s mental disorder tradition, constructivists share a belief in the importance of meaning making in defining abnormality and psychological functioning. In fact, as constructivists we believe that mental health professionals, just like their clients, are engaged in a process of meaning making. When it comes to abnormality, the most prominent product of this meaning making has been the *DSM-IV* constructions of disorder, but other disorder conceptions should be explored, developed, and used should people find them meaningful, predictive, and viable.

Faith in the Talking Cure: The Case of Sharon

Most of the critics of mental disorder mentioned above, with the exception of Masson (1988), believe in the power of conversational psychotherapy as a potentially effective change instrument. However, if one accepts the notion that psychotherapists do not have greater access to universal standards of normality and psychological adjustment than others do, then what is the basis for psychotherapists' expertise? Constructivists often contend that psychotherapists do not know, nor should they pretend to know, what is the correct way for people to live their lives. When it comes to disorder and psychotherapy, constructivism adopts a "not-knowing" approach (Anderson & Goolishian, 1992). Anderson and Goolishian (1992) described this approach as one in which "the therapist's actions communicate an abundant, genuine curiosity" (p. 29), which expresses "a need to know more about what has been said, rather than convey preconceived opinions and expectations about the client, the problem, or what must be changed" (p. 29). In this approach, "the therapist joins with the client in a mutual exploration of the client's understanding and experience. Thus the process of interpretation, the struggle to understand in therapy, becomes collaborative" (p. 30).

The not-knowing approach emphasizes that psychotherapists, when working effectively, are experts at interpersonal communication. Szasz (1965/1988) actually alluded to this kind of expertise for psychotherapists more than 30 years ago in his book, *The Ethics of Psychoanalysis*. Instead of seeing the psychotherapist as someone knowing how people ought to live and what universal standards of adjustment are, the psychotherapist is more effectively perceived as being an expert in interpersonal communication. This seems consistent with many past and current conceptions of psychotherapy. After all, most psychotherapy involves talking, which may explain why Freud, influenced by patient Bertha Pappenheim (more commonly known as Anna O.), adopted Pappenheim's phrase "talking cure" to describe the therapeutic process in the first place (Breuer & Freud, 1895/1956; Freud, 1910/1977). The power of talk is reflected in the following case of Sharon.

> Sharon, a 40-something female, undergoes a free depression screening at a local hotel. The inventory consists of a 10-item depression inventory. After completing the inventory, Sharon is informed that she is suffering from a clinical depressive illness severe enough that it immediately requires medication. Feeling panic over her newly discovered illness, Sharon hurries to a community crisis center and requests antidepressant medication.

Sharon's frightening feelings of unhappiness are strikingly different from the happy (or at the very least, contented and pleasant) presentation one usually expects from people; the noncanonical elements of Sharon's experience produce efforts to make sense of it. Construing Sharon as depressed, and therefore ill, may result in her being prescribed drugs. She may experience this as positive and incorporate the depressed construction into her sense of self. After it is determined that Sharon has a depressive illness, examining her relational difficulties and the ways in which they might isolate her from others is far less relevant as an explanatory hypothesis. Accepting this construction, Sharon may avoid seeing a psychotherapist, instead relying on the medication as the "cure."

> The destruction of client meanings is narrowly averted in the case of Sharon when she happens on a therapist who asks about her current circumstances. Sharon responds by telling the therapist that she recently lost her job and was forced by economic necessity to move in with her older parents. Sharon and the therapist proceed to talk about ways that Sharon's circumstances may or may not be responsible for her feeling depressed. Sharon says that she initially thought her circumstances might be relevant but then concluded that she must have been wrong because the people administering the depression inventory told her she was ill. Without taking a definitive stance on which construction of Sharon's situation is correct, the therapist encourages Sharon to weigh the pros and cons of each position and to decide for herself whether medication is necessary. Ultimately, Sharon decides against medication. She and the therapist proceed to discuss alternative ways that Sharon might manage her sadness. Sharon feels relief from what she perceived to be pressure to take medication; until talking about it with the therapist, she felt like she had no choice. After all, who was she to question the experts? Were it not for the therapist encouraging Sharon to share and flesh out alternative constructions of the situation, Sharon's efforts at meaningful explanation of her very own circumstances might have been foreclosed.

In constructivist psychotherapy, the talking cure involves the psychotherapist helping the client to elaborate and make clear the client's constructions of self, events, and relationships. Although in Sharon's case, this resulted in her rejecting medication, in another client's case a very different outcome might result. What is important here is not just the outcome itself, but also—in keeping with the seminal therapeutic work of White and Epston (1990)—the way in which talking about the problem allowed Sharon to examine and revise her constructions of the problem, with an eye toward how she might resist the "requirements" of the problem. White and Epston (1990) used therapeutic talk in a very novel and creative way by encouraging clients to "externalize" the problem; that is, they encouraged clients to conceive of the problem as an entity external to them rather than as a DSM–IV disorder within them. In this way, they playfully invited clients to map out the way in which the problem, as an independent entity, elicits certain kinds of behaviors and emotional reactions that sustain its existence. In so doing, clients started to identify unique outcomes (i.e., instances when they did not succumb to the requirements of the problem by behaving in the usual way). In identifying unique outcomes, Sharon began to move away from an essentialist conception of herself as having a depressive personality and toward a view of herself as someone able to resist the demands of depression.

> Sharon externalizes depression as the problem; depression, as an independent entity, tries to take over Sharon's life by encouraging her to dwell on areas of her life in which she is encountering obstacles, such as in her difficulty finding a job. Sharon identifies several instances when she is able to resist the requirements of depression by doing something that minimizes or eliminates the depressive feelings. During these times, Sharon avoids cooperating with depression by going for a walk or taking a relaxing bath; she finds she does not feel depressed during these activities. These small instances in which Sharon is able to "outsmart" depression eventually lead to Sharon looking at how she can integrate strategies for resisting the requirements of depression when it comes to larger issues in her life, such as employment and family relationships.

The meaningful functions of language and communication in externalizing the problem are key to White and Epston's (1990) approach and important to constructivist therapy in general (Efran & Fauber, 1995; Gordon & Efran, 1997). How problems are defined and talked about influences the lived experience of those problems. We like White and Epston's (1990) approach because it discourages essentialist, trait-oriented views of clients, which may inadvertently encourage seeing problems as an unavoidable characteristic of personhood rather than as something constructed through interpersonal communication and linguistic meaning construction.

To further elaborate the importance of linguistic meaning construction that occurs in the client–therapist relationship, we turn to personal construct psychology's concept of sociality (Kelly, 1955/1991a, 1955/1991b). *Sociality* occurs when psychotherapist and client construe each other's construction processes. The relationship that results—dubbed a "role relationship" (Faidley & Leitner, 1993)—constitutes a chief experiential component of effective psychotherapy. Perhaps the psychotherapist's part in helping clients elaborate personal meanings through interpersonal communication explains why most therapists pride themselves on providing feedback propositionally rather than dogmatically, using the Rogerian (1961) style of phrasing that is so often parodied but nonetheless effective (e.g., "It seems to me. . .," "What I'm hearing you say is. . .," "From where I sit, it appears that. . ."). In many ways this view also seems consistent with social constructionism, which views therapy as an interpersonal enterprise emphasizing dialogue and negotiation between client and therapist within the context of socially prescribed meanings (McNamee, 1996; McNamee & Gergen, 1992). Most forms of constructivism value relational, conversational meaning making as a therapeutically beneficial endeavor. Although constructivists do not rule out conceptions of disorder that fail to value conversational, interpersonally negotiated meaning making (as might occur with purely biological models), they lean toward therapeutic approaches that incorporate human communication and meaning construction as central to remedying psychological difficulties.

DIAGNOSTIC CONSTRUCTIONS AS ACTS OF MEANING: TWO CONTRASTING CASES

> Dr. Walsh's newest client is Beth, a 20-year-old woman whose behavior in therapy alternates from self-effacing and demure to angry and antagonistic. Dr. Walsh finds dealing with Beth quite stressful and emotionally draining. When talking to colleagues about his new client, Dr. Walsh simply refers to Beth as his "borderline" patient.

Preemptive construing can foreclose therapist meaning making. In the case of Dr. Walsh and his client Beth, preemption is evident in his tendency to refer to Beth as his borderline patient. Borderline personality disorder becomes the all-encompassing and circular explanation for every way that Beth behaves. As a result, Beth is reduced to being a borderline and only a borderline patient. Therapy may become a matter of getting Beth to accept Dr. Walsh's construction of her as a borderline patient and to alter what, in Dr. Walsh's view, is Beth's emotional instability in light of this construction. Of course, this has implications for Beth too. As mentioned previously, when clients internalize *DSM-IV* constructions as the only accurate ones available, their prior personal constructions of the problem may be reconstrued as irrelevant. Ultimately, this can lead to the destruction of these personal but non-*DSM-IV* meanings (Honos-Webb & Leitner, 1997).

The following case provides a contrasting instance in which professional constructions are used in an empowering and multiply meaningful way.

> Dr. Emerich sits down with each client at the start of therapy, and she and the client flip through the *DSM-IV* together. Ultimately, Dr. Emerich and the client collectively decide which *DSM-IV* diagnoses seem relevant for conceptualizing the client's problems. Furthermore, if the client is using insurance to cover the cost of therapy sessions, Dr. Emerich and the client act jointly in determining which *DSM-IV* diagnoses should be submitted to the insurance company.

Dr. Emerich involves clients in the process of *DSM-IV* diagnosis. Instead of seeing the *DSM-IV* as either a scientific certainty dependent on accurate assessment or a scientific sham devoid of meaning, Dr. Emerich uses the *DSM-IV* as a potentially meaningful, but idiographic, self-construction. When clients become active collaborators in the diagnostic process, questions about the *DSM-IV*'s validity become irrelevant. If the diagnostic category chosen is valid to the therapist and client at hand because it allows them to make initial forays into the realm of meaningful constructions of the client's concerns, then so be it. This minimizes concerns about *DSM-IV*'s prepackaged meanings. Legitimate concern about the damaging impact of labels (Scheff, 1984) is defused because client and therapist coopt whatever *DSM-IV* labels are being used and construe the meaning and relevance of those labels within the broader context of encouraging consideration of multiple modes of explanation. This is not that far removed from the tendency of socially oppressed groups to coopt and reconstrue the meaning of derogatory labels that have been socially assigned to them. In such scenarios, a previously negative label becomes redefined in a more personally meaningful and productive manner. What makes the coopting of diagnostic labels different from the acceptance of prepackaged constructions is that the former is not preemptive because it actively encourages construing the *DSM-IV* label at hand idiographically in relationship to the specific clinical situation. Furthermore, coopting a label encourages the view of the label as just a label rather than as the final say on the matter. This encourages continued construing of the problem in an endless variety of ways.

Dr. Emerich's use of the *DSM-IV* is clever, but we would feel more comfortable with it if the *DSM-IV* were not so dominant a construction. When Dr. Emerich and her clients start using the *DSM-IV* labels, can they really separate themselves from the socially constructed meanings attached to those labels? Although we think it is certainly possible to fundamentally reconstrue the meaning of a *DSM-IV* label, we see this as a very difficult task because the metatheory behind the *DSM-IV* is so powerful as a social construction that it is bound to influence the client's therapy. Additionally, both those who like and dislike *DSM-IV* diagnosis may be fooling themselves if they believe that they can use the *DSM-IV* jargon in such a way that they say one thing but mean another. In the words of R. D. Laing (1965),

> dissatisfaction with psychiatric and psycho-analytic words is fairly widespread. It is widely felt that these words of psychiatry and psychoanalysis somehow fail to express what one "really means". But it is a form of self-deception to suppose that one can say one thing and think another. (p. 18)

Constructivism sees the meaning one attaches to words as fluid and amenable to change. In this sense, linguistic meanings are the site of power relations; having one meaning of a term accepted over another leads people using the term to experience particular personal realities (Burr, 1995). Dr. Emerich and her clients cannot avoid problems related to how others are influenced by dominant constructions of mental illness labels; neither can they fully detach themselves from their own internalized social constructions about the meaning of these labels. Although coopting a label for one's own use can be personally empowering, it does not make up for the present tendency to preemptively apply diagnostic labels when discussing those assigned them.

Furthermore, Dr. Emerich's solution does not fully address the intricacies surrounding the inability of a therapist to monitor who can gain access to a client's diagnosis after it has been input into an insurance company's computer system. The client and therapist may have reconstrued the meaning of the diagnostic label in a new and empowering way, but those at the insurance company and in society at large have not. The client needs to be aware of this issue when deciding whether to use his or her insurance. Of course, even if the client decides against using insurance, *DSM-IV* labels can still be coopted, perhaps more effectively because people who are not involved in the client's specific reconstruing of the label are not privy to any part of the process. Even when clients and therapists claim to be using a *DSM-IV* label in their own empowering ways, the current predominance of categorical conceptions of mental disorder is bound to have an impact on the personal realities clients and therapists experience.

DSM-IV AND HUMAN INVOLVEMENT: AVOIDING THE INEVITABLE

We argue that entertaining multiple constructions of disorder is both more personally liberating and clinically useful than relying solely on one specific construction of disorder. This is not a call to a form of atheoretical eclecticism, such as that encouraged in the *DSM* (APA, 1968, 1980, 1987, 1994). In fact, because of constructivism's emphasis on the contextual nature of science and knowledge, constructivists do not believe that any system can be atheoretical—in the *DSM-IV*'s case, even when that system only claims to be atheoretical regarding etiology. By contrast, we tie our approach to personal constructivism's idea of *constructive alternativism* (Kelly, 1955/ 1991a), which holds that the number of potential constructions available is infinite should people choose to examine events in original and creative new ways. This contrasts somewhat from *social constructionist* approaches, which see people as free to mix and match from among the various social discourses about disorder but not free enough to be utterly independent of these discourses as they try to develop alternatives (Burr, 1995). However, even in social constructionism, people are able to combine various social constructions of disorder in fresh, new, and clever ways (Burr, 1995). Thus, both personal constructivism and social constructionism place human involvement in disorder construction at the front and center. We hope this dissolves the perceived opposition between science and political negotiation and prevents the squelching of constructions because they come from an unfamiliar philosophical or scientific paradigm.

Criticizing the *DSM-IV* for being atheoretical seems justified from a constructivist perspective because being atheoretical implies having no point of view. However, some readers might feel that rather than entertain multiple constructions of disorder, we should avoid any or all tendencies to evaluate other people's behavior as "disordered." Although we strongly support the idea that disorder, as a construct, might be redefined out of existence, we do not believe that anyone (clinician or otherwise) is free from making judgments about other peoples' behaviors and experiences. We encourage clinicians to view the inevitable judgments that they are bound to make as simply judgments, not as ultimate truth claims indicative of the defective nature of those judged. In other words, clinicians cannot escape their place of standing in the world and the constructions about human behavior this produces. However, they can acknowledge such constructions as personally and socially devised and of no inherently greater or lesser standing than other constructions about how to live the "good life." Clinicians are still free to believe in their constructions of the good life but not as universals that apply across all people and all contexts. In this way, the phrase *constructions of disorder* emphasizes the notion of constructions and diminishes the idea that there really are disorders of human interaction independent of those creating such disorders.

All too often both the critics and proponents of various constructions of disorder use the name of science as a means to debase one another. Decrying someone else's ideas as unscientific is a call for others to dismiss those ideas. Kitzinger (1990) referred to this as using the "rhetoric of pseudoscience," wherein one's own ideas are upheld as eminently more scientifically defensible than the opposing ideas. People use the rhetoric of pseudoscience to undermine alternative perspectives, although Kitzinger (1990) emphasized that this tactic is as much a discursive strategy as a scientific one. At the risk of engaging in the rhetoric of pseudoscience, we wish to make clear that our approach is not opposed to science; in fact, we believe developing constructions of disorder is indeed a scientific enterprise. In describing therapy clients, Kelly (1955/1991a) conceived of people as scientists, insofar as all people are engaged in a lifelong task of investigating and understanding the world in a meaningful and predictive fashion. If science involves systematic efforts at making meaning of lived experience, in the spirit of constructive alternativism, then there are an infinite number of ways to scientifically conceptualize disorder. We do not advocate for extracting science from the study of meaning. On the contrary, we advocate for acknowledgment of human involvement and meaning in conducting scientific inquiry.

In other words, human involvement in the form of interpersonal negotiation, politics, and rhetoric is impossible to eliminate when one is delineating psychological dysfunction. A psychotherapist's job is not to be a neutral diagnostician because constructivism questions neutrality as an option. Rather, acknowledging human involvement means recognizing that one always has opinions about the morally messy and challenging issues that clients bring to the therapy room, even when proceeding scientifically and systematically in addressing client concerns. All constructions of disorder are philosophically rooted within distinct perspectives, even when developed scientifically. This important but often ignored observation resonates with constructivist therapists such as Efran, Lukens, and Lukens (1990), who argued that the problem with today's psychiatric nomenclature "isn't that value judgments are involved or that causes and purposes are proposed. The problem is that they are disguised as objective assessments that then cannot be debated as philosophical choices" (p. 110).

Philosophical premises, of course, involve value judgments. Constructivism's emphasis on the role of values in concocting definitions of disorder is in keeping with Polanyi's (1958) notion of personal knowledge and Kelly's (1955/1991a, 1955/1991b) emphasis on personal meaning, wherein all people—scientists included—are passionately committed to the constructions they develop for comprehending events. Struggling with how people should best handle certain situations and relationships is a basic component of being human. What people conclude from their struggles is directly tied to what strikes them as dysfunctional. Rather than submerge these ideas in favor of any construction of disorder with claims to universality, constructivism encourages people to take responsibility for their personal constructions of disorder. Sharing these constructions with clients in a nondogmatic and open-minded way allows for the therapist and client to reach consensus about which life issues the client needs to address. Different client–therapist dyads may indeed reach different conclusions. Instead of trying to minimize human involvement and contextual subjectivity, constructivist therapists celebrate them and place them in the forefront. Constructions of disorder are invented, discarded, and reinvented repeatedly in the endless array of productive therapy relationships. When overreliance on any one of these constructions leads to clients and therapists feeling limited, refocusing on human involvement allows for the invention of new alternatives because it emphasizes one's very direct role in both creating and resolving what one construes as disordered. Constructivist approaches strongly emphasize the importance of therapist creativity when it comes to conceptualizing client problems and formulating therapy interventions (Raskin, 1999). This creativity can be found in the work of many constructivist therapists (Hoyt, 1998; McNamee & Gergen, 1992; Neimeyer & Mahoney, 1995; Rosen & Kuehlwein, 1996; Sexton & Griffin, 1997; White & Epston, 1990).

In drawing conclusions about the seemingly contradictory roles of politics and science in the *DSM-IV*, we offer a uniquely constructivist interpretation of events. In our view, the problem with the *DSM-IV* is not its reliance on political negotiation in determining the bounds of normalcy. On the contrary, the *DSM-IV*'s problem is that it fails to rely on such negotiation in any kind of genuine or open-minded way. The *DSM-IV* limits involvement in negotiating constructions of disorder to those who share its basic assumptions about disorder. Each revision of the manual appears to be a product of people with like-minded constructions about what disorder happens to be. Even among like-minded people, there is bound to be some negotiation, but the parameters of such negotiation are prone to be quite narrow because the *DSM-IV* insiders who revise the manual already agree on most elements of the *DSM-IV* construction of disorder. Caplan (1995) spoke to this problem most effectively in relating the way her ideas were dismissed and excluded during her involvement with the development of the *DSM-IV*.

Of course, when protecting a particular construction of disorder, people often find it necessary to limit human involvement. Perhaps much of the anger and frustration attributed to the *DSM-IV*'s critics stems as much from what constructivist therapists have been diagnosing as a far too common problem in the construction of disorder: dominant viewpoints that preempt all alternative interpretations. The *DSM-IV* deserves to stand on its own as a viable construction of disorder. To our sensibility, standing on its own differs markedly from standing in the way of alternative constructions. This volume signifies an exciting effort to share constructions of disorder that grow from constructivist, constructionist, and narrative orientations. The *DSM-IV* is often seen as the ultimate arbiter of disorder. Thus, our intention was to emphasize, in line with the work of Gaines (1992a, 1992b), that the *DSM-IV* is a cultural construction, rooted in the social mores of Western society in general and North American psychiatry and psychology in particular. In other words, the *DSM-IV* is simply one construction developed by particular people at a certain historical time and place. What follows in the remaining chapters of this volume are other constructions.

CONCLUSION

In this chapter, we adopted a constructivist orientation in examining ways in which human communication and negotiation are central in the development of any system for defining psychological abnormality. The notion of disorder as a human construction is particularly salient when considering today's dominant system for conceptualizing a psychological disorder, the *DSM-IV*. Although many critics of the *DSM-IV* direct their attention toward political and interpersonal factors that have played a significant role in the manual's development, we argued that such factors are part of the human construction process behind any scheme of knowledge. In this respect, the *DSM-IV* is no different from any other humanly created system for comprehending experience. We believe that therapists who wish to see alternatives to the *DSM-IV* developed can effectively begin the process by focusing on how human involvement in knowledge creation is crucial and even occurs in endeavors demarcated as scientific. The *DSM-IV*, as a human construction, is not inherently better or worse than potential alternative systems for understanding psychological problems. Rather, such as all systems of meaning, it is a distinctly human endeavor, with all the subjectivity and interpersonal messiness that all human endeavors entail. By taking such a position, we hope to level the playing field so that constructions of disorder that differ drastically from the *DSM-IV* (e.g., those offered by the contributors to this volume) become just as viable as the *DSM-IV*, perhaps even more so.

REFERENCES

American Psychiatric Association. (1968). *Diagnostic and statistical manual of mental disorders* (2nd ed.). Washington, DC: Author.

American Psychiatric Association. (1980). *Diagnostic and statistical manual of mental disorders* (3rd ed.). Washington, DC: Author.

American Psychiatric Association. (1987). *Diagnostic and statistical manual of mental disorders* (3rd ed., rev.). Washington, DC: Author.

American Psychiatric Association. (1994). *Diagnostic and statistical manual of mental disorders* (4th ed.). Washington, DC: Author.

Anderson, H., & Goolishian, H. (1992). The client is the expert: A not-knowing approach to psychotherapy. In S. McNamee & K. J. Gergen (Eds.), *Therapy as social construction* (pp. 25–39). London: Sage.

Anderson, W. T. (Ed.). (1995). *The truth about the truth.* New York: Tarcher/Putnam.

Breggin, P. R. (1991). *Toxic psychiatry: Why therapy, empathy, and love must replace the drugs, electroshock, and biochemical theories of the "new psychiatry."* New York: St. Martin's Press.

Breuer, J., & Freud, S. (1956). *Studies on hysteria* (J. Strachey & A. Strachey, Trans.). London: Hogarth Press. (Original work published 1895)

Bruner, J. (1990). *Acts of meaning.* Cambridge, MA: Harvard University Press.

Burr, V. (1995). *An introduction to social constructionism.* London: Routledge.

Caplan, P. J. (1995). *They say you're crazy: How the world's most powerful psychiatrists decide who's normal.* Reading, MA: Addison-Wesley.

Coleman, L. (1984). *The reign of error: Psychiatry, authority, and law.* Boston: Beacon Press.

Dawes, R. M. (1994). *House of cards: Psychology and psychotherapy built on myth.* New York: Free Press.

Efran, J. S., & Fauber, R. L. (1995). Radical constructivism: Questions and answers. In R. A. Neimeyer & M. J. Mahoney (Eds.), *Constructivism in psychotherapy* (pp. 275–304). Washington, DC: American Psychological Association.

Efran, J. S., Lukens, M. D., & Lukens, R. J. (1990). *Language, structure, and change: Frameworks of meaning in psychotherapy*. New York: Norton.

Epting, F. R., Raskin, J. D., & Burke, T. B. (1994). Who is a homosexual? A critique of the heterosexual–homosexual dimension. *The Humanistic Psychologist, 22,* 353–370.

Faidley, A. J., & Leitner, L. M. (1993). *Assessing experience in psychotherapy: Personal construct alternatives*. Westport, CT: Praeger.

Freud, S. (1977). *Five lectures on psychoanalysis* (J. Strachey, Trans.). New York: Norton. (Original work published 1910)

Gaines, A. D. (1992a). From *DSM-I* to *III-R*; voices of self, mastery, and the other: A cultural constructivist reading of U.S. psychiatric classification. *Social Science and Medicine, 35,* 3–24.

Gaines, A. D. (1992b). Ethnopsychiatry: The cultural construction of psychiatries. In A. D. Gaines (Ed.), *Ethnopsychiatry: The cultural construction of professional and folk psychiatries* (pp. 3–49). New York: State University of New York Press.

Gergen, K. J. (1991). *The saturated self: Dilemmas of identity in contemporary life*. New York: Basic Books.

Gergen, K. J. (1994). *Realities and relationships*. Cambridge, MA: Harvard University Press.

Gordon, D. E., & Efran, J. S. (1997). Therapy and the dance of language. In T. L. Sexton & B. L. Griffin (Eds.), *Constructivist thinking in counseling practice, research, and training* (pp. 101–110). New York: Teachers College Press.

Hayes, R. L., & Oppenheim, R. (1997). Constructivism: Reality is what you make it. In T. L. Sexton & B. L. Griffin (Eds.), *Constructivist thinking in counseling practice, research, and training* (pp. 19–40). New York: Teachers College Press.

Honos-Webb, L., & Leitner, L. M. (1997, July). The *DSM* and the destruction of self-meanings: A client speaks. In T. Anderson (Chair), *Disruptions in the therapeutic relationship: Influences of morality, ecology, diagnosis, and other cutting-edge issues*. Symposium conducted at the 12th International Congress on Personal Construct Psychology, Seattle, WA.

Hoyt, M. F. (Ed.). (1998). *The handbook of constructive therapies: Innovative approaches from leading practitioners*. San Francisco: Jossey-Bass.

Kelly, G. A. (1991a). *The psychology of personal constructs. Vol. 1: A theory of personality*. London: Routledge. (Original work published 1955)

Kelly, G. A. (1991b). *The psychology of personal constructs. Vol. 2: Clinical diagnosis and psychotherapy*. London: Routledge. (Original work published 1955)

Kirk, S. A., & Kutchins, H. (1992). *The selling of DSM: The rhetoric of science in psychiatry*. New York: de Gruyter.

Kitzinger, C. (1990). The rhetoric of pseudoscience. In I. Parker & J. Shotter (Eds.), *Deconstructing social psychology* (pp. 61–75). London: Routledge.

Kuhn, T. (1962). *The structure of scientific revolutions*. Chicago: University of Chicago Press.

Kutchins, H., & Kirk, S. A. (1997). *Making us crazy*. DSM: *The psychiatric bible and the creation of mental disorders*. New York: Free Press.

Laing, R. D. (1965). *The divided self: An existential study in sanity and madness*. Middlesex, England: Penguin Books.

Lyddon, W. J. (1995). Forms and facets of constructivist psychology. In R. A. Neimeyer & M. J. Mahoney (Eds.), *Constructivism in psychotherapy* (pp. 69–92). Washington, DC: American Psychological Association.

Masson, J. M. (1988). *Against therapy*. Monroe, ME: Common Courage Press.

McNamee, S. (1996). Psychotherapy as social construction. In H. Rosen & K. T. Kuehlwein (Eds.), *Constructing realities: Meaning-making perspectives for psychotherapists* (pp. 115–137). San Francisco: Jossey-Bass.

McNamee, S., & Gergen, K. J. (Eds.). (1992). *Therapy as social construction*. London: Sage.

Neimeyer, R. A. (1997). Problems and prospects in constructivist psychotherapy. *Journal of Constructivist Psychology, 10*, 51–74.

Neimeyer, R. A., & Mahoney, M. J. (Eds.). (1995). *Constructivism in psychotherapy*. Washington, DC: American Psychological Association.

Parker, I., Georgaca, E., Harper, D., McLaughlin, T., & Stowell-Smith, M. (1995). *Deconstructing psychopathology*. London: Sage.

Peele, S. (1989). *Diseasing of America: Addiction treatment out of control*. Boston: Houghton Mifflin.

Polanyi, M. (1958). *Personal knowledge: Towards a post-critical philosophy*. Chicago: Univiversity of Chicago Press.

Polanyi, M., & Prosch, H. (1975). *Meaning*. Chicago: University of Chicago Press.

Rabinow, P. (Ed.). (1984). *The Foucault reader*. New York: Pantheon.

Raskin, J. D. (1997). Muddles, myths, and medicine revisited [Review of the book *Cruel compassion: Psychiatric control of society's unwanted*]. *Journal of Constructivist Psychology, 10*, 285–289.

Raskin, J. D. (Ed.). (1999). Constructivism and the creative psychotherapist [Special issue]. *Journal of Constructivist Psychology, 12*(4).

Raskin, J. D., & Epting, F. R. (1993). Personal construct theory and the argument against mental illness. *International Journal of Personal Construct Psychology, 6*, 351–369.

Raskin, J. D., & Epting, F. R. (1995). Constructivism and psychotherapeutic method: Transitive diagnosis as humanistic assessment [Annual edition]. *Methods: A Journal for Human Science*, 3–27.

Rogers, C. R. (1961). *On becoming a person*. Boston: Houghton Mifflin.

Rosen, H. (1996). Meaning-making narratives: Foundations for constructivist and social constructionist psychotherapies. In H. Rosen & K. T. Kuehlwein (Eds.),

Constructing realities: Meaning-making perspectives for psychotherapists (pp. 3–51). San Francisco: Jossey-Bass.

Rosen, H., & Kuehlwein, K. T. (Eds.). (1996). Constructing realities: Meaning-making perspectives for psychotherapists. San Francisco: Jossey-Bass.

Scheff, T. (1984). Being mentally ill: A sociological theory (rev. ed.). New York: de Gruyter.

Sexton, T. L. (1997). Constructivist thinking within the history of ideas: The challenge of a new paradigm. In T. L. Sexton & B. L. Griffin (Eds.), Constructivist thinking in counseling practice, research, and training (pp. 3–18). New York: Teachers College Press.

Sexton, T. L., & Griffin, B. L. (Eds.). (1997). Constructivist thinking in counseling practice, research, and training. New York: Teachers College Press.

Szasz, T. (1974). The myth of mental illness: Foundations of a theory of personal conduct (rev. ed.). New York: Harper & Row.

Szasz, T. (1987). Insanity: The idea and its consequences. New York: Wiley.

Szasz, T. (1988). The ethics of psychoanalysis: The theory and method of autonomous psychotherapy. Syracuse, NY: Syracuse University Press. (Original work published 1965)

Szasz, T. (1994). Cruel compassion: Psychiatric control of society's unwanted. New York: Wiley.

Valenstein, E. S. (1998). Blaming the brain: The truth about drugs and mental health. New York: Simon & Schuster.

White, M., & Epston, D. (1990). Narrative means to therapeutic ends. New York: Norton.

II

DISORDER AS DISRUPTION IN SELFHOOD CONSTRUCTION

3

CORE ORDERING AND DISORDERING PROCESSES: A CONSTRUCTIVE VIEW OF PSYCHOLOGICAL DEVELOPMENT

MICHAEL J. MAHONEY

Many clients are confused, distressed, or disorganized by the limits they perceive in understanding themselves, their worlds, and their lives, particularly the emotional vicissitudes of their lives. Many such individuals may be reassured by a therapist's apparent ability to "make sense of" their stories and to render interpretations that demystify their personal dilemmas. What is often more difficult for clients to accept, particularly clients who struggle with issues of power and control, is the fact that a complete, final, and unequivocal interpretation (and–or answer, rendition, perspective) of their situation is never possible. In this regard, some of the most valuable actions of therapists may include respecting the client's quest to understand and order, or reorder, his or her life while communicating the fact that it is neither a sin nor necessarily an obstacle not to understand their dilemmas completely.

This chapter is based on material from Mahoney (in press).

Order is a central requirement of life as it is known. But what does that have to do with psychotherapy?: in one word, everything. For better or for worse, willingly or otherwise, psychotherapists, myself included, are modern specialists of order. We claim to distinguish between "ordinary" (orderly, "normal") patterns of experience and "disordered" patterns. The latter are then elaborately classified into orderly categories of disorder. Disordered individuals are deemed the primary clients of psychotherapists, and it is the primary responsibility of the therapist to help the client regain a socially condoned and functional semblance of order in his or her experience and activity patterns.

Our status as specialists of order may come as a surprise to some and a given to others. I leave it to other contributors of this volume to pursue some of the fascinating issues raised by the psychotherapist's participation in personal and interpersonal systems of order (see also Foucault, 1970; Halleck, 1971; Szasz, 1970). Instead, I move the level of my dialogue to one of more direct clinical relevance.

My central point is that most psychotherapy clients seek help along similar lines (i.e., lines of establishing, regaining, or improving an order or pattern in their lives). They want to understand what is happening to them. They want to change patterns of experience and activity that are both orderly (i.e., familiar, recurring) and disorderly (in their effects on personal mood, health, functioning, etc.). They want therapists to offer alternatives and to guide them toward practical paths.

The most fundamental principle of human experience, then, is that it reflects uniquely individual attempts to order or "organize" the complex flow of life in process. As if one needed more evidence than oneself, studies of complex phenomena and the life sciences have lent countless illustrations of this basic fact. It is stated in myriad ways. Life requires order. Life creates order. Life is self-organizing. The point is that dynamic (i.e., developmental, interacting, and unfolding in time) patterns of order constitute the "fabric of being" as it is known as the literally unfinished tapestry of personal human experience.

But if order is a permanent need and an ongoing project of basic human being, then disorder and disorganization are likely to be devalued, to be avoided, and, when experienced, powerful sources of activity aimed at control, correction, or eradication. This is, in fact, the implicit message offered by many highly respected experts on psychiatric disorders, emotional disorders, personality disorders, and the like. Major mental illnesses reflect moderate to severe incapacities to maintain various levels of experiential order, ranging from biological self-regulation and perceptual constancy to continuities of attention and the modulation of emotional activity.

In one form or another, virtually all people seeking psychotherapy want assistance in ordering or reorganizing their lives. This is one of the central tenets of constructivism (Hoyt, 1998; Kelly, 1955; Mahoney, 1991; Neimeyer & Mahoney, 1995). The perspective of constructivism questions the wisdom of interventions that seek to quickly dampen or eliminate expressions of systemic disorganization. Such interventions carry a significant risk of danger because such disorganization is essential to ongoing reorganization. This is not to deny, of course, that some people get "stuck" in disorder. Disorder, in the sense of diminished psychological functioning and well-being, becomes the rule for these unfortunate people, and they struggle for years, and sometimes lifetimes, in the same painful patterns. This tragedy contains a central mystery of human development. How and why do episodes and patterns of disorder become important educational "stepping stones" for some individuals and painful prisons for others? How are we, as helping professionals, supposed to know when a particular client is engaged in potentially constructive versus destructive episodes of personal disorganization?

As difficult as they may be, these questions, I suspect, are grossly oversimplified. Still, they speak to the practical tasks of helping. How do therapists help? Or what and how is it that we help when we are most helpful to our clients? Increasingly, the constructivist response to questions like these invokes a reverent respect for the wisdom of the living system in having worked out its own way of dealing with its life circumstances. Even though that wisdom may have involved significant costs of energy and well-being, it is still a wisdom of self-protection and life value. Hence, the living logic of the person is honored, and his or her personal realities are fundamentally affirmed as creative solutions to a complex history of life challenges. Such life logic may need to be explored and expanded to accommodate new possibilities of experiencing, but it is still the hand- and foothold from which such explorations and expansions must be based. The central responsibility of parent, teacher, and therapist is to help other human beings to function viably while also challenging them to develop.

This is a balancing act, not unlike midwifery. Protective functions are critically important, but there may also be phases when the coordinations of the mother and child must be stimulated or accelerated. In psychotherapy, the protective function begins early and remains throughout the relationship. In acute episodes of disorder, the client is likely to fall back on old patterns of coping. Resistance to change is greatest when core ordering processes are challenged, and acute episodes of turbulence shake the very heart of the system (Mahoney, 1991, in press). After addressing urgent issues and establishing a secure base, the therapist challenges the person's core psychological system, and this must be structured and paced to foster development, without undue risk to systemic integrity. Needless to say, this is more easily said than done, and it is unlikely to be captured in a manualized algorithm of strategy.

A promising dimension of constructive psychotherapy involves its appreciation of the role of problems in human life or, more generally, of the dynamics between order and disorder. By way of a preview, I argue that people live their lives literally by trying to keep their balance. Indeed, I assert that disorder and distress are necessary aspects of life in process and that constructivism represents perhaps the only contemporary perspective that (a) respects the wisdom of the living system in its unique history of adaptation, (b) resists the temptation to pathologize all disorder and dysfunction, and (c) reflects a basic resonance with developments in the sciences of complexity, especially chaos theory and models of nonlinear dynamic development in self-organizing systems (Mahoney & Moes, 1995). Here is a condensation of many of the ideas that form the heart of my current practice of constructive psychotherapy.

- Humans are active participants in organizing their experiences of themselves and their worlds. Dynamic and continuous ordering processes construct, maintain, and revise activity patterns.
- Active ordering processes are primarily tacit and unique to each individual.
- Psychological change involves changes in personal meanings, which are relationships among patterns of activity.
- Resistance to change, even desired change, is common, especially when the change is experienced as "too much" or "too quickly." Such resistance reflects basic self-protective processes that serve to maintain the coherence of a living system.
- Self-organizing processes that are vital to individual functioning ("core ordering processes") are given special protection against change.
- Core ordering processes organize experiences and activities along dimensions that include emotional valence (good vs. bad), reality status (is vs. is not, necessary vs. impossible), personal identity (I vs. you or it), and power (control, efficacy, or agency vs. their opposites).
- Interpersonal relationships involving strong emotions are powerful contexts for psychological development. Early-life relationships are formative but not finalizing influences.
- Self-relationships, which emerge in social and symbolic relationships, influence life quality and resilience under stress.
- Learning and development require novel (unfamiliar or unexpected) experiences that challenge older patterns of activity. Such challenges throw the individual off balance and into relative disorder. Initial attempts to regain systemic balance or order reflect the individual's history of responding to challenge.

1. The quest for balance is often experienced as waves, oscillations, or cycles of contraction (tightening) and expansion (loosening).
2. Episodes of intense disorganization include opportunities for dramatic changes in core ordering processes.
3. Chronic disorganization, dysfunction, and distress result when challenges continue to exceed individual capacities for systemic reorganization.
4. The consequences of a strategic change in activity patterns cannot be accurately anticipated. Change is always risky, as is its avoidance. Successful (adaptive) change is facilitated by a rhythmic orchestration of exploratory, selective, and perpetuating activities.

- Life counseling should reflect an appreciation for the history and power of personal realities; the role of interpersonal, symbolic, and self-relational processes in the maintenance and change of personal realities; and the complex existential agency and responsibility of the socially embedded individual.

I next elaborate on a conception of dynamic core ordering processes, followed by a discussion of disorder in development. I conclude this chapter with reflections on the practical implications of such ideas for psychotherapy.

CORE ORDERING PROCESSES

People's personal ordering processes lie at the heart of not only their experience but also their very survival. Only in the presence of some basic regularities are life-seeking processes maintained. In human evolution, two developments are worth noting: (a) the emergence of the eukaryote (or nucleated) cell and (b) homeostasis as in the physiological ability to create partial stability in one's internal (bodily) environment (Bernard, 1865/1957; Cannon, 1932; Nuland, 1997). Boundaries—from the orderly orbits of subatomic particles, through the literal "walls" that separate a cell from its milieu, to the abstract continuities that we call *personality*, *self*, and *culture*—constitute one of the most primitive and powerful of ordering processes. They separate. They "edge." In a literal sense, they "ject" (meaning "to throw off"; Kegan, 1982).

The many tapestries of order that permeate one's daily life become apparent only when one loses them (or oneself in them), and one experiences moments of surprise, confusion, and anxiety over "losing the way." Most people are not aware of the many strands of order that create and maintain the sense of continuity necessary to develop anything resembling basic survival capacities and fundamental intelligence, let alone personality, "life moods," and that ever-changing yet continuous mystery that is called a "self." People are seldom aware of most core orders of primate embodiment: heart rate and breathing; continuous processes of digestion, absorption, and elimination; ever-shifting targets of sensory attention; and so on. People become aware of them, if at all, when such embodiments are "called" to their attention, either by (a) disorder, disease, or distress or (b) symbols (spoken, written, performed) that "re-mind" one of one's bodily being. My point is that a person's powerful ordering processes operate well beyond the range of explicit (expressible) symbols, whether verbal or mathematical. In other words, people live in (as well as from and through) patternings of experience that are predominantly unconscious, even though they play a significant part in their creation.

In the technical terminology of modern cognitive science, people "feed forward" their cumulative experiences onto their future (ranging from the next moment to months, years, and lifetimes). This being the case, people are poorly prepared for events and experiences that are not familiar (e.g., waking up in a strange place or encountering deviations in their daily patterns). As David Hume (1779/1947) aptly noted, the experiences of surprise and ignorance are incompatible (i.e., people are only "surprised" when their presumptions of knowledge are violated). If the violation is minor, they may shrug it off or even laugh at its incongruity. (Such incongruity is, of course, the most common mechanism in jokes. The "punch line," as it is called, is almost always a violation of expectation.) When the violation is significant, people are "thrown" into crisis or shock. I return to this powerful context of disorder after first elaborating on some basics of order.

CORE ORDER: VALENCE, REALITY, IDENTITY, AND POWER

What are core ordering processes and why is their change so challenging? I have spent many years elaborating my own understanding of these questions. I believe that core ordering processes are generally difficult to change but that their change is essential to most individuals seeking significant and enduring developments or improvements in their personal lives. For many years now, I have oscillated around the idea that some of the processes organizing people's experiences are functionally more central or vital than others. Probably inspired by my early readings of Claude Bernard, Charles Sherrington, and Walter B. Cannon, who were among the first to explicitly speak about the "wisdom of the body" (Nuland, 1997), I was impressed with the special protectiveness that the living organism provides for its most vital organs and their functions. In primates, for example, the spinal cord and brain are encased in bone; the lungs and heart are shielded by bony ribs and thick muscle layers. There are also multiple backup systems that allow the organism to switch to other survival strategies when primary ones are impaired. I wondered what such "core psychological systems" might be, pondering their labels, number, interdependence, relative priority, and so on. My pondering has taught me much about my own efforts to understand human self-organization. I do not feel as though I have reached a resting place in those efforts, but I do feel less discomfort in conjecturing some clusters in people's experiential ordering.

Like so many of my constructivist ancestors and colleagues, I believe that people organize their experiencing—create a basic "sensory order"— through processes that are fundamentally categorical or classificatory (Hayek, 1952), hence the haunting practical relevance of the koan that there are two kinds of people in the world, those who believe that there are two kinds of people in the world and those who do not. Whether there are 2 or 20 kinds, the point is that people create contrasts—"kinds"—to help them organize their experience of themselves and their worlds. Core ordering processes, as I understand them, are likely candidates for dynamic "kinds of kinds," or what Gregory Bateson called "metapatterns," the patterns of patterns (Volk, 1995). That is, they are principled patterns of activity attracted to and defined by polar contrasts fundamental to life as people live it.

Emotionality as Core Valencing

Rene Descartes is said to have launched modern rationalism in the 17th century with the statement "*cogito, ergo sum*" (I think, therefore, I am). But a multitude of Renaissance artists, humanists, and scholars had anticipated his self-assertion with a statement even more basic: "I feel, therefore, I am." Neither statement complies with the requirements of formal logic. Neither thinking nor feeling necessarily implies being. However, feeling is almost globally respected as being closer to existential experience than is thinking. Pain, for example, which is an ultimate dimension of feeling, is probably the greatest "common denominator" in human experiencing. People in pain seldom question the fact that they exist. Indeed, the power of pain to assert existence is probably at the heart of many self-mutilating and aggressive patterns (Katz, 1988). The capacity to hurt is associated with the experience of living. People *feel* themselves to be alive. Moreover, they feel their way through life. They navigate their activities with the aids of vision, sound, taste, touch, and smell, but these senses are themselves organized in the service of a much more powerful harmonic than has been yet captured in theories of motivation.

Emotional ordering processes appear to be at the core because they are among the earliest and most powerful distinctions in the emergence of bodily self-regulation (Bowlby, 1988; Schore, 1994). This is illustrated in the differentiation of human emotions in young children. To the limited extent that people can understand and label what infants and young children experience in their first months of postnatal life, a process of progressive differentiation appears to unfold. Heinz Werner (1957) called this process, reflected in all development, the "orthogenetic principle": Development proceeds "from a state of relative globality and lack of differentiation to a state of increasing differentiation, articulation, and hierarchic integration" (p. 126). A person's emotional differentiation begins with a polar distinction between pleasure and pain (joy and distress). They see shades of the aphorism that there are two kinds of people in the world. Are there two basic (polar, valent) ordering processes (good and bad) in life? There are formidable literatures in ethics, philosophy, religion, and spirituality arguing both for and against such an assertion. I hardly presume to judge their relative merits. What I am more interested in here, and what I believe to be most relevant to a therapist's services to his or her clients, is a strong inclination to organize actions in accordance with what feels "good" (right) and "bad" (wrong). As Huston Smith and others (H. Smith, 1976; S. G. Smith, 1988; Wilber, 1998) related in their broad sketches of world religions, all spiritual traditions ultimately appeal to this very basic dimension.

Professional life counseling has traditionally focused on the negative side of the positive–negative differentiation of emotional experience. This is understandable in Western culture and times, when pain has become a universal enemy and its elimination has become the primary goal in "mental health." People in pain understandably seek relief and counsel. People in pleasure also seek counsel (as is common in instantly rich lottery winners). No one is always on one side of the positive–negative divide. I imply here that the seeking is special in itself, whether motivated by biological survival or spiritual longing. Anger and anxiety appear to be the first distinct negative emotional patterns. These primitive affective patterns probably reflect people's biologically most powerful expressions of self-protection and active engagement with their quest to continue being. Cultural and linguistic traditions encourage one to categorize anxiety as a more passive and constraining force (in German, *angst* means "narrowing"), whereas anger is usually deemed more volatile and active. As a formidable force in one's systemic self-organization, anger is often associated with tragic acts of aggression and violence. But this is not a necessary association. Neither anger nor anxiety is bad or inherently dysfunctional. Like their sibling emotions, they are precious expressions of a life-seeking and self-asserting force. My point is to preview the thesis that anger and anxiety (as well as their "positive" contrasts) are likely components in all subsequent forms of emotional development and experience. Thus, one's emotional self-organizing processes are primary and powerful in one's life efforts.

Reality as Existential Assumption

People literally feel their way through life. It is not just blind people who use special tools and companions to help them navigate their movements around the obstacles in their path. All people do it, in many different ways. Undeniably, there *is* something "out there" (i.e., beyond one's mind and imagination), and people are wise to take this fact into account in their movements. Contemporary experts in the sciences of complexity and evolutionary epistemology (the evolution of knowing systems) are drawn to the metaphor of "adaptational landscapes" (Bonner, 1988; Dennett, 1995; Jantsch, 1980; Kauffman, 1993, 1995; Kelso, 1995; Salthe, 1993). In their elaboration of this metaphor, they talk about multiple peaks and valleys that represent a mixture of probabilities and possibilities in the potential movements of a living system. At a more graphic level, and in words more often used by my own clients, there are "walls" that you may suddenly walk into, there are hard rock floors that you hit when you "crash" or "fall," there are tight "traps" where you feel caught and immobilized, and there are sharp edges that cut you, sometimes superficially and sometimes to your heart. (In the metaphorical sense, at least, many life counselors are heart specialists; we often work with "wounds of being.")

In my discussion of reality as a core ordering process, I aim toward a realm of existential organization that has eluded verbal description by the most insightful and eloquent of thinkers and writers (Caputo, 1987; Dreyfus, 1991; Heidegger, 1962; Merleau-Ponty, 1962; Silverman, 1988). Children around the world face off daily in adamant assertions of "is too" versus "is not." But only rare beings have entered the mysteries of the "is" in ways that others can even partially appreciate. Reality is an orderly phenomenon, to be sure, and most cultures teach their children that adaptation and survival require them to act in accordance with (a "natural") order, which may be given a number of names. Indeed, disorder and disease have been most frequently associated with a failure to "contact," respect, or otherwise comply with the demands of reality.

This is not the place to enter into the labyrinthine complexities of *ontology*: theories of reality, theories of "things in themselves." Most relevant to my discussion of core ordering processes in human experience is the nearly universal assumption that reality is an order that lies outside of people. Planetary paradigms, across many millennia of time and vast expanses of space, have almost unanimously placed reality and the world outside the adapting organism. Indeed, a recent scientific revolution reified this external-ization in genuflecting to *objectivism* (observational distance) and *positivism* (public observability). In this portrayal, reality is necessarily something beyond people, and it is common to assume that this real, true order of the universe is singular (i.e., there is only one reality or truth) and permanent (i.e., it is eternal). As a constructivist, I do not believe that reality is singular, permanent, or exclusively outside of people. There is a formidable dimensionality to it. As philosopher Alfred North Whitehead liked to say in his lectures, "there *is* furniture in the universe!" (see Griffin, Cobb, Ford, Gunter, & Ochs, 1993). People are not typically bumping into imaginary obstacles in their lives (although they do have tendencies to create them). There is something beyond them and their imaginings. How are people to anticipate and negotiate those obstacles and opportunities?

Most people act, most of the time, as if their five senses offer reliable and trustworthy information about what lies beyond them. Most of the time, they are warranted in their trust. Vision has earned a special place in the history of science partly because it is such a powerfully shared dimension of sensation. Public observability became the cardinal feature of objectivity and positivism, but people still struggle to free themselves from the conceptual blindness created when only the visible is deemed valid. Touch and olfaction (smell) are arguably as primitive and powerful as vision in human beings' constructions of reality, but this is a recent acknowledgment (Freeman, 1995). Likewise, sound, especially rhythmic sound (e.g., music), and taste bring up the rear, except in some subcultures.

Constructivists contend that a person's sense of reality is greater than the sum of his or her sense data. This is not to deny that sensory capacities are critical channels in the life organization. Touching and being touched, seeing and being seen, hearing and being heard, and lending one's voice and musical skills to the multiple orchestral phonics of life are all activities that define one's uniqueness as life patterns. (Add smell and taste, from breakfast to the bedroom, and one's uniqueness becomes truly intimate.) But the senses, according to constructivists, are more than sensibilities. It is a limiting illusion to believe that people only have five ("n") channels of sensitivity to incoming stimulation. Not only are there more than five, but what is incoming is miniscule compared with what is outgoing. People are not just scanning for signals of an external reality; they are actively recruiting, amplifying or suppressing, and distorting signals. Fernando Pessoa (1991) was not exaggerating when he stated that "we manufacture realities." People are their creators and inhabitants, and they always reside within a "work in progress," whether they label this progress "repair" or "renovation." This creative dance between the organism and its milieu is a symbiotic and developmentally generative one. In such a living complex, reality is neither something outside nor an entity or representation inside. Rather, reality is an ongoing coordination of processes, a continuing order in which each person uniquely participates (Ford, 1987; Guidano, 1987, 1991; Hayek,

1952, 1964; Maturana & Varela, 1980, 1987; Mingers, 1995; Varela, 1979; Weimer, 1982, 1987; Zeleny, 1980).

Self-Continuity as Personal Identity

Because people experience themselves as existing as separate systems, separated by their skin and other boundaries from the ecosystems that afford them, they understandably are inclined to center their sense of life in their interiors. This lies at the essence of the core ordering process of personal identity or "selfing," which has become a central theme in late 20th century theories of life span development, personality, psychotherapy, and psychopathology (Anderson, 1997; Guidano, 1987, 1991; Kegan, 1982; Linville, 1987; Mahoney, 1991, in press; Markus & Nurius, 1986; Neimeyer & Mahoney, 1995; Wurf & Markus, 1991). The spectrum of activity in object relations theory, self psychology, and transpersonal studies testifies to one's fascination with the foundations and frontiers of one's sense of oneself. Psychotherapy clients (and the rest of humanity) often become imprisoned in painful and discouraging constructions of their identities. The psychotherapist is, therefore, confronted with formidable requests to change who his or her clients are as well as how they feel and what is real to them.

I find it difficult to be brief in this discussion of the self as a core ordering process. It is a daunting mystery that speaks to one's most intimate experience, one's innermost experience of oneself. The nature of a self and the merits (and option) of having or not having one, or of having a particular kind of self, these are among the most complicated and controversial topics in contemporary (postmodern) dialogue. Can one change who one is? Can one transcend one's sense of self? Is it selfish or narcissistic to be fascinated with such questions (Zweig, 1980)? How does one's conceptualization of oneself influence one's experience of others and the nested communities within (and probably beyond) the small planet Earth?

I am necessarily biased in my remarks in this domain. I have spent my professional career researching dimensions of selfhood. I began with self-control (weight management, study skills, and habit change) and later diversified into self-regulated thought control, which is the central concern of the cognitive therapies. My personal and professional interests diverged in later years. Control became less interesting to me than something conceptually larger. Perhaps it could be called wisdom, but whatever the label, I found myself pursuing paths and companions who embodied a much larger sense of self than I had previously entertained (Bugental, 1978, 1981; Krippner, 1994; Varela, Thompson, & Rosch, 1991; Walsh & Vaughan, 1980; Wilber, 1998). My therapeutic style drifted toward deeper authenticity, compassionate witnessing, and developmental nurturance rather than clever engineering and technical solutions. My research, which has always mirrored my personal development, shifted in both focus and methodology. I began to study sensory deprivation, contemplation (meditation), stream of consciousness, and the experience of relating to oneself in a mirror.

My continuing studies into consciousness and the personal meanings of spirituality extend this theme. It is a theme of relationships. I do not believe that there are only two kinds of people in the world: those who are self-preoccupied and those who are not. Self-relationships and interpersonal relationships are inextricable. How one relates to oneself is necessarily mirrored in how one relates to others, especially intimate others. Many unhappy individuals hope to find an "other" who will take away the demons of their existential suffering. It is an understandable, although impossible, quest; however, it should be honored for the human heart that it expresses. Shortly before his death, philosopher Bertrand Russell (1967) expressed the power of a loving relationship as one of the passions that had driven his life:

> I have sought love . . . because it brings ecstasy—ecstasy so great that I would often have sacrificed all the rest of life for a few hours of this joy. I have sought it, next, because it relieves loneliness—that terrible loneliness in which one shivering consciousness looks over the rim of the world into the cold unfathomable lifeless abyss. I have sought it, finally, because in the union of love I have seen, in a mystic miniature, the prefiguring vision of the heaven that saints and poets have imagined. (pp. 3–4)

As Erich Fromm (1956), and other sages, recalled, one's capacity to genuinely love another is inseparable from one's capacity to love oneself; this is unfortunately a difficult task for many (Zweig, 1980). One of the central themes in my therapeutic work is self-relationship, ranging from self-awareness and self-acceptance to what might be called "self-actualization" or "self-celebration." These abilities, I believe, are fundamental to an authentic transpersonal engagement with life and with others living, dead, and yet to be. Thus, selfhood and selfing are core processes of experiential order, and all psychotherapy is ultimately self psychotherapy.

Power as Possibility

The complex interdependence of core ordering processes is even more highlighted when the dimension of power is considered. Emotional order (feeling good, bad, or otherwise) is inseparable from one's sense of world order (reality) and one's unique positionality (selfhood or identity) within it. At the opening of his revolutionary *Critique of Pure Reason*, Immanuel Kant (1789/1929) confided that his tome had been driven by three simple questions: What can I know? What may I hope? What should I do? His answers were less simple than the questions, but the questions reflect the basic themes of core ordering processes discussed here. The relationship between hope and action is connected through a sense of power or agency. Can one change things (including one's world, one's self, one's feelings, and one's future)? If not, in an absolute sense, then surrender is probably a wise general posture. If one can change or influence at least some things, however, a prudent course of action is likely to include a more engaged and agentic involvement with daily life. Anxiety and depression (which often oscillate and comingle in actual lives) are relatively active and passive modes of disengagement. When one is more anxious, avoidance tends to be active, sometimes frantic. When one is more depressed, avoidance tends to take on a "heaviness" that makes any effort, even getting out of bed, a formidable challenge. A person who has been chronically depressed often experiences episodes of anxiety because he or she begins to shift toward an active reengagement with life.

Bandura's (1986, 1997) social cognitive theory, with the construct of self-efficacy at its center, is a comprehensive attempt to understand and facilitate the empowerment of individuals, communities, and larger collectives in assuming more active roles in their own lives and futures. Bandura's theory expands Kant's (1789/1929) question of "What should I do?" into "What can I do?" This emphasis on doing is a fundamental issue for all psychotherapists and their clients. Any psychotherapy that grants individuals a degree of power or agency in their movement through the present and into the future is a psychotherapy of action. This emphasis on action need not be on a driven "Type A" struggle for control. Sometimes it is wise to counsel using "Don't just sit there—do something!"; other times it is wise to advise using "Don't just do something—sit there!" Action, as I envision it, is aware engagement, which is often a balanced improvisational dance of effort and surrender according to the prevailing possibilities. "Learned resourcefulness," as Michael Rosenbaum (1990) called it, is as an important a construct as "learned helplessness" in contemporary psychology. Throughout a human life, there are moments and seasons when "trying harder" and "letting go" are each wise courses of action. Part of the challenge of living is knowing when and how to do which.

PRACTICAL IMPLICATIONS

What does all of this mean for your clients? The meaning will vary, of course, but it is likely to include a message about their own personal quests for order. Those quests often represent mixtures of the desire to understand ("What is happening?" "Why is this happening to me?" "How did I get to be this way?") and the desire to predict and control ("What will happen to me?" "What should I do?" "How can I change it?"). Like therapists, clients seek explanations and assurances of order. They want to know (why, how, when, what, who). They seek a "firm" foundation for their beliefs (the origin of the verb *to understand* is to have the intimate knowledge that comes only from "standing under" the object of one's interest). They exert "effort after meaning," as Sir Frederic Bartlett (1932) put it, and create the stories that they live in. Some stories serve them better than others, and some are the source of much pain. It is usually in the face of pain that an individual enters psychotherapy.

Besides serving as a safe and accessible "port in a storm," the therapist often strives to reassure the client about what he or she is experiencing. Episodes of intensely negative emotionality and variability are often frightening to clients, who may describe themselves as "falling apart," "not together," "coming unglued," and so on. In complex systems terminology, these are expressions of their sense that their coherence (systemic integrity) or core may be disintegrating. Feelings of fear, dread, and intense vulnerability are common. In responding to the expression of such feelings, therapists are well advised to respect the phenomenology of their clients. Even if the therapist believes that there is little warrant for a particular feeling, it is the client's psychological reality at that point in time. Challenging the warrant for the feeling may be important at intermediate stages of therapy, but such challenges are usually more effective in the context of a relationship in which the client feels understood and respected. Moreover, the therapist is likely to be capable of greater degrees of reassurance to the extent that he or she is not unduly disturbed, frightened, or destabilized by expressions of emotional intensity and variability. Research comparing more and less successful therapists suggests that the latter often move too quickly or confrontively, given their clients' current accommodative capacities. Such therapists then withdraw in fear when clients display significant destabilization, leaving their clients fundamentally perturbed and then abandoned. Emotional self-awareness, coping skills, interpersonal attunement, and a well-developed sense of timing are, therefore, important assets for therapists.

An important contribution of complexity studies to the conceptualization and practice of psychotherapy is an appreciation for phase transitions and the dynamics of development. Although therapists may not be able to use the technical terminology of chaos and the sciences of complexity to help clients conceptualize what they are experiencing and how it reflects natural processes, we can use developmental metaphors that convey some of that same message. Physical metaphors that invoke bodily experiences are often helpful in reassuring clients, such as "growing pains," "molting," and the like. Metaphors of journeying are also useful, and clients can be encouraged to construct a description of where they have been and where they now are. One client, for example, was very experienced in whitewater canoeing. When an unexpected life event destabilized her, she described her transition into chaos in terms of what she was familiar with, namely, as a slowly moving stream suddenly becoming a torrent of unexpected rapids where she had little control and was desperately struggling just to stay upright and off the rocks. This metaphor helped her regain some sense of familiarity with what she was experiencing, and she felt reassured by realizing that, like river rapids, the rapids in her psychological life were not likely to last forever and that they were likely to be followed by calm waters and opportunities to rest.

But this is not always the outcome in life, and this is one of the necessary acknowledgments of practicing psychotherapy with an appreciation for complex systems. Happy endings are not guaranteed. Indeed, theory, research, and clinical experience all converge on the inevitable realization that no one can predict or control what is coming next in life. Neither can one ever completely know the consequences of a particular course of action. One may feel that one understands the operative principles and the processes that they describe, but there is a world of difference between principles and particulars. Psychotherapists, among others, learn that well-reasoned plans of action often lead to consequences and later choice points that were never anticipated. Thus, periods of destabilization are not always preludes to the emergence of a healthier and happier system. At many levels, research indicates that variability in activity is at least a prerequisite to change and often an integral element in the creative solutions or expressions that may emerge. This has been illustrated in studies ranging from infants' motor development to psychotherapy process (Hager, 1992; Mahoney & Moes, 1995; Masterpasqua & Perna, 1995; Robertson & Combs, 1995; Suedfeld & Bluck, 1993; Thelen & Smith, 1994).

Of particular importance for the practitioner is an appreciation for individual and temporal differences in clients' needs for support and challenge. During periods of intense destabilization, clients may need highly structured experiences to help them deal with their phenomenological chaos. In moments of panic or hysteria, for example, clients may need very simple, specific, and straightforward directions, such as "look at me, listen to my voice, and breathe slowly like I am doing." The stabilizing aspects of such instructions draw on the visual system as a primary source of perceptual order, the potential power of voice, and the usefulness of focusing on a basic bodily rhythm, such as breathing. During more protracted episodes of destabilization, clients may benefit from generous and patient reassurance, combined with the practice of daily routines that contribute to a familiar sense of order. Focusing on "what needs to get done when" may also help the destabilized client feel more like a participant than a victim in his or her current episode of distress. Needless to say, it is important that these "grounding" or stabilizing routines be order maintaining and initially easy to achieve.

The issue of therapeutic challenge is a complex one. Most clients find themselves in therapy because they are having difficulties with the challenges in their lives. The amount of challenge is important. Too little challenge may encourage "business as usual," which may be neither satisfying nor functional for the individual, whereas too much challenge may result in clients displaying patterns of withdrawal punctuated by extreme distress. If they feel overwhelmed, they are likely to exhibit more frequent and intense cycles of activities, which may jeopardize their functioning. Even more important than the absolute quantity of challenge, however, may be its timing and its meaningfulness (relatedness) to the individual's core ordering processes. The skilled therapist attempts to remain attuned to his or her client's "intellectual (systemic) respirations" and to offer appropriately timed encouragements and challenges toward elaboration. Although it is more easily described than achieved, this level of attunement and modulation is essential to constructive psychotherapy.

CONCLUSION

I tried in this chapter to briefly outline the relevance of conceptualizing psychotherapy as an endeavor that embraces both the human quest for order and the inevitable presence of disorder in complex developing systems. I believe that one of the most valuable contributions of constructive approaches in psychotherapy is their ability to avoid the pathologizing and problem-focused traditions that have been dominant in the profession. Viewing individuals as active and resourceful participants in their own experiencing patterns can help to empower them in the face of life challenges. Moreover, viewing disorder as a natural expression of human development can shift energies toward learning the valuable skills required to navigate through rough seas. As illustrated in the other chapters in this volume, such views of the person and of life carry far-reaching implications for how therapists practice.

REFERENCES

Anderson, W. T. (1997). *The future of the self: Inventing the postmodern person*. New York: Tarcher/Putnam.

Bandura, A. (1986). *Social foundations of thought and action*. Englewood Cliffs, NJ: Prentice-Hall.

Bandura, A. (1997). *Self-efficacy: The exercise of control.* New York: Freeman.

Bartlett, F. C. (1932). *Remembering.* Cambridge, England: Cambridge University Press.

Bernard, C. (1957). *An introduction to the study of experimental medicine.* New York: Dover. (Original work published 1865)

Bonner, J. T. (1988). *The evolution of complexity by means of natural selection.* Princeton, NJ: Princeton University Press.

Bowlby, J. (1988). *A secure base.* New York: Basic Books.

Bugental, J. F. T. (1978). *Psychotherapy and process: The fundamentals of an existential–humanistic approach.* Reading, MA: Addison-Wesley.

Bugental, J. F. T. (1981). *The search for authenticity: An existential–analytic approach to psychotherapy.* New York: Irvington.

Cannon, W. B. (1932). *The wisdom of the body.* New York: Norton.

Caputo, J. D. (1987). *Radical hermeneutics: Repetition, deconstruction, and the hermeneutic project.* Bloomington: Indiana University Press.

Dennett, D. C. (1995). *Darwin's dangerous idea: Evolution and the meanings of life.* New York: Simon & Schuster.

Dreyfus, H. L. (1991). *Being-in-the-world: A commentary on Heidegger's Being and time, Division I.* Cambridge, MA: MIT Press.

Ford, D. H. (1987). *Humans as self-constructing living systems: A developmental perspective on behavior and personality.* Hillsdale, NJ: Erlbaum.

Foucault, M. (1970). *The order of things: An archeology of the human sciences.* New York: Random House.

Freeman, W. J. (1995). *Societies of brains: Mind, morals, and the meaning of life.* Hillsdale, NJ: Erlbaum.

Fromm, E. (1956). *The art of loving.* New York: Harper.

Griffin, D. R., Cobb, J. B., Ford, M. P., Gunter, P. A. Y., & Ochs, P. (1993). *Founders of constructive postmodern philosophy: Peirce, James, Bergson, Whitehead, and Hartshorne.* Albany: SUNY Press.

Guidano, V. F. (1987). *Complexity of the self: A developmental approach to psychopathology and therapy.* New York: Guilford Press.

Guidano, V. F. (1991). *The self in process: Toward a post-rationalist cognitive therapy.* New York: Guilford Press.

Hager, D. (1992). Chaos and growth. *Psychotherapy, 29,* 378–384.

Halleck, S. L. (1971). *The politics of therapy.* New York: Harper & Row.

Hayek, F. A. (1952). *The sensory order.* Chicago: University of Chicago Press.

Hayek, F. A. (1964). The theory of complex phenomena. In M. Bunge (Ed.), *The critical approach to science and philosophy: Essays in honor of K. R. Popper* (pp. 332–349). New York: Free Press.

Heidegger, M. (1962). *Being and time.* New York: Harper & Row.

Hoyt, M. F. (Ed.). (1998). *The handbook of constructive therapies*. San Francisco: Jossey-Bass.

Hume, D. (1947). *Dialogues concerning natural religion* (N. K. Smith, Trans.). New York: Bobbs-Merrill. (Original work published 1779)

Jantsch, E. (1980). *The self-organizing universe: Scientific and human implications of the emerging paradigm of evolution*. Elmsford, NY: Pergamon Press.

Kant, I. (1929). *The critique of pure reason* (N. K. Smith, Trans.). New York: Macmillan. (Original work published 1789)

Katz, J. (1988). *Seductions of crime: Moral and sensual attractions in doing evil*. New York: Basic Books.

Kauffman, S. A. (1993). *The origins of order: Self-organization and selection in evolution*. Oxford, England: Oxford University Press.

Kauffman, S. A. (1995). *At home in the universe*. Oxford, England: Oxford University Press.

Kegan, R. (1982). *The evolving self: Problem and process in human development*. Cambridge, MA: Harvard University Press.

Kelly, E. A. (1955). *The psychology of personal constructs*. New York: Norton.

Kelso, J. A. S. (1995). *Dynamic patterns: The self-organization of brain and behavior*. Cambridge, MA: MIT Press.

Krippner, S. (1994). Humanistic psychology and chaos theory: The third revolution and the third force. *Journal of Humanistic Psychology, 34*, 48–61.

Linville, P. (1987). Self-complexity as a buffer against stress-related illness and depression. *Journal of Personality and Social Psychology, 52*, 663–676.

Mahoney, M. J. (1991). *Human change processes: The scientific foundations of psychotherapy*. New York: Basic Books.

Mahoney, M. J. (in press). *Constructive psychotherapy: Exploring principles and practices*. New York: Guilford Press.

Mahoney, M. J., & Moes, A. J. (1995). Complexity and psychotherapy: Promising dialogues and practical issues. In F. Masterpasqua & P. A. Perna (Eds.), *The psychological meaning of chaos: Self-organization in human development and psychotherapy* (pp. 177–198). Washington, DC: American Psychological Association.

Markus, H., & Nurius, P. (1986). Possible selves. *American Psychologist, 41*, 954–969.

Masterpasqua, F., & Perna, P. A. (Eds.). (1995). *The psychological meaning of chaos*. Washington, DC: American Psychological Association.

Maturana, H. R., & Varela, F. J. (Eds.). (1980). *Autopoiesis and cognition: The realization of the living*. Boston: Reidel.

Maturana, H. R., & Varela, F. J. (1987). *The tree of knowledge: The biological roots of human understanding*. Boston: Shambhala.

Merleau-Ponty, M. (1962). *Phenomenology of perception* (C. Smith, Trans.). London: Routledge & Kegan Paul.

Mingers, J. (1995). *Self-producing systems*. New York: Plenum Press.

Neimeyer, R. A., & Mahoney, M. J. (Eds.). (1995). *Constructivism in psychotherapy*. Washington, DC: American Psychological Association.

Nuland, S. B. (1997). *The wisdom of the body*. New York: Knopf.

Pessoa, F. (1991). *The book of disquiet*. New York: Pantheon.

Robertson, R., & Combs, A. (Eds.). (1995). *Chaos theory and psychology in the life sciences*. Mahwah, NJ: Erlbaum.

Rosenbaum, M. (Ed.). (1990). *Learned resourcefulness: On coping skills, self-control, and adaptive behavior*. New York: Springer.

Russell, B. (1967). *The autobiography of Bertrand Russell: 1872–1914*. Boston: Little, Brown.

Salthe, S. N. (1993). *Development and evolution: Complexity and change in biology*. Cambridge, MA: MIT Press.

Schore, A. N. (1994). *Affect regulation and the origin of the self: The neurobiology of emotional development*. Hillsdale, NJ: Erlbaum.

Silverman, H. J. (Ed.). (1988). *Continental philosophy: I. Philosophy and non-philosophy since Merleau-Ponty*. London: Routledge.

Smith, H. (1976). *Forgotten truth: The primordial tradition*. New York: Harper.

Smith, S. G. (1988). *The concept of the spiritual: An essay in first philosophy*. Philadelphia: University of Pennsylvania Press.

Suedfeld, P., & Bluck, S. (1993). Changes in integrative complexity accompanying significant life events: Historical evidence. *Journal of Personality and Social Psychology, 64*, 124–130.

Szasz, T. S. (1970). *The manufacture of madness: A cooperative study of the inquisition and the mental health movement*. New York: Harper & Row.

Thelen, E., & Smith, L. B. (1994). *A dynamic systems approach to the development of cognition and action*. Cambridge, MA: MIT Press.

Varela, F. J. (1979). *Principles of biological autonomy*. Amsterdam, The Netherlands: Elsevier North-Holland.

Varela, F. J., Thompson, E., & Rosch, E. (1991). *The embodied mind: Cognitive science and human experience*. Cambridge, MA: MIT Press.

Volk, T. (1995). *Metapatterns: Across space, time, and mind*. New York: Columbia University Press.

Walsh, R. N., & Vaughan, F. (Eds.). (1980). *Beyond ego: Transpersonal dimensions in psychology*. Los Angeles, CA: Tarcher.

Weimer, W. B. (1982). Hayek's approach to the problems of complex phenomena: An introduction to the theoretical psychology of *The sensory order*. In W. B. Weimer & D. S. Palermo (Eds.), *Cognition and the symbolic processes* (Vol. 2), (pp. 241–285). Hillsdale, NJ: Erlbaum.

Weimer, W. B. (1987). Spontaneously ordered complex phenomena and the unity of the moral sciences. In G. Radnitzky (Ed.), *Centripetal forces in the sciences* (pp. 257–296). New York: Paragon House.

Werner, H. (1957). The concept of development from a comparative and organismic point of view. In D. B. Harris (Ed.), *The concept of development: An issue in the study of human behavior* (pp. 125–148). Minneapolis: University of Minnesota Press.

Wilber, K. (1998). *The marriage of sense and soul: Integrating science and religion.* New York: Random House.

Wurf, E., & Markus, H. (1991). Possible selves and the psychology of personal growth. *Perspectives in Personality, 3,* 39–62.

Zeleny, M. (Ed.). (1980). *Autopoiesis, dissipative structures, and spontaneous social orders.* Washington, DC: American Association for the Advancement of Science.

Zweig, P. (1980). *The heresy of self-love: A study of subversive individualism.* Princeton, NJ: Princeton University Press.

4

THE ORDER IN CLINICAL "DISORDER": SYMPTOM COHERENCE IN DEPTH-ORIENTED BRIEF THERAPY

BRUCE ECKER AND LAUREL HULLEY

Constructivist thought captured the imagination of whole new segments of the psychotherapy world, ourselves included, when it emerged in the nonpathologizing brief and systemic therapies of the 1970s. Organizing therapy around the view that people think, feel, and act according to how they construe the context of experience yielded a nimbleness of process and a swiftness of change that was revolutionary.

This refreshing efficacy was achieved with methodologies that by design avoided any work with the unconscious and emotional construction of symptoms. Yet why should constructivist thought not achieve high levels of dexterity when applied to in-depth therapy? This question was the guiding spirit of our work over many years of clinical practice. It progressively became apparent that there was a predictable pattern in our clients' unconscious constructions, a well-defined, four-level structure of order and coherence generating the surface manifestation of clinical "disorder." With increasing understanding of this specific structure, it became clear which aspects of methodology contributed to in-depth resolution most effectively and why.

The resulting leap in therapeutic effectiveness bore out our original intuition of what would be possible if constructivism were fully operationalized. We call this system of psychotherapy depth-oriented brief therapy (DOBT; Ecker & Hulley, 1996, in press).

After a capsule summary of the constructivist basics that are DOBT's point of departure, we give in this chapter a succinct account of its model of symptom production. We then discuss four clinical case examples intended to show concretely how DOBT ushers the client into a richly experiential process that reveals and uses psychological deep structure to bring about resolution. We begin with the following foundational notions of constructivism.

1. The internal "representations" that make up experiential reality are subjective renditions actively constructed by the individual, not passively received stored copies of an objective reality (Guidano, 1995a; Mahoney, 1988b; Mahoney, Miller, & Arciero, 1995; von Glasersfeld, 1979, 1988). The mind's constructs are the person's knowledge structures; that is, they define what the individual takes as reality and how to anticipate and respond to that reality (Kelly, 1955; Piaget, 1937/1971).

2. Symptoms and problems presented in psychotherapy are, like all features of experiential reality, products of the constructs individuals are using for knowing and responding to the flux of experience. Because the mind itself forms its personal store of constructs (either originally creating them or installing those received socially), it can also dissolve or discard them. People ordinarily are not conscious of having and using these native capacities to create, maintain, or dissolve constructs, but it is a constructivist psychotherapist's task to be skilled in prompting the use of these capacities.

3. The constructs that govern personal experience and behavior most broadly and potently are unconscious (Hayek, 1978; Polanyi, 1966; Turvey, 1974; Weimer, 1982a; the terms *implicit* and *tacit* are used by some constructivist writers).

4. The mind is understood as being self-organizing, using "core ordering processes" or "nuclear morphogenic structure" (Hayek, 1952, 1978; Mahoney, 1988a, 1988b, 1991; Mahoney et al., 1995; Weimer, 1977, 1982a, 1987). These phrases refer to an hierarchical arrangement in which the surface structure of overt thoughts, feelings, and behaviors is constrained and shaped by a deep structure of more abstract, unconscious, and nonlinguistically held constructs.

SYMPTOM COHERENCE

The core concept of DOBT is *symptom coherence*: A symptom or problem is produced by a person because he or she harbors at least one unconscious construction of reality in which the symptom seems compellingly necessary to have, despite the suffering or trouble incurred by having it. Symptom coherence dictates a methodology in which the therapist focuses on discovering the client's unconscious construction of emotional reality that requires having the symptom and makes complete sense of having it. When there is no longer any construction within which the symptom is necessary to have, the person ceases producing it. Embedded in this model of symptom production is the constructivist view of the self as having profound if unconscious agency in shaping experience and behavior.

The direct evidence for symptom coherence is DOBT's explicit, phenomenological mapping of the deep structure of symptom-necessitating constructions. A universal pattern, not previously delineated, is revealed, namely, a four-level hierarchy of constructs of different logical types: unconscious, core ontological themes; unconscious, urgent life purposes based on those themes; unconscious contexts or frames construed and applied to the concrete situation according to those purposes; and conscious, manifested responses (including clinical symptoms) produced within those contexts. Recognizing and skillfully using this deep order in the consulting room can bring new levels of accuracy, effectiveness, and swiftness to in-depth psychotherapy.

Moreover, this same four-level hierarchy is responsible for the manifestation of all thoughts, feelings, and behaviors, not only those considered symptomatic by psychiatric or sociocultural standards. That is, most clinical symptoms conventionally viewed as pathology and dysfunction are produced by the normal functioning of this core scheme of order self-maintained by the mind. Identifying this order within an apparent disorder further develops the constructivist challenge to standard notions of psychopathology.

As mentioned, a construct of vital purpose proves to be a key part of every unconscious construction maintaining a clinical symptom. It is this governing purpose that renders the presenting symptom "necessary" to have in one of two ways: the symptom is either functional, itself directly carrying out the crucial purpose, or functionless, an incidental by-product necessitated by the way in which the vital purpose is being carried out. What has historically seemed to be the opposing views of functional versus functionless symptom production (see, e.g., Bogdan, 1986; and Hoffman, 1981) are unified within DOBT's conceptual framework as two subtypes of symptom coherence.

The order just described within any one construction of reality exists in tandem with another pattern of order governing the relationship between different constructions. DOBT phenomenologically shows that unconscious constructions operate as isolated, parallel, state-specific knowledge modules, each pertaining to a specific narrow context and determining the person's behavioral response and subjective experience within that zone of personal meaning. This description corresponds closely with the findings in the fields of cognitive science (e.g., Fodor, 1983; Johnson-Laird, 1988; Rumelhart & McClelland, 1986) and psychoneurology (e.g., Gazzaniga, 1985; Posner & Raichle, 1994). DOBT works specifically with this aspect of psychic order by bringing out of isolation the construct modules that maintain symptoms, integrating them into the network of conscious knowledge structures. This qualitative shift in how the constructs are held, with no attempt to change the constructs themselves, proves to be the key condition for their transformation, thereby resolving the problem.

Four examples of anxiety symptoms show how DOBT reveals and uses the hidden order that produces clinical symptoms. The first two examples show the coherence of functionless symptoms of anxiety and of panic attacks; the next two are instances in which these same kinds of symptoms prove to be functional. The overall similarity of symptoms is intended to make it particularly clear that even within the predictable deep structure of symptom coherence, the specific constructs driving symptom production are unique in each case and require a phenomenological, noninterpretive approach.

Assessment in DOBT, therefore, consists of carrying out the phenomenological methodology of discovery to identify the unique constructions maintaining symptom production. (In other writings, we refer to this methodology as "radical discovery" or "radical inquiry" to underscore its specialized design for direct accessing of root constructs, *radical* deriving from the Latin *radix*, meaning "root.") Treatment then consists of ushering the client into making permanent changes in those constructions (with a methodology we elsewhere called "experiential shift").

Functionless Anxiety

We worked with a woman who wanted therapy to relieve her symptoms of ongoing raw anxiety and paralyzing feelings of being helplessly vulnerable to disaster. She was in the midst of intense extrafamilial conflicts, legal battles, and various health crises within her family, all posing serious consequences for her young children, her husband, and herself.

The extent to which this woman was beseiged in her external circumstances nearly drew the therapist into viewing her anxiety and overwhelmed state as a natural reaction to such a threat, but the therapist managed to pursue the internal construction necessitating her symptoms and, by the end of the first session, had found it. This woman had a powerful, fully unconscious emotional theme and purpose which, once discovered experientially, was then put into phrases, such as "My life is supposed to be the life of a Good Girl. I'm not willing to give that up! If I get fierce, to fight a battle, I'd seem like a troublemaker or crazy and no longer be a Good Girl. So, I'm not going to be a fighter and get fierce, even if that leaves me so endangered and so unable to protect us that I'm full of anxiety."

These phrases verbalize what we term the emotional truth of the symptom: the (until now) unconscious but well-defined construction of personal meaning that produced symptomatic levels of anxiety and helplessness. As the phrasing illustrates, a symptom's unconscious emotional truth contains a reality-defining theme (a Good Girl gets to have a certain kind of life) and a compelling purpose stemming from that theme (be a Good Girl to have that life), with a general design for carrying out that purpose (have only the qualities of a Good Girl and avoid having qualities that disqualify one from being a Good Girl). The symptom of terrified vulnerability is necessitated by how the client carries out that ardent purpose (maintain the role of a nonfierce nonfighter, even when under attack). Symptom coherence means that the symptom is produced as a necessary feature of a cogent construction of reality.

When a client knows, feels, and actually voices the whole construction comprising the symptom's emotional truth, she experiences it as being her own *position:* her own view of reality, own purpose within that view, and own way of carrying out that purpose. It is, in a very real sense, the client's discovery of having a powerful, life-organizing position, which he or she has had all along but did not know he or she had. There is much therapeutic value in recognizing this as the client's position because of how strongly this term spotlights his or her discovered agency in relation to the problem. We refer to the position that necessitates the symptom as the client's "pro-symptom position," simply because it is entirely in favor of producing the symptom. This contrasts with the position sharply against having the symptom that the client feels and expresses at the start of therapy: his or her "anti-symptom position," in which the symptom is construed as completely senseless, valueless, and undesirable and is something to eliminate; an involuntary experience, making one a powerless victim; and evidence of pathology, disorder, deficiency, defectiveness or badness of self, others, or the world. Obviously, it is from this position that a person seeks therapy, and virtually all psychotherapies are designed to stop the symptom by strengthening this position against having it. The strategy of DOBT is along a fundamentally different line.

Within the emotional reality of the client's unconscious, pro-symptom position, eliminating the symptom means not carrying out the ardent purpose necessitating it. Not carrying out that purpose is expected to bring dire consequences and a suffering much worse than the familiar suffering accompanying the symptom. Without knowing it, the client is caught between the "devil and the deep blue sea." The client arrives in therapy having already unconsciously and powerfully opted for the suffering with the symptom, over the even worse suffering without it. In the current example, the client came to the session cleaving to the role of a Good Girl who never fights, unconsciously choosing to suffer the raw anxiety of defenselessness rather than be a tough fighter who protects herself but suffers the loss of the life of a Good Girl.

Note that being in a state of anxiety is not in itself how she carries out her governing purpose of having the life of a Good Girl. It is by not fighting even when under attack that she carries out that purpose, and anxiety then necessarily arises as a functionless by-product of being (purposefully) defenseless.

For a functionless symptom, the process of discovery that most efficiently reveals the client's pro-symptom construction has three steps. First, the therapist's concrete, vivid, and evocative verbal prompts (Martin, 1991; Watson, 1996) help the client bring to mind a typical occurrence of the symptom or problem as if it were happening in the present. For example, "If you're willing, would you imagine you're right there in that situation you told me about: It's Tuesday morning, it's raining, you've just opened up a piece of mail from your lawyer and you've just read that the other party has made a tricky new legal maneuver. And you start to feel a whole new wave of vulnerability and fear."

Next the client is asked to carry out this task: "Right in that very situation, just as you're experiencing it right now, let your imagination show you whatever view, attitude, or behavior you could have that would make that fear and vulnerability [i.e., the presenting symptom] diminish or stop happening." The woman in the current example got in touch here with "fighting back" as the shift that would diminish her feelings of frantic vulnerability.

The third step then consists of having the client find and experience his or her unconscious position that opposes making the shift that would diminish the symptom because of unacceptable consequences anticipated from the new view, attitude, or behavior. To assume the presence of such a position is simply to assume symptom coherence. The therapist says, "Okay, now imagine that you're really fighting back in various ways. And you're really having an effect on people by how you're fighting back. It's really making a difference. [pause] How is that, for you? Are you entirely okay with that?" To her surprise, the unconscious urgency of maintaining her Good Girl identity now stirred consciously. Her unwillingness to do anything contrary to that identity surfaced, and the coherent emotional truth of the symptom became poignantly apparent, including her agency in maintaining the problem.

An unconscious construction is truly accessed and made available for immediate change only by subjectively experiencing the reality it defines, not by having cognitive insight about it based on the therapist's interpretation or suggestion. It is for this reason that all stages of DOBT's methodology are predominantly experiential and phenomenological. These stages consist of ushering clients into (a) "bumping into" their own governing pro-symptom themes and purposes, discovering them (as illustrated in the previous paragraph); (b) more and more fully "trying on," "inhabiting," and "living from" these themes and purposes in a first-person, present-tense manner during and between sessions, integrating them; and (c) then transforming (revising or dissolving) this pro-symptom position by experiencing it simultaneously with incompatible constructs brought into in the same field of awareness (which often occurs spontaneously as a result of integration, or else can be deliberately prompted by the therapist). A single pass through these stages is sometimes sufficient, but more typically the process has alternating steps of discovery and integration incrementally until the pro-symptom position is sufficiently conscious for transformation to occur.

Near the end of the session, as a postsession task to foster integration, the therapist gave her an index card inscribed with her phrases of emotional truth (quoted above). She was to read this every morning and night for 7 days to reconnect repeatedly in her day-to-day life with the way she actually felt it in the session. Integration in DOBT means that whenever the client produces the symptom, the client is routinely conscious of his or her purpose for doing so—a purpose so important that the pain or hardship of having the symptom is worth enduring.

This client lived thousands of miles from the therapist, so she had only this one session. At a 6-month follow up, she said her symptoms of anxiety and paralyzing feelings of vulnerability and pending disaster had been and still were "hugely eliminated" by the session; she had taken assertive action and was fighting back on a number of fronts.

Note that the therapist did nothing in an attempt to prevent or eliminate the symptoms other than have her subjectively experience and "own" her powerful position that necessitated them. Once she became conscious of her pro-symptom position of preserving the identity of a Good Girl at all cost and conscious of the high emotional cost of that position, she spontaneously revised her priorities. This illustrates one of DOBT's major principles: to best promote change, one should first find and take the governing position one actually has—the unconscious position of needing the presenting symptom as it is. Change is blocked by unawareness of having that position. People are able to change positions they consciously experience having but are unable to change positions they do not consciously experience having.

Table 4.1 (see the column labeled "Example 1") shows the structural relationship of the constructs composing the pro-symptom position discovered in this session. It is apparent that the constructs are of different logical types because they belong to distinct, hierarchically related domains or orders, as described in the lefthand column of the table. Each order of construct creates an emotional reality within which the next-lower order of construct exists; that is, each order is superordinate to (the prior ground of existence of) the constructs below it and subordinate to (dependent for existence on) the constructs above it.

As a rule, only some of the first-order constructs of a pro-symptom position, the presenting symptoms, are conscious at the start of therapy. The unconscious third- and fourth-order constructs constitute the emotional truth of the symptom, namely, the themes and purposes that are discovered, integrated, and transformed in the course of therapy. Therefore, this is a therapy of third- and fourth-order change, which is a technical definition of its "depth" and its inherent capacity for achieving resolution beyond symptom relief. Those third- and fourth-order constructs operate as the context governing how the client unconsciously construes or frames the meaning of the immediate, concrete situation, which is the second-order construct. The person's first-order presenting symptoms of thought, mood, or behavior then follow from that construal of the situation.

Our conceptualization of the hierarchical organization of constructions and the corresponding levels of change continues a tradition of applying the theory of logical types (Whitehead & Russell, 1963) in tandem with general systems theory (Ashby, 1952) to human psychology. Created initially by Bateson (1951, 1972), this approach was developed into a constructivist methodology for a brief psychotherapy of second-order change by Watzlawick, Weakland, and Fisch (1974). It is an indication of the richness of this conceptual tradition that whereas Watzlawick et al. use it to avoid working with unconscious material, we find this same framework superbly suited to mapping unconscious constructions in DOBT.

Functionless Panic

At the beginning of her first session, a 34-year-old single woman described intense, almost daily, panic attacks. She said, "objects in the room swell and shrink and get halos around them." Her limbs get rubbery, her heart pounds violently, she feels cold and lightheaded, and her breathing becomes rapid and shallow—all of the classic physical symptoms of a panic attack. She explained that she had been suffering these baffling symptoms since adolescence, if not longer, but had learned to endure them. The intensity had recently increased after she landed a new job with a significant amount of responsibility for making decisions that would directly affect

Table 4.1.
Organization of Constructs Constituting Clients' Pro-Symptom Positions in Depth-Oriented Brief Therapy

Order of Construct	Example 1: Functionless anxiety	Example 2: Functionless panic	Example 3: Functional panic	Example 4: Functional anxiety
4th: Nature of the self, others, and the world (ontology)	A girl who is good never makes trouble and is always nice, gets good things, and has a happy life. Bad things will not happen to her.	I am a dangerously harmful, even lethal, presence. My harmfulness can come out without my knowing or controlling it.	The universe requires intense suffering in every house and will actively inflict it if not enough suffering occurs.	I cannot survive feeling my hurt, grief, and anger over how utterly unloving and cruel daddy always was.
3rd: Broad purposes and strategies (teleology)	Never be unnice, make trouble, or fight, or I won't be that Good Girl and have that good life.	Avoid being the focus of others' attention to keep my lethality from harming anyone.	Always deliberately suffer enough so the universe won't uncontrollably inflict harm on our family.	Always keep my attention away from those feelings.
2nd: Meaning of the concrete situation	Bad things happening means I haven't been good enough. My only protection is failing! I've got to try hard to be truly good!	At this job, I am completely visible in directly affecting others. My lethality could harm someone at any moment!	My husband driving home is a prime moment of vulnerability, so I must quickly suffer enough to make calamity unnecessary.	Worrying over my baby's medical condition is how I can totally occupy my attention.
1st: Response (overt thoughts, feelings, behaviors)	Feelings of raw anxiety, vulnerability, and helplessness (the presenting symptom)	Panic attacks (the presenting symptom)	Panic attacks (the presenting symptom)	Continuous anxiety over baby daughter's health (the presenting symptom)

Note.   Each order of construct is the basis for the existence of constructs at lower levels. Shaded cells represent unconscious, nonverbal constructs cast in verbal form.

others. She obsessed all evening about her actions at work, could not sleep at night, and in general was living in almost continuous misery.

The therapist set out to find the unique construction of meaning generating this woman's repeating experience of panic. In the third session, the emotional truth of the symptom emerged. Each time the therapist drew her into actually experiencing themes involving her own needs, feelings, and so on, she became uneasy, subtly changed the subject, or shifted out of felt experience and into ideas. When the therapist commented on this, the client said, "Well, that's how I was brought up." She then explained in an offhand manner that throughout her childhood, the family revolved around her mother's physical and emotional fragility. The continual message to her from both parents was that causing mother any trouble or stress would make mother's health collapse catastrophically. Several incidents appeared to prove this. For example, when she was 15 years old, she "lost control" one day and had an intense altercation with her mother. The very next day she found her mother curled up on the floor in excruciating pain (which turned out to be appendicitis). This sequence of events gave immediate, powerful reinforcement to her sense of being dangerously harmful.

Therefore, it always felt urgent never to attract attention to herself, and she lived in the fear that anything she might inadvertently say or do would trigger the stress that gravely harms or even kills her own mother. Clearly, this emotional construction was still operating, generating the evasive action she took whenever the therapist invited sustained self-expression. She also still felt fear, she said, that telling her mother about any of her own current problems would make mother's health collapse.

In the information just revealed by the client, the therapist recognized a pro-symptom construction: her position of knowing she is a serious danger, of feeling terror that she will somehow harm others, and of striving always to be unnoticed to avoid causing such a disaster but still knowing she could fail to efface herself sufficiently at any time. Her new job brought panic because it required not only that she make decisions that directly affect others but also that she be highly visible, which eliminated staying unnoticed as her main solution to the problem of being so harmful.

The client was talking intellectually about her family-of-origin themes and was not yet conscious at all of how they were living in her emotionally and governing her thoughts, mood, somatic state, and behavior. Furthermore, she had no inkling of any connection between these themes and her panic attacks at work.

With the end of the hour approaching, as a step that would begin to draw her into direct experience of these emotional constructs, the therapist asked her to picture Mom and to "straightforwardly tell her what you've been telling me." She said to Mom, "You know, I'm always afraid to mention any of my problems because I'm afraid I'll make your health fall apart." The technique we use here is called *overt statement*: As a result of overtly voicing the emotional truth of his or her position in highly personal terms directly to the relevant person, the client deepens into a direct subjective experience of this position. This indeed occurred here. The client became teary and was in touch with a complex mixture of emotions involved in the theme she had verbalized. The therapist then gave her an index card with those words written on it and suggested a between-session task: She would make her usual weekly telephone call to mother; when talking, she would have the card in front of her and stay in touch with the option of actually saying those words to Mom. The therapist emphasized that the purpose was not to confront, challenge, or blame Mom in any way, or even say anything at all, but only to consciously feel and be aware of having this position right in the moment when in this position with her mom. Doing this would help her feel and integrate her normally unfelt emotional truth of anxiety over being dangerous to Mom.

At the start of the fourth session, she reported that she had phoned her mother and after a few minutes had actually said the words on the card. Her mom gave a very quick, tight denial ("Oh, that's nonsense!") and abruptly changed the subject to superficial matters. Several minutes later, the client mentioned that she was seeing a therapist. Her mom responded tensely, "Why are you doing *that*! There's nothing *wrong* with you!" She explained what happened next. Her mother's voice tones were an all-too-familiar signal that she was now doing something exceedingly bad that was threatening to Mom. But because she was keeping her eyes on the card, she experienced something unprecedented, a kind of double awareness of in fact being very gentle and caring in how she was speaking to Mom, yet simultaneously regarding herself as dangerously harmful, in agreement with Mom's apparent view of her. She said it felt very peculiar to suddenly see this big discrepancy and added, "I realized it's that I've simply always been given the message that I'm dangerous."

Her awareness of the theme in this panic-generating pro-symptom position, "I am dangerous and could gravely harm Mom at any time," had deepened from intellectualizing into genuine experiential accessing. Then, having accessed it, she spontaneously began dissolving this construction when an incompatible one ("I am caring and gentle") came into the same field of awareness experientially. This typifies how the construct-module generating a symptom is shifted out of isolation and into semantic contact with other, disconfirming constructs (integration leading to transformation).

For integration to be enduring, it is important for the therapist to persist in prompting the client to relate to the problem actively from and in that pro-symptom emotional reality, until that construction has lost every bit of its unconscious autonomy and compellingness. The therapist, therefore, offered a trial sentence by saying, "Would you be willing, just as an experiment, to try out saying to me, 'It has always seemed to me that I am a lethal person'?" The use of the word *lethal* was very deliberate. It is essential for the verbalization to capture fully and vividly the passionate emotional truths and high stakes that constitute the pro-symptom position (for research on use of vivid language, see Martin, 1991; and Watson, 1996).

She again became teary in voicing the trial sentence and said, "Yes, that's what I felt I was, but I didn't actually think it. I always felt I was lethal and had to struggle to keep it from actually coming out and hurting her." This experientially verified that the phrasing was accurately capturing her pro-symptom position that until now had been held nonlinguistically and unconsciously. The therapist next prompted her again to hold the old construal of herself as lethal in the same field of awareness as the new one—the condition for transformation—by saying empathically, "You've realized that you've actually been very gentle and caring with your mom. [pause] What's it like to know this and look back now, and see all those years of growing up, knowing this?" She said after a silence, "I just see this child who's always trying so hard to do the right thing. Who's really always very caring and helpful and trying so hard not to cause any trouble for anyone." The therapist responded, "mm-hm. [pause] And see her also as thinking of herself as harmful and lethal." After a short silence, she said with tears, "It's so sad to see that. Really, really sad that all those years that's how I felt I was."

In the next session, she reported that at work, she now felt no panic or anxiety at all. For example, she felt completely confident as she negotiated with board members to define her responsibilities in her job description. She also described how her posture and walk had changed and become more upright; she had to readjust her rearview mirror. A friend asked if she had something done with her face because of the new vitality in it. This kind of neuromuscular release in the body is an important indicator of the real depth of the psychological work.

She explained the change at work in this way: "Now I can admit to myself how much I care about things going well, and I feel I'll be able to make decisions so they *will* go well." The therapist asked what she meant by that, and she explained that her view of herself had changed, from someone whose anxious moment means she is harmful and will probably do the wrong thing and who, therefore, feels a collapse of confidence, to someone whose anxious moment means she cares greatly about how she affects others and who, therefore, will do the right thing. This change in how she construes her own nature—an ontological or fourth-order change—had completely eliminated the panic attacks.

By mutual agreement, this fifth session was the last. The therapist made sure she knew she could have more sessions if and when needed. Six months later, on her own initiative, she sent the therapist a letter that opened with the following: "Before I become so used to it that I forget I was ever any different, I want to tell you that the narrowly focused change I thought I was seeking [eliminating panic attacks] has ended up affecting my whole life in ways I never expected! I've become more comfortably gregarious [she had always been very 'shy,' a manifestation of the need to avoid attention] but also more comfortable with the fact that I truly enjoy doing many things alone. I've lost 25 pounds, and even my handwriting has changed. And perhaps more important, I find I am now basically an optimist and tend to assume all problems can be solved somehow." Almost 2 years after these sessions, she sent a holiday greeting card in which she indicated that the changes had held.

Table 4.1 (see column labeled "Example 2") maps the constructs making up this woman's symptom-generating position. The panic symptom was functionless because it was necessitated as a by-product of how she had tried to carry out the purpose in this construction. The cessation of panic attacks resulted from dissolving a highly superordinate construct that had particularly sweeping influence over personal reality. It is not surprising, then, that a range of other spontaneous changes accompanied "the narrowly focused change I thought I was seeking."

Functional Panic

In contrast, another client's panic attacks were found to be the functional means by which she carried out her pro-symptom purpose. This woman, 35 years old, said the most common trigger of a panic attack was knowing that her husband was on the road. She thought of him having an accident and then her panic would rapidly build up, especially if he was a few minutes late in arriving home. She wanted therapy to dispel these panic attacks and to diminish the "strong sense of danger" she always felt. Staving off the dangers, she said, is "like a war." She had "never felt understood" by her parents. Both parents were very religious Christians, although she herself since childhood had been an agnostic and "very turned off to religion." As a result, she said, the universe seems chaotic to her: "If you don't have a belief in God, you don't know what's controlling things."

Her panic attacks had begun 5 years previously. "Before the panic attacks started, I had strong depressions that lasted weeks at a time. The panic attacks replaced the depression." A subsequent experience of an earthquake significantly increased the intensity and frequency of panic.

During the second session, the therapist used the DOBT discovery technique of *symptom deprivation*; this technique consists of having the client imaginally experience being without the symptom in the very circumstance in which normally the client produces the symptom. If the symptom is functional, this is a highly effective way to bring to light the unconscious purpose carried out by producing it. When the symptom is disallowed, the resulting difficulty or distress reveals the driving purpose. (Symptom deprivation is also part of the accessing process with a functionless symptom, but it is preceded in that case by other steps, as outlined earlier.)

With her eyes closed, she imagined being in a recent situation that triggered panic but now saw what she experienced if panic did not arise. She said, "Well, I start to feel panicky over *that*. I know it sounds strange but that's what it is. I start to feel scared over *not* having the panic." Clearly, she was beginning to access a position in which the panic was important to have—a pro-symptom position—so the therapist continued along this line, asking her to stay in the imaginal scene without the panic and to see if she could notice what was scary about not having the panic. What happened without it? Finally, she said, "It just feels kind of darker, like something bad will happen, but I don't know what or why."

The session was nearing its end, so the therapist gave the next step of discovery as a between-session task, with these instructions: "When you notice you're starting to have a panic attack, just for a moment see if you can glimpse what you'd experience instead, if you didn't have panic. I'm not asking you to learn how to stop going into panic. Just see if you can glimpse, even for a moment or two, what would start to happen if panic didn't develop when it normally would. It might be hard to do, but I wonder if you could give it a try between now and our next session." She was willing to try, and the therapist wrote the task on an index card.

In the next session, her third, she described an evening when her husband was late coming home from work. As the panic began, she took out the card, did the task, and made an experiential discovery, which she described by saying, "If I don't worry, then I feel it means I believe we'll live forever and nothing bad will happen—and having *that* belief *will* make bad things happen. I really feel that if I panic, it keeps it from happening. I feel I believe I can get away with nothing happening if I just suffer."

These words give a complete account of a pro-symptom position she had experientially glimpsed in herself. Table 4.1 (see column labeled "Example 3") lays out this position. It was now apparent that this woman had the unconscious ability to "whip up" a state of panic whenever that seemed necessary to protect her family members, according to her unconscious view of how the world works. This also explained the intriguing mystery of how her former depressions could be "replaced" by panic attacks: She had simply switched to a more preferable type of intense suffering; she preferred the high-energy electricity of panic to the low-energy deadness of depression.

The therapist asked whether she viewed her newly discovered "beliefs" as being in any sense religious or similar to her parents' beliefs. The sense of connection was immediate for her, and she was surprised and somewhat disoriented to realize this because in her conscious position, she was adamantly agnostic and did not have such beliefs.

The therapist went on to observe, "What you've told me seems to mean there are two ways you could stop having panic attacks: You could switch to a different type of suffering to keep bad things from happening, or you could reassess your beliefs and decide that your suffering has no effect over what happens; then you wouldn't have to suffer." She was silent with eyes closed, then said it was clear to her that this belief "is in my guts" and could never change, so the only alternative was to find a different type of suffering. The therapist accepted this and suggested that she think seriously about what type of suffering she could switch to and report on this at the next session.

At the beginning of the fourth session, she said there had been no panic attacks for several days. She had not yet identified a different suffering that she wanted to adopt. The therapist asked how it was for her since her last session to be aware now of having the strongly felt, religion-like convictions that she had discovered. It soon became apparent from the intellectual way she talked about those beliefs that she was now in touch with them as only ideas. The therapist, therefore, focused on having her review her earlier discovery of her beliefs and then invited overt statements that once again deepened her into experiencing their emotional reality, which she verbalized by saying, "I really feel that if I think we'll be happy and fine, the universe will smash us in some way, so to protect us from that I *have* to suffer by feeling terrified every day or two and expecting disaster." She was again left with the task of finding an alternate form of suffering.

At the fifth session, 10 days later, she reported that there had now been no panic attacks at all for 2 weeks, which was unprecedented. She added, "Panic attacks seem silly to me now. They never used to. But it really seems silly to have a panic attack." Even an earthquake that had occurred locally since the last session did not induce panic, and she said, "Earthquakes seem managable now." She said she had not implemented an alternate suffering.

Doing no more than making the emotional truth of her panic attacks conscious had resulted in their cessation, again illustrating that people usually can change their symptom-generating position after they experientially know they have that position. The therapist persisted nevertheless in requesting her to come up with an acceptable, sufficiently intense form of alternate suffering, not because such an actual behavioral change was necessary but because her focus on that task was helping to sustain her integration of her pro-symptom position, eliminating the symptom.

She then went on to describe other significant changes stemming from the sessions. She had become aware of having the assumption and expectation that the world would and should always "correct itself" whenever she expressed dissatisfaction. She said she was realizing that the world was not going to comply with her wishes and that she was now beginning to accept this. The client's panic attacks were her attempt to get the world to behave the way she wanted, and her particular ontological (fourth-order) construct of how the world was manipulable by the self became conscious as part of her pro-symptom position. Her comments indicated that she was revising or dissolving this ontological construct. Moreover, she had stopped her main way of manipulating the world (by suffering panic attacks) yet was feeling no anxiety over loss of control, as would be expected if those ontological constructs were still intact and real to her.

She decided not to schedule another session at this point, feeling she wanted to see how she would do on her own. The therapist, recognizing the genuineness of the in-depth changes that were now in progress, agreed but emphasized that she could always call for another session if needed. She did not. In response to a follow-up query mailed to her 9 months later, she reported the following: "After our sessions ended, a number of interesting revelations occurred to me. I still experience a panic attack once in a while, but the sessions made me realize some things I'm still working on. The sessions were very helpful. I'll call you if I want to speed things along."

Functional Anxiety

Worrisome, high-anxiety preoccupation with her baby daughter's health was the presenting symptom of a 28-year-old female client. She wanted her husband present in the sessions for emotional support, and the therapist agreed, holding open the question of whether the work would need to be individual or systemic. In DOBT the therapist relies on phenomenological methods to reveal whether the symptom is maintained by an individual's constructions, by a systemic ecology of constructions, or both. (For DOBT case examples of couple and family work, see Ecker & Hulley, 1996, 1998a, 1999a, 1999b.)

Her daughter, "Jenny," 20 months old, had had a life-threatening condition for many months following her birth. The doctors had recently assessed the problem as no longer critical, although it still required vigilance and a rapid response to symptoms that were difficult to distinguish from an ordinary cold or upset stomach. A considerable level of parental anxiety was clearly appropriate under the circumstances, but both the client, "Nina," and her husband, "Rick," viewed her almost nonstop, fearful worry and preoccupation as excessive and out of control.

What follows is a condensed account of only the segments of therapy directly relevant to Nina's pro-symptom position, in which anxiety had a crucial function. The work also addressed positions of low self-esteem and other themes that more tangentially maintained anxiety functionlessly, but the full complexity of this case is beyond our present scope.

Nina described her childhood as devastatingly unhappy because of a harshly critical, alcoholic father who went into daily screaming rages and never expressed positive feelings toward family members. Her parents had long ago separated, and she now had virtually no contact with her father. In contrast, she had almost daily contact with her mother and relied on her heavily for child care.

With several hypotheses tentatively in mind, the therapist wanted to probe first for a possible connection between Nina's anxiety and what seemed from her description to be a completely unresolved experience of emotional abuse in childhood. It soon became apparent that it was extremely distressing for Nina to experience her feelings and memories of her childhood and of her father. She would try to follow the therapist's prompts and begin experiencing her feelings but would very soon dissociate and "shut down" because, as she explained, "It just hurts way too much. It's overwhelming."

The pace of the therapy had to be adjusted to what Nina could handle, and the therapist gingerly maintained focus on experientially discovering her emotional themes relevant to anxiety. At the start of the fourth session, Rick made an important comment: "I've known for a long time that Nina never gets into her childhood and all the pain she has from it. I've really begun to wonder about how much she focuses on worrying about Jenny instead." The therapist, careful not to allow Rick to slide into a cotherapist role, nevertheless took his spousal perspective seriously. In DOBT, a therapeutic hypothesis such as this—that Nina's anxiety had the vital function of blotting out unresolved feelings about her father—is always converted into an experiential exercise in which the client finds whether the hypothesis is emotionally true.

Therapist:	Spouses usually do have ideas about what makes the other one tick. Well, let's see—I wonder if you'd be willing to try something. Just for 10 or 15 seconds, go back and picture your dad raging around the house [pause] and back into feeling just some of the overwhelming hurt that you feel with that. [pause] Got that?
Client:	[Nods. Gets teary.]
Therapist:	Okay, good. Now, add in some thoughts about Jenny, some worrying about how much the flu is going around now and how endangered she is by it. [pause] Can you do that?

Client:	Oh yeah!
Therapist:	Okay. And when you've got that going [pause], tell me how much pain over Dad is still there.
Client:	[pause] Hn! [laugh of recognition] It's completely gone.
Therapist:	So you were feeling some of those really strong feelings over Dad, but then, when you started to focus on worrying over Jenny, you stopped feeling any of that pain over Dad. Is that right?
Client:	Yeah—it is!
Therapist:	This could be really important, so let's get this really clear. Would you be willing to do it one more time? [Essentially the same steps are now repeated, with the same results]
Therapist:	Let me see if I understand what you just experienced. Tell me if I've got this right. You're always carrying around feelings over your dad that you need to somehow not feel because they're unbearable. And you just found that being in anxiety over Jenny blots out those feelings. Is that what you just discovered?
Client:	Yeah, it is.
Therapist:	Obviously you don't like feeling that anxiety, but did we just find that "parking" yourself there keeps you from feeling things you really don't want to feel? All that hurt and anger over your father?
Client:	God, I had no idea! So how do I stop doing this?
Therapist:	Maybe we need to start looking at how you could approach all those unresolved feelings about your dad, without it feeling overwhelming. Then you wouldn't need to mask it with something else. How would that be?
Client:	I don't know. I told Rick last week that I feel like there's a big closet door, and I'm standing at the door and I'm trying to push it shut, but all this stuff is coming in around the edges. And I feel like I'm gonna get buried by all the crap that's coming in.
Therapist:	What a good image for what's happening. Okay, I have an idea for a task that's a really small step, based on what we've learned today: You would keep trying to shut that door in the same ways, but now you'll *know* you're keeping it shut by worrying real hard about Jenny. Let's write that down on a card.

The card read, "I need to keep this door shut against all my hurt and grief and anger over Dad because it just feels overwhelming. I don't like staying in anxiety over Jenny instead, but that's not as awful as feeling overwhelmed by all that hurt." Within symptom coherence, the client would much rather endure the suffering with the symptom than the suffering unconsciously expected without it. Table 4.1 (column labeled "Example 4") shows how the constructs discovered in the sessions make up Nina's pro-symptom position.

Nina reported at the fifth session that she had made much use of the card and had had a "difficult" 2 weeks because "I don't know where to turn. I don't like any of my options: either facing my childhood and my issues with my Dad or staying in anxiety." Clearly, her purposeful use of anxiety to avoid her feelings related to her dad was becoming integrated. With this growing awareness of her agency in producing anxiety, less and less could anxiety seem like something happening to her as a helpless victim of a mysterious internal state.

Toward the end of the session, Nina made some comments that indicated real progress in tolerating her unbearable feelings over her father: "A few years ago, my sister told me something that I just never let in. She told me that our father had molested her. I had always thought, 'At least there was never *that*,' and when she told me, it's like it never felt real to me. I just couldn't deal with it. Maybe now I will."

The therapist recommended that she continue her previous task but rephrased it in this way: "Every time you notice yourself going into anxiety over Jenny, take a moment and ask yourself, 'Is there something I just got away from by plunging into worry over Jenny?'" Those words also went on an index card, and the therapist explained, "When you find there is some feeling or thought you're getting away from, just acknowledge to yourself what it is, and then you can either go back into the anxiety or not, whichever way it goes." The goal of this task of integration was for her to become thoroughly and routinely conscious of her purpose and agency in resorting to anxiety.

At the next session 2 weeks later, Nina reported that for the first full week she had consistently stayed in feeling her hurt and anger over her father's abusiveness. At the end of that week, she had abruptly "shut it down completely and didn't go back to it. During the second week, I got anxious about Jenny." The therapist asked how much anxiety over Jenny she had felt during the first week. "None at all," said Nina. Her purposeful production of the anxiety to block the other feelings was now blatantly obvious to her.

The therapist focused the rest of the session on learning from her what she was experiencing at the end of the first week that had made it necessary to resort to that screen of anxiety. It emerged that being in touch with her feelings about her father no longer felt overwhelming to her. What now made it necessary to shut down those feelings was her mother's great taboo on any feelings of sadness and unhappiness. During that week, Nina had had daily contact with her mother, and finally the stress of keeping her own emerging grief and anger contained and hidden was too much.

Although anxiety had initially seemed to be the problem, Nina now knew it to be actually her solution to the real problem of having grief and anger that seemed unworkable. Therapy became a matter of establishing a real solution to that problem, rendering forbidden feelings viable and engaging Nina in the retrieval of major themes of personal meaning. Over the next few sessions, she resorted to anxiety over Jenny less and less, and she and Rick soon felt that the much reduced level of anxiety still present was now appropriate to their child's medical circumstances. Her long-stuck grieving went forward.

CONCLUSIONS

Depth-oriented brief therapy could equally be called coherence psychology. In the course of our clinical work over the past 2 decades, we have found symptom coherence to be the core structure of a broad spectrum of clinical symptoms. This includes not only anxiety and panic but also depression, attachment problems, attention difficulties, low self-esteem, sexual problems, complicated bereavement, underachieving, procrastination, eating and weight problems, sequelae of childhood abuse, and a range of couple and family problems (Ecker & Hulley, 1996, 1998a, 1998b, 1998c, 1998d, 1999, in press).

Table 4.1 makes explicit the symptom coherence in each of our four examples by detailing the emotional truth of the symptom: the person's passionate, purposeful, unconscious version of reality in which the symptom is necessary to have, despite the suffering it entails. (For a fifth anxiety-spectrum example, a case of agoraphobia, see Ecker & Hulley, 1996, pp. 28–37.) Note that the concept of *secondary gain*, with its inherent reference to primary pathology (see, e.g., Fenichel, 1945, p. 126), has no place within DOBT because symptom coherence is a primary gain model of symptom production.

The four-level schema of symptom coherence appears to be native to the psyche, a universal order that underlies apparent clinical disorder. Seemingly irrational symptoms prove to have this full coherence, symptoms considered dysfunctional prove to be the functioning of this hidden order, and a vast array of symptoms regarded as psychopathology fail to betray any broken or diseased structures. Over many years of practice, we have yet to encounter a symptom-generating construction that departs from this hierarchical form. The question then arises as to whether there exist any symptoms with deep structure that deviates from this four-level schema (perhaps some psychoses and organicity conditions). If so, this class of conditions would more appropriately be termed disorder.

Furthermore, the methodology that has allowed us to see into the unconscious four-level structure of symptoms shows that all overt thought, feeling, and behavior has the same underlying structure. This means that the question of whether there is any intrinsic difference between the deep structures of symptomatic versus nonsymptomatic manifestations can now be answered in the negative: Virtually all clinical symptoms actually express the normal functioning of the core ordering scheme of the mind.

The principle of symptom coherence is encountered in varying degrees, explicitly or implicitly, in a range of psychotherapies, including those of Bandler and Grinder (1979), Bateson (1972), Dell (1982), Enright (1980), Jung (1964), Laing (1967), Papp and Imber-Black (1996), Satir (1972), Schwartz (1987), Sullivan (1948), and Watzlawick et al. (1974). The notion has widespread acceptance among psychotherapists but is usually held as an ad hoc truism or axiom of faith with unsystematic application to clinical methodology. DOBT centrally and systematically organizes both the conceptualization and the methodology of psychotherapy around it.

Our examples also demonstrated the immediate accessibility of unconscious constructs. For a person to access and experience symptom-related unconscious constructs, passage of time per se is not an intrinsic requirement. Constructs formed in childhood and maintaining symptom production for decades can as a rule be brought into experiential awareness in minutes during a therapy session through methods that accurately bring attention to these habitually or purposefully unattended constructs. However, if the therapist assumes a priori that therapy will require much time, then he or she will not apply methods designed for relatively swift accessing and transformation of constructs, and the assumption will be self-fulfilling.

As a final point, we briefly locate DOBT in relation to other developments in constructivist psychology (see Neimeyer, 1993, 1995a, 1995b, 1997; and Mahoney, 1995a, 1995b; for full reviews of the evolution and diversity of constructivist orientations).

Although DOBT is a system of personal construct therapy, it is quite different from that developed by Kelly (1955; Neimeyer, 1985, 1986), although it is entirely in accord on fundamental constructivist principles. DOBT's closest cousin theoretically is dialectical constructivism (Greenberg & Pascual-Leone, 1995; Greenberg, Rice, & Elliott, 1993); the two conceptual models have close correspondences although couched in very different terms. By working directly with the higher orders of meaning, DOBT is pragmatically and philosophically a therapy of applied ontology, teleology, and epistemology, as are other in-depth constructivist therapies (Keeney, 1983; Mahoney, 1995a). However, to a new degree, DOBT makes one of constructivism's most central intuitions concrete, well defined, and empirically verifiable and susceptible to research: the view that an individual's unconscious, nonlinguistic, abstract ordering rules (higher order constructs) shape and constrain conscious thoughts, feelings, and behaviors without appearing in them (see Mahoney, 1988b; and Guidano, 1995a, for excellent articulations of this position and references to the constructivist literature on it). This "primacy of the abstract" (Hayek, 1978) has been assumed to imply an inherent ambiguity or indistinctness (Weimer, 1982b), but DOBT explicitly shows the sharply defined and accessible nature of both the schema of construct organization and the high-order constructs themselves. In the psyche, abstract evidently means general, inclusive, overarching, and supervening but not ill defined.

In relation to the narrative and social constructionist perspectives and their focus on the discursive and sociolinguistic construction of meaning, it is curious that most exponents of these approaches not only affirm the importance of this domain but also deny the importance of unconscious, stable, nonlinguistic knowledge structures (see, e.g., Coale, 1992; and Harré & Gillette, 1994). Consequently, on this point, DOBT stands as a challenge to these orientations (as does a formidable array of the findings in cognitive science; see, e.g., Epstein, 1994; Baars, 1988; Reber and Lewis, 1977; and Wegner & Smart, 1997).

The four-level hierarchy of construct domains organizes all content areas, including the critical areas of identity, reality, power, and values, which Mahoney (1991) identified as being particularly important zones of self-organization and, therefore, most strongly held against change. Indeed, the more globally a construct defines and structures experiential reality, the more strongly it must be protected (Kelly, 1955; Guidano, 1987, 1991; Guidano & Liotti, 1983; Liotti, 1987; Mahoney, 1991). Still, rapid therapeutic change even in such high-order, global constructs can often occur, as our examples show. In the concept of position and in methodologies designed for working with positions therapeutically, DOBT operationalizes recognition of the modular organization of mind and brain, establishing a common ground with the findings of cognitive science and psychoneurology, as noted previously. DOBT posits a seemingly paradoxical blend of relativism and objectivism. On the one hand, it shares the fundamental relativism of constructivism in accepting that an objective reality is never directly known or perceived by the individual. On the other hand, we find that each person has a native ability to apprehend directly his or her own mental constructs. A person's unconscious constructs behave phenomenologically as well-defined and highly durable mental objects that are discovered in therapy, not invented, and are then manipulable in accordance with equally well-defined principles. Any two competent therapists would usher a particular therapy client into discovering the same constructs necessitating the symptom. (Of course, the verbal renditions of these constructs would not be identical, although equally true to the essential meanings.) In DOBT's objectivistic relativism, the only kind of entity the mind can know directly is its own created construct as a construct rather than as a true representation of anything.

Our focus was primarily on the underlying static order producing so-called disorder, the structural arrangement or architecture of constructs at any given time. It is due only to our limited scope here that we less systematically addressed the mind's dynamic order in managing its constructs, the conditions under which knowledge structures are transformed or dissolved in the flow of experience (Guidano, 1991, 1995a, 1995b; Mahoney et al., 1995; Piaget, 1937/1971; von Glasersfeld, 1979, 1988). Likewise, many of the methods and concepts of DOBT have not been touched on here at all, including the nature of the self, the therapist's stance and trustworthiness, and the existence of constructs of fifth and higher order from which derive the lower four orders most relevant to psychotherapy. We hope that a clearer understanding of psychological self-organization has emerged, with great practical relevance for dramatically enhancing the effectiveness of in-depth psychotherapy.

REFERENCES

Ashby, W. R. (1952). *Design for a brain*. New York: Wiley.

Baars, B. J. (1988). *A cognitive theory of consciousness*. Cambridge, England: Cambridge University Press.

Bandler, R., & Grinder, J. (1979). *Frogs into princes: Neuro linguistic programming*. Moab, UT: Real People Press.

Bateson, G. (1951). Information and codification: A philosophical approach. In J. Ruesch & G. Bateson (Eds.), *Communication: The social matrix of psychiatry* (pp. 168–211). New York: Norton.

Bateson, G. (1972). *Steps to an ecology of mind*. New York: Ballantine Books.

Bogdan, J. (1986). Do families really need problems? Why I am not a functionalist. *Family Therapy Networker, 10*(4), 30–35, 67–69.

Coale, H. W. (1992). The constructivist emphasis on language: A critical conversation. *Journal of Strategic and Systemic Therapies, 11*(1), 12–26.

Dell, P. (1982). Beyond homeostasis: Toward a concept of coherence. *Family Process, 21*, 21–41.

Ecker, B., & Hulley, L. (1996). *Depth oriented brief therapy*. San Francisco: Jossey-Bass.

Ecker, B., & Hulley, L. (1998a). Briefer and deeper: Addressing the unconscious in short-term treatment. *Family Therapy Networker, 21*(1), 75–83.

Ecker, B., & Hulley, L. (1998b). Compulsive underachieving: Video and viewer's manual. *Depth oriented brief therapy video demonstration and training series* (497E). Oakland, CA: Pacific Seminars.

Ecker, B., & Hulley, L. (1998c). Down every year: Video and viewer's manual. *Depth oriented brief therapy video demonstration and training series* (1097SP). Oakland, CA: Pacific Seminars.

Ecker, B., & Hulley, L. (1998d). Stuck in depression: Video and viewer's manual. *Depth oriented brief therapy video demonstration and training series* (1096T). Oakland, CA: Pacific Seminars.

Ecker, B., & Hulley, L. (1999). DOBT: Insights in a small space. *Family Therapy News, 29*(7), 27–28.

Ecker, B., & Hulley, L. (in press). Depth oriented brief therapy: Accelerated accessing of the coherent unconscious. In J. Carlson & L. Sperry (Eds.), *Brief therapy with individuals and couples*. Redding, CT: Zeig, Tucker.

Enright, J. B. (1980). Change versus enlightenment. In S. Boorstein (Ed.), *Transpersonal psychology* (pp. 217–231). Palo Alto, CA: Science & Behavior Books.

Epstein, S. (1994). Integration of the cognitive and the psychodynamic unconscious. *American Psychologist, 49*, 709–724.

Fenichel, O. (1945). *The psychoanalytic theory of neurosis*. New York: Norton.

Fodor, J. A. (1983). *The modularity of mind*. Cambridge, MA: MIT/Bradford Books.

Gazzaniga, M. (1985). *The social brain*. New York: Basic Books.

Greenberg, L. S., & Pascual-Leone, J. (1995). A dialectical constructivist approach to experiential change. In R. A. Neimeyer & M. J. Mahoney (Eds.), *Constructivism in psychotherapy* (pp. 169–191). Washington, DC: American Psychological Association.

Greenberg, L. S., Rice, L., & Elliott, R. (1993). *Facilitating emotional change: The moment-by-moment process*. New York: Guilford Press.

Guidano, V. F. (1987). *The complexity of the self: A developmental approach to psychopathology and therapy*. New York: Guilford Press.

Guidano, V. F. (1991). *The self in process: Toward a post-rationalist cognitive therapy*. New York: Guilford Press.

Guidano, V. F. (1995a). A constructivist outline of human knowing processes. In M. J. Mahoney (Ed.), *Cognitive and constructive psychotherapies* (pp. 89–102). New York: Springer.

Guidano, V. F. (1995b). Constructivist psychotherapy: A theoretical framework. In R. A. Neimeyer & M. J. Mahoney (Eds.), *Constructivism in psychotherapy* (pp. 93–108). Washington, DC: American Psychological Association.

Guidano, V. F., & Liotti, G. A. (1983). *Cognitive processes and emotional disorders*. New York: Guilford Press.

Harré, R., & Gillette, G. (1994). *The discursive mind*. Thousand Oaks, CA: Sage.

Hayek, F. A. (1952). *The sensory order*. Chicago: University of Chicago Press.

Hayek, F. A. (1978). *New studies in philosophy, politics, economics, and the history of ideas*. Chicago: University of Chicago Press.

Hoffman, L. (1981). *Foundations of family therapy*. New York: Basic Books.

Johnson-Laird, P. (1988). *The computer and the mind*. Cambridge, MA: Harvard University Press.

Jung, C. G. (1964). *Man and his symbols*. Garden City, NY: Doubleday.

Keeney, B. (1983). *The aesthetics of change*. New York: Guilford Press.

Kelly, G. (1955). *The psychology of personal constructs*. New York: Norton.

Laing, R. D. (1967). *The politics of experience*. New York: Pantheon.

Liotti, G. (1987). The resistance to change of cognitive structures: A counterproposal to psychoanalytic metapsychology. *Journal of Cognitive Psychotherapy: An International Quarterly, 1*, 87–104.

Mahoney, M. J. (1988a). Constructivist metatheory: I. Basic features and historical foundations. *International Journal of Personal Construct Psychology, 1*, 1–35.

Mahoney, M. J. (1988b). Constructivist metatheory: II. Implications for psychotherapy. *International Journal of Personal Construct Psychology, 1*, 299–315.

Mahoney, M. J. (1991). *Human change processes: The scientific foundations of psychotherapy*. New York: Basic Books.

Mahoney, M. J. (1995a). Theoretical developments in the cognitive and constructive psychotherapies. In M. J. Mahoney (Ed.), *Cognitive and constructive psychotherapies* (pp. 3–19). New York: Springer.

Mahoney, M. J. (1995b). Continuing evolution of the cognitive sciences and psychotherapies. In R. A. Neimeyer & M. J. Mahoney (Eds.), *Constructivism in psychotherapy* (pp. 39–65). Washington, DC: American Psychological Association.

Mahoney, M. J., Miller, H. M., & Arciero, G. (1995). Constructive metatheory and the nature of mental representations. In M. J. Mahoney (Ed.), *Cognitive and constructive psychotherapies* (pp. 103–120). New York: Springer.

Martin, J. (1991). The social–cognitive construction of therapeutic change: A dual coding analysis. *Journal of Social and Clinical Psychology, 10*(3), 305–321.

Neimeyer, R. A. (1985). Personal constructs in clinical practice. In P. C. Kendall (Ed.), *Advances in cognitive–behavioral research and therapy* (Vol. 4, pp. 275–329). San Diego, CA: Academic Press.

Neimeyer, R. A. (1986). Personal construct therapy. In W. Dryden & W. Golden (Eds.), *Cognitive behavioural approaches to psychotherapy* (pp. 98–127). London: Harper & Row.

Neimeyer, R. A. (1993). An appraisal of constructivist psychotherapies. *Journal of Consulting and Clinical Psychology, 61*, 221–234.

Neimeyer, R. A. (1995a). Constructivist psychotherapies: Features, foundations, and future directions. In R. A. Neimeyer & M. J. Mahoney (Eds.), *Constructivism in psychotherapy* (pp. 11–38). Washington, DC: American Psychological Association.

Neimeyer, R. A. (1995b). Limits and lessons of constructivism: Some critical reflections. *Journal of Constructivist Psychology, 8,* 339–361.

Neimeyer, R. A. (1997). Problems and prospects in constructivist psychotherapy. *Journal of Constructivist Psychology, 10,* 51–74.

Papp, P., & Imber-Black, E. (1996). Family themes: Transmission and transformation. *Family Process, 35,* 5–20.

Piaget, J. (1971). *The construction of reality in the child.* New York: Ballantine. (Original work published 1937)

Polanyi, M. (1966). *The tacit dimension.* Garden City, NY: Doubleday.

Posner, M. I., & Raichle, M. E. (1994). *Images of mind.* San Francisco: Freeman.

Reber, A. S., & Lewis, S. (1977). Implicit learning: An analysis of the form and structure of a body of tacit knowledge. *Cognition, 5,* 333–361.

Rumelhart, D. E., & McClelland, J. L. (1986). *Parallel distributed processing: Explorations in the microstructure of cognition* (2 vols.). Cambridge, MA: MIT Press.

Satir, V. (1972). *Peoplemaking.* Palo Alto, CA: Science & Behavior Books.

Schwartz, R. (1987). Our multiple selves. *Family Therapy Networker, 10*(2), 25–31, 80–83.

Sullivan, H. S. (1948). The meaning of anxiety in psychiatry and in life. *American Journal of Psychiatry, 11,* 1–13.

Turvey, M. T. (1974). Constructive theory, perceptual systems and tacit knowledge. In W. B. Weimar & D. S. Palermo (Eds.), *Cognition and the symbolic processes* (pp. 56–95). Hillsdale, NJ: Erlbaum.

von Glasersfeld, E. (1979). Radical constructivism and Piaget's concept of knowledge. In F. B. Murray (Ed.), *The impact of Piagetian theory on education, philosophy, psychiatry, and psychology* (pp. 109–122). Baltimore: University Park Press.

von Glasersfeld, E. (1988). The reluctance to change a way of thinking. *Irish Journal of Psychology, 9*(1), 83–90.

Watson, J. C. (1996). The relationship between vivid description, emotional arousal, and in-session resolution of problematic reactions. *Journal of Consulting and Clinical Psychology, 64,* 459–464.

Watzlawick, P., Weakland, J., & Fisch, R. (1974). *Change: Principles of problem formation and problem resolution.* New York: Norton.

Wegner, D. M., & Smart, L. (1997). Deep cognitive activation: A new approach to the unconscious. *Journal of Consulting and Clinical Psychology, 65,* 984–995.

Weimer, W. B. (1977). A conceptual framework for cognitive psychology: Motor theories of the mind. In R. Shaw & J. Bransford (Eds.), *Perceiving, acting, and knowing: Toward an ecological psychology* (pp. 267–311). Hillsdale, NJ: Erlbaum.

Weimer, W. B. (1982a). Hayek's approach to the problems of complex phenomena: An introduction to the theoretical psychology of *The sensory order.* In W. B. Weimer & D. S. Palermo (Eds.), *Cognition and the symbolic processes* (Vol. 2, pp. 211–242). Hillsdale, NJ: Erlbaum.

Weimer, W. B. (1982b). Ambiguity and the future of psychology: Meditations *liebniziennes*. In W. B. Weimer & D. S. Palermo (Eds.), *Cognition and the symbolic processes* (Vol. 2, pp. 331–360). Hillsdale, NJ: Erlbaum.

Weimer, W. B. (1987). Spontaneously ordered complex phenomena and the unity of the moral sciences. In G. Radnitzky (Ed.), *Centripetal forces in the sciences* (pp. 257–296). New York: Paragon House.

Whitehead, A. N., & Russell, B. (1963). *Principia mathematica* (2nd ed., 3 vols.). Cambridge, England: Cambridge University Press. (Original work published 1913)

5

EXPERIENCE, EXPLANATION, AND THE QUEST FOR COHERENCE

GIAMPIERO ARCIERO AND VITTORIO F. GUIDANO

Since the celebrated "cognitive revolution" of the 1970s, psychology has taken as its basic strategy the explanation of human feeling and acting according to predictive causal laws. The presumed point of reference for the study of human knowing has accordingly been the "rational man,"[1] who can logically infer the validity of his actions and emotions from "clear and distinct" premises. As an extension of this model of rationality, cognitive science translates this prevailing metaphor into a still more specific operational metaphor of the "computational man." Although this translation maintains the principles of rationalism, the computational approach emphasizes that valid knowing is the product of "representing" an observer-independent world. The correspondence between representations and "external reality" is presumed to be ensured by one's ability to (a) causally

---

[1]We consciously use the masculine form in this opening discussion of the "rational man," in deference to the traditional form in which this metaphor is phrased, not only in psychology but also in related disciplines such as philosophy and economics. Moreover, we suspect that this model of "rational supremacy" and its concomitant distrust of emotion implies a masculine epistemology that contrasts, for example, with "women's ways of knowing," which tend toward greater holism (e.g., Belenky, Clinchy, Goldberger, & Tarule, 1986). Our shift to more gender-neutral language in the remainder of this chapter therefore represents not only a transition to more contemporary nonsexist language but also an attempt to envision an epistemology that transcends this rationalistic, computational, and masculine bias.

explain the relationships between observed facts and (b) verify the explanations empirically across contexts and observers. Accordingly, explanations of mental events try to confirm causal hypotheses by reproducing conditions that generated the events themselves. As a consequence, the community of observers can recognize mental acts as such only when they fulfill such criteria.[2] This prevailing epistemological attitude assumes the existence of rational observers and impersonal mental events. But can we substitute the impersonal analysis of experience by rational observers for the personal meanings of lived experience?

In the past decade, developments in cognitive psychology and psychotherapy have led to a new perspective known as "constructivism." This approach emphasizes the personal and social aspects of human meaning making and is incommensurable with rationalist theories. In the first part of our chapter, we outline this perspective, offering a set of basic assumptions grounded in the tradition of evolutionary epistemology and hermeneutic phenomenology. In the second part of this chapter, we address processes of personal identity regulation in the course of living. In the third part, we briefly outline postrationalist principles of psychopathology and psychotherapy. Finally, in the fourth part, we present a clinical case intended to illustrate the implications of this postrationalist perspective for understanding disorder and psychotherapy.

A CONSTRUCTIVIST PERSPECTIVE

Constructivism's fundamental point of departure from rationalist theories is the acknowledgment that rational laws do not organize knowing systems. "Our actions," noted Hayek (1988), "are governed by rules adjusted to the type of world we live in, that is, to circumstances we are not well aware of, that determine the structure of our successful actions" (p. 81). Every knowing system is an integral part of a community history of practices and of shared senses to which individuals contribute through their own involvement. The loss and renewal of traditions, the death of entire civilizations, and the disappearance of entire languages demonstrate the intrinsically historical nature of human knowledge processes.

However, if one thinks of each individual as biologically unique, one's perceptual–motor scaffolding cannot be separated from one's body (Maturana, 1986; Maturana & Varela, 1987; Merleau-Ponty, 1962). Therefore, being embodied biologically has basic ontological implications: Acts of knowledge are not impersonal; they reflect the experiential order on which

---

[2] The possibility of reproducing "mental acts" is at the core of the extensive use of computational technology in cognitive psychology.

they are based, and they are inseparable from the vital units that bring them forth (Guidano, 1987; Guidano, 1991a; Guidano & Liotti, 1983).

Rather than being purified through the control and governance of reason, cognition is an action inextricably connected to one's participation in a shared social–historical matrix as well as to one's personal history and to the ways one is biologically embedded and organized. Knowing becomes the continuous construction of a world that makes one's ongoing experience contextually consistent (Arciero, 1989; Arciero & Mahoney, 1989; Varela, 1987; Winograd & Flores, 1986). This contrasts with thinking of knowing as a more or less valid representation of external reality.

Language and Experience

If the worlds one brings forth are codependent on one's experiences, the ordering of one's experiential scaffolding takes shape through social interaction. This makes it possible to coordinate one's feelings and actions with those of others. The reordering of experience through language permits a level of self-reflection and mutual coordination that is different from the level of action to which it refers.[3] The possibility of constructing and sharing the meaning of one's own experience through the use of language fosters remarkable human adaptation. Even in primitive societies, linguistic coordination of activity permits human beings to better exploit environmental resources, evaluate opportunities and dangers, and convey experiences through storytelling in ways that promote both immediate survival and intergenerational transmission of knowledge. Hence, if one considers language as a whole, it is impossible to distinguish the contribution of each participant. Instead, from this standpoint, language takes place as a spontaneous order, on a level different from the individuals who use it.

However, if one considers the individual, one arrives at a different view of "subjectivity" than that offered by rationalism. In fact, the meanings one attaches to one's life experiences, rather than being generated by an isolated, self-reflective consciousness, emerge from the interaction of individuals and their cultural context (Ricoeur, 1983). Self-consciousness is not a given; it surfaces through developing and (linguistically) articulating the experience of existence. Knowledge of the self, therefore, takes shape through a circular interplay between the continuous "happening" of one's life and one's recomposing it through shareable meanings that allow its stable ordering. These two levels of experiencing are irreducible. Thus, "feeling like this" in a given situation amounts to a way of being and, at the same time,

---

[3] Studies in different fields clearly show how language, in preliterate societies, was characterized by a complete adherence to the acting dimension (Havelock, 1963; Ong, 1982).

a way in which the world happens. It is because of this cobelonging that the way one feels one is and one's immediate experience of the world cannot be mistaken. One is always how one feels one is (Guidano, 1991b; Olafson, 1988). On the other side, one orders lived experience into a more-or-less coherent life story. One configures (and continually reconfigures) one's experience into a consistent plot that allows one to make attributions about self and others. This generates the boundaries between one's own identity and the identities of others. Through this linguistic imposition on lived experience, people coconstruct their existence. As Madison (1995) noted, "the reflecting subject in search of meaning, self-understanding, is a linguistic subject, a subject which is given to and which knows itself by means of the language it inhabits" (p. 81).

Personal Identity

Personal identity is constructed in the mutual relation between lived experience and the ongoing composition of one's life story. This gives rise to two ways of ordering experience over time, two ways of perceiving oneself in the continuity of living. On the one hand, one has a sense of "permanence" or sameness across lived experiences. On the other hand, one has a sense of "cohesion" or narrative identity as one orders one's experiences (Ricoeur, 1990). The relationship between these two ways of ordering experience generates a number of related problems. First, what relationship exists between variations in one's lived experience (selfhood) and sense of self-permanence? Second, how does one's reordering of moment-to-moment feeling and actions generate a sense of cohesive experience (narrative identity)? Third, how does the mutual coordination between these aspects of personal identity take shape?

As for the first issue, it is necessary to distinguish two aspects of identity that are often confused and overlapping: the *immediacy* of happening in specific circumstances and the "condensed" perception of one's own *continuity*, regardless of the contingent situation. These two polarities reflect different emotional manifestations: episodic affective states and enduring traits or predispositions. In the last 2 decades, several authors have underlined the transient aspects of the former and the recurrent nature of the latter, distinguishing between emotional states and traits. In particular, studies based on a functionalist perspective of discrete emotions (Ekman, 1984; Izard, 1991; Malatesta, 1990) show how patterns of emotional predisposition (traits) correspond to a stable, recurrent, and unitary emotional organization (e.g., seeing oneself as characteristically anxious or generally happy), which ensures the continuity of one's sense of self. In these studies, discrete emotional events (e.g., being afraid of a particular event) seem to be more related to concrete situations and may not be integrated in a sense of personal continuity.

What relationship exists between these two dimensions of the emotional domain? In terms of personal continuity, recurrent emotional states reflect overlap of one's sense of self-stability and one's immediate experience: one's moment-to-moment feelings "fit" with one's self-permanence. An event is integrated into one's perceptions through the identification of those properties that match one's sense of personal continuity. This means that the emotional biases that develop provide the coordinates for all subsequent engagement with the world. Attachment-avoidant children, for instance, develop a stable sense of rejection or loss, accompanied by a personal emotional organization centered on anger and sadness. Once stabilized, this pattern not only leads them to anticipate rejection–loss across situations but also guides their immediate experience in terms of both perception and action. Therefore, any event is immediately decoded through the identification of properties that refer to loss and rejection, thereby leading them to act in ways that can only be understood as responses to loss and disappointment (Guidano, 1987). An illustration of this progressive consolidation of a coherent emotional style organized around the anticipation of loss is provided in the clinical case study below.

The near overlap between the sense of personal continuity and immediate experience is supported by a number of studies on the organizing role of emotions on perception and behavior. These studies show how personal emotional biases influence whether one experiences affect-specific perceptual readiness for comprehending certain types of emotional expression in others (Tomkins & McCarter, 1964). These studies also show how one's affect-specific readiness allows one to express certain emotions (Malatesta, 1990; Malatesta, Fiore, Messina, & Culver, 1987; Malatesta & Wilson, 1988). The emotional continuity of one's life constitutes a story. In this story, the recurrent sedimentation and integration of experience regulates how one perceives and responds to events.

Yet this emphasis on emotional continuity conflicts with one's day-to-day and moment-to-moment variability in mood as one encounters various events. In fact, the contingency and unpredictability of one's emotional life led Gadamer (1976) to contend that "the self that we are does not possess itself; one might say it just happens" (p. 5). How, then, does one reconcile this scattering of the self with one's sense of personal continuity, which time does not alter? Here, we come to the second issue alluded to above. This is where symbolic mediation of life experiences comes into play; in fact, it is through the reconfiguration of experience in a story that the multiplicity of one's happening can be integrated with a sense of self-permanence.

Cohesively organizing events into an intelligible totality is perhaps the most important function of self-narratives. Integration takes place through the plot of a story, in which the discontinuity of happening is combined into a meaningful whole. From this perspective, every life story maintains its coherence and identity as long as it imbues unexpected life events with a sense of personal meaning (Neimeyer, chap. 8, this volume). Reconfiguring the praxis of living into a personal narrative involves constructing a character to whose actions and emotions the narrative refers. In fact, composing a story entails attributing experience to oneself, configuring situations in terms that are uniquely significant for one as the subject. In this respect, as one constructs unique stories, one constructs unique images of oneself as protagonist. Thus, the continuity or discontinuity of one's life stories reflects the dialectic between recurrent emotional patterns that provide a sense of self-permanence and discrete situations triggering discordant feelings that disrupt any sense of personal continuity. Self-narratives attempt to integrate and unify disturbing emotions to maintain, moment-by-moment, one's sense of continuity and personal uniqueness. The dialectical interplay between these stabilizing and destabilizing patterns gives rise to personal identity. The attempt to assimilate perturbing experiences in a way that coheres with one's self-narrative is illustrated in the case study presented later.

PERSONAL IDENTITY AND REGULATION OF INNER COHERENCE

The process of narrative construction changes the experiences on which it depends; in so doing, it transforms that which it seeks to explain. The way one organizes one's emotional domain grows from the way one organizes early life relationships with emotionally reciprocating others, such as parents. The sedimentation of emotional events into a sense of self-permanence is shaped within these stable, balanced relationships; these relationships are centered on a child's proximity to a safe base of emotional attachment. The attunement of and to caregivers allows an infant to organize sensory–motor inflow into feelings that fall somewhere on a continuum of approach to avoidance. Attachment, therefore, plays a critical role in (a) differentiating and organizing a range of basic emotions and (b) modulating the frequency, intensity, and duration of emotional states by regulating the oscillations between arousal-inducing patterns (e.g., exploration and play) and arousal-reducing patterns (e.g., security and clinging; Fox & Davidson, 1984; Malatesta & Wilson, 1988; Schore, 1994; Suomi, 1984; Thompson, 1990).

One's sense of self-permanence is organized around recurrent emotions whose ordering and regulation depend on the quality of ongoing patterns of attachment; these emotional traits provide the key perceptual–affective features for assimilating ongoing experiences. Additionally, the consistency of one's relationship with caregivers helps stabilize and articulate the prototypical sense of self-permanence achieved during early stages of development. These self-organizing and self-regulatory capabilities are clearly demonstrated by the presence of avoidant, ambivalent, and secure attachment organizations from the earliest stages of development (Ainsworth, Blehar, Waters, & Wall, 1978; Bretherton, 1985, 1995). For instance, an avoidant child of a rejecting parent characteristically develops self-perceptions centered on a sense of detachment from others, whether passive or imposed (as in a sense of helplessness) or active and self-generated (as in anger and aggressiveness). However, an opponent process regulation keeps the child's emotional arousal within critical limits, so that excessive movement toward withdrawal and loneliness is "corrected" by the activation of outward, contact-seeking behavior (connected to anger) and vice versa. Thus, any particular form of self-permanence establishes a range of permissible variations within which the individual can shift. In this model, the activation of extreme feeling states triggers a precipitous movement to the contrasting extreme. A detailed clinical example of this emotional self-regulatory process is described later.

From our perspective, emotional organization is both regulatory and self-regulated. It is regulatory in that it modulates the individual's proximity to an attachment figure (interpersonal domain), and it is self-regulated because it integrates new emotional experiences into a unitary perception of the self (personal domain). This mutually defining and regulating relationship involving an emotionally reciprocating figure is supported by studies examining the influences on the development of a sense of self-permanence in infancy and early childhood. Among these influences are changes in caregiving patterns (e.g., loss of an attachment figure) and harsh life circumstances that jeopardize the stability of attachment relationships (e.g., in disadvantaged families; Crittenden, 1985; Magai & McFadden, 1995; Thompson, Lamb, & Estes, 1982).

The composition of one's own narrative identity allows one to distinguish feelings from the flow of immediate experiences. This permits one to understand and explain feelings and experiences, making an implicit "sense of things" explicit. This is how "in the course of ontogenesis[,] individuals develop biases—ideoaffective organizations—around certain emotions which figure as prominent features of personality and which influence a broad spectrum of behaviors, including information processing and coping strategies" (Magai & Hunziker, 1993, p. 250).

The organization of behavioral–affective patterns, made stable through reciprocity with attachment figures, guides narrative framing by providing, from the earliest stages of linguistic development, the recurrent context to which one's symbolic reconfiguration is anchored. As shown by several studies on attachment narratives in early and middle childhood, children's stories reflect both the content of their attachment style and the ways in which they construct and communicate affective themes (Oppenheim & Waters, 1995). For example, Cassidy and Kobak (1988) found that secure 6-year-olds told stories in which the main character was valuable, the relationship with the mother was warm, and the mother was available for help. By contrast, avoidant children depicted the same character as rejected and self-reliant, thus denying the importance of affective relationships and the need for help. Avoidant children tried to withdraw or evade discussion of emotionally laden topics. In another study assessing the internal working models of 6-year-olds, Main, Kaplan, and Cassidy (1985) found that not only did avoidant children have difficulties communicating separation experiences, but they also struggled to remain behaviorally and emotionally regulated when confronted with emotionally evocative interpersonal themes.

These studies indicate that in early and middle childhood, the narrative ordering of experience coordinates the relationship with a more advanced partner. It also modulates the emotional experiences it refers to through a more or less coherent reconfiguration. The parents' ability to provide emotional support facilitates the modulation of emotions and the integration of more complex situations into a sense of self-coherence. This promotes the child's ability to distinguish internal states and elaborate them in an increasingly differentiated way, while allowing the maintenance of a manageable level of emotional activation. The stability of the sense of the self is made possible through the active search for intermediate emotional states (Guidano, 1987) and through direct or indirect exclusion of emotional tonalities that cannot be integrated into the narrative identity constructed (Bowlby, 1980, 1985; Bretherton, 1985; Guidano, 1987, 1991b). This finding implies that fundamental difficulties in accessing emotional tonalities concerning critical areas of personal experience complicates the integration of one's own internal states. If feelings cannot be identified and articulated, they remain outside the story of one's experience and appear alien to who one is. Psychotherapy is therefore concerned with helping clients to access these unarticulated feeling states and promoting more adequate assimilation of them in a revised and expanded self-narrative.

CONTINUITY AND DISCONTINUITY

Beginning in adolescence, self-narratives become more autonomous from the flow of life, even though their stability and direction are related to ongoing experience. Although basic emotional themes continue to guide adult development, their composition into meaningful plots is linked to the unfolding circumstances of life, making that life and that story unique. Therefore, narrative identity elaborates the emotional themes to which it is anchored, integrating discordant emotions and unexpected events into a sense of uniqueness and unity. The core feature of the narrative act is the relation it establishes between the structuring of the plot of one's life story and its ability to modulate affect. This implies that the more effectively one can articulate experience in an intelligible way, the more one can modulate disturbing emotional oscillations and integrate them into one's sense of self. Thus, the symbolic reconfiguration of experience and the ability to recognize different emotional tonalities are interdependent. As Taylor (1985) noted,

> At each stage, what we feel is a function of what we have already articulated and evokes the puzzlement and perplexities which further understanding may unveil. But whether we want to take the challenge or not, whether we seek the truth or take refuge in illusion, our self-(mis)understanding shapes what we feel. This is the sense in which [humans are] self-interpreting animals. (p. 65)

What happens when an unforeseen event challenges narrative identity by generating feelings that interfere with a sense of personal continuity? The integration of the event into the ongoing self-narrative reactivates emotional themes and, with them, internal cues, images, scenes, action sequences, and thoughts. This integration changes the direction of the story by modifying the horizon of expectations regarding future events. One's current story fluctuates between memory and fiction, modulating discordant feelings to square them with one's sense of personal continuity.

Often, developmental transitions and life stages trigger new self-perceptions and constitute an opportunity, for most, to engage in some form of self-narrative revision. How well one integrates these developmental challenges influences one's ability to solve later developmental demands (Cicchetti, 1998). Less frequently, life events may be so unexpected and discordant with respect to one's own story and the ongoing sense of self that they call for a major reorganization of narrative identity. The impossibility of integrating the event triggers a radical break in one's sense of continuity. This break has a retroactive effect on the ordering of experience and inevitably on one's life expectations. The disorganization of the self-narrative that follows is accompanied by a more intense activation of core ordering processes. The profound stirring of basic emotional themes at this critical time helps to reestablish a sense of self-permanence and guides the person's effort to totally reelaborate a familiar narrative identity. However, disruptive life experiences can trigger major transformations and discontinuities in addition to a magnification of preexisting basic personality dispositions (Caspi & Moffit, 1991).

A global reorganization of the sense of self depends on the ability to reach a new balance—one more flexible and abstract than its predecessor—between one's critical experience and one's life outlook. Every personal revolution is matched by a deep reinterpretation of one's own past, a reconstruction of existential projects, and the very praxis of living. An inability to complete this reelaboration prevents a person from reintegrating the emotional discrepancy into a sense of personal continuity. When this happens, the strong activation of basic emotional themes aroused by a persistent discrepancy produces rigidity and concreteness in the life narrative. It also produces a sense of strangeness of the critical experience. The onset of psychopathology may reflect extreme attempts by individuals to maintain the sense of managing of their own feelings. The goal of postrationalist constructivist therapy is to assist clients facing such transitions to achieve viable reordering of self-narratives by expanding their range of affective experiences and behavioral responses.

DISORDERS AND THERAPY

Principles of Psychopathology

This perspective calls for a drastic reconsideration of current methodology in psychopathology and clinical psychology. If experience is considered in terms of its meaning to the individual, the explanation of clinical disorders inevitably changes. Rather than arising from an impersonal etiology (perhaps having neurocortical or biochemical origins), the genesis of disorder must be sought in the client's history of transforming his or her narrative identity throughout the life cycle. Such an approach contrasts fundamentally with an "objective" diagnosis of psychopathology in terms of signs and symptoms associated with traditional psychiatric nosology. It likewise contrasts with a rationalistic cognitive approach that defines criteria for the rationality or irrationality of human cognitive activity irrespective of who brings it forth.

If the construction of one's personal identity involves constructing a reliable world that can render experience recognizable as one's own (Guidano, 1987), then clinical disorder becomes comprehensible only in light of the fundamental dialectic between the domain of acting and feeling and its recomposition in a self-narrative. Although different core emotional organizations lead, in the course of life, to assimilating experience in different ways, those same personal meaning patterns may develop in a normal, neurotic, or psychotic direction, depending on how effectively experience is assimilated into a unitary, cohesive self. Although normality coincides with a flexible and generative processing of critical events, in a neurotic condition the discordant situation is elaborated outside the sense of cohesion of the self, which causes the following:

- less flexibility in personal meaning organization, thereby constraining both the development of the story and its character
- the repetitive surfacing of critical emotions that cannot be articulated in a cohesive fashion and must be crudely and concretely managed (e.g., the attempt to "control" unwanted anger)
- attributing the "neurotic condition" to negative self-elements or elements external to the self, maintaining the discrepancy from which the problem arose.

Finally, in a psychotic situation the inability to elaborate the conflicting event produces disintegration of any sense of self-cohesion and narrative identity. This estrangement of the self from itself has repercussions for the two polarities of personal identity. On the one hand, the inability to reorder one's own feelings and actions into a consistent plot structure precludes one from articulating a variety of experiences and identifying them as one's own. This explains why images, perceptions, thoughts, and emotions are felt as elements "outside" of oneself. This gives rise to a set of symptoms that is typical of psychotic states, defined conventionally as hallucinations, ideas of reference, flattened affect, and so on. On the other hand, the conflicting event can trigger an intense polarization of emotional themes. The magnification of emotional traits steers subsequent cognitive dynamics, in effect preserving a sense of continuity while excluding any possible variation in the psychotic individual's ongoing sense of self, as in delusional and paranoid states.

In disorganized forms, the psychotic identity continuously changes with shifting situations, thereby losing any anchorage with a sense of self-permanence. This effectively produces a neutralization of the variety of the event's meanings (reflected in the lack of integration of experience) and, at the same time, a loss of self-cohesion (so that the subject of the story cannot be identified as the same). In both cases, the progressive stabilization of the disordered patterns generates a gradual loss of a shareable sense of the personal meaning of experience. The path taken—toward self-narrative reification or disintegration—depends on the status of the personal meaning system prior to exposure to the critically disruptive event. Depending on the level of flexibility and generativity achieved in the course of personal development, a personal meaning organization may be elaborated in different directions. For instance, in attachment-avoidant individuals, the same loss experience can be understood as (a) a turning point that prompts a review of one's personal history and life expectations (normal direction); (b) a confirmation of one's unlovability attributed to concrete aspects of the self (neurotic direction); or (c) delusions of personal inadequacy or persecution (psychotic direction).

Postrationalist Psychotherapy: Methodological Aspects

The principles of psychopathology outlined above carry direct therapeutic implications, requiring that the therapist focus attention on the dialectic between the experience of living and its (joint) reconfiguration into an intelligible narrative of events.[4] From the outset, the therapeutic process aims to help the client distinguish between the two polarities of personal identity. On the one hand, this allows the client to grasp any current emotional tonalities and recurrent activation patterns; on the other hand, the client can recognize the basic interpretation processes he or she uses to give meaning to life experiences. In reconstructing a significant event with the client, the therapist orients the client's attention alternately toward either the praxis of living or its dialectic explanation.

As studies on recovery from emotional difficulties demonstrate, to be effective the joint reelaboration of an event should focus on in-depth exploration of feelings triggered by the event rather than on objective "facts" about the situation that triggered it (Philippot & Rimé, 1998). In this way, the therapist and client gradually determine three things: how immediate understandings of the event led to a discrepancy between felt emotions and perceptions of the situation, the effect that the event had on the client's ongoing sense of personal identity, and how the client intelligibly integrates emotional themes and situations.

Through the joint reelaboration of event sequences, the therapist gradually shows the client that behind the apparent strangeness of critical emotions, there exists an internally coherent organizing framework. The therapist's goal is to facilitate the acquisition of those emotions that interfere in a self-narrative to integrate the meaning of disturbing emotions with the client's sense of personal continuity. By assimilating these apparently disruptive emotional experiences into the self-narrative, a client can achieve an expanded and more coherent sense of self.

The therapist involved in this process has two basic considerations in mind. First, people try to reorganize the meaning of their stories in a way that preserves their own continuity as protagonists, not in accordance with objective truth. Consequently, client resistance is triggered by events jeop-

---

[4] Because of space restrictions, we do not discuss in detail the nature of the therapeutic relationship per se, which also provides an emotionally resonant context within which the client can identify various feeling tonalities and develop a more adequate narrative account of them. We refer the reader to Guidano (1991b) for further details.

ardizing a sense of continuity. Such resistance should be articulated rather than opposed by the therapist. As Mahoney and Lyddon (1988) emphasized, respect for the implicit wisdom of systemic processes is more likely to facilitate psychological development than attempts to constrain their expression. Second, the client's ability to articulate feelings is mostly determined by the understanding that he or she has developed rather than by the professional skill of the therapist. This explains the common observation that different clients with the same externally defined disorder can in some cases reintegrate discrepant emotional experiences in a few sessions and in other cases require a considerable amount of time, which implies that the client's reordering processes constitute the fundamental constraint on the therapy's length and course.

In terms of method, self-observation is the essential strategy for both assessment and intervention. In a cinematographic–literary metaphor, the therapist "rewinds the tape" to a discordant situation and encourages the client to "replay" the scene in slow motion. In this "moviola" technique (Guidano, 1991b), the client is trained to review critical scenes from his or her past, alternately "zooming out" and "zooming in" on events. Zooming out helps the client to create meanings consistent with a unified self-narrative. Zooming in helps the client to reinsert problematic scenes into the overall narrative sequence once the scenes are conceptualized in more significant and meaningful ways. Reintegrating critical scenes into an intelligible story shifts the emphasis and meaning of other scenes composing the drama of the client's life. The new emotional tonalities that this process allows the client to recognize can therefore be transformed into many variations of his or her own sense of self and narrative identity. The use of this moviola technique represents the central form of therapeutic intervention in the case study that follows.

In the early stages of therapy, therapist-driven self-observation enables the client to distinguish between lived experience and its reconfiguration in a self-narrative. Through a joint analysis of scene sequences, the therapeutic team reconstructs both the client's patterns of inner coherence and patterns of problematic events, as well as the way the client uses them to refer to him- or herself. Later in the course of therapy and during the subsequent analysis of the client's affective style and developmental story (from infancy through adulthood), this reframing process may be further facilitated by training the client to adopt alternately the role of a protagonist, spectator, and author. The protagonist's role involves the *subjective* viewpoint, emphasizing how the client perceives experience. The spectator's role involves the *objective* viewpoint or focusing on recurrent situations. Finally, the author's role requires a *reflective* viewpoint that helps the client to become aware of how he or she integrates experiences. Reading emotionally significant life episodes from several viewpoints reactivates critical emotions while changing the way they are assessed and self-referred. This leads the client to recompose new sets of immediate answers at subjective, expressive, and physiological levels, generating a greater flexibility of his or her ongoing sense of personal stability. However, reframing a sequence of scenes in an intelligible manner triggers the emergence of new memories, new connections between events, and new emotional tonalities related to them. This translates into a recomposition of the relation between specific autobiographical memories (unique to a single event), general event knowledge (over the period of a lifetime), and life themes. This is matched by a shift in expectations about the future. This gradually restructures the client's self-image by fostering the acquisition of new experiences that are integrated into a new sense of self-cohesion. Greater flexibility unfolds through an increased integration of experience, matched by more articulate modulation of the emotional domain; this is at the heart of effective psychotherapy.

A CASE ILLUSTRATION

This form of psychotherapy is illustrated by the case of Ricardo, a client who requested professional help because of depressive symptoms. His therapy consisted of three phases: helping Ricardo to distinguish between the praxis of living and its narrative reconfiguration, aiding him in the recomposition of his affective style, and working with him on the reelaboration of his developmental story. Although this is a simplified account, it provides a "roadmap" to orient readers to the primary emphases of Ricardo's personal reconstruction.

Ricardo was a 45-year-old Italian writer and film director whose deadpan expressions and slow movements conveyed the impression of significant depression. He spoke with apparent difficulty as he related that for 2 or 3 years, he had been in a state of dejection from which he could not emerge. He was extremely worried because he was neglecting his work. He was also neglecting his wife, Maria, who was 12 years Ricardo's junior, and Bruno, his 13-year-old son. What disheartened Ricardo most was discovering himself to be "another person" in these last few years, a "weakling" who was frightened by anything, above all by his own reactions to circumstances. The most troubling of these reactions took the form of intense desperation when he was faced with even minimal failures or disappointments, alternating with explosions of uncontrollable rage. Ricardo stated that he was not really aware at moments of what made him angry. His anger could be triggered by trivial disagreements with a friend over a soccer match or with his son over choosing a television program. These reactions led him to feel that he was becoming an "impossible" person who, through no one's fault but his own, would be abandoned even by those he held dear.

As Ricardo presented his situation, the therapist listened actively, asking for periodic clarifications of the painful emotion experienced but without revealing any worry or perplexity about the despairing conclusions at which the client regularly arrived. At the end of this initial exposition of the problem, the therapist noted that Ricardo's feeling himself to be another person seemed, at that moment, to be the most important aspect of the experience to investigate, given how much it shocked and depressed him. The therapist, therefore, began by asking if at other times Ricardo had felt sensations and moods analogous to those that brought him to therapy. Ricardo, as if disoriented, seemed not to understand the question and, growing sadder, stated that he had been depressed many times in his life. The therapist pointed out that he was not interested in compiling a diagnostic inventory of Ricardo's symptoms but rather in reconstructing this sense of feeling himself to be another person and that the best way to begin this exploration was to see if Ricardo had felt similarly on other occasions.

After reflection, Ricardo noted several such occasions. The first had occurred at the age of 19, after going abroad, against the advice of his parents. The second had immediately followed his getting married at the age of 32. In both cases he had felt "turned upside down," quite different from how he had felt shortly before. He also had felt great desperation and anxiety. He felt that he used to have "more guts" and will to struggle, which had allowed him to live through these disorienting experiences more effectively than now. Although these earlier episodes were associated with great suffering, they also had contributed to important changes in Ricardo's life. Indeed, after the journey abroad, he never returned to the bosom of his family, acquiring autonomy and an ability to "go it alone." He was still proud of this ability. Nevertheless, his marriage had radically changed his nomadic habits, deeply affecting his private and professional life.

The therapist pointed out how these remembered situations seemed to correspond to those transformations of his sense of self that commonly appear in the course of individual life span development. The therapist suggested that such periods were commonly experienced as painful "overturnings of the self," which were usually upsetting and nearly always resisted because of the human need for continuity. The therapist also wondered aloud whether Ricardo's present feelings expressed a transformation in progress. In Ricardo's case, the main difference between the earlier experiences of self-transformation and the present situation seemed to be that although the earlier transformations had followed decisions he had made, the present transformation was spontaneous. It was perhaps because of this that he felt it was involuntary. Ricardo and his therapist agreed to reconstruct what was changing in Ricardo to understand and help him. They began this reconstructive process by focusing on times when Ricardo had felt sudden desperation or uncontrollable rage; such incidents were hypothesized to be possible signs of a transformation in progress. Ricardo's uncommon ability to immediately grasp the essence of this interpretation, combined with the establishment of a strong collaborative climate in therapy, made it possible for a reformulation of the presenting problem to be completed during the first session.

Focusing and Reconstructing the Praxis of Living

The first phase of therapy began with the therapist's request that Ricardo note weekly events that seemed meaningful. For Ricardo, this entailed attending to experiences of helplessness and anger as well as the memories triggered spontaneously by these experiences and the conclusions he drew about himself and his life as a result. As therapy unfolded, Ricardo noticed that his uncontrolled outbursts of anger toward others, far from expressing a resigned preference to live alone, expressed Ricardo's dissatisfaction with his perceived emotional detachment of others. This was particularly evident where his wife Maria was concerned because he sensed a cooling in their relationship (a topic he found difficult to address). Significantly, Ricardo experienced the most intense outbursts of rage with her.

After 3 months of approximately weekly sessions, Ricardo was able to distance himself from episodes of helplessness and anger, to the point where these intrusive emotions became generally less frequent and intense. Ironically, the situation with Maria appeared little changed, if not worse. With her, Ricardo's outbursts of anger and his desperate reactions to her "abandonment" became even more intense and repetitive. Despite the reluctance he had shown in talking about the marital relationship, he agreed, out of necessity, to examine his emotionally charged exchanges with Maria using the moviola technique. Shifting continuously from a subjective to objective viewpoint, Ricardo showed that his outbursts of rage were replete with grudges and accusations against Maria, ignited whenever he interpreted her as refusing his sexual overtures. Such refusal characteristically triggered a sense of abandonment in Ricardo, associated with the feeling that he did not deserve her. Of interest is that this was immediately followed by a profound sense of indifference, when Ricardo would not have batted an eyelid if Maria had suddenly announced that she wanted a divorce. Ricardo was astonished to discover that his outbursts of anger were chiefly made up of sexual grudges toward Maria, given that he had decided more than 2 years previously to discontinue a sexual relationship with her.

By focusing on how this decision came about, the therapist saw the critical event emerge. About 3 years ago, Maria had heedlessly let slip that she had had an affair with a colleague Ricardo knew only by sight. At the moment of this revelation, Ricardo was stunned, but immediately afterward he exploded into such a violent rage that his wife considered calling the police. He quickly calmed down, took Maria into the bedroom, and in a peremptory, contemptuous fashion, forced her to give him technical demonstrations of all the erotic interactions she had had during every single meeting with her lover. Although his intention had been to humiliate her, he unexpectedly found himself aroused to a level of sexual excitement he had never known before. Thus, in his words, he "couldn't help" transforming all of this into a ritual repeated every night. After this had gone on for a few weeks, Maria burst into tears, threatening divorce because of "sexual incompatibility" due to his obvious "perversion." This led to a reversal of the situation, with Maria attributing her extramarital affair to Ricardo's sexual "oddity," which she always sensed but only now fully comprehended. More convinced that he was despicable and shamefully perverted, Ricardo announced that he was willing to give up all sexual activity between them and would allow Maria sexual freedom as long as she withdrew her threat of divorce.

Several sessions were needed to examine these events using the moviola technique, which involved analyzing specific scenes and shifting between subjective and objective viewpoints. Through this technique, Ricardo tied stunned and enraged feelings to the invalidation of his image of Maria as an "innocent child," an image that was contradicted by the disclosure of her sexual liaison with another man. Only when he could render her submissive and humiliated by his oppression could he reestablish the sense that she was "his baby." This solution had drawbacks, because it also revealed Ricardo as a "bad father," quite incapable of protecting Maria from the perils of the world. After Maria threatened divorce, Ricardo felt himself "no longer worthy of her." He was ready to do anything to keep them together, although he no longer felt that he deserved it. The event triggering Ricardo's difficulties was the unexpected change in his image of Maria and the successive strategies by which he sought to negate this change. Ricardo's sexual perversions were a self-deceiving pattern that, although radically altering his own self-image, restored Maria's positive image.

During the session in which this became clear to Ricardo, he underwent a strong emotional reaction. Unable to hold back his tears, he said he could never imagine making himself into a "monster" to preserve his image of Maria. This key session instigated a significant change in Ricardo's behavior. He became less resigned, less desperately fixed in an "abandoned for life" role, and more enterprising in carrying on the exploratory work that had "awakened" him. This yielded related insights. He discovered that his thoughts of suicide corresponded to afternoons when he suspected Maria was meeting her boyfriend, resulting in angry outbursts when she came home. A moviola review of subsequent scenes from his life made it evident to him that he had sustained the expectation of a *coup de theatre* in which Maria would come back to him, ready to accept even his perversion (which had vanished on the threat of divorce). Although illusory in some respects, this "storybook ending" had allowed him to project a livable future.

Reconfiguration of the Client's Affective Style

After 4–8 months of therapy, clients typically undergo an appreciable change in their view of themselves, accompanied by a substantial remission of the disturbances that led them to therapy. The second phase of therapy begins by focusing on this reformulation and explicating the way in which the client structures affectional ties with others to maintain the perceived coherence of his or her current sense of self. In Ricardo's case, this began with a detailed analysis of the following:

- his "sentimental debut," that is, his earliest memories of events that shaped his sense of self in intimate relationships
- his sequence of meaningful relationships since the debut, including a reconstruction of the criteria by which he differentiated meaningful from unimportant relationships
- the way in which each meaningful relationship was formed, maintained, and broken and the ways in which they were experienced, appraised, and self-referred.

Ricardo's affective history began with a first love affair with Analisa at the age of 17. At this point in his life, Ricardo was a somewhat solitary young man, dedicated to the study of literature and cinema. This inwardness, combined with his thick dark hair, led peers to teasingly call him the "brown bear." Analisa, by contrast, was a bit older, was more socially experienced, and had many friends. Despite his fantasies about her, Ricardo was quite bashful in her presence. He was astonished when Analisa asked him if they could start dating. Ricardo's disbelief transformed almost immediately into elation mixed with a sense of being specially chosen, making him even more awkward and clumsy. This state of exaltation lasted a very short time because it soon seemed impossible that this could have really happened to him. He immediately closed himself up in his usual retiring and detached manner. The affair lasted only 1 week because he found it hard to tolerate Analisa's ironic little comments about his being a "clumsy bear" and disliked seeing her enjoying herself with her friends—something he felt she did not do with him. One afternoon, Ricardo had an outburst of uncontrollable rage for a reason he could not remember, after which Analisa never talked to him again. Ricardo had an intense and prolonged depressive reaction to this breakup, which kept him for months shut up in his room. After nearly

1 year, he slowly began to feel the desire to start doing something again. To avoid the environment that had caused so much trouble, he decided to go abroad, despite the opposition of his parents.

After leaving home, Ricardo led an adventurous life. He had relationships with many women but had difficulty involving himself emotionally in these affairs. There were two relationships he felt were meaningful: The first, between the ages of 25 to 29; the second, when he met Maria at age 31. He saw these relationships as meaningful because he felt unconditionally chosen by these partners, and reliable.

At 25, Ricardo was living abroad, had finished a course in film directing, and had begun working professionally with some success. This was what he called the "best moment of my life." He felt he was a leader who functioned well and was sought after in social situations, despite his tendency toward a retiring existence. The affair with Sandra, a slightly older woman from a well-to-do family, began passionately when during what seemed like a banal flirtation, she suddenly decided to leave her family of origin and live with him. Ricardo accepted the situation as a *fait accompli*, with little enthusiasm, maintaining that it was "impossible" and destined to "vanish like a soap bubble" at any moment. Little by little, however, his habits changed, which he attributed to his showing "elementary good manners" toward his partner. He dedicated less and less time to work and study, reaching the point where this relationship became the central element of his life structure. For a couple of years, this situation continued. Ricardo appraised every moment as if it marked the end of the relationship, only to find further confirmation that he was Sandra's choice in the way she fought pressure from her family to break off the affair. At the end of the 2nd year, the situation suddenly cooled. Sandra became vague and elusive, held her own less and less against her family, and after a time packed her bags and went back to them. For several days, Ricardo suffered deep depression, when suddenly he realized, as if a spell had finally broken, that it was precisely his passive attitude of being "condemned and awaiting the verdict" that had caused Sandra to leave. He then began a desperate chase that lasted for 2 years, continually running after her and blaming himself for everything. This ended only when he received a definitive warning from Sandra's family lawyer.

Ricardo's love affair with his wife, Maria, began differently. Ricardo returned for good to Italy, where he made a brilliant start as a television director. The outcome of his relationships with Analisa and Sandra had emphasized the futility of overwhelming intense affairs, bringing about the feeling that his life as a bachelor was coming to an end and that he "had to get his head together." Maria, who was 12 years younger than he, was one of his students. After about 1 year, she finally asked him if there was any chance of their getting together. Ricardo did not consider it an obstacle that he felt neither passion nor enthusiasm for Maria; indeed, it seemed to him like a situation offered by fate to enable him to start living just like everybody else. During their 1st year of marriage, however, he felt progressively more disappointed by his wife, whose simplicity began to strike him as immaturity. When Maria became pregnant, Ricardo went into an intense depressive crisis, characterized by a disturbing sense of feeling like another person. He came out of this depression convinced that his life must center on Maria and his son Bruno. He saw them as his "two children," as if he had suddenly changed from a bachelor to a widower with two dependents. As a consequence, he relegated his career as a television director to a distant second place in his scheme of priorities.

By repeatedly reconstructing this sequence of critical events, the therapist helped Ricardo see the essential ingredients on which Ricardo had based his self-organized affective style. In the first place, the central theme of loss seemed to recur in his structuring of affective relationships. Relationships began with the anticipation of their loss. His relationships with Analisa and Sandra served as evidence for this. This theme also applied to his relationship with Maria; his lack of enthusiasm and passion had been the very condition permitting the formation of the relationship. In perceiving himself as the "cause" of the relationship because he was Maria's object of choice, he concluded that he would also cause the anticipated demise of the relationship as well. His continuous anticipation of loss seemed to give him a key for reading negative trends in each of his partner's responses to him (feeling mistreated by Analisa, condemned and awaiting the verdict with Sandra, and a widower in his marriage to Maria). This confirmed his ongoing sense of being alone, abandoned, and inexorably separate from others. At the same time, he minimized the life changes that accompanied his relationships by attributing them to external factors, such as "good manners" or the "childishness" of his wife, thereby deceiving himself about the range and intensity of his own emotional involvement. This self-deception served an important function: In a world in which loss appeared inevitable, "being unattached to anybody" seemed to be the most effective way to mitigate the intensity of disruptive feelings resulting from anticipated future rejections. His keen experience of loss unmistakably marked all the crises and eventual dissolutions of his affective relationships.

It was invariably the partner who initiated the relationship's end. Ricardo passively experienced abandonment that provided the confirmation of his presumed unlovability, despite his periodic suspicion that he himself had played a role in being abandoned. After each breakup, reaffirming his unlovability was the only way to recover a more active role, supplying an explanation of what had happened that would be sufficiently consistent with his sense of self and that would at the same time allow him to struggle to recover what had been lost. The episode of sexual perversion with his wife, which had played an important part in the first part of the work, was where this attitude stood out most clearly.

Reelaboration of the Developmental Story

The third phase of Ricardo's therapy followed the disappearance of his depression, desperation, and anger. Therapy shifted to reconstructing how Ricardo's development had led him to structure his life along the lines discussed above. Ricardo traced the sense of sadness that had always accompanied him to his earliest memories, going back to age 2 or 3. He attributed his sadness to the fact that his parents had had him at a fairly late age, when they were resigned to not having children and to leading an unexciting existence. His first images of life were of "gray surroundings," animated only by the slow movements of "lifeless" older people who were entirely detached from his world of childhood. Significantly, Ricardo was unable to recall any images of interacting with others during these years. His most tranquil moments were those spent alone in the garden. In contact with his parents, he was always upset by their financial worries, which they discussed continually. His clearest memory of this period was when he was 4 and his father leaned toward him with a worried look on his face and said, "How are we going to be able to give you a future with the situation we're in?" This memory still perturbed him so deeply that every time he talked about it, more than 40 years later, his voice was broken with sobs. This was the first time it became clear to him that his birth had created an unbearable burden for his parents, who otherwise would have been able to lead a relatively peaceful life less beset by financial concerns.

Focusing on multiple scenes with his mother and father using the moviola technique, the therapist was struck by Ricardo's lack of emotional contact with his parents. Ricardo attributed this to his parents' being preoccupied by "far more important things than slobbering over their son." Indeed, with his birth they had had to intensify their efforts to earn money, despite uncertain employment. Ricardo being a "sickly" child, whose needs preempted possibilities for carefree moments of affection, complicated this. Because of his delicate health, he was forced to forgo nursery school and postpone meeting peers until the beginning of school. However, just before the beginning of primary school, the family doctor discovered that Ricardo had a "weak" heart and dissuaded his parents from sending him to school. Consequently, during his primary school years, Ricardo stayed at home to study, aided by a retired teacher who came wearily to him every day with the sole aim of adding to a meager pension. This additional unforeseen expense naturally worsened the already precarious family budget.

Ricardo saw himself as burdening his old and tired parents, who surely deserved a better son. He felt this responsibility particularly with his father, who aroused his tenderness and respect while also seeming "unreachable" and preoccupied with worries primarily caused by Ricardo. Ricardo put forward much effort in his studies, partly to repay his father for all the troubles he had unwittingly caused. He did not feel the effects of his isolation in those years because of a total commitment to his studies. This gave him a sense of being "one of the family." He did so well on middle school entrance exams that he received a cash prize, which he proudly presented to his father, feeling that he had finally "earned" his place in the family. However, his parents reacted by sending him to a renowned boarding school, so he could take full advantage of his academic talents, stressing that this was yet another sacrifice on their part. Although Ricardo tried to conceal his true reaction, he experienced the imminent separation from his parents with a deep sense of desperation and a pervasive anxiety that he might never see them again. His mother embraced and kissed him for the first time when Ricardo boarded the train to his new school, confirming for Ricardo that this was a definitive, irreversible separation. With this "realization," Ricardo burst into uncontrollable tears, despite his father's repeated admonition to "be a man."

Ricardo's transition to the new school was difficult. He arrived with a reputation of being "clever" but "different" and "sickly." Moreover, the complexity of the new environment relative to his secluded home setting left Ricardo feeling clumsy and unequipped with even the most elementary norms of social behavior, prompting him to keep mostly to himself. He immersed himself in literature, which allowed him to "live parallel lives in books." Gradually, however, Ricardo gained acceptance from peers, eventually becoming an indisputable leader. This period, from age 13 to 15 years, corresponded to a period of well-being that Ricardo had never felt before. He discovered that he had qualities that others appreciated and a way of being and of seeing the world that differed from what he had experienced at home.

However, this period of academic and social success eroded between the ages of 15 and 17, when Ricardo began to do less well at school. He was hard pressed for an explanation of this. He attributed it simply to a "reawakening of the senses" that he began to feel during this period, coinciding with an emergence of adolescent sexuality. When his father, on rare visits, treated him coldly as if he were a "degenerate," Ricardo felt a mixture of humiliation, remorse, and rage. This threw him into despair for weeks afterward. The situation culminated when his father withdrew Ricardo from the boarding school and sent him to a stricter and more rigorous one. Ricardo at first felt despair, followed by a fury he never imagined possible. He refused to continue school and shut himself in his room, immersing himself as much as possible in the literature that had become his "real life." A year of tension and despair followed.

From that moment, his father did not speak to him again and referred to him in the past tense as if he were dead, even though he tacitly assented to his mother's sending him food and a little money. As a child, Ricardo had merely felt that he was a burden; now he felt a "cosmic" solitude. He concluded that his attempts to be different had been useless folly and that the only thing that might have mattered, "making an effort for the Old Man's sake," had turned out to be a colossal failure for which he alone, as usual, was responsible. By age 20, he had decided to fully play his role as degenerate son, abandoning his family to travel abroad. He dreamed about the day when, as a famous director, he would return home welcomed with affection, recognition, and his father's apologies. The fact that both his parents had died before he established himself as a director confirmed to him that he had been a disgrace to them and that he might also be a disgrace to all those who loved him.

Repeatedly passing affect-laden scenes through the moviola made it a fairly straightforward matter to reconstruct the gradual self-organization of Ricardo's depressive meaning while reordering his appraisal of the past. For Ricardo, clearly from his earliest years, solitude and the sense of affective loss were the connecting threads along which his entire history had unfolded. What was less clear was how attachment dynamics and the role played by his parents had influenced this. As is characteristic of helpless children, Ricardo tended to minimize the experience of distressing affect (e.g., that associated with his almost total isolation). He also dismissed the idea that his relationship with his parents was not a source of comfort, arguing that "they had more important things to think about." Ricardo's tendency to reduce the level of affective experience left him feeling perturbed by experiences that were inadequately appraised and self-referred.

His memory from the age of 4, in which his father expressed grave concern about his future, clearly fit this pattern. Faced with the discrepancy between his stated indifference to his childhood and his being moved to tears by this image, Ricardo repeatedly processed this and similar recollections through the moviola technique. The result was an intense emotional experience accompanied by various discoveries about himself and his parents. Shifting between viewing himself and his father from internal and external perspectives, what struck him most about his father's attitude was his "making him a participant in the problems of the household, as if he were an adult." Ricardo appraised this as a crushing responsibility, denying him the experience of a childhood characterized by protection, affection, and attention. Moreover, as the focus broadened to include the whole sequence of critical images of childhood, it became clear how this theme of not deserving affection, confirmed moment-by-moment by his parents' inattention, was articulated into more complex meaning structures. On the one hand, this stance left open the possibility that "succeeding for his parents" would one day allow him to fully recover their affection. On the other hand, he was able to look after himself efficiently in situations that would be difficult for any child, such as pursuing his studies alone and still managing to come out on top (thereby establishing his pattern of compulsive self-reliance).

It gradually became clearer to Ricardo that his parent's behavior, rather than resulting from their advanced age, instead corresponded to a rigid strategy of upbringing that allowed them to have complete control over him, with a minimum of emotional investment. For a strategy of this nature to maintain its efficacy over the years, it was necessary that the moment Ricardo fulfilled any responsibility, another was immediately presented that required even more effort and devotion. Thus, when Ricardo thought he had managed to earn a place in the home with the brilliant middle school admission exam results, he suddenly found himself alone on a train to boarding school, an event that seemed more than he could handle. In this way, the experience of never attaining secure emotional attachment slowly became the defining aspect of his world. Loneliness, anger, and a sense of unlovability became his core features of self-reference. This supported the continuity of his patterns of self-perception. It also structured new domains of experience, such as his attitude toward studying, literature, and the development of love relationships.

As Ricardo's therapy was shifted to focus on his period of academic decline, two things became clear. First, Ricardo began to distinguish themes and interests that he would subsequently develop. Second, another world different from home was possible. His decision to go it alone was a tacit bid to be praised by and reconciled with his father and with the world at large. His despair was the price he had to pay for the eventual understanding and acceptance that he had assumed would one day follow from his success.

Faced with his parents' decision to change his boarding school, Ricardo thought he had lost both the new world he had conquered and the family world to which he had once belonged. As his anger gradually diminished, his despair intensified to the point that it seemed he could mitigate it only by suicide or a complete withdrawal from the world. As Ricardo and the therapist ran the subsequent period through the moviola, it became evident to him that his father's withdrawal of support was a power maneuver to bring him back under control. Furthermore, Ricardo viewed this separation as a real abandonment, similar to what he had felt with his wife. Ricardo's guilt and self-blame for being a degenerate son permitted him to maintain his image of his father, thus preserving emotional reciprocity with him while constructing the fantasy of a prodigal son's return. Ricardo realized how his own self-blame prevented him from attributing his father's historical indifference to the Old Man himself. It became painfully clear to Ricardo that his father had always thought him to be an intrusion and that only this painful but liberating interpretation could explain the absence of even the most elemental paternal feelings across the course of their lives together. The consequent change in his image of his father triggered an intense emotional reaction on Ricardo's part, so much so that he could not hold back the tears associated with his sense of irreparable loss. As his tears continued, however, they changed in character and gradually came to express exaltation in feeling himself released from the solitude and personal ruin to which he long felt condemned. Building on this sense of liberation, he was able to revisit his strained relationship with Maria with less panic over her abandoning him, and less tendency to torment himself with the conclusion that her withdrawal was a just punishment for his faults and unlovability. Although much work on their marriage remained, Ricardo felt a fresh sense of optimism about his future, accompanied by the growing conviction that he could form new affectional bonds, even if his fears of divorce were realized.

CONCLUSION

In this chapter, we tried to outline the essential features of a postrationalist therapy that is informed by both an understanding of the central role of coherence in the construction of a self-narrative and the importance of affectional bonds in shaping one's appraisals of both one's self and world. In doing so, we underscored the delicate interplay between levels of tacit experiencing and explicit explanation, focusing particularly on the genesis of clinical disturbance when an individual's appraisals of self and circumstance contribute to recurrent and problematic affective and behavioral patterns of adaptation. By extension, we presented therapy as a process by which such appraisals are gradually revised, through the emotionally charged and painstaking review of both contemporary and more remote scenes from a client's life. This review helps clients to challenge the narrative intelligibility used to make sense of such scenes. Our detailed discussion of this moviola process in the case of Ricardo illustrates the potential power of a constructivist therapy to promote profound change in a client's most fundamental meaning structures. It also conveys our conviction that such change can promote a more genuine and liberating sense of coherence in the self-narratives of clients who once experienced only their constraints.

REFERENCES

Ainsworth, M. D. S., Blehar, M. C., Waters, E., & Wall, S. (1978). *Patterns of attachment*. Hillsdale, NJ: Erlbaum.

Arciero, G. (1989, January). *From epistemology to ontology: A new age of cognition.* Paper presented at the American Association for the Advancement of Science Conference, San Francisco.

Arciero, G., & Mahoney, M. J. (1989). *Understanding and psychotherapy.* Unpublished manuscript, University of California, Santa Barbara.

Belenky, M. F., Clinchy, B. M., Goldberger, N. R., & Tarule, J. M. (1986). *Women's ways of knowing.* New York: Basic Books.

Bowlby, J. (1980). *Attachment and loss. Vol. 3: Loss, sadness and depression.* London: Hogarth.

Bowlby, J. (1985). The role of childhood experience in cognitive disturbance. In M. J. Mahoney & A. Freeman (Eds.), *Cognition and psychotherapy* (pp. 181–189). New York: Basic Books.

Bretherton, I. (1985). Attachment theory. *Monographs of the Society for Research in Child Development 50*(1–2, Serial No. 209).

Bretherton, I. (1995). A communication perspective on attachment relationships and interval working models. *Monographs of the Society for Research in Child Development, 60*(2–3, Serial No. 244), 310–329.

Caspi, A., & Moffit, T. E. (1991). Individual differences are accentuated during periods of social change: The sample case of girls at puberty. *Journal of Personality and Social Psychology, 61,*157–168.

Cassidy, J., & Kobak, R. R. (1988). Avoidance and its relation to other defensive processes. In J. Belsky & T. Nezworski (Eds.), *Clinical implications of attachment* (pp. 300–323). Hillsdale, NJ: Erlbaum.

Cicchetti, D. (1998). The development of depression in children and adolescents. *American Psychologist, 53,* 221–241.

Crittenden, P. (1985). Maltreated infants: Vulnerability and resilience. *Journal of Child Psychology and Psychiatry, 26,* 85–96.

Ekman, P. (1984). Expression and the nature of emotions. In K. Scherer & P. Ekman (Eds.), *Approaches to emotion* (pp. 319–341). Hillsdale, NJ: Erlbaum.

Fox, N. A., & Davidson, R. J. (Eds.). (1984). *The psychobiology of affective development.* Hillsdale, NJ: Erlbaum.

Gadamer, H.G. (1976). *Philosophical hermeneutics.* Berkeley: University of California Press.

Guidano, V. F. (1987). *Complexity of the self.* New York: Guilford Press.

Guidano, V. F. (1991a). Affective change events in a cognitive therapy system approach. In D. J. Safran & S. L. Greenberg (Eds.), *Emotion, psychotherapy, and change* (pp. 120–135). New York: Guilford Press.

Guidano, V. F. (1991b). *The self in process.* New York: Guilford Press.

Guidano, V. F., & Liotti, G. (1983). *Cognitive processes and emotional disorders.* New York: Guilford Press.

Havelock, E. (1963). *Preface to Plato.* Cambridge, England: Cambridge University Press.

Hayek, F. A. (1988). *The collected works of F. A. Hayek.* London: Routledge.

Izard, C. E. (1991). *The psychology of emotions.* New York: Plenum Press.

Madison, G. B. (1995). Ricoeur and the hermeneutics of the subject. In L. E. Hahn (Ed.), *The library of living philosophers. Vol. 22: The philosophy of Paul Ricoeur* (pp. 75–89). Chicago: Open Court.

Magai, C., & Hunziker, J. (1993). Tolstoy and the riddle of developmental transformation. In M. Lewis & M. Haviland (Eds.), *Handbook of emotions* (pp. 241–260). New York: Guilford Press.

Magai, C., & McFadden, H. S. (1995). *The role of emotions in social and personality development.* New York: Plenum Press.

Mahoney, M. J., & Lyddon, W. J. (1988). Recent developments in cognitive approaches to counseling and psychotherapy. *The Counseling Psychologist, 16,* 190–234.

Main, M., Kaplan, N., & Cassidy, J. (1985). Security in infancy, childhood and adulthood. *Monographs of the Society for Research in Child Development, 50*(1–2, Serial No. 209).

Malatesta, C. Z. (1990). The role of emotions in the development and organization of personality. In R. A. Thompson (Ed.), *Nebraska Symposium on Motivation. Vol. 36: Socioemotional development* (pp. 1–56). Lincoln: University of Nebraska Press.

Malatesta, C. Z., Fiore, M. J., Messina, J., & Culver, C. (1987). Affect, personality, and facial expressive characteristics of older individuals. *Psychology and Aging, 1,* 64–69.

Malatesta, C. Z., & Wilson, A. (1988). Emotion–cognition interaction in personality development: A discrete emotions, functionalist analysis. *British Journal of Social Psychology, 27,* 91–112.

Maturana, H. (1986). *Ontology of observing. The biological foundations of self-consciousness and the physical domain of existence.* Unpublished manuscript, University of Chile, Santiago.

Maturana, H., & Varela, F. (1987). *The tree of knowledge.* Boston: Shambhala.

Merleau-Ponty, M. (1962). *Phenomenology of perception.* London: Routledge.

Olafson, A. F. (1988). *Heidegger and the philosophy of mind.* New Haven, CT: Yale University Press.

Ong, W. (1982). *Orality and literacy.* London: Methuen.

Oppenheim, D., & Waters, S. H. (1995). Narrative processes and attachment representations. *Monographs of the Society for Research in Child Development, 60*(2–3, Serial No. 244, pp. 197–216).

Philippot, P., & Rimé, B. (1998). Social and cognitive processing in emotion. In F. W. Flack, Jr., & D. J. Laird (Eds.), *Emotions in psychopathology* (pp. 114–129). London: Oxford.

Ricoeur, P. (1983). *Temps et recit* [Time and narrative]. Paris, France: Editorial du Seuil.

Ricoeur, P. (1990). *Soi-meme comme un autre* [Self as other]. Paris, France: Editorial du Seuil.

Schore, N. (1994). *Affect regulation and the origin of the self.* Hillsdale, NJ: Erlbaum.

Suomi, S. (1984). The development of affect in rhesus monkeys. In N. Fox & R. Davidson (Eds.), *The psychobiology of affective development* (pp. 150–172). Hillsdale, NJ: Erlbaum.

Taylor, C. (1985). *Human agency and language.* Cambridge, England: Cambridge University Press.

Thompson, R. A. (1990). Emotion and self-regulation. In R. A. Thompson (Ed.), *Nebraska Symposium on Motivation. Vol. 36: Socioeconomic development* (pp. 336–467). Lincoln: University of Nebraska Press.

Thompson, R. A., Lamb, M. E., & Estes, D. (1982). Stability of infant–mother attachment and its relationship to changing life circumstances in an unselected middle-class sample. *Child Development, 53,* 144–148.

Tomkins, S. S., & McCarter, R. (1964). What and where are the primary affects? *Perceptual and Motor Skills, 18,* 119–158.

Varela, F. (1987). Laying down a path in walking. In W. J. Thompson (Ed.), *Gaia: A way of knowing* (pp. 48–64). Great Barrington, MA: Lindisfarne Press.

Winograd, T., & Flores, F. (1986). *Understanding computer and cognition.* Norwood, NJ: Ablex.

III

DISORDER AND ASSESSMENT OF PERSONAL MEANINGS

6

LINGUISTIC AMBIGUITY AS A DIAGNOSTIC TOOL

JAY S. EFRAN AND PAUL F. COOK

For us, psychotherapy is fundamentally a diagnostic venture—more sleuthing than healing. It is most applicable to clients who suffer from linguistic confusions and hypocrisies. It is why Efran and Heffner (1991) argued that psychotherapy "is the treatment of choice only for problems that hinge on self-deception" (p. 61). Such dilemmas tend to clear up as clients' underlying assumptions and hidden agendas are brought to light.

Our perspective differs from the traditional view that diagnosis is a process that precedes and guides treatment. Instead, we see diagnosis as the primary ingredient of the therapeutic recipe. In other words, what we offer clients is a sharply focused collaborative examination of the language they use in talking to (and about) themselves. The accounts people give of their actions—their "stories"—seem plausible only when viewed at a certain aesthetic distance. Under closer scrutiny, it becomes clear that their rhetoric contains unexamined suppositions and glaring inconsistencies that have ordinarily been ignored, minimized, or explained away. If such linguistic glitches are allowed to persist, they tend to block the creative solution of interpersonal difficulties.

We thank Elsa R. Efran for her assistance in the preparation of this chapter.

Our description of therapist-as-diagnostician calls to mind the story of the master ship's plumber who is called on to repair an ocean liner's hydraulics. After tapping on various pipes, he finally "whacks" one of them with his wrench. Although the ship owner is delighted to have his engines running smoothly again, he is appalled by the plumber's $5,000 fee. He complains that the man spent only a few minutes in the engine room and did little more than bang on a pipe. In response to the owner's concern, the plumber offers to provide an itemized bill. It says: "For hitting a pipe with a wrench, $1. For knowing where to hit, $4,999." Psychotherapists, too, earn their pay by providing diagnostic expertise.

We hasten to add that our interest is generally not in the diagnostic categories of the *Diagnostic and Statistical Manual of Mental Disorders* (fourth edition [*DSM-IV*]; American Psychiatric Association, 1994). Most of those classifications are too broad gauged to guide our linguistic inquiries. Our work demands a finer grained analysis of the way clients interact and how they portray their interactions to themselves and others. This method explores the details of people's introspective experience. By contrast, the *DSM-IV* situates the diagnostician as an extraspective observer of objective medical "facts" (Rychlak, 1981). Furthermore, the *DSM-IV*'s disease—entity approach perpetuates misleading reifications of pseudomedical terms such as *symptom*, *disorder*, *patient*, *cure*, and *treatment*. As personality theorist and psychotherapist George Kelly (1955) was fond of pointing out, terms such as *patient* imprison clients in a passive role, implicitly communicating that they need to wait patiently for their doctors to cure them.

PSYCHOTHERAPY AS SOCIAL INFLUENCE

The term *psychotherapy* is itself a misnomer. In keeping with the dualistic doctrines of the day, physicians at the turn of the century reasoned that there should be treatments for the mind to parallel those that had been developed for the body. They coined the word *psychotherapy* by combining the terms *psyche* (for mental) and *therapie* (for treatment). It was difficult, however, to find any concrete referents for such a label. Physicians were unable to show that the mind (vs. the brain) could become "diseased." Even to this day, the psychiatric establishment stretches metaphorical license to the limit in a tortured attempt to convert communal, linguistic, moral, and interpersonal conflicts into distinct, identifiable disorders (Carson, 1991; Kirk & Kutchins, 1992; Kutchins & Kirk, 1997).

Moreover, there is still no consensus about how the mind can be "treated" or made "healthier" (e.g., Szasz, 1974, 1996). Philosopher and psychotherapist Robert Fancher (1995) argued that today's competing schools of therapy represent little more than distinct moral and aesthetic preferences—philosophical discourses disguised as scientifically validated techniques. These so-called "cultures of healing" do not cure anything. Instead, they simply indoctrinate clients into particular worldviews, each of which advocates a specific blueprint for the good life. If Fancher were correct, psychotherapies would be simply contexts for discussing customs and values.

Similarly, when asked about the form of treatment he practiced, psychiatrist Thomas Szasz (1998) insisted that he had never treated anyone because those who came to see him were not sick. His secret formula was simply "to talk and to listen." From our perspective, Szasz was absolutely correct in describing the therapeutic craft as dialogic. Regardless of one's orientation, whether behavioral, psychoanalytic, solution focused, or any of the 400 or so other modalities (Karasu, 1986), there is no escape from the proposition that therapy is conversation, thereby a social influence process.

The therapeutic process must be social because interpersonal problems are communal creations. They derive from the fact that people have multiple social allegiances (Rabkin, 1970). Because of the many different "clubs" to which people belong, people are constantly forced to juggle partially contradictory role demands. For instance, an adolescent must decide how to act with his friends when his parents are watching. A therapist is conflicted about whether to say hello to a client she sees at a party. A salesman is torn about how truthful to be when a loyal customer asks for his honest opinion.

"Symptoms" appear when the rules of one club require people to violate the rules of another. As Szasz (1973) noted, "symptoms are actually declarations of [social] independence and dependence" (pp. 88–89) by individuals feeling the strain of conflicting group norms. Ironically, people can suffer from such clashes even when they are alone. This is because such disputes are encoded in words and symbols, and people continue to use the vocabulary of their reference groups even when no one else is physically present.

Whenever a client describes a "problem" or reports a symptom, the astute clinician can discern evidence of incompatible role expectations and unexamined club commitments. For instance, one of us saw a college student who was trying to avoid studying but could not admit to himself that he preferred working in the family business over remaining in school. Dropping out would have dishonored his immigrant father, who had sacrificed to finance his son's education. In this case, the therapeutic task was not to improve the client's study habits but to help him find ways to be true to his own desires, without abrogating implicit family responsibilities.

Mediating such club conflicts requires a careful balance of bluntness and empathy. Perhaps that is why Szasz (1973) once described therapists as "modern-day court jesters": They bring crucial but potentially unpleasant truths to their patrons' attention. Like a court jester, the therapist must have permission to skirt some of the usual rules of etiquette to explore possibilities that break social taboos and go beyond club boundaries. For example, a depressed individual may need to be reminded that she retains the "right" to commit suicide, even though such a choice would not be considered politically correct in other settings. As Rabkin (1970) pointed out, the value of a therapeutic encounter derives specifically from the fact that the therapist, having different patterns of club affiliation, can discuss matters the client is unable to broach elsewhere.

In this chapter, we further explicate our model of psychotherapy as a linguistically focused diagnostic process. First, we define language as a form of social action. Second, we describe how social and linguistic processes combine to generate interpersonal and psychological problems. Then, we detail two types of client quandaries: unexamined hypocrisies and confusions of logical type. Finally, we discuss "orthogonal interaction" (Efran, Lukens, & Lukens, 1990) as the essential element of the therapeutic process.

LANGUAGE AS SOCIAL ACTION

"Words," said Aldous Huxley (1937), "form the thread on which we string our experiences" (p. 84). Through verbal interchange and symbolic expression (i.e., language), human beings turn otherwise meaningless circumstances into life's triumphs and defeats, problems and solutions. In that sense, language is both friend and foe. On the one hand, it enables people to create and sustain social processes of great subtlety and complexity. On the other hand, it also opens the door to a plethora of uniquely human predicaments and vexations. As essayist William Hazlitt (1969) related, "man is the only animal that laughs and weeps; for he is the only animal that is struck with the difference between what things are and what they ought to be" (p. 1). Language is what makes such comparisons both possible and inevitable.

Verbal and symbolic expression are the human equivalents of grooming in chimps; they help to establish and maintain the social order. Perhaps this is why Szasz (1973) said that "in the animal kingdom, the rule is, eat or be eaten; in the human kingdom, define or be defined" (p. 20). Although members of other species coordinate social activities and sustain rudimentary forms of communal organization, language enables human beings to orchestrate far more complex and variable social sequences. Cockatoos and marmosets gather berries for their daily sustenance, but people evaluate the day's harvest and draft plans for the future. In other words, humans not only coordinate their actions but also coordinate their coordinations. Language is the specialized form of communal action that permits such second-order coordination.

The importance of language-based coordinations cannot be overemphasized. Language is what allows humans to formulate purposes, distinguish and label objects, and carve identifiable "events" out of the continuous flux of the universe. Using words and symbols, people devise and exchange stories. In fact, according to mathematician and philosopher James P. Carse (1986), "if we cannot tell a story about what happened to us, nothing has happened to us" (p. 167). It is only in the context of such narratives that people develop a sense of self.

Recently, one of the authors reread an old portfolio of family correspondence. Included in a series of letters that the author's parents had exchanged when his father was away on a business trip were frequent allusions to someone named "Snookums." The author was startled when he deduced from the dates on the letters that *he* was the Snookums in question. This realization forced him to grapple with a brand new identity; he had certainly never thought of himself as a Snookums before.

Note that being a Snookums or a Honeybun is different from being a "mister," "missus," "doctor," or "professor." Names and titles have functional significance; they license certain interactions and inhibit others. Words are a core component of the communal choreography. Even wearing a name tag at a social gathering alters the range of permissible intimacies. Words are, therefore, never simply descriptive or epiphenomenal. Moreover, words have no true synonyms. Every concept that "survives" in a language points to a distinctive form of social coordination. That is why therapists must be alert to the precise language clients use in describing their circumstances (Efran & Fauber, 1995). For instance, claiming to be "depressed" is different from maintaining that one's circumstances are "hopeless" or saying that one "feels sad" about a loss.[1]

We are careful to define language as communal action rather than purely internal behavior. Contrary to what everyone learns in school, the so-called higher cortical functions do not take place inside one's head; they take place in the community (Maturana & Varela, 1987). Of course, people require a sufficiently plastic nervous system, including a neocortex, to participate in communal "language games" (Wittgenstein, 1922/1971). However, the use of words and symbols is fundamentally a team sport.

---

[1]Words sometimes appear to be synonymous when the differences in their connotations have no relevance to the purpose at hand. For example, most people loosely interchange terms like *robber*, *burglar*, and *thief*, but criminal justice workers must understand the conceptual distinctions between them.

It is difficult to comprehend how one might experience life if one did not operate in language. Once one has "joined" the language community, all of one's sensations, perceptions, and experiences are colored by linguistic judgments, comparisons, and evaluations. In other words, people do not just taste a particular hamburger, they experience it in terms of their concepts and expectations about hamburgers. As a child, one of the authors was happily eating a chopped tongue sandwich until a classmate happened to explain why it was called tongue. The author could not bring himself to take another bite. The label, with its multiple associations, had dramatically altered his experience.

If it were truly possible to strip away the verbal and symbolic labels that color people's experience, people would be left with what biologist and cyberneticist Humberto Maturana (1988) described as a meaningless "structural drift." Within that drift, a person's life trajectory is determined entirely by how his or her biology happens to "fit" the structure of the surrounding environment. Picture a boat without oars, rudder, motor, or sail. Its course is solely a function of the intersection of its shape with the currents and the wind. Its drift lasts until it finally breaks up and disintegrates—what Maturana calls a "destructive interaction." Similarly, everyone drifts through life until encountering an event that destroys his or her class identity as a living human being.

Although the boat in our analogy is just drifting, without purpose or direction, it would—if it could speak—spin a fascinating yarn about its voyage. Because humans operate in language, however, they regale each other with just such tales, celebrating their achievements and cursing their misfortunes. Moreover, whatever people talk about "enters" their drift, continuously altering the environment to which their systems respond. For instance, a teacher's evaluation of a pupil can have an important influence on the pupil's future performance (e.g., Rosenthal & Jacobson, 1968).

Furthermore, even seemingly trivial comments can have profound impacts. We recall a couple who broke up shortly after the boyfriend made an offhand comment about an earlier relationship. He had thought he was just being "honest." However, his girlfriend kept picturing him in bed with the other woman, which spoiled any sense of being special with him.

Because life never doubles back on itself, the things people say to one another create changes that can never be entirely reversed. In the historical drift of linguistic influences, each utterance becomes part of the context for everything that follows. As Maturana's colleague Francisco Varela (1979) noted, "everything said is said from a tradition" (p. 268). In other words, "every statement reflects a history of interactions from which we cannot escape" (p. 268).

GENESIS AND MAINTENANCE OF PROBLEMS

Linguistic embellishments are what transform simple circumstances into personal and interpersonal problems. In this respect, human predicaments are quite different from those faced by other animals. A bear in the woods that gets its paw caught in a trap does not have a problem in the human sense: Bears do not operate in language, do not make value judgments, and do not philosophize about their lives. They never ask, "Why me?" Thus, there is not much call for bear therapists. To a bear, even death is just a circumstance.

People, however, invariably use language to make something of their circumstances. They react to their own behavior on the basis of their labels, goals, images, standards, and expectations. For example, some students will be distraught over grades that others would be thrilled to receive. Some people react to the demise of a relationship by withdrawing for months; others begin dating again within the week. Some shoppers enjoy haggling for discounts, and others are uncomfortable even mentioning the topic of price. In each of these situations, raw circumstances are transformed into meaningful events as significances are added. When negative evaluations are involved, the events also become problems.

Although it is unfortunate when a person's home is washed away in a flood, this is still just a set of circumstances until the person starts grieving over lost mementos, contemplating the difficulties of rebuilding, chastising himself or herself for feeling overwhelmed, and so on. As problems mount, the person may decide to seek the services of a psychotherapist. However, it is only *second-order significances*—how people interpret their own reactions using the linguistic conventions of their interpersonal clubs—that qualify for therapeutic assistance. For instance, people may be upset that their hard work has not produced happiness because they believe that life should be fair. In the East, such linguistically fostered illusions would be called "attachments," in the West, "entitlements." In that sense, therapy is perhaps analogous to the Eastern meditation practices that help people transcend *maya*, the veil of illusion that keeps them stuck in their egocentrism. Whereas Sigmund Freud described therapy as a process that replaces id with ego, we think of it as a process that replaces self-deceptive ambiguity with linguistic clarity.

Because self-deception is so crucial to the diagnostic picture, we divide it into two broad categories: unacknowledged hypocrisies and confusions of logical type. *Hypocrisies* are lies one tells oneself and others as one attempts to maintain consistency in one's social performances (Goffman, 1959). Included are euphemisms, half truths, partial omissions, justifications, rationalizations, and distractions. *Confusions of logical type* are more complex;

they derive from the rapidity and imprecision with which people shift up and down the ladder of abstraction. Among the errors that result are reifications, self-referential paradoxes, and misconceptions about the nature of change.

Ubiquity of Hypocrisy

According to an old Chinese proverb, "birds are entangled by their feet and men by their tongues." As we indicated, the exigencies of social life virtually guarantee that people will lie to each other and to themselves rather continuously. We agree with Hazlitt (1914) that people only cease being hypocrites in their sleep and also with Maturana (1993) that people save their lives many times over through hypocrisy. Despite the fact that virtually all social codes contain formal injunctions against lying, the reality is that all human enterprises, from international diplomacy to Sunday dinner, absolutely require people to overlook each other's dissimulations.[2]

Because only unacknowledged hypocrisies are of therapeutic relevance, distinguishing between responsible and irresponsible lying is a crucial diagnostic issue. A responsible lie is one in which the perpetrator fully understands and accepts the risks of his or her chicanery. Drug dealers, for instance, often lie responsibly, intentionally deceiving family, friends, and authorities in the pursuit of their occupational goals. If caught, they are usually candidates for prison, not psychotherapy.[3]

Irresponsible liars, however, are either unaware of their duplicity or in denial about its consequences. Here, the therapist has an important job to do. He or she must use every means available to call attention to inconsistencies and evasions in the client's narrative. In a way, the therapist working with an irresponsible liar is like a nosy houseguest who keeps picking up knickknacks and asking questions about them. At first, these inquiries may be annoying, but eventually they help the host recover forgotten memories and relive important experiences. Similarly, the therapist's questions draw the client's attention to assumptions and interpersonal agreements that have become "invisible" over time but now need reexamining (Efran, 1994).

The smallest details of the client's narrative may be worthy of therapeutic attention. Therapists who work in this mode quickly develop a "sixth sense" about the kinds of statements that mask hidden elements in the client's story. Recently, for example, one of our clients excused being short of cash for his therapy session by saying "I just don't know where my money

---

[2] The hazards of brutal honesty are illustrated in the popular film *Liar, Liar*, in which actor Jim Carrey plays a lawyer compelled to tell the unvarnished truth.
[3] Note that individuals can lie responsibly even in the service of goals that society finds reprehensible.

goes!" This cliché is a perfect example of what psychotherapist Roy Schafer (1976, 1983) labeled "disclaimed action." By intentionally keeping himself in the dark about his finances, the client was able to indulge his spendthrift ways yet deny any accountability. The therapist's strategy involved challenging this client's pronouncement with a series of questions. We wanted to know what prevented him from keeping better track of his finances, who was present when his money was being spent, and who had the job of setting his financial priorities. These queries helped the client notice that his spending patterns were choices, not accidents. Our technique in this case is an example of what therapists sometimes call "spitting in the client's soup." In other words, he was free to continue spending his funds as he pleased, but it was no longer possible for him to assume the role of an innocent victim with regard to handling his finances.

Often a single choice of word or phrase tells volumes. For instance, a client who says "yeah" or "I guess so" communicates something different from one who uses the more decisive "yes." Similarly, subtle disqualifying gestures, such as a shoulder shrug or an aversion of the eyes, can alter or even reverse the meaning of a communication. In interpreting verbal and nonverbal cues, we make use of the "codebooks" developed by Weiner and Mehrabian (1968; Mehrabian, 1981). Their research on nonimmediacy provides a compendium of the ways people distance themselves from their own messages. For instance, people who are lying or discomforted may focus excessively on trivial details or speak in broad generalizations. They may also be unexpectedly laconic or inappropriately verbose.

In addition, Weiner and Mehrabian (1968) described how people adjust their psychological distance from their messages by selecting words such as *that* rather than *this*, *there* instead of *here*, and *then* in place of *now*. A person's discomfort may be "tipped" by his or her use of the past tense when the present will do or by the substitution of the third person for the first. "I love you" communicates more immediacy than "It was nice to have seen you." "This is great" is more immediate than "That's not too bad." Although neither speakers nor listeners are necessarily aware of the "rules" of immediacy, Weiner and Mehrabian demonstrated that people respond intuitively to this "language within language." For the therapist, linguistic nonimmediacies are diagnostic markers for pockets of irresponsibility.

A case seen by one of the authors contains multiple examples of irresponsible lying. A couple had been having such vicious fights that their neighbors sometimes called the police. Most of their scuffles were the end result of a predictable scenario: He would drop hints about being considered for a promotion at work, and she would discover that he was not telling the truth. He claimed to have made up such tales solely because she desperately wanted to believe he was on his way up the corporate ladder. In fact, he had little motivation to change jobs. Frankly, he had been happiest when, earlier in his life, he had held a low-paying mechanic's job. However, she had expensive tastes and constantly wanted him to earn more money and pursue a higher status position.

As so often happens, this couple's conflicts represented a clash of backgrounds and family allegiances. Her parents were wealthy and influential; his roots were working class. They had met, by chance, when she was having her car repaired at the garage where he worked. During their on-again, off-again courtship, both had tried to downplay their obvious differences in upbringing. Her family initially worked to block their wedding and might have succeeded if she had not unexpectedly become pregnant. Although the husband and wife clearly loved each other, the differences in their value systems continued to create tensions and antagonisms.

Throughout their relationship, both spouses had lied to themselves, to each other, and to members of their families. For instance, the wife placated her parents by telling them how well her husband was doing at work, even though she was livid about his lack of drive. At the same time, he pretended to be looking into better job prospects. On one occasion, he found himself putting on his best suit to go on an imaginary job interview. When his charade fell apart, his wife felt violated and betrayed. Each time they fought, he promised to tell her the whole truth from then on, a promise he usually broke almost immediately. Of course, she made being honest much more difficult; she would go on a rampage whenever he tried to level with her about his actual career interests (or lack thereof). He was embarrassed by his wife's lies to her parents, but ironically he believed he had no choice but to tell similar lies to her. She savagely resented being misled but felt it would crush her parents if they learned the truth.

The therapist's job was to clarify for this couple the costs and payoffs of their tandem duplicities. The husband was shown how his small initial appeasements merely fueled his wife's false hopes and eventually escalated into major falsehoods. With the therapist's encouragement, he was able to declare, once and for all, that he would never be the competitive go-getter of his wife's dreams. Simultaneously, the wife was encouraged to talk to her parents about the couple's true financial situation. Furthermore, the couple's discussions with the therapist prompted an exploration of nontraditional marital role assignments. The husband realized that he would be quite content to putter around the house, and the wife decided that she would not be averse to a corporate career. They agreed that they would experiment with those options once their children got a bit older.

This case illustrates a basic clinical principle: "Whatever you resist, persists; whatever you let be, lets you be." Each time this couple attempted to forestall a showdown, they merely contributed to additional strife. Their emphasis on pleasing everyone amplified everyone's displeasure. Matters improved when they began to tell the truth and to accept each other's actual strengths and weaknesses.

The hazards of broken agreements and promises are also well illustrated by this case. The wife, for instance, broke an implicit promise to herself and her parents: she would marry someone at her own socioeconomic level. The husband, when he proposed, implicitly promised that he would be able to surmount the differences in their backgrounds. Of course, both of them also made and broke many explicit promises concerning their relationship.

Whenever a commitment, implicit or explicit, is abrogated, repair work is needed. The interpersonal mess created by breaking a pledge must be cleaned up. Sometimes this requires little more than acknowledging one's transgressions. At other times, it necessitates more actively making amends and renegotiating unfulfilled contracts. Although owning up to broken agreements can be painful, it is almost always less costly than burying transgressions beneath further layers of hypocrisy. In the final analysis, all people have in life is their word; it is prudent to let it mean something.

Before leaving the topic of hypocrisy, we should mention clients whose motives for seeking therapy are partly or wholly fraudulent. These individuals discovered how to gain social advantage by claiming to be sick, confused, or "in treatment." Included in this category are many clients referred by the court system, some individuals seeking welfare or disability payments, and spouses who come to treatment merely to placate their partners. For such individuals, therapy can be a way to "buy time," evade disciplinary action, or obtain "exemptions" from various social consequences.

Diagnosing inauthentic motives usually involves inquiring about the immediate precipitants of the client's decision to initiate therapy; general claims about wanting to improve, getting one's life in order, and so on will not do. These are insufficient grounds on which to base a therapeutic contract. Specifics, not generalities, are what move people from where they are to someplace else. Without knowing why a person picks up the telephone to make an appointment on a given day, the therapist runs the risk of becoming simply another pawn in the client's social game. However, encouraging the client to lay all his or her cards on the table gives therapy at least some chance of success.

An addiction counselor of our acquaintance had his own rule of thumb for assessing client motivations. He listened to what his clients said but paid attention mostly to what they did. Our diagnostic formula is similar. We distinguish between what people say they want and what their behavior actually produces. For instance, a person may talk for years about returning to college without going anywhere near the registrar's office. Anyone who is not progressing, stepwise, toward his or her stated goal is probably being motivated by other, partially concealed, purposes. Therapy is most effective when such covert agendas are identified.

We recall a case in which the therapist was able to convert an inauthentic therapy contract into a very useful encounter. The client, who had been labeled "difficult" by previous therapists, was attending sessions to maintain his eligibility for Veterans' Administration benefits. Quickly sizing up the situation, the clinician told him that he could keep coming to sessions as long as he wanted and that he did not have to keep "proving" his need for help. However, as long as they were going to be spending time together, the therapist would be happy to talk about any questions the client might have about himself, his family, other people, or life in general. Note that this approach leaves the subject matter entirely up to the client, but it disentangles the session content from the client's hidden agenda.

Therapists can never force clients to relinquish apparently useful hypocrisies. The bottom line is that people change only when their current behaviors no longer work, when lower cost alternatives come into view, or when their basic preferences shift in valence or intensity. A man may stop drinking, for instance, if (a) his wife threatens to leave (and shows that she means it), (b) a former drinking buddy offers to be his Alcoholics Anonymous sponsor, or (c) he wants to get in shape for an upcoming marathon. Even if certain hypocrisies are currently too valuable to abandon, therapy can still assist clients by helping them turn their irresponsible lies into responsible ones.

Confusions of Logical Type

Although people's participation in multiple social groups generates many self-deceptions, some confusions result more directly from the slippery nature of the linguistic medium. The self-referential property of language means that words and symbols can refer to other words and symbols, creating a potentially dizzying array of logical levels. Language enables people to comment on their comments, and even to comment on their having commented on them. The complexity surrounding these nested "logical types" (Whitehead & Russell, 1963) makes it virtually inevitable that people's lives (and stories) will contain a series of paradoxes, "strange loops," and reifications (Hofstadter, 1979). Thus, for example, people are apt to find themselves worrying about their anxiety, expressing intolerance toward those who are prejudiced, and blaming their tardiness on procrastination.

Reification

Reifications arise when people confound names and processes, maps and territories (Korzybski, 1941; Varela, 1979). Language constantly lures human beings to attribute independent psychological or physical existence to mere abstractions. For instance, one slips into talking about gravity as if it were a thing, a force, or a quantity rather than simply the description of an observed relationship. Similarly, one tends to reify concepts such as *poverty, intelligence, impulsivity,* and *mental health.* Frequently, one turns observed behavioral patterns into trait labels. Thus, one is likely to attribute "courage" to a person who reenters a burning building and to ascribe "laziness" to someone whose assignments are usually overdue.

Reification is a pernicious master, seducing one to strive toward imaginary goals, to accept spurious explanations, and to covet mythical abilities and characteristics. Clients, for example, often insist that they need more "self-esteem" if they are to be successful. In truth, self-esteem is neither a cause nor a mechanism; it is a description of post hoc approval for one's own accomplishments (Dawes, 1994). Similarly, self-confidence generally comes from success, not the other way around. Novice skiers would, therefore, be foolish to wait at the top of the slope for self-confidence to arrive. If they would get on with their skiing, confidence would be their automatic reward. Even then, it would be better to describe what they acquired as practice and expertise, not confidence or self-esteem.

Therapists often fall into the same reification traps that bedevil their clients. Bandura (1984, 1989, 1991), for example, discussed self-efficacy as if it were an internal characteristic, a commodity that can empower people to overcome their phobias and accomplish other miraculous feats.[4] Yet he defined *self-efficacy* solely as an individual's announcement of readiness to tackle a previously avoided task. Thus, the theory of self-efficacy is a simple tautology, an exercise in linguistic sleight of hand. It reifies a description into a pseudomechanism (Smedslund, 1991), capitalizing on the fact that people can partially predict their own proximal behavior.

Unfortunately, theories such as self-efficacy are not neutral in their effects: They encourage clients (and therapists) to pursue goals that are illusory and to add unnecessary steps to solving life's problems. Recently, for example, a client arrived complaining of a "lack of self-control." She hated her tendency to procrastinate about cleaning the house, paying bills, getting paperwork done, and so on. She hoped we could suggest ways for her to become more disciplined. She also thought that perhaps one of the newer medications could increase her "willpower." Our therapeutic approach to this case was two pronged. First, we demonstrated to the client that she already possessed all the self-control she would ever need. Then, we helped her find better ways to achieve her goals, taking into account her basic

---

[4]For critiques of this circular reasoning, see Eastman and Marzillier (1984), Marzillier and Eastman (1984), and Meichenbaum (1990).

desires and propensities. It was easy to show her that she only "procrastinated" when the task at hand was aversive and her level of commitment to it was minimal. Her enthusiasm for housework, for instance, waxed and waned, dependent on who was expected for dinner. Overall, her housekeeping was probably no worse than that of the average person living alone. But she had a Martha Stewart complex and desired to run the "perfect" household.

We could not increase this client's self-control; nor could we remove the unpleasantness surrounding particular tasks. But we could show her how to get things done by subtly manipulating her environment to fit her preferences. For instance, we encouraged her to enlist a friend's assistance with her backlogged paperwork. Inviting the friend over made the job more social and, therefore, more pleasant for her. Moreover, the friend's presence created a "behavioral trap," ensuring that the job would actually get done. At the therapist's suggestion, the client arranged to commemorate the completion of the task by taking her friend out for a celebratory dinner.

Life works best when one recognizes that one is a preferential creature. Therefore, it always pays to begin by assessing one's priorities, proclivities, and dispositions. One can then find ways to use these to advantage rather than wasting time chasing after presumed attributes that turn out to be nothing but reifications (Efran, Greene, & Gordon, 1998).

One of the most common reifications clinicians encounter is the concept of *habit*. People like to talk as if they are compelled by their habits to gamble, drink, smoke, overeat, and so on. This choice of language obscures the specific consequences that maintain such activities. Note that people rarely attribute their admirable actions to habit. In other words, people are willing to call their nail biting a habit but not their philanthropy. Moreover, individuals fail to notice how easily they can "break" habits of many years' duration. For instance, although most people brush their teeth twice a day, refraining from doing so would hardly require "kicking the tooth-brushing habit." In general, people do what they want to do and adjust their language descriptions to shield themselves from social blame.

Trying is another term frequently used to put a better face on less-than-commendable conduct. By claiming, for instance, to have "tried and failed" to lose weight, a person can get credit for the effort but still be overweight. Yet words like *trying* mask a multitude of sins. For instance, a man who is late but claims to have tried to arrive on time neglects to mention that he slept in, took a lengthy shower, answered the telephone on his way out the door, and left no extra time for rush-hour traffic. The "I tried" disclaimer hides the facts and lets people avoid disapprobation. However, it also falsely portrays them as pawns of uncontrollable internal needs and irresistible external forces. Therefore, clients' use of such terms should always become a diagnostic and therapeutic issue.

Terms like *dependency, impulsivity, compulsivity,* and *anxiety* are also familiar and counterproductive reifications. For example, clients often claim that their panic attacks are caused by anxiety or that they are unassertive because of their dependency needs (Efran, Germer, & Lukens, 1986). Again, logical levels are crossed whenever such descriptive terms are pressed into service as causal hypotheses.

We recall a client explaining that her boyfriend had sent her to therapy because she was too "clingy." Of course, like many people who present themselves as needy and compliant, she was much more interpersonally powerful than she liked to appear. For instance, she managed to ignore, reject, or sabotage—ever so sweetly—most of the therapist's suggestions. Frequently, as in this case, dependency claims camouflage the pursuit of particular preferences, coerce support from others, and delegitimize attempts at retaliation. Therapy helps by clarifying the hidden costs of controlling through weakness. The client can then decide whether the perks of the victim role are worth the associated risks. This particular case actually turned into couples counseling. In that context, the boyfriend could express his frustration with his partner's passive–aggressive tactics. He understood more clearly that he was free to leave the relationship at any time, and she recognized that she would prefer him to stay with her through choice rather than obligation. The increased clarity of their positions put their relationship on a much firmer footing.

In assessing relationship conflicts, it is also useful to be on the lookout for "conversations of characterization, accusation, and recrimination" (Mendez, Coddou, & Maturana, 1988, p. 158). Such conversations consist of a lapse into characterological name calling that spells an end to constructive problem solving. Such conversations pathologize actions and impugn motivations as people accuse each other of being vindictive, argumentative, stubborn, malicious, aggressive, crazy, stupid, and so on.

For instance, a couple we saw nearly came to blows while working on a kitchen remodeling project. The husband was a doer: He wanted to start hammering and knocking down walls. The wife was a planner: She wanted to interview consultants and visit home improvement stores. When her husband balked about coming along on these trips, she immediately launched into a flurry of recriminations, branding him as selfish and accusing him of purposely trying to undermine her plans. He retaliated by condemning her for being overly cautious and pathologically perfectionistic. It was helpful to point out to this couple that they were not purposely attempting to annoy each other; they simply had antithetical approaches to work. Once they understood that their disagreements were not personal, they could focus on developing a plan to take advantage of their complementary skills and abilities. She agreed to leave him out of her preliminary window-shopping ventures, and he agreed to wait until she had a final plan before going into high gear.

Finally, Maturana described self-recriminatory reifications that typify people "living in emotional contradiction" (see Efran & Greene, 1996). Such individuals experience being "stretched" between two legitimate but conflicting motives. For example, a student who needs to study for tomorrow's exam is tempted by his fraternity brothers to join them for a few beers. If he stays, he will feel lonely and rejected. If he goes, he is apt to castigate himself for being immature, suggestible, lazy, and so on. In fact, he is simply facing mutually incompatible social obligations. His peers want him to be sociable, and his parents and professors expect him to be studious. Reification stigmatizes one or both sides of the equation, causing the student to interpret a legitimate social conflict as a characterological defect (Akillas & Efran, 1989). Resolving such contradictions can be a difficult balancing act, but it is not helped by name calling.

Paradoxes of Self-Reference

Because language permits people to talk to themselves as if they were two separate people—a speaker and a listener—they come to believe that they can order themselves about. Consider, for instance, the debate people sometimes have with themselves over whether to get out of bed. One voice appears to urge for getting up, while a second argues for staying put. Sometimes, a third "presence" seems to hover on the sidelines, waiting to see which of the first two voices will win the argument. If people reflect on such discussions, they may find themselves unsure about who each of the voices represents and which has final authority. In truth, because getting out of bed is a systemic process, none of the voices actually make any of the decisions. In other words, the discussion the person "overhears" is simply an aspect of the process, not the cause of it. Despite appearances to the contrary, there is no commanding voice with the power to make one's body rise on cue.

Although people like to think of their cognitive processes as being in charge of their feelings and behavior, this notion violates the well-accepted cybernetic principle that no system component can unilaterally control the system of which it is a part. To the casual observer, the governor of a machine may look as if it gives instructions about speed and acceleration to the rest of the motor. However, despite its name, the governor has no more autonomy (and exercises no more executive function) than any other component. In fact, it is itself entirely governed by its shape and how it meshes with other engine parts. Analogously, there is no captain at the helm of the ship of self; everyone on board is just another passenger. Even those wearing executive uniforms are merely playing dress-up. As novelist Annie Dillard (1977) observed, "we are most deeply asleep at the switch when we fancy we control any switches at all" (p. 62).

The false belief that one controls oneself through one's cognitions has been referred to as the "doctrine of rational supremacy" (Mahoney, 1991, p. 446). Fancher (1995) called this "one of the grand myths of Western culture" (p. 244). It reifies the operation of the organism into three subsystems: thoughts, feelings, and actions. Moreover, it presupposes that the higher cognitive functions (logic and reason) control the lower functions (feelings and behavior). Therapies based on this myth assume that if people can somehow change their thoughts, their lives will change. Of course, other therapies are founded on the equally fallacious myth of irrational supremacy. From that perspective, feelings are the kingpins of the system, and powerful impulses frequently overwhelm the intellect to dictate what one does and believes. Therapists who adhere to that philosophy typically urge people to unblock their feelings and "pay attention to their gut."

Both the doctrine of rational supremacy and the myth of irrational supremacy perpetuate the classical Aristotelian split between cognition, affect, and conation (Efran & Blumberg, 1994). However, from our point of view, thoughts are never separate from actions; they are, in fact, particular kinds of actions. Emotions, however, are not internal quantities or forces. They are bodily postures and calibrations that support various classes of behavior. For example, being affectionate calls for one set of hormonal and musculoskeletal settings, but fighting calls for another. What people "feel" (and label as "emotion") is the shifting calibrations of their bodily equipment. According to Maturana (1988), all linguistic behavior requires an emotional setting—a body posture—and languaging and emotioning are continuously "braided" together in a reciprocal process. Talking about food, for instance, begins to produce salivation and feelings of hunger; being hungry provides a context conducive to thinking about food.

From this perspective, rationality is an emotional state, not a cognitive achievement. A unique set of calibrations supports calm deliberation and logical problem solving. It is literally the embodiment of a particular set of values, distinguishable from those associated with other goals and activities, such as nurturing, copulating, escaping, or resting. Although rationality is sometimes said to be a "neutral" state, like any other emotion it represents a distinct bias and proceeds from certain a priori assumptions, preferences, and starting points.

Because they subscribe to the doctrine of rational supremacy, clients often believe that something is "wrong" with their thoughts or their feelings. Unfortunately, therapists too often subscribe to the same point of view and, therefore, join clients in the foolhardy project of "fixing" system functions that are not really broken. For the structure determinist, a client's reactions always accurately reflect the fit between his or her structure and the surrounding environment. The therapeutic task is not to repair cognitive or emotional machinery but to mediate conflicts between personal desires and social demands.

We once saw a client who feared flying but whose job was about to require him to travel abroad. We maintained that there was nothing whatsoever wrong with the client's feelings or his thoughts. His system simply responded to flying as a threat to his survival. In fact, the one time he had flown, the plane had run into some frightening turbulence. This client was not particularly naive about planes. He understood, for instance, that (statistically speaking) flying is safer than driving. Nonetheless, he was still more comfortable behind the wheel of his car.

Rather than trying to alter this client's feelings or "challenge" his cognitions, we convinced him to experiment with a few very brief flights, accompanied by a close friend who was an experienced traveler. These trial runs permitted his system to accommodate to the experience of riding in an aircraft. This was particularly enlightening for him because today's jets create such different sensations from those of the small propeller planes he flew in years before. It would have been more difficult to make progress in this case if we had not first accepted the client's protective reactions as inconvenient but perfectly legitimate responses to his flying history.

Change, Instructive Interaction, and Orthogonality

Note that in the case we just described, the client's system adapted to various changes in environmental circumstances. First, a new social context was created by our conversation with the client. Second, there was a juxtaposition between the client and the plane he boarded. Both of these novel "couplings" produced shifts in the client's responses and beliefs. Although neither we nor the client could directly change his thoughts, feelings, or behaviors, the conversational process did all of those things, opening the door to new possibilities.

Therapy is no exception to the general principle that life is a codrift. People's responses always result from the mesh between their structures and the environment, each of which is changed by the unfolding interaction. In this constant flux, people use language to decide what to call a cause, what to call an effect, and what to label a change. For instance, therapists might see an event as an effective intervention (a cause), which could alternatively be described as the therapist's inevitable response to a particular client statement or action (an effect). As Varela (1979) noted, "if we consider a conversation as a totality, there cannot be distinction about what is contributed by whom" (p. 269). Therapy sessions, like other conversations, are coherent, recursive aggregates. Thus, most of our traditional thinking about therapeutic "change" has been too lineal. Sessions, techniques, and outcomes cannot be teased apart and separated from the larger context of the client's life. Perhaps all we can usefully say about therapy is that it hinges on what Maturana (1993) called orthogonal interaction.

Theoretically, orthogonal interaction denotes the trigger that enables a system to adapt to changing circumstances. Consider a spark plug removed from an automobile's engine by a mechanic. By adjusting its gap, the mechanic interacts orthogonally with the plug. That is, he subjects the plug to a different set of conditions—a different "conversation"—than it would encounter in the environment of the motor. Furthermore, the mechanic interacts with the plug in a way that does not exceed its structural capabilities; spark gaps can, after all, be adjusted. Once the plug is reseated in the engine, the changes in it lead to modifications in the overall operation of the engine (and the automobile). In a nutshell, the orthogonal interaction between mechanic and spark plug changes the relationship of the plug to its adjacent parts, generating novel adaptations in all the other system components.

By creating a new miniculture with its own rules (Rabkin, 1970), therapy potentially generates orthogonal interaction. It is a context in which clients can experiment with statements and actions that would rarely be elicited in their usual clubs. The changes in structure produced by this orthogonal interaction eventually necessitate accommodations in the larger social systems to which clients belong. However, if client and therapist are too similar or remain together for too long, their conversation will contain fewer opportunities for orthogonality and the process of change will slow to a crawl (see, e.g., Sharma, 1986).

In our clinical work, we are always looking for ways to introduce orthogonal elements. Ironically, simply urging clients to report the truth of their experience often stimulates an orthogonal interaction. Telling the truth differs from the client's initial orientation. Clients usually come to therapy speaking the language of deficiency and change, but we tutor them to adopt the language of acceptance and responsibility.

A fearful 68-year-old chemist once sought our advice. Much of his life consisted of exercising, following health-food fads, avoiding germs, and reading about various obscure medical conditions. He was so busy surviving that he had little time to live. Throughout his life, he had always taken the "safe" path, indulging his hypochondriacal obsessions and avoiding a number of career opportunities because he feared that they might create undue stress. He abruptly ended a romantic involvement because he was not sure he could be comfortable adjusting to another person's living habits. He had recently joined a macrobiotic group, and he would eat only organically grown foods. He insisted on living near a major medical center so that he could quickly obtain assistance should an emergency arise. All in all, this client fit Otto Rank's (1945) description of an individual who "refuse[s] the loan (life) in order to avoid the payment of the debt (death)" (p. 126).

The more this client attempted to preserve his health, the more preoccupied he became with minor health fluctuations—a good example of the principle that "what you resist, persists." He hoped that with a therapist's assistance, he could decrease his anxiety and perhaps lower his blood pressure. Yet at another level of analysis, seeking therapy was just one more symptom of his obsessive concern with health.

Our interventions in this case were highly orthogonal. We quickly called into question this client's basic life premises, including the idea that the objective of life is to live a long time. We raised subjects that no one else dared discuss with him, such as why he wanted to stay alive, how long he intended to live, and what he thought would eventually do him in. We wondered aloud whether the members of his macrobiotic club ever got sick and whether any had died. We even asked him what epitaph he wanted engraved on his tombstone. As one can imagine, this line of questioning was perturbing to the client. In fact, he was initially astonished and angered that therapists would be tactless enough to broach such matters. Much to his surprise, however, he had to admit that he began to experience relief almost immediately. (A skeptical colleague suggested that this was simply the comfort of being free of us between sessions.) Still, he kept returning for more. Therapy was the one context in which the "bugaboo" of mortality could be openly confronted, and he could reexamine what he was giving up in his exaggerated attempts to preserve his physical existence.

CONCLUSION

In our model of therapy, clinicians function as linguistic detectives, identifying the language traps within which people have imprisoned themselves. Although the notion of change is a therapeutic mainstay, we argued that psychotherapists never produce change directly. Instead, they engage clients in Maturana's (1993) "orthogonal interaction": a conversation that expands clients' options beyond the limits established by their ordinary social affiliations. By generating novel experiences, orthogonality yields fresh perspectives on how life might be lived. Because they are partly outside their clients' social networks, therapists can stimulate exchanges that usefully highlight the reifications, contradictions, hypocrisies, and paradoxes embedded in their clients' stories. In other words, therapy, as a diagnostic venture, is fundamentally an opportunity to sort through the implications of people's semantic falsehoods.

Although many other approaches discuss clients' problems by using a language of deficiency, we operate from the supposition that clients are "sufficient" and that their responses and preferences are fully legitimate. Moreover, we do not work to restore mental health because the problems our clients bring us are not symptoms of mental illness. They are interpersonal conflicts disguised and sustained by linguistic ambiguities. Such dilemmas are well on their way to resolution when their hidden elements have been parsed. As magician and memory expert Harry Lorayne noted, "most problems precisely defined are already partially solved" (as quoted in Millman, 1994, p. 21). Merely identifying domains of confusion is often sufficient to produce therapeutic movement. Thus, when in doubt, clients can always begin by acknowledging what they do not know. As they say in the East, "confusion is a very high state."

As Rabkin (1970) suggested, therapy is basically about candor and authenticity rather than insight or change. In therapy, as we envision it, clients are afforded the opportunity to take responsibility for their preferences and to face up to how they have shortchanged themselves by denying, minimizing, or negating aspects of their own experience. By enabling clients to transcend self-deception, we help them with therapeutic conversations that free them to discover more effective solutions to their interpersonal problems.

REFERENCES

Akillas, E., & Efran, J. S. (1989). Internal conflict, language and metaphor: Implications for psychotherapy. *Journal of Contemporary Psychotherapy, 19,* 149–159.

American Psychiatric Association. (1994). *Diagnostic and statistical manual of mental disorders* (4th ed.). Washington, DC: Author.

Bandura, A. (1984). Recycling misconceptions of perceived self-efficacy. *Cognitive Therapy & Research, 8,* 231–256.

Bandura, A. (1989). Human agency in social cognitive theory. *American Psychologist, 44,* 1175–1184.

Bandura, A. (1991). Human agency: The rhetoric and the reality. *American Psychologist, 46,* 157–162.

Carse, J. P. (1986). *Finite and infinite games.* New York: Ballantine Books.

Carson, R. C. (1991). Dilemmas in the pathway of the *DSM-IV*. *Journal of Abnormal Psychology, 100,* 302–307.

Dawes, R. M. (1994). *House of cards: Psychology and psychotherapy built on myth.* New York: Free Press.

Dillard, A. (1977). *Holy the firm.* New York: Harper & Row.

Eastman, C., & Marzillier, J. S. (1984). Theoretical and methodological difficulties in Bandura's self-efficacy theory. *Cognitive Therapy & Research, 8,* 213–230.

Efran, J. S. (1994). Mystery, abstraction, and narrative psychotherapy. *Journal of Constructivist Psychology, 7,* 219–227.

Efran, J. S., & Blumberg, M. J. (1994). Emotion and family living: The perspective of structure determinism. In S. M. Johnson & L. S. Greenberg (Eds.), *The heart of the matter: Perspectives on emotion in marital therapy* (pp. 172–204). New York: Brunner/Mazel.

Efran, J. S., & Fauber, R. L. (1995). Radical constructivism: Questions and answers. In R. A. Neimeyer & M. J. Mahoney (Eds.), *Constructivism in psychotherapy* (pp. 275–304). Washington, DC: American Psychological Association.

Efran, J. S., Germer, C. K., & Lukens, M. D. (1986). Contextualism and psychotherapy. In R. L. Rosnow & M. Georgoudi (Eds.), *Contextualism and understanding in the behavioral sciences: Implications for research and theory* (pp. 169–186). New York: Praeger.

Efran, J. S., & Greene, M. A. (1996). Psychotherapeutic theory and practice: Contributions from Maturana's structure determinism. In H. Rosen & K. T. Kuehlwein (Eds.), *Constructing realities: Meaning-making perspectives for psychotherapists* (pp. 71–113). San Francisco: Jossey-Bass.

Efran, J. S., Greene, M. A., & Gordon, D. E. (1998). Lessons of the new genetics. *The Family Therapy Networker, 22*(2), 26–32, 35–41.

Efran, J. S., & Heffner, K. H. (1991). Change the name and you change the game. *Journal of Strategic and Systemic Therapies, 10,* 50–65.

Efran, J. S., Lukens, M. D., & Lukens, R. J. (1990). *Language, structure, and change: Frameworks of meaning in psychotherapy.* New York: Norton.

Fancher, R. T. (1995). *Cultures of healing: Correcting the image of American mental health care.* New York: Freeman.

Goffman, E. (1959). *The presentation of self in everyday life.* Garden City, NY: Doubleday.

Hazlitt, W. C. (1914). *The plain speaker: Opinions on books, men, and things.* New York: George Bell.

Hazlitt, W. C. (1969). *Lectures on the English comic writers, delivered at the Surry Institution.* New York: Russell & Russell.

Hofstadter, D. R. (1979). *Gödel, Escher, Bach: An eternal golden braid.* New York: Basic Books.

Huxley, A. L. (1937). *The olive tree and other essays* (2nd ed.). New York: Harper.

Karasu, T. B. (1986). The specificity versus nonspecificity dilemma: Toward identifying therapeutic change agents. *American Journal of Psychiatry, 143,* 687–695.

Kelly, G. A. (1955). *The psychology of personal constructs* (Vol. 1). New York: Norton.

Kirk, S. A., & Kutchins, H. (1992). *The selling of DSM: The rhetoric of science in psychiatry.* New York: Aldine de Gruyter.

Korzybski, A. (1941). *Science and sanity: An introduction to non-Aristotelian systems and general semantics* (2nd ed.). Lancaster, PA: Science Press.

Kutchins, H., & Kirk, S. A. (1997). *Making us crazy. DSM: The psychiatric bible and the creation of mental disorders.* New York: Free Press.

Mahoney, M. J. (1991). *Human change processes: The scientific foundations of psychotherapy*. New York: Basic Books.

Marzillier, J. S., & Eastman, C. (1984). Continuing problems with self-efficacy theory: A reply to Bandura. *Cognitive Therapy & Research, 8,* 257–262.

Maturana, H. R. (1988). Reality: The search for objectivity or the quest for a compelling argument. *Irish Journal of Psychology, 9,* 25–82.

Maturana, H. R. (1993, November). *The biology of knowing.* Paper presented at the Conference of the American Society of Cybernetics, Philadelphia, PA.

Maturana, H. R., & Varela, F. J. (1987). *The tree of knowledge.* Boston: Shambhala.

Mehrabian, A. (1981). *Silent messages: Implicit communication of emotions and attitudes* (2nd ed.). Belmont, CA: Wadsworth.

Meichenbaum, D. H. (1990). Paying homage: Providing challenges. *Psychological Inquiry, 1,* 96–100.

Mendez, C. L., Coddou, F., & Maturana, H. R. (1988). The bringing forth of pathology. *Irish Journal of Psychology, 9,* 144–172.

Millman, D. (1994). *The inner athlete: Realizing your fullest potential.* Walpole, NH: Stillpoint.

Rabkin, R. (1970). *Inner and outer space: Toward a theory of social psychiatry.* New York: Norton.

Rank, O. (1945). *Will therapy and truth and reality.* New York: Knopf.

Rosenthal, R., & Jacobson, L. (1968). *Pygmalion in the classroom: Teacher expectation and pupils' intellectual development.* New York: Holt, Rinehart & Winston.

Rychlak, J. F. (1981). *Introduction to personality and psychotherapy* (2nd ed.). Boston: Houghton Mifflin.

Schafer, R. (1976). *A new language for psychoanalysis.* New Haven, CT: Yale University Press.

Schafer, R. (1983). *The analytic attitude.* New York: Basic Books.

Sharma, S. L. (1986). *The therapeutic dialogue: A theoretical and practical guide to psychotherapy.* Albuquerque: University of New Mexico Press.

Smedslund, J. (1991). The pseudoempirical in psychology and the case for psychologic. *Psychological Inquiry, 2,* 325–338.

Szasz, T. S. (1973). *The second sin.* Garden City, NY: Doubleday.

Szasz, T. S. (1974). *The myth of mental illness: Foundations of a theory of personal conduct* (rev. ed.). New York: Harper & Row.

Szasz, T. S. (1996). *The meaning of mind: Language, morality, and neuroscience.* Westport, CT: Praeger.

Szasz, T. S. (1998, March). *The meaning of mind.* Paper presented at the 21st Annual Family Therapy Network Symposium, Washington, DC.

Varela, F. J. (1979). *Principles of biological autonomy.* Amsterdam, The Netherlands: Elsevier North Holland.

Weiner, M., & Mehrabian, A. (1968). *Language within language: Immediacy, a channel in verbal communication*. New York: Appleton-Century-Crofts.

Whitehead, A. N., & Russell, B. (1963). *Principia mathematica* (2nd ed., Vols. 1–3). Cambridge, England: Cambridge University Press.

Wittgenstein, L. (1971). *Tractatus logico-philosophicus* (2nd ed.). London: Routledge & Kegan Paul. (Original work published 1922)

7

CONSTRUCTING AND DECONSTRUCTING TRANSITIVE DIAGNOSIS

THOMAS J. JOHNSON, DAVID T. PFENNINGER, AND REID E. KLION

The destabilization created by the rapid pace, ease of communication, and mixing of cultures and viewpoints that characterize the postmodern world is perhaps nowhere more apparent than in the raging controversies about health care. Psychologists and the public are alarmed by the threat of diluted access to high-quality mental health care. Concerns about cost containment, efficacy, and accountability will continue to be constraints for the practitioner, and they have forced a basic review of nearly every aspect of clinical service delivery. Follette (1996) noted that the "tentacles" of the *Diagnostic and Statistical Manual of Mental Disorders* (*DSM*; American Psychiatric Association, 1994) diagnostic system have extended from managed care (in the form of requirements for classifying clients to gain reimbursement for services) to funding agency requirements to organize research around *DSM* constructs, all "despite the fact that *DSM* has not been particularly successful as an organizing principle for guiding science, and its assumptions about how to interpret behavior seem inadequate from many perspectives" (p. 1117). Nonetheless, there is still an urgent need for theoretical and diagnostic frameworks to facilitate clinical work, inform "change management" strategy, and integrate technically eclectic practice.

Against this backdrop, we present for consideration a diagnostic system based on personal construct theory (PCT). Called "transitive diagnosis," the system—despite being more than 40 years old, in its original incarnation—offers a viable alternative for contemporary and future clinicians. We review the key tenets of PCT, present the transitive diagnostic model, situate the model with reference to historical and current developments in clinical diagnosis, and offer case material illustrating the approach in practice.

PERSONAL CONSTRUCT THEORY

The American psychologist George Kelly (1905–1967) authored one of the most comprehensive personality theories of the 20th century, known as the psychology of personal constructs or PCT (Kelly, 1955). Kelly developed a psychology that represented a radical departure from the mainstream behaviorist, psychoanalytic, and biopsychiatric theories of his day. PCT also encompasses a remarkably complete diagnostic and therapeutic system, anchored by the concept and process of transitive diagnosis.

The central philosophical position of Kellian PCT is *constructive alternativism*: This philosophy assumes that the universe is real, in constant flux, and both integral (ultimately interconnected) and temporal (unfolding along an axis of time) yet can never be known directly "in and of itself." Human beings individually and jointly construct versions of reality that permit them to understand their world. An infinite range of such constructions is theoretically possible. All events are therefore subject to revision and reconstruction; those constructions, including diagnostic systems, that are useful tend to be retained, whereas those that offer little predictive value tend to be revised or discarded.

PCT maintains that people understand and create meaning through personal construct systems. Kelly defined the basic process and goal of psychological activity (and more broadly, life) as one of anticipation. As stated in the PCT fundamental postulate, "a person's processes are psychologically channelized by the ways in which he [or she] anticipates events" (Kelly, 1955, p. 46). A *construct* is defined as a dichotomous or bipolar dimension abstracted from and subsequently imposed on the raw perceptual and ideational experience of life. Recurrent themes across time are perceived, abstracted, and organized into a meaning system that features hierarchical relations and includes subsystems that have a specific range of convenience (e.g., apply to a limited class of events). Constructs define and constrain the interpretation and relationships of elements available in one's perceptual field. The perceptual field itself varies on a continuum of *constricted* (fixed and closed) to *dilated* (shifting and open). PCT does not draw sharp lines among cognition, behavior, and affect. Thus, anticipation involves not only cognitive expectancies and emotional evaluations of events or outcomes but also concurrent behaviors aimed at manipulating reality to create those outcomes.

TRANSITIVE DIAGNOSIS IN PERSONAL CONSTRUCT THEORY

Transitive diagnosis represents both a general principle and a set of diagnostic constructs. Kelly (1955) rejected diagnostic labels referring to static disease entities presumed to reside within a person. He thought that diagnoses should carry pragmatic implications for change and transition in the client's life. What does lie within the individual is that person's construct system. Kelly developed a system of diagnostic terms that refer to structural aspects of one's construct system and processes involved when one's construct system is used to anticipate events in one's life. Transitive diagnosis involves exploring the client's construct system and then using Kelly's diagnostic constructs to map out the structures and processes of that construct system. In PCT, a disorder is conceptualized as the continued use of constructs that have been invalidated. Thus, transitive diagnosis is the process of identifying where or how a client is "stuck" so that the therapist might help the client more successfully predict and control his or her world. The PCT therapist helps the client explore alternative ways of construing to make more appropriate and adaptive transitions. To understand transitive diagnosis, one must first become familiar with Kelly's view of how construct systems operate.

Construing Everyday Life

In the simplest of cases, individuals impose meaning on an element or event by rendering it on one pole or the other of a bipolar construct. For example, consider Jack, who anticipates that his supervisor will be irritable (vs. pleasant) in an upcoming meeting. If the supervisor acts in a fashion that meets Jack's criteria for irritability, then Jack's expectation will have been validated. However, if the boss behaves in a manner that Jack sees as pleasant, his anticipation will have been invalidated. This may create some confusion or anxiety for Jack, perhaps prompting him to explore his understanding of his supervisor in more depth or even stimulate an alteration in the structure or implications of his irritable versus pleasant construct.

Under these conditions, Jack may survey his previous encounters with his supervisor and conclude that there have been frequent unpleasant exchanges. In this light, he may be resistant to viewing his boss as anything but irritable and difficult. Any pleasant behavior on the part of the boss might be construed as an anomaly or linked with another construct (e.g., that his apparent friendliness is an aspect of phoniness or manipulation).

On the whole, this irritable versus pleasant construct may have had a reasonably good track record of predictive efficacy for Jack, allowing him to make decent probability estimates about what to expect in exchanges with his supervisor. The friendliness today was not enough to alter Jack's general appraisal of his supervisor. Hence, Jack retains both the construct and its pattern of application toward his supervisor.

Alternatively, it may turn out that Jack tends to view all authority figures as irritable, regardless of their particular style or behavior. Perhaps it is *polarized*, an "either–or" preemptive construct with little room for nuance or "shades of gray." This sort of construct may be highly *permeable*, readily applied to new elements and situations (vs. impermeable and applicable only to a narrow range of situations or people). Because of its centrality to the entire personality system, the construct is applied *impulsively*, without consideration of alternative constructions before making a decision. The construct may serve a definitional rather than an extensional function, preserving the status quo rather than pursuing innovation. Perhaps it exists in a state of *fragmentation*, cut off from or diffusely linked with other important construct systems. It may be tight (as opposed to loose) in its unwavering reliability and constancy across time and circumstance. It could be deeply imbued with difficult emotions, such as guilt and anxiety, or have powerful implications for Jack's expressions of social dependency.

Suppose further that Jack is so strongly wedded to this construal of "authority-as-irritable" (perhaps from early experience in relation to caregivers) that he refuses to see them otherwise. He construes them preemptively as irritable and rejecting. Even supportive authority figures are construed in such a way that they are made to "fit" the construct. Evidence that the construction is ineffective, or even damaging to self and others, may be ignored through selective inattention on Jack's part, if not aggressive efforts to distort the "validational evidence" and force situations and people to conform to the construct. He may also alter his own perceptual field to preserve the construct, screening out contradictory information. These responses may be facets of psychological *hostility*, the refusal to modify a social construct that has been repeatedly invalidated. Additionally, because one's basic interpersonal or core role constructs literally define who one is, one will defend them vigorously. Prospective change in core roles almost always implies *threat*, the potential that an event may invalidate a deeply valued belief.

In the example of Jack, it is important to note that each of the PCT concepts is applicable to both healthy and disordered psychological processes. None of the dynamics in his case were necessarily disordered, abnormal, or even dysfunctional. That is, the concepts are used as broad dimensions for discerning both intra- and interindividual change. The dividing line between a "normal" and "disordered" pattern is not absolute. These judgments can be assessed only relative to the context of the individual client's life and values and, as postmodern psychologists have demonstrated, to the context of the diagnostic situation itself.

Alternative Constructions of Transitive Diagnosis

Kelly (1955) thought that a theory should be reflexive: It should be possible to apply the theory to itself and explain the existence of competing theories. If PCT is truly reflexive, then it should be subject to constructive alternativism. Although the theory was "put forward as a complete and formal statement by one man at one time" (Bannister & Fransella, 1986, pp. 3–4), Kelly also invited readers to revise or completely discard his theory if it did not prove fruitful. In the spirit of constructive alternativism then, herein we elect to elaborate several construals of transitive diagnosis.

We first consider transitive diagnosis as a reaction to conditions that prevailed in psychiatry and psychology in the period from the 1930s through 1955 and formulate transitive diagnoses of both Kelly and the field of psychiatry during this period. Next, we present transitive diagnosis as a description of reality and the reality of applying transitive diagnosis, including further discussion of the diagnostic constructs Kelly created. We then attempt to construe transitive diagnosis as a prescription for evaluating and improving clinical work. Finally, we treat transitive diagnosis as part of a metatheoretical perspective, which may be a useful guide for practitioners of many theoretical orientations.

TRANSITIVE DIAGNOSIS AS HISTORY

The history of the personal and cultural events that influenced the development of Kelly's theory have been documented by Kelly (1955, 1969a) himself and others (Fransella, 1995; R. A. Neimeyer, 1985; Zelhart & Jackson, 1983). We focus primarily on the development of Kelly's approach to diagnosis. It is worth noting that DSM-I (1952) appeared just 3 years before Kelly's 2-volume opus. Writers have attempted to describe and categorize mental and behavioral symptoms for several centuries, forming in the process the discipline of descriptive psychopathology. Although a complete history of the development of nosological systems is not possible here, a broad overview explains some of the influences on Kelly's work.

Diagnostic Systems Prior to World War II

Before the 19th century, concepts of insanity were based on observable behaviors. During the 19th century, physical symptoms (e.g., cold and blue extremities was a sign of catatonic schizophrenia) and self-reports (e.g., mood, thought content, hallucinations) were also used to define categories (Berrios, 1996). In addition, through postmortem examinations, scientists attempted to identify brain lesions that were presumed to be associated with disturbed behavior. At approximately the same time, the discovery of microorganisms and the development of microbiology further stimulated interest in the identification of organic causes for psychopathology. Early successes included the identification of syphilis as the cause of general paresis and lesions in specific brain regions underlying specific forms of aphasia. When a lesion, microbe, or toxin could not be identified and associated with a particular pattern of symptoms, heredity typically was invoked (Clark, 1973). The failure to identify additional organic causes contributed to the decline in interest in descriptive psychopathology for several decades early in the 20th century.

In Europe, a distinction was made between the form of a symptom (e.g., the "fact" that the patient presented with an hallucination vs. a delusion) and the content of a symptom (e.g., the content of the hallucination or the specific delusional belief). Descriptive psychopathology concentrated on form so that "the psychopathologist could . . . not be accused of 'constructing' symptoms: he just carved out behavior at the joints" (Berrios, 1996, p. 20). European interest in nosology culminated in the detailed nosological systems of Kraepelin (1913/1919, 1913/1921) and Bleuler (1911/1950).

Kelly (1958, 1969d) was fond of noting that theories or systems are inventions rather than discoveries or "things," and he recommended that the proper role of empiricism in science was "the discovery of what things ensue from the courageous application of invented ideas" (Kelly, 1958, p. 323). Just as constructive alternativism was antithetical to an emphasis on delimited categories of psychopathology, Kelly was also interested in the content of "symptoms." Although his diagnostic constructs could be thought of as representing forms, the forms in question were processes rather than static conditions. Kelly was interested in content because the content of an individual's construct system allows that person to successfully anticipate events. Despite these breaks with tradition, Kelly (1955) did pay homage to Kraepelin and Aristotle as "great contributors to psychological thought" (p. 775). Although Kelly recognized the limitations of nosological systems, he apparently also thought that an approach relying on detailed description of behavior was possible at some point in the future, noting, however, that the job of "collecting and classifying normative data along the base lines of human behavior has yet to be done" (p. 779).

For most of the 19th century, alienists (the 19th-century term for psychiatrists; people with "mental illness were thought to be 'alienated,' not only from the rest of society but from their own true natures"; Carr, 1995, p. vii) in the United States had little interest in developing complex nosological systems. Opinions differed widely concerning causes and categories of insanity, generally favoring organic explanations but often emphasizing the uniqueness of the individual case (Grob, 1991). The U.S. Bureau of the Census, however, was very interested in keeping track of the "insane," the "feeble-minded," and other "dependents." The census bureau's concern with insanity reached its apex in the late 1800s and early 1900s, stimulated in large part by sociopolitical concerns (e.g., the eugenics movement, fears about immigrants; Grob, 1991). In the late 19th century, the Bureau of the Census received input from several different psychiatrists; by 1908, it had formally requested input from the American Medico Psychological Association. A committee on statistics was created by the association in 1913; in 1918, the first *Statistical Manual for the Use of Institutions for the Insane* (cited in Grob, 1991) was released. Of the 22 categories in this manual, 20 emphasized biological causes, and most categories represented forms of psychosis (Grob, 1991). This manual went through various revisions, but it was the primary diagnostic document in the United States until World War II.

From 1910 through the 1940s, the most influential figure in American psychiatry was Adolf Meyer (Clark, 1973; Grob, 1991). Meyer had little use for diagnosis by "legislation" or for nosological systems in general (Grob, 1991). Meyer remained committed to the importance of biological determinants, but he also emphasized the importance of an individual's life experiences. Thus, for most of the first half of the 20th century, classification systems in the United States served mainly as assistance with statistics records rather than as aids to treatment.

Early Development of Kelly's Theory

Numerous authors (e.g., R. A. Neimeyer, 1985; Kelly, 1969a) have noted that the uniqueness of Kelly's theory may be due at least in part to his broad background (i.e., training in engineering, sociology, education, psychophysiology; experience teaching drama, speech, and government) and relative lack of formal training in clinical psychology. Nonetheless, when Kelly began teaching at Fort Hayes State University in Fort Hayes, Kansas, in the fall of 1931, he almost immediately became involved in opening a free psychological clinic. Zelhart and Jackson (1983) documented the origins and history of Kelly's clinic at Fort Hayes, which essentially began as a class project and evolved into a traveling "road show," carrying diagnostic and treatment services far out into rural Kansas. Kelly's (1955) statement of his theory had its origins in the handbook he wrote to guide policies, procedures, and services for this clinic.

Kelly (1955) himself provided therapy to Fort Hayes students, including those who worked for his clinic (Zelhart & Jackson, 1983). The activities of the clinic included not only assessment and therapy but also training in academic skills, vocational training and guidance, and services to both physically and mentally handicapped children (Zelhart & Jackson, 1983). In contrast to the fear of marginalized and "defective" people shown by the eugenics movement and the census bureau's classification efforts, Kelly was dedicated to providing services for all.

The list of books Kelly required clinic workers to read (documented by Zelhart & Jackson, 1983) included a detailed neurology text (Herrick, 1931), although it is not clear whether this reflected Kelly's experience in psychophysiology or an early allegiance to organic explanations of psychopathology. Another required text included 11 categories of "maladjustments," 7 of which are noted to "depend upon some physical condition of disease" (Morgan, 1936, p. 26). This suggests that Kelly's early thinking regarding diagnosis was rather traditional.

Kelly also included on his reading list works by Sigmund Freud and Alfred Adler. Although Kelly's (1969a) initial impression of Freud was that his writing consisted of "elastic meanings and arbitrary syntax" (p. 47), the orientation of his clinic was largely psychodynamic. For example, Zelhart and Jackson (1983) presented a "Schema for the Psychopathology of the Neuroses" (p. 142) that Kelly had prepared for his clinic handbook. This system included formulations for 10 diagnostic categories, including Freudian stages and conflicts associated with each category.

Thus, Kelly (1969a) appeared to have relied initially on organic and psychodynamic formulations of disorder. Gardner (1993) noted that individuals who formulate creative breakthroughs in science and the arts may begin by attempting to create a work within the dominant symbol system of their time (e.g., Freud's *Project for a Scientific Psychology*, 1895/1966, or Stravinsky's *Firebird*), only to find that these symbol systems do not contain an adequate "vocabulary" to express the themes with which they grapple. Kelly's attempt to use Freudian dynamics as the basis for a (not entirely original) diagnostic system may represent such an attempt on his part. It is probable that the clinical problems Kelly encountered could not be explained or categorized to his satisfaction using Freudian dynamics regarding neurosis or the contemporary nosology that emphasized psychosis and was designed to facilitate the compilation of statistics rather than to serve as a guide for treatment.

Kelly (1969a) recounted that through his clinical work, he discovered that not only did Freudian interpretations seem beneficial to his clients but also just about any interpretation that "account[ed] for the facts as the client saw them and . . . [carried] implications for approaching the future in a different way" (p. 52). Kelly's initial construction of a detailed structure for his clinic, followed by his "playing" with interpretations, can be construed as tight and loose phases of a cycle of creativity. Kelly's attention was clearly drawn to the process of change, so it was natural that he might formulate a diagnostic system with a similar emphasis.

Through his work with children, Kelly found that traditional labels could actually serve as a barrier to change. Classroom teachers were a major source of referrals for Kelly's (1969b) clinic.

> A teacher complained about a pupil. . . . If we kicked the pupil around long enough and hard enough[,] we could usually find some grounds to justify any teacher's complaint. This procedure was called in those days, just as it is still called, "diagnosis." In Kansas we diagnosed pupils and, having impaled ourselves and our clients within our diagnoses, we cast about more or less frantically for ways of escape. (p. 75)

Through these experiences, Kelly came to the conclusion that the diagnosis often said more about the teacher than about the student. Similarly, Kelly (1955) noted that IQ test scores pigeonhole a child "rather than opening up a fertile source of plans, opportunities, and methods of teaching" (p. 454). His concern with client integrity and the potentially pernicious effects of syndromal labeling presaged by several decades the later intense interest in social labeling theory (e.g., Conrad & Schneider, 1980; Rosenhan, 1973; Sarbin & Mancuso, 1980; Scheff, 1975).

The 1940s and Beyond

In 1942, Carl Rogers published *Counseling and Psychotherapy: Newer Concepts in Practice*, marking the beginning of his nondirective approach. The nondirective movement in counseling typically asserted that diagnosis had no implications for treatment (Berdie, 1950). Perhaps because his personality included a penchant for system building, Kelly saw diagnostic practice as having the potential to inform clinical practice but only if a diagnostic system carried implications for change. Kelly (1955) thought that the proper question regarding diagnosis was " 'What is to become of this client?' rather than 'In what category should this case be classified?' " (1955, p. 776).

From slightly before World War II and continuing throughout the 1940s, psychiatry was increasingly dominated by psychoanalytic clinicians who brought with them classifications based on psychodynamics rather than observable symptoms or hypothesized organic causes (Grob, 1991). The concerns of psychoanalytic clinicians would be expressed in many of the categories that were included in the *DSM-I* (APA, 1952). Kelly toyed with such psychodynamic classifications approximately a decade earlier, and he again appeared to have been ahead of his time. However, by 1955 Kelly thought that psychoanalytic constructs were "only a few short steps removed from primitive notions of demoniacal possession and exorcism" (p. 776). Although he appreciated the Freudian recognition that "there was something going on in the client" (p. 776), at this point Kelly was bound to resist any diagnostic system influenced by psychodynamic dogma.

World War II also proved to be a turning point for diagnostic systems because the existing system did not include categories adequate for the problems presented by battle-weary soldiers (Grob, 1991; Klerman, 1986). Several branches of the armed services responded by developing their own manuals, precursors to the *DSM-I*. To an extent, psychiatry in the 1940s may have faced a situation somewhat similar to that facing Kelly in the 1930s. The concepts of *disorder* and *systems of classification* that both Kelly and psychiatrists of that period had to work with were deemed inadequate to the task. Kelly referred to the experience of facing events outside of the range of convenience of one's construct system, events one cannot adequately anticipate or categorize, as "anxiety." Kelly faced such anxiety in the 1930s, initiating a creative cycle of loosening and tightening, culminating (but not ceasing) with the 1955 2-volume set.

It is tempting to construe psychiatry's response to the situation it faced in the 1940s as hostility, defined by Kelly (1955) as a "continued effort to extort validational evidence in favor of a type of social prediction which has already proved itself a failure" (p. 510). Despite pressures that might have allowed a radical reinvention of diagnostic systems, the *DSM-I* simply represented a more grandiose version of previous systems. The foreword to the *DSM-I* notes that in the late 1920s, the existence of multiple systems was "effectively blocking communication and the collection of medical statistics" (p. v). That situation arose again during WWII, when various branches of the armed services created their own systems. In the face of competing systems and with cases that could not be classified adequately within existing systems, hostility might involve eliminating rival systems or entrenching existing ones or, in Kelly's terms, a "hardening of the categories."

Postwar Clinical Psychology

Some clinical psychologists in the 1940s and 1950s continued to deny the role of economic deprivation or wartime trauma as contributing to psychopathology (Dorcus & Shaffer, 1945)—a position clearly antithetical to that of Kelly (1955). Many, however, acknowledged that no one theory of psychopathology or abnormal behavior was dominant or adequate (Coleman, 1950; Conklin, 1944; O'Kelly & Muckler, 1955). This acknowledgment was at least somewhat consistent with Kelly's principle of constructive alternativism. Contemporary clinical psychologists were also aware of the limitations of diagnostic systems and the dangers of labeling. For example, Coleman (1950) noted that "more dynamic and flexible classification schemes have been worked out, which are useful for guiding therapy and research rather than pigeonholing patients in the Kraepelinian tradition" (p. 56). However, the system Coleman chose to follow was the U.S. Army classification scheme, which was one of the principal sources for the development of *DSM-I*—hardly a radical deviation from Kraepelinian nosology.

The importance of diagnosis for clinical practice was taken as a given during the period. McKinney (1948) noted that an evaluative attitude can weaken the clinicians' acceptance of the client, but he stated that an early diagnosis was necessary because "this impression partly determines the nature of the therapeutic approach, hence its accuracy is vital" (p. 452) and because "the counselor must determine early [on] whether he is competent to handle the problem before him" (p. 452) or if a "referral to other professional workers is indicated" (p. 452). McKinney's emphasis on accurate diagnosis presupposes a valid diagnostic system that cuts nature at the joints and includes implications for treatment. As seen, Kelly thought that neither of these conditions existed in the diagnostic systems then available. Kelly (1969a), who never accepted fees for his services, was also critical of what he termed the "referral game" (p. 50) or "pinning pathological diagnoses" (p. 50) on people. He noted that this game "has to be played in metropolitan areas where there is a suitable proliferation of agencies and specialists on whom you can unload your less profitable clients. In western Kansas when a person came to me we were pretty much stuck with each other" (p. 50).

In considering Kelly's approach to diagnosis as an historical document, we see that he probably began with rather conventional notions regarding the importance of organic sources of pathology and systematized nosologies. However, in confronting situations outside the range of convenience of his construct system, he was forced to formulate new constructs. He elected to focus on the role of anticipation in adaptation and developed a system of diagnostic constructs that focused on transitions or failures of anticipation. When psychiatry and psychology faced similar anxiety during the postwar period, many professionals opted to continue to attempt to validate concepts, such as discrete disease entities and organic or psychodynamic pathologies, for which evidence was sparse at best.

TRANSITIVE DIAGNOSIS AS REALITY

Kelly intended for his diagnostic system to provide a flexible set of conceptual tools and procedural maps for the practicing psychotherapist. Aware of the human tendency toward "reification" of concepts, he cautioned against taking the transitive diagnostic system literally. Kelly (1955) wanted therapists in their clinical diagnoses to avoid the preemptive labeling of an individual as this-or-that category or type, and he referred to traditional diagnosis as an "attempt to cram a whole living struggling client into a nosological category" (p. 775). Such labeling reduces freedom of movement and options for the client. Kelly designed transitive diagnosis as an integral part of PCT's constructivist model of reality. However, Kelly explicitly developed his diagnostic system with the goal of assessing anticipatory processes and change at a sufficient level of abstraction to allow for relevant assessment of the full range of individualized personal realities.

Transitive Diagnosis

Transitive diagnosis "suggests that we are concerned with transitions in the client's life, that we are looking for bridges between the client's present and his future" (Kelly, 1955, p. 775). Kelly's diagnostic approach is focused on elucidating the pathways of change clients might follow in resolving their difficulties. To this end, "if the clinician wishes to free himself from the restrictions of fixed nosological pigeonholes, he must start examining clinical situations with an eye for the practical potentialities" (p. 776). The question to answer by a transitive diagnosis is not What is wrong with this client? but How is this client going to get well?

Part of the challenge in reading and understanding PCT is Kelly's seemingly idiosyncratic use of diagnostic terms. We already listed some of Kelly's (1955) general diagnostic constructs (e.g., loose vs. tight construing). The following is a brief review of some of the more prominent constructs and dimensions used in transitive diagnosis. The dimensions and constructs related to transition in Kelly's theory do not necessarily constitute disorders. Disorders typically occur when a person's construct system is confronted with events or information that cannot be adequately anticipated or explained. If that person continues to apply invalidated constructs, it constitutes disorder from Kelly's perspective. Kelly was concerned with the underlying processes that lead an individual to continually use a construct, even when it has been repeatedly invalidated. In this spirit, he attempted to define emotional reactions in terms of those transitions that people experience in their struggles to infuse their world with meaning.

Threat occurs when an individual becomes aware of an imminent comprehensive change in his or her core construct structures. Core structures define an individual's identity and most basic processes. Death is often threatening because it has immediate implications for one's core identity. People's core roles define who they are as individuals, and people often will defend them with their lives. Landfield (1976) argued that suicide might be understood as a person's ultimate attempt to preserve his or her core structure from further invalidation. However, if the change only has incidental (vs. comprehensive) implications for one's core roles, the result is fear.

Guilt is experienced when one is dislodged from one's core role. It should be noted that this acting out of character or loss of a social role need not imply immoral behavior but simply actions that deviate from one's core role structure. Anxiety is the awareness that one is confronted with events that are not well accommodated by one's current construct structure. Thus, with the notion of transitive diagnosis, anxiety is often a sign that a construction may be in need of a revision. Clinically, the most appropriate intervention might be to assist the client in exploring what it is he or she is having difficulty making sense of rather than immediately launching into techniques such as relaxation exercises or the identification of irrational beliefs simply to reduce the "signs" of the disorder. As Winter (1992) argued, what seem to be negative emotions may simply be very healthy signs that one's construing is in need of a revision.

Aggression is the active elaboration of one's perceptual field (e.g., attempting to expand the range of elements to which one applies one's constructs). Aggression is not necessarily pathological and, indeed, is often necessary for growth. Hostility is the continued use of a construct that has already been invalidated. Although hostility can be problematic, it can also represent a healthy engagement with the world and an attempt to make desired outcomes come to pass (see Pfenninger & Klion, 1995). McCoy (1977) conducted further work in conceptualizing affect as signs of construct system transition.

Construct system transition and evolution occur through the circumspection–preemption–control cycle (CPC cycle). *Circumspection* is the phase in which an individual considers how an event may be understood in a propositional way. For example, when one meets new neighbors, there are many initial hypotheses and hunches about them that one might entertain when one first meets them. When one moves to *preemption*, one rules out some of the initial hypotheses and reaches toward a decision about one's anticipations of these individuals. Are these "good" neighbors, "nice" people, or people with whom one feels uncomfortable? *Control* is the point at which one makes an ultimate decision about how to construe an event and acts on that construction. If one construes the neighbors as nice, one may not hesitate to let them borrow a rake or one may bake them a cake as a welcome. If one feels uncomfortable, one may avoid eye contact when one passes them on the street. When a person selects a particular construction of events and acts on that construction, that person is effectively conducting an experiment, testing the validity of that construction. This brings the CPC cycle full circle, as one must then circumspect regarding the outcome of one's behavioral experiment.

Any number of difficulties can arise in the CPC process. For example, *impulsivity* is understood as the tendency to foreshorten the circumspection phase without considering all of the options. One may jump to a conclusion about the neighbors, without really getting to know them. Difficulties in preemption are evident in the individual who has substantial difficulty reducing a problem to a critical issue, perhaps ruminating about options rather than adopting one construction of events to guide his or her behavior. One may not be able to make up one's mind about the neighbors and, therefore, remains unsure as to how one should act. One may then avoid them or be inhibited in their presence. To successfully adapt, one must not only preempt and adopt a particular hypothesis but also act on the basis of that hypothesis and consider the outcome of one's actions. In PCT terms, the "socially unskilled" person may be failing to effectively act on his or her constructions of events (deficits in control), whereas the sociopath may fail to reflect on the outcomes of his or her behavior (failing to return to circumspection).

Assessment

An important aspect of the pragmatic reality of transitive diagnosis is the actual steps one takes to gather information, to formulate the diagnosis, and to develop a plan of action. Kelly's *The Psychology of Personal Constructs* (1955) retains much of its origins as a treatment manual. Kelly included an extensive discussion of assessment techniques; chapters on assessment of a client's cultural and personal experiences, behavior, and activities; and a detailed list of steps in the diagnostic process. The chapter on appraisal of activities includes many techniques that would today be called "behavioral assessment" but with the goal of developing or testing hypotheses about a client's personal construct system rather than identifying contingencies.

Kelly's (1955) list of diagnostic steps is also very contemporary and could easily serve as a training model today. Diagnosis began by one creating a list of the specific presenting symptoms or behaviors, including temporal patterns of symptoms, cultural and personal context of symptoms, and work and family issues. Assessment then moved to an attempt to specify the client's understanding of what he or she believed to be the problem and what the client believed that others thought was going on. The client's perception of his or her life role or core identity structures is also assessed. Additional steps include assessment using the transitive diagnostic constructs (see below), assessment of socioeconomic contexts, consultation with other professionals, and making plans for treatment and case management.

The most crucial phase of transitive diagnosis is the identification of the constructs clients use to construe themselves and others as well as the patterns in which those constructs are applied. Contemporary clinicians have a number of options in assessing clients' construct systems. Kelly's (1955) original techniques include the role construct repertory test (REP grid) and the self-characterization sketch. The REP grid, used in hundreds of studies since 1955, is a technique for identifying the constructs that an individual uses in construing or categorizing a set of elements. In the initial version of the REP grid, clients list a number of important people in their lives and then compare those people in groups of three. In each group, clients identify one important way that two of the people are alike yet different from the third. For example, one's mother and one's favorite teacher might be different from a successful acquaintance because they both are "kind," whereas the acquaintance is "indifferent." This procedure allows for a generation of a sample of the client's relevant constructs. The client then rates each person on the original list, using all of the constructs generated. This allows the therapist to make inferences about the organization of the clients' construct system, such as which constructs are correlated. Kelly and others developed detailed procedures for scoring REP grids, however a complete discussion of this technique is beyond the scope of this chapter. We suggest that interested readers consult specific texts on the topic, such as those by Fransella and Bannister (1977), Landfield and Epting (1987), and G. J. Neimeyer (1993).

The self-characterization sketch is a written description of the client's self in the third person, as if it were by someone who knew him or her intimately. Another way of framing the task is to describe the self-characterization sketch as the information an actor would need to play the role of the client. The ways the client describes him- or herself are thought to offer glimpses of that client's personal construct system. The self-characterization sketch is most generally treated in an informal way as a type of projective technique, but recommendations and procedures for analyzing the sketch have been offered (G. J. Neimeyer, 1993).

These two formal techniques may not always be necessary. Much may be gained by a therapist simply questioning and interacting with the client. Several specific verbal techniques have been developed, such as the downward arrow, "ABC technique," and laddering (Fransella & Dalton, 1990; G. J. Neimeyer, 1993), but a basic approach is to listen for the terms the client consistently uses to describe him- or herself and others. The therapist should attempt to get the client to elaborate on the personal meaning of such terms. Additional important questions include the following: What social or occupational roles are most important to the client? What values and beliefs does he or she cherish? What is the client's explanation of his or her problem and how strongly does he or she hold to that conceptualization? If the explanation has become part of the client's core role (e.g., "I am an alcoholic"), attempts to modify the client's view of his or her "disorder" could result in a Kellian threat (dissolution of the core role or self).

Traditional cognitive therapy assessment devices such as the Automatic Thoughts Questionnaire (Hollon & Kendall, 1980) or Social Interaction

Self-Statement Test (Glass, Merluzzi, Biever, & Larsen, 1982), might also be used, but the PCT clinician focuses on groupings of items that suggest particular constructions of self or others (e.g., factor scores or idiosyncratic sets of items) rather than rely on a total score or a simple list of isolated automatic thoughts. Standardized norm-based tests of symptoms and personality patterns also are readily incorporated into the constructivist's assessment repertoire (Pfenninger & Klion, 1997), provided that they are interpreted heuristically and contextually as alternative constructions of the client rather than as preemptive "reality." Finally, a client's behaviors also offer important clues to his or her construct system. Impulsiveness may be apparent in a client's speech or repetitive behavior patterns. The client's interactions with the therapist may offer clues as to his or her interpersonal roles and constructs. Only after some assessment of a client's construct system has been made can potential transitive diagnoses be explored.

Disorders of Construction and Transition

Kelly (1955) defined psychological disorder in terms of the continued use of invalidated constructs, constructs that do not allow one to adequately anticipate events. A variety of factors may contribute to a client's continued use of invalidated constructs, including structural aspects of his or her construct system (e.g., excessively loose or dilated construction, impermeable constructs) or the process of applying his or her construct system (e.g., responses to threat, lack of adequate circumspection). The PCT therapist should be technically eclectic (Kelly, 1969c), using interventions from a number of theoretical traditions but guided by the premises of PCT.

Disorders of construction refer to the nature of the client's construct system. For example, loose construction is analogous to the fragmented thinking associated with the traditional diagnostic category of schizophrenia, whereas tight construction resembles the rigid, inflexible thinking seen in some organically impaired individuals or associated with the traditional diagnosis of obsessive–compulsive disorder. Loose (or tight) construction is not in and of itself a disorder. Loose construction allows one to "tolerate ambiguity" (Kelly, 1955, p. 855). Tight construction allows one to focus on details. Loose construction is similar to the notion of divergent thinking because a loose construct may lead to different predictions, even across variations of the same situation. This ability to see things in different ways is part of Kelly's creativity cycle (alternating between loose and tight construing). However, if loose thinking continues over time, it leaves a client unable to successfully predict what is going to happen in his or her world, and it meets the PCT definition of a disorder (i.e., continued use of invalidated constructs).

In treating the loose client, the therapist must establish a relationship with the client and attempt to become at least one predictable element in that client's life (Kelly, 1955). Immediately presenting the client with information that disconfirms his or her loose thinking might precipitate a crisis. Tightening must be accomplished gradually, while attempting to build on any remnants of tight construction present in the client.

Kelly (1955) described disorders of transition as involving PCT constructs, such as aggression, threat, anxiety, guilt, hostility, or problems with the CPC cycle. A therapist might use a variety of interventions with a client conceptualized as having difficulties with the CPC cycle. *Problem-solving training* (D'Zurilla & Goldfried, 1971) is a behavioral intervention aimed at explicitly identifying the stages in a problem-solving process and training the client to move through these stages in a controlled fashion. Cognitive interventions might include labeling impulsivity as a cognitive distortion ("jumping to conclusions") and generating alternative conclusions using rational analysis, examining the evidence, or using other techniques (Beck, 1976). Kelly's approach is similar in principle to (and predates) that of Beck; but rather than attempting to modify isolated automatic thoughts, Kelly attempted to modify systems of constructs by having clients experiment with coherent alternative roles. This experimentation allowed clients to test specific aspects of their construct system or try on alternative ways of anticipating events. When treating the impulsive client, Kelly (1955) recommended helping the client explore the consequences of alternative courses of action through use of role-play or helping clients to develop "social techniques" (what might today be called "social skills") through group therapy experiences or experiments outside of therapy.

A Clinical Illustration

The following case example demonstrates the integration of transitive diagnosis with more traditional diagnostic schemes. *DSM-IV* or *International Classification of Diseases* diagnoses are often the "starting point" for treatment. Clinicians who use various approaches and models may then further refine their diagnostic formulations to provide a specific plan to address a client's difficulties.

> Robert is a 37-year-old gentleman who was troubled for the past 2 years with what he described as "bad nerves" and "hearing voices." He sought treatment at the encouragement of his wife, who saw him as depressed and "hateful" (her term for irritability and hostility). Across a series of diagnostic interviews, it became apparent that Robert had been experiencing severe depressive symptoms for the past 2 years. He had become increasingly isolated from others, had lost interest in almost

all activity, found it difficult to keep his mind on anything for more than a few minutes, and was "hearing" the voice of his deceased father making disparaging comments to him. It took Robert hours to fall asleep at night, as he "worried about nothing and everything," and he had developed numerous physical complaints that had no apparent medical etiology.

In the eyes of his treating psychiatrist, he met the *DSM-IV* criteria for major depressive disorder, severe with psychotic features and generalized anxiety disorder. Proceeding from this initial diagnostic formulation, the target symptoms of auditory hallucinations and insomnia were first addressed with psychopharmacology because these were the most acutely upsetting symptoms to Robert. Although some moderate degree of progress was made in limiting the auditory hallucinations and the sleep disturbance, he continued to have great difficulty getting along with his family. Robert also found leaving the family home for any extended period of time difficult and therefore was unable to return to his work as an electric utility lineman.

Robert was then referred to one of us for psychotherapy. Transitive diagnosis had begun with psychiatric syndrome classification and was now continued through interviews, psychological testing, and family discussions. In his own eyes, Robert felt totally unable to "cope with the world" because of his "bad nerves." As a result, he would do virtually nothing, spending much of the day in his room in bed or looking out the window. In PCT terms, he was anxious because he felt wholly unable to make sense of the world or people around him. As a result, he worked very hard at controlling his world (constricting his perceptual field). Because he was relying solely on his family for support, his access to social validation was quite limited, and his dependency needs poorly dispersed. He was also unaware of how his physical symptoms might be related to his emotional difficulties, fluctuating as a function of his acute degree of distress.

After some initial psychotherapy sessions, it was mutually decided that Robert would attempt to engage in an "experiment" in expanding (or elaborating) his social world (in PCT terms, "exploring alternate roles"). Although initially resistant, he did recognize the need to expand his horizons beyond his immediate family and bedroom. To do so, he began helping out with yard work and later volunteered to help an older neighbor by raking leaves. Although seeing little connection between his physical and emotional problems, he did agree to exercise 20 minutes daily. Indeed, after some weeks of effort, he was regularly leaving the home to go on neighborhood walks, assisting his wife in grocery shopping, and even driving short distances (on "good" days).

However, despite what his therapist saw as good progress, Robert again became quite anxious and agitated, doing little but pacing around his home. Although he initially wanted an immediate medication adjustment, this was not possible for scheduling reasons. As such, he raised these concerns in psychotherapy. After discussion, it became evident that much of his current distress was due to his perceived inability to provide for his family, something he had always prided himself in (although Robert had improved, continuing difficulties with concentration prohibited his returning to work). In PCT terms, this shows guilt, dislodgement from what he saw as one of his core roles, that of being a "good provider" for his family. He felt threatened by his own guilt, aware that he was undergoing a comprehensive change in his personal identity. For Robert, this was particularly important given his deceased father's struggles with alcohol and abandonment of the family. Thus, the auditory hallucinations were interpreted as important and relevant symptomatic experiences, linking his own currently injured self concept with the contrasting and shameful memories of his father.

Robert was becoming so focused on his inability to return to work (constriction) that he soon found himself becoming isolated again—in his words, "backsliding into the black hole." Attention was then directed toward helping him to develop a more comprehensive set of core role constructs for his self-definition as a good provider. With additional counseling and considerable effort on Robert's part, he was eventually able to find work that was less perilous and made fewer cognitive demands. Able to again live according to his own core role, albeit modified in terms of greater flexibility and comprehensiveness, his depressive, anxious, somatic, and psychotic symptoms gradually remitted. His new core role had to incorporate, at a high level of awareness, the fact that he had had a "nervous breakdown." This forced him to acknowledge limitations and vulnerability for the first time in his life, but it also oriented him to taking "better care" of himself.

TRANSITIVE DIAGNOSIS AS CLINICAL PRESCRIPTION

Elaborations

Heeding Kelly's (1955) caution against reifying PCT constructs and methods, constructivists have been creative in extending transitive diagnostic concepts (Landfield & Epting, 1987; G. J. Neimeyer, 1993). For example, Leitner explored qualitative diagnosis of disorders involving sociality (Leitner & Pfenninger, 1994) and framed "dispositional assessment" (Leitner, 1995) as an explicitly process-oriented engagement with the client as a full partner in the initial diagnostic formulation and its revision across time. Mahoney (1991) bridged the gap between cognitive–behavioral strategies and constructivist diagnosis in his focus on "human change processes," significantly enriching each tradition. Pfenninger and Klion (1995) critiqued the pivotal PCT diagnostic concept of hostility and demonstrated how assessment tools from many clinical traditions can be useful in evaluating client defensiveness and hostile construction. Kegan (1982) used Piagetian dialectical constructivism and Feixas (1995) was influenced by systems theory in their respective illustrations of how the individual and his or her environment interact to drive development.

Kelly (1955) dispensed with traditional diagnostic entities, such as schizophrenia and depression, and reconceptualized other constructs, such as anxiety. However, PCT has also been applied to some traditional categories of diagnosis, including depression and anxiety (Sanz, Avia, & Sánchez-Bernardos, 1996), panic disorder (Pfenninger & Klion, 1997), eating disorders (Button, 1983; Marsh & Stanley, 1995; G. J. Neimeyer & Khouzam, 1985), schizophrenia (Bannister, 1963; Carroll, 1983), obsessions (Rigdon & Epting, 1983), chemical dependency (Klion & Pfenninger, 1997), and many other conditions (R. A. Neimeyer & Neimeyer, 1987; Winter, 1992). PCT constructs may be used to offer an explanatory model of the etiology of a disorder or as a descriptive model of the processes of individuals with a particular diagnosis.

For example, Yelich and Salamone (1994) argued that the DSM concept of attention deficit hyperactivity disorder (ADHD) represents an atheoretical consensual reality arrived at by committee. They offered numerous critiques of neurobiological formulations of ADHD, including the fact that the disorder has a habit of manifesting itself only when the child is placed in social contexts outside of the immediate family. In addition, ADHD seems to be concentrated in families of lower socioeconomic status who are likely to be subject to numerous social and financial stressors.

Yelich and Salamone (1994) proposed that ADHD arises when children have not been able to develop adequate schemas or construct systems to regulate their autonomic arousal in a socially acceptable manner. In their modified constructivist model, ADHD children, like all children and adults, act on the basis of their construct systems in such a way as to maintain an optimal level of arousal. School situations continually present the child with new and likely discrepant information, thus increasing arousal that the child attempts to modulate using previously learned, but not situationally appropriate, strategies. ADHD children's attempts at arousal modulation are labeled as misbehavior by adults in their environment, offering further invalidation and leading to still more arousal and dyscontrol. Activities that are consistent with a low level of arousal, such as remaining seated and attentive, may lead to attempts to self-regulate to a higher, more optimal level of arousal through engaging in off-task behaviors or motor activity. Over time, the child's self-construals come to resemble those of the adults who label them as "problem children," "lazy," or "unintelligent" (Yelich & Salamone, 1994). Kelly viewed motivational constructs, such as arousal modulation, as unnecessary. Concepts of transitive diagnosis might, therefore, be able to explain ADHD characteristics, such as inattention, impulsivity, and hyperactivity, without the use of motivational terms.

In PCT terms, impulsivity represents a lack of circumspection. Construing includes behaving, so an impulsive application of a construct also includes impulsive behavior. Various environmental circumstances might contribute to a child's adopting an impulsive style of construction. If a child's environment is chaotic, fast paced, or even dangerous, shortened circumspection might be highly adaptive, allowing the child to rapidly adjust to changing circumstances. If a child's environment is so chaotic as to be inherently unpredictable, impulsive construction might represent an attempt by the child to impose order on his or her world by immediately applying particular constructs across situations. Alternatively, a child who is confronted with an impoverished, nonstimulating environment may have few opportunities to develop new constructs. Therefore, the child may fail to consider alternative construals simply because of a limited range of different constructs in memory or limited experience with behavioral experiments. Such an impoverished construct system might also account for other aspects of ADHD.

A child who lacks a range of constructs from which to draw might have great difficulty attending to a variety of environmental inputs and stimuli. One cannot adequately attend to an event for which one has no relevant constructs. Without a broad range of constructs, there is no basis for categorization and interpretation of experience. When a child has limited constructs to use in understanding his or her world, he or she may be frequently confronted with anxiety (the realization that events lie outside of the range of convenience of his or her construct system). Anxiety can produce confusion (Kelly, 1955) or loosening, both of which could be observed as deficits in attention. Anxiety may also lead to impulsivity, as one attempts to "bring some semblance of structure to bear upon his [or her] problems" (Kelly, 1955, p. 527). Kellian aggression might also result from anxiety, as one tries to elaborate or develop one's construct system. Aggression implies activity, perhaps even to a degree that is intrusive to others.

Even if stronger evidence of neurobiological substrates of ADHD is identified, PCT constructs might be descriptively useful in understanding the phenomenology and cognitive style of someone who receives that diagnosis. Kelly (1955) commented on the inflexible styles of construal shown by head-injured individuals. Idiographic assessment of an ADHD child's or adult's construct systems would be useful to cognitive or cognitive–behaviorally oriented therapists. The transitive diagnostic constructs described above might also offer a glimpse into the phenomenology of someone for whom the world may seem a confusing or perhaps slow and unstimulating place.

Broader Clinical Applications

R. A. Neimeyer (1988) proposed that PCT serve as an integrative theory for clinicians who hold constructivist metatheoretical assumptions. Kelly (1955) himself noted that in the future, "clinicians [will be] choosing treatment measures from a much bigger bag of tricks" (p. 777). Most practitioners describe themselves as eclectic. Even Freud appeared to have applied interventions that could be described only as multisystemic (see Yalom, 1980, p. 4). As R. A. Neimeyer, and others (e.g., Lazarus, 1992), pointed out, technical eclecticism without the guidance of an integrative theory may degenerate into picking cards at random from a deck of interventions and dealing them to an unfortunate client.

R. A. Neimeyer (1988) used tight versus loose construing as an example of a PCT construct that offers integrative potential. The entire range of transitive diagnostic constructs that we discussed offers similar potential. Construction is expressed in behavior, so the use of behavioral techniques in response to a transitive diagnosis is internally consistent. Even behavior therapists have noted the similarities between Kelly's fixed-role therapy and behavioral interventions, such as modeling (Bandura, 1969), and behavioral rehearsal (Goldfried & Davison, 1976). Transitive diagnostic constructs might be used as guidelines to form plots for use in narrative therapies. Many other types of intervention, from art therapies to skills training to emotive techniques, could be used with guidance from transitive diagnosis.

Two additional applications of transitive diagnosis are worth noting. As we outlined above, transitive diagnostic constructs may be applied to systems or elements within systems, thus providing family and systemic therapists with additional conceptual tools. In addition, transitive diagnostic constructs may be applied to the therapist just as easily as to the client. What clinician has not experienced anxiety when confronted with a case he or she construed as beyond the range of convenience of his or her constructs and skills? Transitive diagnostic constructs might be useful training and supervisory tools, offering ways to characterize the therapist's movement (or lack of movement) that are more personal than archaic, dehumanizing notions, such as countertransference.

Reflexive Application to Contemporary Professional Behavior

Kelly intended his theory to be applicable to a variety of contents, therefore a transitive diagnosis could be applied to an entire diagnostic system or even an organized group of professionals. For example, those who have proposed alternatives to the *DSM* (e.g., Benjamin, 1996; Follette, 1996; McCrae, 1994) would be diagnosed as engaging in Kellian aggressiveness, attempting to expand the use of their systems. The predictable response from proponents of the *DSM* is likely to be a threat ("awareness of imminent comprehensive change in one's core role structures"; Kelly, 1955, p. 489). Even without such a perception of threat, proponents of the *DSM-IV* are engaged in acts of overt Kellian hostility by promoting the supremacy of the *DSM*, despite social and empirical invalidation of many of its core constructs.

Both psychiatry and clinical–counseling psychology face such a threat in the current mental health climate. Psychologists' attempts to obtain prescription privileges might be conceptualized as aggressiveness in response to managed care initiatives that threaten psychologists' self-construals as providers of therapy. These attempts by psychologists in turn threaten psychiatrists' core self-construals as dispensers of medical wisdom and chemical agents of control. Only time will tell whether the involved parties will respond with circumspection, preemption, and control—creatively loosening and tightening—or simply disintegrate into further hostility.

TRANSITIVE DIAGNOSIS AS METATHEORY

Constructivist metatheory has been the subject of numerous articles (Botella, 1995; Chiari & Nuzzo, 1996; R. A. Neimeyer, 1995). For example, Mahoney's (1988) critical constructivist position claims that one can know reality only imperfectly, human cognition constrains and orders one's experiences, reasoning and logic are most useful in critical rather than confirmatory analysis, and scientific data do not necessarily provide ever-closer approximations to "the truth" but rather selectively eliminate less viable models. R. A. Neimeyer (1995) emphasized knowledge as the organized product of the experiences and actions of goal-directed humans. Knowledge can be evaluated only in terms of viability and internal consistency rather than correspondence with reality. Many cognitive and cognitive–behavioral therapists have been moving in the direction of constructivism for some time (Hollon & Beck, 1994). Such therapists may find that constructivist metatheory actually offers a more comfortable home than the objectivist metatheory under which they had been attempting to operate. Experiential, interpersonal, and narrative therapists, among others, are also likely to feel comfortable in constructivist shoes. For those first dipping into the waters of constructivism, we offer the following list of metatheoretical issues and practical implications that follow from them.

Constructive Alternativism

Although constructive alternativism represents a particular philosophical position, Kelly (1955) did not intend to develop it into a "complete philosophical system" (p. 16). Constructive alternativism reminds us of the "subject–predicate error," wherein one ascribes the qualities used to construe people and things to the people and things themselves rather than understanding such designations to be rooted in and reflective of one's own psychological processes and values. In this way, Kelly was anticipating the considerable contemporary interest in biases in clinical judgment (Arkes, 1981; Dumont & Lecomte, 1987). Although Kelly might have applauded contemporary discussions of debiasing techniques, he adopted the solution of getting information straight from the "horse's mouth" (e.g., asking a client directly, using a self-characterization sketch). In this way, constructive alternativism reminds us to explore alternative interpretations of events, to consider alternative diagnostic constructs, and to treat the client as a primary source of data.

Diagnosis Equals Preemptive Construction

The PCT clinician is aware that electing to make a transitive diagnosis is selecting one construction of reality to focus on and temporarily excluding other possibilities. Preemptive construction is choosing one explanation of an event over others. To move, one must make a choice; as such, a clinician must eventually propose a hypothesis to guide the therapeutic endeavor. However, the constructivist clinician typically treats diagnoses as hypotheses or temporary choices to guide clinical work, not as permanently fixed reality statements. Such an attitude may facilitate developing habits of searching for disconfirming information and help mitigate the well-known confirmation bias. The PCT clinician also acknowledges responsibility for rendering the diagnosis. This implies a commitment to ongoing critical review of not only the therapist's diagnosis of a specific client but also his or her overall patterns of diagnostic practice.

Human Growth

Transitive diagnosis is conducted with the primary goal of advancing the developmental processes of the client. Diagnosis in the service of statistical epidemiology alone (without intervention), institutional coercion, or pressured social conformity violates the tenets of the PCT system and is an anathema to genuinely transitive diagnosis. Kelly (1995) conceptualized transitive diagnosis as "the planning stage of client management" (p. 774). Rather than traditional diagnostic categories, which have a static quality of describing the client's present state, Kelly preferred constructs with implications for change, hence transitive diagnosis. Reification of diagnostic constructs tends to freeze or deanimate the elements construed by means of such constructs. In the case of reified psychodiagnostic systems, the "elements" being construed are people. Reified people are diagnosed as "types," or as isomorphic with their presumed disease syndrome, and are in effect preempted and stereotyped. Thus dehumanized, these clients are vulnerable to control and institutional "degradation ceremonials" (Goffman, 1961).

At times, clinicians may tell clients they have a "chemical imbalance." Actually, this is a rather meaningless term because one may state that a chemical imbalance occurs when one's bladder fills and leads to a subsequent urge to urinate. What is important, for good or ill, about such a statement is what it implies for change in the client. Psychoeducational approaches often attempt to educate clients about their diagnosis as if the therapist really knew what was wrong with them. Clients who adopt "patient" as part of their core role may constrict their perceptual field and become less able and less attuned to notice opportunities to act in ways inconsistent with their role. Clients who identify with their diagnosis may reject or fail to notice evidence of their own competence and limit their activities in accordance with their assumed role. However, if clients view their diagnosis as a challenge to be overcome (e.g., in interpersonal psychotherapy for depression; Klerman, Weissman, Rounsaville, & Chevron, 1984) or as merely an incidental part of them (vs. part of their core self), even a traditional diagnosis may serve a transitive function.

CONCLUSION

Most therapists today are in a position where they may have to assign a *DSM-IV* diagnosis to a client and perhaps even communicate this diagnosis to the client. Given the prevalence of books and other media addressing specific diagnoses, clients may even enter the therapy room having already diagnosed themselves. However, even in the face of such situations, the metatheoretical assumptions we summarized outline ways in which any diagnosis might be used in a transitive fashion and as a catalyst for change.

It is particularly important to attempt to elucidate the meaning the client attributes to the diagnosis. For example, Orford (1973) found better treatment outcomes associated with nonacceptance of the "alcoholic" label prior to treatment. If a diagnosis is communicated to a client, the therapist and client should share an understanding of what that diagnosis means and what it does not mean. This might involve explaining one's philosophical position that diagnostic constructs are hunches or outlining how current scientific knowledge of psychopathology is and always will be incomplete, thus making it clear that there are many ways of understanding a client's problem. A therapist who makes a *DSM-IV* diagnosis should avoid reifying that diagnosis and consider alternative conceptualizations and diagnoses for the client.

To the constructivist, it is encouraging that therapists of different orientations are calling for the development of theoretically coherent alternatives to the *DSM* (Follette, 1996). We think that Kelly's transitive diagnostic constructs may be one of the most useful additional ways for therapists to conceptualize change. These constructs have the advantage of stemming from an existing coherent theory and being applicable not only to the individual client but also to family or social systems, organizations, or even to a therapist who feels stuck with a particular case. Transitive diagnosis offers a theoretically rigorous process psychology for guiding the work of technically eclectic therapists who wish to transcend the limitations of current diagnostic systems.

REFERENCES

American Psychiatric Association. (1952). *Diagnostic and statistical manual of mental disorders*. Washington, DC: Author.

American Psychiatric Association. (1994). *Diagnostic and statistical manual of mental disorders* (4th ed.). Washington, DC: Author.

Arkes, H. A. (1981). Impediments to accurate clinical judgment and possible ways to minimize their impact. *Journal of Consulting and Clinical Psychology, 49*, 323–330.

Bandura, A. (1969). *Principles of behavior modification*. New York: Holt, Rinehart & Winston.

Bannister, D. (1963). The genesis of schizophrenic thought disorder: A serial invalidation hypothesis. *British Journal of Psychiatry, 111*, 377–382.

Bannister, D., & Fransella, F. (1986). *Inquiring man: The psychology of personal constructs* (3rd ed.). London: Croom Helm.

Beck, A. T. (1976). *Cognitive therapy and the emotional disorders*. Madison, CT: International Universities Press.

Benjamin, L. S. (1996). *Interpersonal diagnosis and treatment of personality disorders* (2nd ed.). New York: Guilford Press.

Botella, L. (1995). Personal construct psychology, constructivism, and postmodern thought. In R. A. Neimeyer & G. J. Neimeyer (Eds.), *Advances in personal construct psychology* (Vol. 3, pp. 3–33). Greenwich, CT: JAI Press.

Berdie, R. F. (1950). Counseling methods: Diagnostics. *Annual Review of Psychology, 1*, 255–266.

Berrios, G. E. (1996). *The history of mental symptoms: Descriptive psychiatry since the nineteenth century*. Cambridge, UK: Cambridge University Press.

Bleuler, E. (1950). *Dementia praecox or the group of schizophrenias*. New York: International Universities Press. (Original work published 1911)

Button, E. (1983). Construing the anorexic. In J. Adams-Weber & J. C. Mancuso (Eds.), *Applications of personal construct theory* (pp. 305–316). New York: Academic Press.

Carr, C. (1995). *The alienist*. New York: Random House/Bantam.

Carroll, R. C. (1983). Cognitive imbalance in schizophrenia. In J. Adams-Weber & J. C. Mancuso (Eds.), *Applications of personal construct theory* (pp. 285–303). New York: Academic Press.

Chiari, G., & Nuzzo, M. L. (1996). Psychological constructivisms: A metatheoretical differentiation. *Journal of Constructivist Psychology, 9,* 163–184.

Clark, R. A. (1973). *Mental illness in perspective: History and schools of thought.* Pacific Grove, CA: Boxwood Press.

Coleman, J. C. (1950). *Abnormal psychology and modern life.* Chicago: Scott, Foresman.

Conklin, E. S. (1944). *Principles of abnormal psychology.* Holt.

Conrad, P., & Schneider, J. (1980). *Deviance and medicalization: From badness to sickness.* St. Louis, MO: Mosby.

Dorcus, R. M., & Shaffer, G. W. (1945). *Textbook of abnormal psychology.* Baltimore: Williams & Wilkins.

Dumont, F., & Lecomte, C. (1987). Inferential processes in clinical work: Inquiry into logical errors that affect diagnostic judgments. *Professional Psychology: Research and Practice, 18,* 433–438.

D'Zurilla, T. J., & Goldfried, M. R. (1971). Problem solving and behavior modification. *Journal of Abnormal Psychology, 78,* 107–126.

Feixas, G. (1995). Personal constructs in systemic practice. In R. A. Neimeyer & M. J. Mahoney (Eds.), *Constructivism in psychotherapy* (pp. 305–337). Washington, DC: American Psychological Association.

Follette, W. C. (1996). Introduction to the special section on the development of theoretically coherent alternatives to the *DSM* system. *Journal of Consulting and Clinical Psychology, 64,* 1117–1119.

Fransella, F. (1995). *George Kelly.* London: Sage.

Fransella, F., & Bannister, D. (1977). *A manual for repertory grid technique.* London: Academic Press.

Fransella, F., & Dalton, P. (1990). *Personal construct counseling in action.* London: Sage.

Freud, S. (1966). Project for a scientific psychology. In J. Strachey (Ed. & Trans.), *The standard edition of the complete psychological works of Sigmund Freud* (Vol. 1, pp. 283–387). London: Hogarth. (Original work published 1895)

Gardner, H. (1993). *Creating minds.* New York: Basic Books.

Glass, C. R., Merluzzi, T. V., Biever, J. L., & Larsen, K. H. (1982). Cognitive assessment of social anxiety: Development and validation of a self-statement questionnaire. *Cognitive Therapy and Research, 6,* 37–55.

Goffman, E. (1961). *Asylums.* Garden City, NY: Doubleday.

Goldfried, M. R., & Davison, G. C. (1976). *Clinical behavior therapy*. New York: Holt, Rinehart & Winston.

Grob, G. N. (1991). Origins of *DSM-I*: A study in appearance and reality. *American Journal of Psychiatry, 148,* 421–431.

Herrick, C. J. (1931). *An introduction to neurology*. Philadelphia: Saunders.

Hollon, S. D., & Beck, A. T. (1994). Cognitive and cognitive–behavioral therapies. In A. E. Bergin & S. L. Garfield (Eds.), *Handbook of psychotherapy and behavior change* (4th ed., pp. 428–466). New York: Wiley.

Hollon, S. D., & Kendall, P. C. (1980). Cognitive self-statements in depression: Development of an automatic thoughts questionnaire. *Cognitive Therapy and Research, 4,* 383–395.

Kegan, R. (1982). *The evolving self: Problem and process in human development*. Cambridge, MA: Harvard University Press.

Kelly, G. (1955). *The psychology of personal constructs* (Vols 1 & 2). New York: Norton.

Kelly, G. (1958). Theory and technique of assessment. *Annual Review of Psychology, 9,* 323–352.

Kelly, G. (1969a). The autobiography of a theory. In B. Maher (Ed.), *Clinical psychology and personality: The selected papers of George Kelly* (pp. 46–65). New York: Wiley.

Kelly, G. (1969b). Man's construction of his alternatives. In B. Maher (Ed.), *Clinical psychology and personality: The selected papers of George Kelly* (pp. 66–93). New York: Wiley.

Kelly, G. (1969c). The psychotherapeutic relationship. In B. Maher (Ed.), *Clinical psychology and personality: The selected papers of George Kelly* (pp. 216–223). New York: Wiley.

Kelly, G. (1969d). The role of classification in personality theory. In B. Maher (Ed.), *Clinical psychology and personality: The selected papers of George Kelly* (pp. 289–300). New York: Wiley.

Klerman, G. L. (1986). Historical perspectives on contemporary schools of psychopathology. In T. Millon & G. L. Klerman (Eds.), *Contemporary directions in psychopathology: Toward the DSM-IV* (pp. 3–28). New York: Guilford Press.

Klerman, G. L., Weissman, M. M., Rounsaville, B. J., & Chevron, E. (1984). *Interpersonal psychotherapy of depression*. New York: Basic Books.

Klion, R. E., & Pfenninger, D. T. (1997). Personal construct psychotherapy of addictions. *Journal of Substance Abuse Treatment, 14,* 37–43.

Kraepelin, E. (1919). *Dementia praecox and paraphrenia* (R. M. Barclay, Trans.). Edinburgh, UK: E & S Livingstone. (Original work published 1913)

Kraepelin, E. (1921). *Manic-depressive insanity and paranoia* (R. M. Barclay, Trans.). Edinburgh, UK: E & S Livingstone. (Original work published 1913)

Landfield, A. (1976). A personal construct approach to suicidal behavior. In P. Slater (Ed.), *Explorations of intrapersonal space* (pp. 93–108). London: Wiley.

Landfield, A., & Epting, F. (1987). *Personal construct psychology: Clinical and personality assessment*. New York: Human Sciences Press.

Lazarus, A. A. (1992). Multimodal therapy: Technical eclecticism with minimal integration. In J. C. Norcross & M. R. Goldfried (Eds.), *Handbook of psychotherapy integration* (pp. 231–263). New York: Basic Books.

Leitner, L. (1995). Dispositional assessment techniques in experiential personal construct psychotherapy. *Journal of Constructivist Psychology, 8*, 53–74.

Leitner, L., & Pfenninger, D. (1994). Sociality and optimal functioning. *Journal of Constructivist Psychology, 7*, 119–135.

Mahoney, M. J. (1988). Constructive metatheory: I. Basic features and historical foundations. *International Journal of Personal Construct Psychology, 1*, 1–36.

Mahoney, M. J. (1991). *Human change processes*. New York: Basic Books.

Marsh, M., & Stanley, R. (1995). Assessment of self and others during treatment for anorexia nervosa. *Journal of Constructivist Psychology, 8*, 97–116.

McCoy, M. (1977). A reconstruction of emotion. In D. Bannister (Ed.), *New perspectives in personal construct theory* (pp. 93–124). London: Academic Press.

McCrae, R. R. (1994). A reformulation of Axis II: Personality and personality-related problems. In P. T. Costa, Jr., & T. A. Widiger (Eds.), *Personality disorders and the Five-Factor model of personality* (pp. 303–309). Washington, DC: American Psychological Association.

McKinney, F. (1948). Directive techniques. In L. A. Pennington & I. A. Berg (Eds.), *An introduction to clinical psychology* (pp. 443–464). New York: Ronald Press.

Morgan, J. J. B. (1936). *Psychology of the unadjusted school child*. New York: Macmillan.

Neimeyer, G. J. (1993). (Ed.). *Constructivist assessment: A casebook*. Newbury Park, CA: Sage.

Neimeyer, G. J., & Khouzam, N. (1985). A repertory grid study of restrained eaters. *British Journal of Medical Psychology, 58*, 365–367.

Neimeyer, R. A. (1985). *The development of personal construct psychology*. Lincoln: University of Nebraska Press.

Neimeyer, R. A. (1988). Integrative directions in personal construct therapy. *International Journal of Personal Construct Psychology, 1*, 283–297.

Neimeyer, R. A. (1995). Constructivist psychotherapies: Features, foundations, and future directions. In R. A. Neimeyer & M. J. Mahoney (Eds.), *Constructivism in psychotherapy* (pp. 11–38). Washington, DC: American Psychological Association.

Neimeyer, R. A., & Neimeyer, G. J. (Eds.). (1987). *Personal construct therapy casebook*. New York: Springer.

O'Kelly, L. I., & Muckler, F. A. (1955). *Introduction to psychopathology*. Englewood Cliffs, NJ: Prentice-Hall.

Orford, J. (1973). A comparison of alcoholics whose drinking is totally uncontrolled and those whose drinking is mainly controlled. *Behavior Research and Therapy, 11*, 565–576.

Pfenninger, D., & Klion, R. (1995). Re-thinking hostility: Is it ever better to fight than switch? In R. A. Neimeyer & G. J. Neimeyer (Eds.), *Advances in personal construct psychology* (Vol. 3, pp. 271–289). Greenwich, CT: JAI Press.

Pfenninger, D., & Klion, R. (1997, August). *Toward a constructivist model of panic*. Paper presented at the 105th Annual Convention of the American Psychological Association, Chicago, IL.

Rigdon, M. A., & Epting, F. R. (1983). A personal construct perspective on an obsessive client. In J. Adams-Weber & J. C. Mancuso (Eds.), *Applications of personal construct theory* (pp. 249–263). New York: Academic Press.

Rogers, C. R. (1942). *Counseling and psychotherapy: Newer concepts in practice*. Boston: Houghton Mifflin.

Rosenhan, D. (1973). On being sane in insane places. *Science, 179,* 250–258.

Sanz, J., Avia, M. D., & Sánchez-Bernardos, M. L. (1996). The structure of the construct system in social anxiety: Qualifications due to affective confounding. *Journal of Constructivist Psychology, 9,* 201–212.

Sarbin, T., & Mancuso, J. (1980). *Schizophrenia: Medical diagnosis or moral verdict?* Elmsford, NY: Pergamon Press.

Scheff, T. (1975). (Ed). *Labeling madness*. Englewood Cliffs, NJ: Prentice-Hall.

Winter, D. (1992). *Personal construct psychology in clinical practice: Theory, research, and applications*. London: Routledge.

Yalom, I. D. (1980). *Existential psychotherapy*. New York: Basic Books.

Yelich, G., & Salamone, F. J., Jr. (1994). Constructivist interpretation of attention-deficit hyperactivity disorder. *Journal of Constructivist Psychology, 7,* 191–212.

Zelhart, P. F., & Jackson, T. T. (1983). George A. Kelly, 1931–1943: Environmental influences on a developing theorist. In J. Adams-Weber & J. C. Mancuso (Eds.), *Applications of personal construct theory* (pp. 137–154). New York: Academic Press.

8

DIAGNOSING HUMAN MEANING MAKING: AN EXPERIENTIAL CONSTRUCTIVIST APPROACH

LARRY M. LEITNER, APRIL J. FAIDLEY, AND MARK A. CELENTANA

Sociality is a fundamental tenet of human existence. Throughout life, a person experiences life through relationships, albeit in myriad forms and expression: the ecstasy of unity with and completion by another or heart-wrenching abandonment, estrangement, or mistreatment; the delight of acceptance and validation from another or the inscrutability and pain of being misunderstood or attacked; the awe of the reverence of others or the degradation of the baseness of others. George Kelly (1955/1991a) addressed the basic sociality of our existence in his corollary "to the extent that one person construes the construction process of another, he [or she] may play a role in a social process involving the other person" (p. 66). Experiential personal construct psychotherapy has evolved by pursuing the profound implications arising from this sparse and skeletal corollary (Leitner, 1988).

This chapter is an elaboration of a paper presented at the 102nd Annual Convention of the American Psychological Association, Los Angeles, CA, in August 1994. All clinical material has been distorted to protect client confidentiality. We acknowledge Elgan Baker for his discussions of structural arrests. We thank Lara Honos-Webb for her comments on an earlier version of this chapter.

Other people are not merely dispassionate objects that inhabit a neutral space and with which someone periodically interacts as he or she goes about living. Rather, others always have the potential to validate or invalidate a person. As John, for example, perceives and construes his contact with others, he constantly evaluates, either consciously or at a lower level of awareness, the texture and quality of his relationships to others: What are the meanings of the others' words, actions, facial expressions, gestures, and tone? After all, John has been learning to filter his experience along these dimensions from the moment he was born, when his very survival depended on others. The terror an infant must feel if he or she is ignored or mistreated contrasts strikingly to the feelings of security, contentment, and fulfillment of being cherished and nurtured with care. The same potential for terror or fulfillment exists for all throughout life. This fundamental issue in human relationships is the central theme of experiential personal construct psychotherapy.

Vital, significant relationships based on a mutual, deep revealing of selves are essential for meaning and richness in life. In experiential personal construct terms, these relationships are referred to as "ROLE relationships" (Leitner, 1985). This condenses what can be only descriptively explained in two words. The term ROLE *relationship* distinguishes deeply significant relationships from those based solely or primarily on the social roles the participants assume with one another. Although such an intimate relationship offers the promise of fulfillment and profound satisfaction, it also poses terrifying threat. The more deeply intimate a relationship, the more the relationship's partners are mutually revealing and coming to know the most central meaning-making processes of one another. Each person in a ROLE relationship permits the other to know something of her or his core being. If you affirm or validate another's most central processes of creating meaning and maintaining existence, the relationship can be extremely enriching. However, should you disconfirm the most fundamental definers of who that person is, she or he can be overwhelmingly invalidated (Epting & Leitner, 1994; Leitner & Faidley, 1995). Thus, everyone is confronted with this basic dilemma: A person can protect the self from the terror of invalidation by revealing less of oneself and lead an empty but safe existence or risk (and invariably also experience) the terror of invalidation to gain the richness and depth that life in a ROLE relationship can bestow. The depth of terror around potential injury leads people to find ways of retreating from the genuine ROLE experience of person-to-person engagement. Experiential personal construct psychotherapy explores the ways that clients risk and retreat from ROLE relationships. In particular, this therapy challenges the client to struggle with trying to connect with (or avoid) the potential ROLE relationship with the therapist, placing the interpersonal struggle into the "living relationship" (Epting & Leitner, 1994, p. 141) of the therapy room.

Ideally, this genuine encounter allows both therapist and client to grow within the relationship.

All attempts to aid people begin with a diagnosis of some sort. Raskin and Epting (1993) showed how the approach used in the *Diagnostic and Statistical Manual of Mental Disorders* (DSM; American Psychiatric Association, 1994) for labeling psychopathology is problematic. In addition to the conceptual problems inherent with the *DSM* labels, these labels tell very little about understanding a person in ways that lead to treatment options. In his discussion of transitive diagnosis, Kelly (1955/1991a, 1955/1991b) clearly stated that diagnosis is a useful and valuable enterprise *when it points to ways of understanding the client that facilitate personal growth.* (Faidley & Leitner, 1993, and Leitner, 1995, discuss this issue more fully.)

Because treatment can be understood as the application of theory to distress, any diagnostic system must be relevant to the theory being used by the clinician. From an experiential personal construct perspective, a useful diagnostic system must illuminate how the client negotiates ROLE relationships and, thus, must point to ways of helping the client in his or her life struggles. In this chapter, we describe such a system of understanding others. We expect this system to evolve because we are open enough to learn more from our clients and from our own lives about the complex interplay among risk, safety, and meaningfulness in ROLE relationships. We make no claims that this system is, or ever will become, the ultimate understanding of human struggles.

We present this system by focusing on three interrelated components of diagnosing human meaning making. (We provide a summary of these components in Table 8.1.) First, we describe some ways of understanding

Table 8.1.
Diagnostic Axes of Human Meaning Making

Developmental–structural issues	Interpersonal components	Experiential components
Construct of self versus other Self–other permanence Self–other constancy (Attachments)	Undispersed dependency Excessively dispersed dependency Dependency avoidance Physically distancing self Psychologically distancing self	Discrimination Flexibility Creativity Responsibility Openness Commitment Courage Forgiveness Reverence

Note: The system assumes that in cases where developmental–structural arrests have occurred, many of the interpersonal and experiential struggles over ROLE relationships are linked to the arrest. The traumas associated with the arrest would need to be reconstrued before any meaningful change could occur on the interpersonal and experiential axes. In cases where the developmental–structural arrests have not occurred, therapy can be more time limited and address the interpersonal and experiential issues more directly.

developmental traumas that necessitate truncation of ROLE relating. Understanding these developmental sources of crippled ROLE relating is vital because most core constructs are developed early in life (Kelly, 1955/1991a, 1955/1991b) and any new core processes will either account for or, at least, be shaded by experiences in one's life. Furthermore, if the therapist does not have an understanding of the processes that led to his or her client's choice of emptiness, he or she will have failed to establish a ROLE relationship in the therapy room and experiential personal construct psychotherapy will likely fail. Next, we discuss some interpersonal presentations of client struggles. Finally, we describe ways that the client's struggles can be seen through the client's experiences in the world.

Before beginning, we would like to point out that theoreticians and therapists from many diverse orientations have struggled with systematically understanding the process of human meaning making. The reader may find that aspects of our system are similar to others who have attempted to understand human subjectivity. Examples of these other approaches include attachment theory (e.g., Bowlby, 1969), psychoanalytic theory (e.g., Luborsky & Crits-Cristoph, 1990), and dialogical theory (e.g., Friedman, 1985), among many others. We believe that similarity to theoretical systems with similar goals provides external validity for aspects of our system.

DEVELOPMENTAL STRUCTURAL ISSUES

Core constructs are developed early in life, primarily through interactions with family and caretakers; these include central experiential graspings of self and of others that facilitate or hinder ROLE relating. Because new meanings must account for the experiences subsumed under older core structures and to the extent that the therapist cannot grasp his or her client's core processes, he or she is limiting the ROLE relationship (and hence therapy). An understanding of the development of the construction of self and other is important in psychotherapy. We begin this section with a theoretical overview. Next, we discuss various aspects of self and other that can be arrested because of overwhelming personal disconfirmation early in life.

Theoretical Overview

Beginning with Bannister and Agnew (1977), personal construct psychologists have found that children's construing is fundamentally different from adult's. For example, Barratt (1977) discovered that children's construing developed from physical descriptions of others (e.g., "tall") through social role meanings ("my father") and behavioral descriptions ("spanks me") into more personality-oriented understandings ("tough hearted") by adolescence. Given the relatively unsophisticated nature of childhood construing, many events either will be understood in simplistic ways or, if too far beyond the current meaning system, not construed at all. Kelly (1955/1991a, 1955/1991b) described the process as suspending events that are too incompatible with one's existing meaning system. Events that are suspended are still capable of being construed at a later time after the person through his or her construct system is able to grasp them more completely. Until such a time arrives, they remain at a lower level of awareness.

For Kelly (1955/1991a), suspension was related to threat. "In contrast with some notions of repression, suspension implies that the idea or element of experience is forgotten simply because the person can, at the moment, *tolerate no structure* within which the idea would have meaning" (p. 349, emphasis added). He emphasized this later when he stated that "ideas are not suspended because of their intrinsic nature but rather because their implications are *intolerable*" (p. 350, emphasis added). Kelly was describing events that are not merely painful and threatening, rather they are so overwhelmingly threatening as to be intolerable. We use the term *trauma* to describe such events, although other events may be traumatic that have not been suspended. (Note the ways that a constructivist understanding of trauma is based more on the interaction between events and inner meanings than on an "objective" classification of traumatic events. In this way, a constructivist conceptualization of trauma has greater therapeutic richness.)

Leitner (1999) described how when exposed to such traumas, the very process of meaning making itself can "freeze" around such issues. Because childhood construing is more simple and concrete, one may be less able to tolerate the implications of events that threaten the very nature of one's relationships with parents and other people who can literally hold one's lives in their hands (see discussion on dependency below). This implies that the freezing of the process of meaning making is more likely to occur around issues of childhood traumas rather than ones that occur later in life. Because, for Kelly, the process of meaning creation is the essence of psychological life itself, one winds up with a numbed existence instead of being psychologically alive (Leitner, in press). Finally, events that one sees as resembling the initial traumas also may be frozen because of the overwhelming terror evoked by one's remembrance of the original horrors (Leitner, 1999).

Because people are fundamentally ROLE relationship seeking, they are from early on in their childhood seeking understandings of themselves and others that allow for the intimacy they need. In their early ROLE relationships, they use the rudimentary construals we have so far formulated. If one was traumatized severely during the time when these rudimentary meanings were dominant, the freezing of one's construing process may place one in serious trouble throughout life. *Structural arrests* (Leitner, 1997) are the freezing of the meaning-making process, such that self, other, and relationships are predominantly experienced as they were in these earlier periods of life. Psychotherapy for people who are more severely disturbed is difficult without a grasp of these fundamental early constructions. Without such understandings, the world of the severely disturbed person could be so confusing and chaotic that the therapist may tend to reach for toxic chemicals (i.e., psychotropic "medications") to control and numb the client. In this section, we briefly summarize three understandings of self–other meanings described in more detail elsewhere (Leitner, 1997). We also briefly explore the implications of these self–other constructions for the attachment process, which is so vital in truly connecting with other humans.

Self Versus Other

If experiences of the world are based on constructions, a person cannot create constructions of self, other, and relationships before having a construct of self versus other in place. Without such a construct, the world is chaotic, stormy, and unpredictable because without the ability to separate self from other, one cannot even recognize the existence of others, much less connect to another in any meaningful way. As a matter of fact, much of psychological life can be seen in terms of the elaboration of a construct of self–other (Kegan, 1982). Should interpersonal aspects of the meaning-making process be frozen prior to the development of this basic construction, a person would probably not survive outside of a highly structured, institutional setting.

One's initial construction of self–other is based on the sensory–physical meaning system that begins to be developed early in life (Barratt, 1977; Klion & Leitner, 1985). One possible basis for the beginnings of this self–other construct is the existence of a "skin barrier," which allows one to experience certain events inside of the self and other events outside of the self (Leitner, 1997). However, defining self and other in terms of the skin barrier can be problematic; psychological boundaries between people are more complex, permeable, and changeable than physical ones. To the extent that understandings of self and other are frozen around the physical "inside of me–outside of me" construction, ROLE relationships are drastically limited. One may tend to construe people as totally self-contained organisms who bump into one another rather than beings who interconnect. In so doing, the ROLE experience of psychologically intertwining is experienced as a massive invasion of self, resulting in "psychotic" terror around connection.

Alternatively, a person can be unaware of the impact of his or her being on others who attempt to connect with the person. One can be emotionally neglectful of another and not grasp the reasons why that other feels empty and isolated in the relationship. The other's injuries around such neglect are experienced as the other's responsibility rather than the other's, the person's, and theirs in different ways. The net result is experiencing extreme internal emptiness as the relational world is experienced more as using the other to meet one's needs or, at best, giving the other what he or she needs so that he or she will give back to one what one needs. This objectification of others and relationships has been linked to profound emptiness within personal construct psychology (Leitner, 1985).

Self–Other Permanence

Similar to object permanence, self–other permanence is based on the fact that because ROLE relationships involve commitments over time (Leitner, 1985; Leitner & Pfenninger, 1994), they are difficult or impossible until one creates a sense of permanence of self and other. If a person has no sense of another's permanence, the other literally ceases to exist when outside of the person's awareness. Thus, a person is extremely fearful of any separateness in relationships. When a person is apart from the other there is no *other* out there who cares for, is invested in, and loves that person. The relationship is gone, and the person is absolutely alone. Without self-permanence, a person may cease to exist (experientially) as he or she becomes aware of the reality of the other. Thus, the person lacking self–other permanence cannot resonate with and empathically respond to the other's needs and may experience the other's needs as massively invasive.

During childhood, when making the transition from one manner of construing to another (e.g., from behaviors to personality construing), the child may lose the ability to use the newer ways of meaningfully grasping the world at times of greater psychological stress. (Klion & Leitner, 1985, provide data consistent with this assertion.) Applied to the struggle for self–other permanence, there would be a period where as long as things were not too complicated or stressful, one would be able to grasp self and others as permanent. However, this newly acquired ability would be lost if life were to become too stressful. Should a person experience severe trauma and freeze the process of meaning making at this transition point, he or she may look quite healthy when life is calm and peaceful but look extremely disturbed when life is hard and stressful. Because much of life involves considerable stress, people injured in this way never quite live up to the potential they show during the better times. As they age, the mounting guilt over failed potentials can become overwhelming. Writing from a family systems perspective, Bowen (e.g., 1976) provided a similar conceptualization in his discussion of functioning being tied to both the level of anxiety and the degree of integration of self.

Self–Other Constancy

Because ROLE relationships fundamentally are connections between people who are constantly evolving and changing in the process of creating meaning, they cannot flourish without a sense of self–other constancy. Without constancy, one cannot integrate new experiences of self and other into a coherent sense of identity. Absent constancy, if one sees another as caring for one, then the other is wonderful, nurturing, and connected. If one construes the other as angry, then the other becomes evil, malevolent, and rejecting. The other person cannot be a caring person who loves but also is angry. Likewise, when one is angry at another, one loses contact with the parts that love and nurture the other and may modify or transform one's anger.

Obviously, lack of self–other constancy limits relational depth because significant aspects of experience cannot be admitted into the relationship. How intimate can a relationship be if when one is sad, angry, bitter, or bored, the other's experience of their connection is destroyed? How horrifying are relationships where, each time the other becomes bitter or angry, the person loses touch with the security of knowing the other cares about him or her? How much self-knowledge can one have if the experience of anger or intense jealousy means the loss of all integrity and goodness as a person?

Once again, as this important construction of self and other is developing, there is a time at which it has been created but is not well integrated into the meaning-making system. At this point, one can experience constancy when things are going well but can lose this experience when life gets too stressful. If the construing process is frozen at this point, a person may look very healthy during the good periods of life. Intellectually, a person knows that the other can care for and be angry with him or her also. However, when the stress of construing the other as angry continues or increases, a person loses touch with the "whole" other and cannot be calmed, soothed, and cared for in the relationship. All that a person experiences is the "angry" other. After a person has mastered this new way of construing self and other, it is no longer lost during times of stress.

Attachments

As their understandings of self and other develop, people become more able to attach to others in significant ways. Attachment is closely related to dependence because the other is a vital validator of one's meanings. However, attachment has more to do with the felt sense of the dependence than whether one is over- or underdispersed or avoidant of one's dependence (see below). If a person reaches the point of well-integrated self–other constancy, attachments to others are based on a sense of security and confidence. A person can trust central others in life to care for and nurture him or her. The points at which a person feels frightened and insecure may be useful messages about the frailty or temporariness of the current relationship.

If a person does not develop constructions of self and other that allow for a sense of others as permanent and constant, attachments are more insecure. One may approach others always feeling anxious and frightened because of the likelihood of abandonment. A person may attempt to be so nice, unassuming, and nonburdensome that others will not abandon or betray him or her. (If one does not have self–other constancy, any experience of the other as inconsistent with nurturing can be experienced as abandonment and betrayal.) A person may implicitly or explicitly construe the relationship between the world and the self as "If I am nice enough, you will love me." This construction has much in common with Horney's (1945) "moving toward people" interpersonal style.

Insecure attachment style also may manifest itself in anger and hostility. If John cannot trust another's being there for him, then he may respond to any relational failures on another's part by becoming outraged. Anger may be the basic mode through which he experiences the world. John senses others as being concerned only for themselves; he is going to do what it takes to make sure they give him what he needs and will not injure him. (Once again, without self–other constancy, any experience of another as inconsistent in an affirmation of John may be experienced as betrayal.) John may, implicitly or explicitly, be construing the world, such that "If I am on my guard and am powerful enough, you will not betray me." This construction has much in common with Horney's (1945) "moving against people" interpersonal style.

Finally, insecure attachments may be revealed by one's seeming indifference to others as validating agents (Landfield, 1988). In this style, others' confirmation causes no joy and their disconfirmation causes no pain. Rather a person seems independent, aloof, and unresponsive to human emotions. One seems to be operating from a construction of the world that communicates with "If I am distant and uncaring enough, you cannot hurt me." This construction has much in common with Horney's (1945) "moving away from people" interpersonal style.

DIAGNOSING HUMAN MEANING MAKING: INTERPERSONAL COMPONENTS

ROLE relationships involve more than construing the meaning-making process of another. They involve actions based on one's understandings, actions in the real world of relational risk and awe (Leitner, 1985). In this section, we discuss a major principle within experiential personal construct psychotherapy: the interpersonal component of diagnosis. We also show the use of this organizing principle through a discussion of a few interpersonal styles. This principle can be seen in a discussion of a significant paradox inherent in our discussion of ROLE relationships: the reasons one seeks such relationships in the first place.

ROLE relationships are essential to the experience of richness and meaning in the world. Without them, a person is left with an existence that is empty and impoverished. However, to the extent that one attempts to connect with others to reduce emptiness, one fails to develop a ROLE relationship. Such connections use the other as a means to the end of being less isolated and empty. To this extent, the other is not a unique, evolving, subjective creature in his or her own right; the other is there to meet one's needs. This relative objectification of the other contradicts an essential component of ROLE relationships. A person must engage in a ROLE relationship because of a genuine caring for another, not because of emptiness and aloneness. Emptiness disappears as a by-product of the ROLE relationship because the emptiness was present as a communication to one's self that one had failed to develop mutually affirming ROLE relationships.

This paradox (emptiness without ROLE relationships yet the impossibility of forming a ROLE relationship if one does so to reduce emptiness) forms the basis of the interpersonal components of the diagnostic system. Interpersonal actions can be conceptualized in terms of the ways they use another to reduce a person's experience of emptiness. Actions where significant others are used as a means to an end can be seen as pathological. Alternatively, actions that grasp the wonder of the other can be viewed as healthy. We now illustrate this principle with some examples of interpersonal styles that we view as problematic.

Undispersed Dependency

Kelly defined *dependency construing* as construing on which one's very survival as a person is based. Dependency constructs, whose formation begins very early, are originally based on literally needing adults to feed and care for one to live. These constructs then become the framework for structuring relationships that enliven people, as well as keep them physically alive. Rather than viewing dependency as problematic, Kelly (1955/1991a, 1955/1991b) was more interested in how clients allocated their dependencies. In particular, he believed that people who did not disperse their dependencies over a number of others could easily experience psychological distress. Should George place his dependencies on another or a limited number of others and be abandoned, he would be in crisis. Affirmation of central meanings enlivens him and George's only source of affirmation becomes a source of disconfirmation. In other words, to the extent that George does not disperse his dependencies, another's meeting of his needs is so critical that it is very difficult to tolerate the other's separate evolution; to this extent, the other is objectified, despite the depth of George's passions about the relationship. Walker (1990, 1993) provided a more detailed account of the problems with undispersed dependency.

Excessively Dispersed Dependency

Other people show problems in ROLE relating through excessively dispersing dependencies. Rather than counting on another or an extreme few people to affirm their most central meanings, these people allow many people to confirm or disconfirm their cores. The excessively dispersed dependent person often shows problems with *under*discrimination (see below). In other words, rather than arranging others along a hierarchy from minor strangers to profound validating agents (Landfield, 1988), most people are significant validating agents and capable of threatening the very survival of such a person. Life can be a chaotic roller coaster of intense joys and great devastations as any and all others touch this person's central meanings.

The excessively dispersed person views most others as major confirmers of his or her meanings. Because no one is able to establish extensive ROLE relationships with a large number of people (it takes too much time), such a person's view of most people is more along the lines of an object to affirm the self rather than a unique, evolving other. In other words, the need to experience validational feedback is so large that others cannot be seen in their own right. For example, if Sue disconfirms Bob's meanings and Bob is counting on Sue for his very survival, he will find it difficult to understand, even celebrate, their differences. To the extent that Sue is an "affirmation machine" for Bob's dependencies, Bob cannot see Sue as someone who needs confirmation and understanding for herself.

Dependency Avoidance

Still other people show struggles with ROLE relationships through avoiding most or all dependencies. In some ways, such a person resembles someone who has excessively dispersed dependencies because no one will hold a more central place as a confirmer or disconfirmer of life meanings than any other person. In other ways, this person resembles someone who struggles with undispersed dependencies because most people's validational reactions have little effect on the person's meaning-making process. However, it would be a clinical error to see the person who is avoiding dependencies as similar to the person who struggles with dependency through under- or overdispersion.

Dependency is inherent in ROLE relationships. To the extent that Sue allows another into her most central meanings, she is dependent on the other's confirmations and disconfirmations. Although Sue may be able to use other ROLE relationships to deal with the devastation of another's invalidations without losing all psychological balance and stability, there is no protection from painful disconfirmation in a ROLE relationship. The person described as avoidant of dependency allows no others into the central processes of his or her existence. There is no mutual subjectivity and interaction. Rather than viewing dependency as potentially healthy, all of this person's feelings of dependency are signs of inadequacy and weakness. Although others may be allowed to lean on the self, the avoider cannot reciprocate. In so doing, the avoider denies others the opportunity to be in a reciprocal ROLE relationship and is using others as a means to an end.

Physically Distancing Self

Because physical proximity can provide greater contact and therefore greater potential for relational confirmation and disconfirmation, people can manifest struggles with ROLE relationships through physically retreating from the other. These people literally flee the relationship when the potential for a ROLE connection is present. For example, a man was excited about a relationship and pursued its growth and development through months as his significant other made her way through her separation and divorce, only to end the relationship when all of the obstacles were gone and they began to talk about marriage. People who physically distance themselves may or may not tell the other that the relationship is terminated. Sometimes they leave the area; other times they merely leave the relationship.

Other people use physical distance as a way of limiting intimacy without actually ending the relationship. These people may find reasons to be physically absent for excessive periods of time, use external justifications (e.g., job, other friends, volunteer commitments) for the lack of time spent in a relationship, or subtly absent themselves even when they are in the same residence (e.g., by engaging in a hobby, talking on the telephone, or going to bed early). Clinically, one can infer such a style when a person is unwilling to consider alternatives that would decrease the physical distance, is unwilling to give up responsibility to be with the partner in an activity desired by the other, and does not experience sadness at the loss of time together. The physically distancing defense is often manifested as a stoic, "that's the way life is," attitude.

Psychologically Distancing Self

A person does not have to physically leave a relationship to distance the self from another. One can also distance oneself while living with the other. Such psychological distancing is much more common than the physical distancing discussed above. One can objectify the other in innumerable ways. For example, Susan can be a source of sexual gratification. Ed can be someone to cook meals. Jana can be someone to handle domestic responsibilities, leaving the other person free to pursue alternate goals. Bill can be the worshiper and cheerleader. Mike can be the provider of financial security. This is problematic not when such functions are a part of an ongoing role relationship but when they displace a deeper going ROLE relationship.

Clinically, psychological distancing can be inferred from the inability or unwillingness of one person to see the other as an evolving, subjective entity, with rights and dignity of his or her own. The purpose of relating to another is to solve a particular problem, meet a specific need, and so on. A person does not take joy in meeting another for its own sake. The other is nothing more than a collection of drives, attitudes, and behaviors, and one's relationship is little more than a set of activities. The mutual subjectivity inherent in ROLE relating has been sacrificed for a safe pseudo-connection.

Role of Symptoms in Diagnosis

Although we are well into our discussion of diagnosing human meaning making, we have yet to mention "symptoms." Clearly symptoms have an entirely different place in experiential constructivist diagnosis than in the *DSM*, where clusters of symptoms determine a diagnosis. Although we acknowledge that symptoms are a part of the experience of psychological difficulties, we understand their presence other than as annoying manifestations to eradicate.

The objectification of others in interpersonal life serves the valuable function of protecting one from the terrors of ROLE relating. In so doing, a person numbs the self to the joys and terrors of the ROLE experience of profound connection and profound separateness (Leitner, in press). Even the person who is undispersed in his or her dependencies is numbing the self to the experience of the separateness of the other. In other words, people experience psychological numbing when they retreat from ROLE relationships. For many people (typically called "normal"), ways of numbing "become the accepted way of living life[,] and they are able to go through life ignoring the faint whispers, coming from someplace deep within, that there must be more than what they are experiencing" (Leitner, in press).

However, others cannot ignore these whisperings. In this regard, a fundamental tenet of experiential personal constructivism is that all experiences, rather than being symptoms to eradicate, can be better understood as communications from the self to the self about the self. In other words, all experiences should be attended to and honored to learn more about aspects of the meaning-making process. The primary experiences that communicate about the retreat from ROLE relationships are the symptoms of "psychopathology" (Leitner, in press). In other words, if one has the ability to attend to them, symptoms tell others about one's struggles in ROLE relationships. As a person learns to hear them, what they are telling the person can be expressed in other ways (thus leading to the alleviation of the symptoms). This discussion leads naturally to the experiential components of ROLE relationships.

DIAGNOSING HUMAN MEANING MAKING: EXPERIENTIAL COMPONENTS

Leitner and Pfenninger (1994) developed nine interrelated aspects of empathic sociality: discrimination, flexibility, creativity, responsibility, openness, commitment, courage, forgiveness, and reverence. All people can be understood ("diagnosed") in terms of the issues associated with these concepts. However, these diagnoses are not static labels as much as descriptions of the ways a person can facilitate or retreat from ROLE relationships. Furthermore, all people show great strength as well as significant struggles in these areas. An empathic therapist resonates to the strength and integrity of the client at least as much as to the "pathology." Finally, by exploring the experiences a person has in these areas, the therapist can develop rich understandings of the experiential meanings of the issues impeding the formation of ROLE relationships.

Discrimination

Discriminating is construing the differences between two people and evaluating the subsequent impact those differences will make in a ROLE relationship (Leitner & Pfenninger, 1994). The potential in ROLE relating for massive disconfirmation and fundamental affirmation has far-reaching implications. Discrimination means that Sue, for example, anticipates the ways others may injure and affirm her. In so doing, she may choose not to enter into a ROLE relationship with another if the potential risks seem too great, and she may optimize the possibilities for healthy, mutually satisfying relationships.

There are two basic difficulties with discrimination (Leitner & Pfenninger, 1994). Some people underdiscriminate: They are willing to form ROLE relationships with most anyone, not looking at how individual differences in meaning making may lead such relationships to be difficult or impossible. However, other people overdiscriminate. These people use any differences in the other's process of meaning making as a reason for avoiding or limiting a ROLE relationship. They may be very good at initiating relationships; however, they rarely manage to maintain relationships for any period of time.

Flexibility

Not only do people differ in their personal meanings, they continue to evolve and change. A person cannot see the differences between oneself and another (necessary for discrimination) or experience another's changing without being flexible, having the "ability to construe alternative constructions" (Leitner & Pfenninger, 1994, p. 122). In other words, if Sue rigidly clings to certain meanings, she cannot enter into the world of other people to any great extent. Examples of inflexibility are bringing the same set of construals to every relationship under every circumstance and forcing all relationships into those boundaries or being frozen in the constructions formed early in a relationship, with little ability to recreate the relationship as it evolves.

One aspect of flexibility involves suspending one's meanings around an issue to see another's meanings. However, to the extent that Sue gives another's meanings total control in defining her interpersonal reality, she ceases to be a cocreator of her relationship. In so doing, her "excessive" flexibility results in being less able to make value judgments about the ways another's meaning making is helpful or harmful to her. Taken to an extreme, this flexibility can lead to an "anything goes" psychological relativism in which taking a stand is very difficult. Perhaps a better way of putting it is that flexibility involves simultaneously holding one's meanings and the meanings of another in one's awareness. The rigid person cannot make room for the meanings of the other; the acquiescent person loses self-meanings in the face of the reality of the other.

Creativity

Because humans continue to evolve, old meanings, no matter how flexibly applied, eventually lose their ability to do justice to the developing new realities of ROLE relating. Thus, people in intimate relationships create new ways of seeing self, other, and relationships and are able to move the relationship to new places (Leitner & Pfenninger, 1994). Kelly (1955/

1991a, 1955/1991b) defined creativity as a process of "loosening" (allowing meanings to be more elastic, vaguely held, fuzzy) and "tightening" (allowing meanings to be more specific, precise, and unchanging within the context). The first part of this process allows for the creation of alternative ways of structuring one's experience of the world; the second part allows one to try out these alternative structures to see if they are workable (i.e., if they allow for the meaningful understanding of self, other, and relationship).

Obviously, a person may have difficulty at any point in the creativity cycle (Kelly, 1955/1991a, 1955/1991b). If Sue cannot loosen her meanings, for example, she is unable to experience the "fertile chaos" (Leitner & Pfenninger, 1994, p. 124) that reinvents self, other, and relationship and brings variety, spice, and vigor to relating. However, if she cannot tighten her construing, her ways of structuring experience are too wavering either to test their utility or to use as a basis for launching herself into the future and her relationships stagnate.

Responsibility

Leitner and Pfenninger (1994) defined *responsibility* as the willingness to examine one's construct system and its implications for others. Experiential personal constructivism explicitly assumes that meanings are created in the "between" of the person–environment (frequently self–other) dynamic reality. Thus, there are ways in which a person is responsible for the meanings he or she creates; there are also ways in which the context plays a role in the meanings that have been created. Negating either side of this dynamic reality can create problems.

For example, many people are willing to discount the "person–self" side of this dynamic, particularly when they have engaged in actions that are troublesome, either to themselves or to others. People can find it easy to construe the bases of their actions, experiences, and relationships in terms of genetics, biochemistry, conditioning history, traumas, parental pathology, or societal oppression, to name a few. However, when people openly look at the meanings they have cocreated, as the definition of responsibility requires, they have to acknowledge that these factors are only a small part of the reason they developed their unique meaning system. In other words, because the universe is open to an endless variety of constructions, people have to acknowledge that although their understandings of the realities they confront in life are a reasonable and valid possibility, another person may have created quite different understandings. Denying that disempowers the person, negating the person–self side of the person–environment dynamic, and, in so doing, is pathological. Being responsible implies openly considering the reasons people chose to create their unique construct systems.

Alternatively, the "environment–other" side of this dynamic reality can be discounted by ignoring the role of the other, social context, and so on in the meanings created. For example, Sue may assume that the problems with her spouse, children, parents, and boss are entirely her fault. In this situation, not only is she injuring herself by ignoring the other half of the "between" so vital in meaning making, but she is also disempowering the other by refusing to experience him or her as capable of creating meanings that affect her.

Openness

Openness is defined as the willingness to reconstrue when invalidated (Leitner & Pfenninger, 1994, p. 127). A person cannot know the world directly; it always exists just beyond the meanings created to understand it. Therefore, one tests one's meanings continuously through interaction with the world. Not infrequently, events in the world apprise a person that certain ways of understanding are not working well. Kelly (1955/1991a, 1955/1991b) termed this experience "invalidation." One's willingness to reconstrue when invalidated is an important aspect of continuing to derive meaning from the world.

Many destructive human interactions involve an unwillingness to reconstrue when invalidated. Kelly (1955/1991a, 1955/1991b) defined *hostility* as extorting validational evidence to continue to use meanings that have proven themselves predictive failures; that is, Bob insists that Edward be the way he wants or needs him to be. For example, a man may have a construction of a child as obedient. Inevitably, as the child grows, there will be times when this construction is invalidated. If the father refuses to reconstrue, he may begin to force the child to obey him in increasingly violent ways. He may also accuse the child of being "bad," resulting in the child disliking parts of the self having to do with taking stands independent of his or her parental demands.

However, a person might be too willing to reconstrue when invalidated. If Bob's core meanings are involved, he may be caught invalidating his own most central meanings in a desperate attempt to incorporate the meanings of another or trying to simultaneously hold mutually exclusive meanings. Such dilemmas can pose a threat to the most basic construals Bob uses to structure his existence. Thus, excessive openness can severely fracture the integrity and wholeness of a person. Typically, these meanings involve moral or value issues. Some people do not have meanings so central that they may be worth fighting to protect or even dying for. A person without such core meanings cannot form highly intimate ROLE relationships because, by definition, such relationships involve sharing one's core structures with another. (Pfenninger & Klion, 1995, discussed this in more detail.)

Commitment

Commitment can be defined as the willingness to validate the other's process over time (Leitner & Pfenninger, 1994). Thus, in a ROLE relationship, not only must Sue be willing to touch another (experience and affirm another's process), she must be willing to maintain this level of contact in the future. This component of ROLE relationships is the source of both richness and difficulty.

On the one hand, Sue may be unwilling to make such a commitment. She lives for the day, and Joe may have little confidence in her willingness to affirm him in the future. Although Sue may initiate relationships quite well, problems occur when she is faced with the demands of maintaining a relationship. Thus, when things get rocky between Sue and another, she is ready to end the relationship or retreat to a kind of relationship that is less intimate. Such a person may have a history of multiple short-term relationships. In so doing, she deprives herself of the richness of deepening mutual affirmation that can be experienced over time.

On the other hand, Sue may find it difficult to terminate a relationship that she has committed to despite the ways in which it is destructive for her. Perhaps the other originally affirmed aspects of her process, and they have grown in incompatible ways; perhaps the other never validated her in any profound way. In either case, the other no longer affirms her core processes in ways that allow her to feel rich, to feel a valued part of the world, to grow. However, Sue finds it difficult to admit that a healthy resolution to this dilemma may be the termination of the relationship with the other. Instead, she continues to stay in a relationship with little experiential vitality.

Courage

ROLE relationships involve risking the terror of exposing one's most central meanings, one's very life process, to potential confirmation or disconfirmation. Furthermore, one does not occasionally take such a risk; one risks over extensive periods of time and must be responsibly open to the outcomes of such ventures. Obviously, then, courage is critical, and diagnosing struggles with courage can be important for the psychotherapist.

Courage is not limited to bravery in life-threatening situations like combat. It certainly is not linked to the experience of not being afraid. As a matter of fact, if courage is defined as engaging in an activity despite the clear recognition of the dangers involved, the experiences of fear, threat, and indeed terror are essential for an act to be courageous. Thus, Sue offers herself to another, despite her cognizance that the other person may (indeed, sometimes certainly will) cause her great pain.

As with the other experiential components of meaning making, one can have many difficulties with courage. George can allow his awareness of the terror of disconfirmation to stop him from risking with others. In so doing, George retreats from another and they do not have the experience of a ROLE relationship. Such people typically view feelings of fear, threat, vulnerability, and so on as "bad" feelings, to be avoided at all costs. They typically lead sheltered lives in which safety is the first, foremost, and indeed only concern.

However, Tom may distort courage by denying the experience of fear. He adopts the position that potential devastation either is an impossibility or nothing to worry about. In some ways, he leads an expansive life in which he engages in all sorts of activities and takes on all sorts of challenges. However, in terms of ROLE relationships, Tom's life is as sheltered and protected as people who allow the experience of fear to prevent them from engaging in any activities. By not admitting to the real terror inherent in ROLE relating, he cannot bring a central part of his experience to the relationship. Such an impediment prevents him from participating fully in the coconstruction of a mutually satisfying, intimate relationship.

Forgiveness

Invalidations, sometimes of devastating proportions, are not uncommon in ROLE relationships. All people must find ways of living with the pain and injury of disconfirmation that allow them to continue to risk into the future. Sometimes, this future involves risking again with the same person; at other times, it involves risking again with other people. Forgiveness is a way of reconstruing self and other, such that major invalidations are not allowed to hinder the development of future ROLE relationships (Leitner & Pfenninger, 1994, p. 132).

A person may, implicitly or explicitly, assume that the injury experienced in one relationship portends similar injury in all future interpersonal relationships. Psychologically armed with bitterness, the person relates to others with apprehension and guardedness. A stasis ensues that blocks personal and relational growth. If John cannot reconstrue himself beyond being the injured party, he becomes mired in the role of victim, with all of the limitations that places on him. As he holds onto his pain, John misses the opportunity to learn what it may have to teach him. If he cannot reconstrue the other, his views of all others may be constricted to their potential to be "abusers," "jerks," "losers," and so on. John is no longer willing or able to understand the others' needs, fears, hopes, or desires. He also may not look at the ways his needs, desires, hopes, and fears contributed to the disconfirmations he experienced. Ways he might have actively or passively contributed to the limitations of the previous relationship are very likely to be repeated in future ones.

Forgiveness is not an easy process. Before Sue can forgive a devastating injury, she needs to clearly look at the ways she was injured and mourn the invalidation of vital meanings structuring her very life. If she attempts forgiveness prior to understanding the injury, Sue does not know what she is forgiving. If she attempts forgiveness absent grieving the core invalidations, she dishonors the importance of those meanings in maintaining herself in the world. Because tightly construing and mourning devastations are very painful, it is not surprising that many people attempt to preempt the process and claim to have forgiven as a way to not deal with such terrible pain. Such "premature forgiveness" does not facilitate ROLE relationships.

Reverence

ROLE relationships, so central to a rich life, involve more than merely sharing core meanings with another. In a mutually enriching relationship, the other also shares his or her experiences with Sue. If a major part of the other's experience is the profound wonder and richness of Sue's affirmation, she has to be able to allow the other to share this with her. Leitner and Pfenninger (1994) defined *reverence* as the awareness that one is affirming the core ROLE process of the other.

Limitations in the ability to affirm the core processes of others preclude the experience of reverence for others. A person fails to glimpse the mystery of the other, the wonder of each person's uniquely creative engagement of life. Instead, others are seen more narrowly in terms of actions, cognitions, and attitudes. A person also fails to experience the awe of the other's courageously choosing to risk with him or her, a vulnerable, fallible, human being.

Alternatively, struggles with reverence may lead to a lack of revering oneself. For example, John cannot experience the fact that he is the person Kate chooses to affirm her most central processes. He cannot understand his vitalness to Kate. He may even feel unworthy of such vitalness because he knows the ways he has retreated from ROLE relationships in the past and the ways he has hurt others within those relationships. However, without this self-revering, John is limiting the unfolding ROLE relationship as he inevitably discounts central parts of the other's experience, the revering of him.

Leitner and Pfenninger (1994) argued that transpersonal reverence develops out of the experience of interpersonal reverence. A person learns to revere all people for their unique humanness. It is therefore possible to explore and understand a person's transition from interpersonal to transpersonal reverence. Indeed, it is possible to consider the lack of transpersonal reverence as pathological.

A Case Illustration

We illustrate the use of our diagnostic framework by describing Carrie, a 31-year-old, single, White woman. She presented for therapy because of unrelenting depression and recurrent suicidal desires. Carrie's mother and father were married when they were still in their teens, and her mother became pregnant. When Carrie was 2 years old, her father broke both of her legs. She and her siblings were removed from the home; Carrie was placed with relatives. Because this was never discussed in the family, Carrie knew very little about it.

The family was reassembled 2 years later. Carrie recalls her mother being constantly critical of the children and fearful of her husband. Sometimes in the middle of the night, her mother would awaken all of the children, urgently telling them they needed to hurry and leave. They would go to the car and drive aimlessly about town with her until she returned home. Carrie's father was unpredictably explosive and frequently physically abusive to his wife and his children. In contrast to this home life, Carrie's parents were highly respected in the conservative Christian church they attended and often were praised for their well-behaved and accomplished children.

Carrie had several corrective eye surgeries during her childhood, beginning when she was 6 years old. After her first surgery while her eyes were still bandaged, her father began to sexually abuse her. Although the episodes initially involved only caressing, his actions gradually escalated to intercourse. He would tell her that she owed him sex as a substitute for her mother and that Jesus would want her to submit to his demands. This abuse lasted until Carrie was 13 years old when she threatened to tell others. She became depressed and anorexic when she was a teenager. Although she managed to graduate from high school and attended college for 2 years, she was eventually sent home because of her dangerously low weight.

Her parents did not acknowledge her problems or try to get help for her until she attempted suicide. At that point, a long series of various types of "treatments," both inpatient and outpatient, began. Carrie was given a number of diagnoses, mostly revolving around mood disorders (depression or bipolar) and personality disorders (borderline). Physical abuse continued at home until Carrie's mother called friends of the family and begged them to take Carrie in before her father killed her. At one point, she spent several weeks living on the street. At another point, she was hospitalized for 2 months in a state psychiatric hospital. Her parents cut off all contact with her. She eventually got help from a church and now lives alone in a small apartment on Social Security disability income.

Conceptualization of Developmental Structural Issues

Although Carrie has a construction of self versus other, her history of early traumas led her to struggle with self–other permanence. For example, she frequently has to call her therapist between sessions for issues that can routinely be handled during either her regular appointment or regular business hours (e.g., rearranging an appointment time, asking if her minister can talk to the therapist). Carrie begins most of these conversations feeling panicked. However, after hearing her therapist's voice and getting in touch with the calming, soothing components of therapy, she can relax. The development of Carrie's ability to count on the therapist's caring commitment between appointments or when her therapist is out of town will be an important therapeutic accomplishment. This development of self–other permanence will open the door to her being able to direct her courage toward risking deeper ROLE relating through the beginning of the struggles around self–other constancy.

Carrie's interpersonal attachments tend to combine being nice and sacrificing herself for others with an angry, hostile discounting of others. For example, if her minister wonders whether therapy with a non-Christian therapist can be helpful, Carrie anxiously considers whether she should terminate therapy to stay in her minister's favor. However, there are times, particularly when she is feeling suicidal, that she will discount and rebuff all therapeutic interventions. These attachment styles are not surprising, given her struggles with self–other permanence. From Carrie's perspective, at any moment one of these significant others in her life could cease to be connected to her and she would experience the terror of absolute, total aloneness.

The maintenance of physical safety, let alone psychological safety, was precarious for Carrie throughout her entire childhood and young adulthood. It was nearly impossible to find any way to get her needs met from her parents; it certainly was not possible to get them met by directly expressing them, a sure trigger for derogation and abuse. Thus, she developed hidden, indirect, even convoluted interpersonal interactions for extracting validation from her relationships. For example, she feigns physical illnesses, complete with fabricating detailed stories of life-threatening diseases and desperate medical treatments, to get caring from others. Others may think that these behaviors on Carrie's part are "manipulative." However, it would be antitherapeutic for Carrie's therapist to confront Carrie with intentionally endeavoring to use or manipulate their relationship. Understanding the fragility of

Carrie's self–other permanence helps the therapist grasp the ways Carrie would experience such a confrontation as the total loss of her caring therapist because anything other than "caring" means that she would lose contact with the person of the therapist. Such a confrontation might precipitate a massive crisis for Carrie. The fragility of her construction of self–other permanence provides an understanding of her manipulative behavior as an attempt to elicit affirmation without risking the violent loss of the caring therapist should the therapist be unable or unwilling to affirm some aspect of her experience.

This understanding also clearly shows the path of growth Carrie's therapy needs to pursue for her to reach the point where she can rely enough on the presence, stability, and care of others that she can relate her needs to them more directly. For example, her therapist could respond to her manipulations with direct statements about the ways Carrie fears the loss of the therapist between sessions. The therapist could conclude crisis phone calls with reassuring statements, such as, "I look forward to when we can celebrate you knowing that I am still present for you between our sessions," "I know that when you do not see me, you get very frightened. That's okay. We will understand that terror as a feeling, not a reality."

There are indications that Carrie is starting to develop constructions of self–other permanence. For example, during low-stress times, she can go for several days without contacting her therapist. Furthermore, there are sessions during those times in which she feels the caring and commitment of the therapist. Even more important, she sometimes lets the therapist know when she has been hurt in their relationship and when she has felt the therapist's investment. This movement between having self–other permanence during low-stress times and losing it during periods of higher stress is a sign of transition between older, simpler construals and newer ways of meaning making.

Conceptualization of Interpersonal Components

Because she does not have constructions of self–other permanence and constancy, Carrie has significantly limited ROLE relationships. For example, she appears quite undispersed in her dependencies at the present time. She leans on her therapist and a friend who helps handle her finances for most of her emotional support. With others, she seems quite avoidant of dependent relationships. At the same time, she can become quite panicky about her feelings of dependence and may both physically and psychologically distance herself from others. Frequently, these distancings take the form of hospitalizations because of suicidal impulses. When she is in the hospital, she is spared some of the intimacy and the consequent terror of a live, face-to-face relationship in therapy. Her suicidal symptoms, then, provide some protection from the horrors of intimate relationships without a sense of self–other permanence and constancy.

The interpersonal conceptualization also points to ways the therapist can helpfully interact with Carrie. For example, the therapist can make empathic comments on how frightening it must be to depend on others, and together they can explore the ways that Carrie modulates that fear by depending heavily on a few people while keeping all others at a distance. After Carrie has weathered a period of strong suicidal temptations, the therapist may wonder about the relational implications of the feelings. Keeping in mind the ways in which Carrie may experience these thoughts and react to them because of her tenuous grasping of a self–other permanence, the therapist might sow the seeds for future growth in meaning making by introducing the following thoughts: In what ways is being suicidal a way that Carrie distances herself from her therapist? In what ways might Carrie's suicidal tendencies serve to enhance the therapeutic relationship (e.g., allowing her to get away until she can tolerate more intimacy)? These areas will be repeatedly (and carefully) introduced as Carrie's ability to explore them matures. Such conversations may help Carrie to continue to risk intimacy with her therapist as she learns what her suicidal ideation is communicating to her. They also help Carrie understand that her suicidal impulses, rather than being experiences that descend on her and are beyond her control, can communicate many things to her, one of which is the important relational purposes they serve for her.

Conceptualization of Symptoms

Carrie's symptoms point to other important truths about her life. The continuous despair and suicidality are messages about the emptiness of her present life and her capacity to enter into ROLE relationships. Her pervasive sense that life is not worth living reflects the truth that a life without ROLE relationships is an empty facade of true living. In this regard, her symptoms can be seen as a courageous reminder to her that she needs to address the core aspects of her interpersonal reality. In other ways, Carrie needs to trust herself and her therapist to explore the meanings behind the symptoms, rather than assuming that the truth they communicate is a literal one. Having the ability to take perspective on her symptoms will be vital if Carrie is to grow toward deeper ROLE relationships (Landfield, 1980).

Conceptualization of Experiential Components

Carrie's struggles with the construction of self–other permanence also result in significant problems in the experiential realm of meaning making.

Her issues with discrimination are linked to her history of severe invalidation. Trusting others to affirm her is an act of greater courage than she is capable of much of the time, and thus she typically overdiscriminates. This is especially evident in her relationships with men. She literally dislikes being in the presence of many men, even some whom she has known and related to for years. She also underdiscriminates with people, especially women, assuming a more intimate relationship than there has been time to develop and making demands for time and attention that the woman is likely to experience as inappropriate or excessive. For example, she often has her friend drive her to numerous appointments throughout the day, with little recognition of the friend's need to do things other than care for Carrie.

She inculcated the values of her father and mother so thoroughly during her childhood (i.e., she adopted their meanings as her meanings) that she has not been able to develop optimal flexibility. She is readily suspicious of others abandoning her; thus, she can be seen as transferring her experience with her parents inflexibly onto people currently in her life. However, in relationships with extremely significant others, she is excessively flexible. The other person's meanings have greater power in the relationship than her own.

Carrie shows both strength and problems with creativity. Her current life situation shows a creative solution to the horrors of her life. Having achieved this solution against great odds, she is not as actively engaging in the creation of new meanings, meanings that might free her from her current despair. Until she can feel more comfortable and stable in her current situation, she will find it difficult to loosen her meaning system and entertain new possibilities. Carrie's tendency to accept blame for every problem in her relationships shows her struggling with overresponsibility. She spends a lot of time in therapy trying to understand what she did that led to her family abandoning her. She has a very hard time elaborating on the possibility that it was not her fault.

There are ways that Carrie is willing to invalidate her own core meaning in her desperate attempts to connect with her parents. However, when events happen that affirm her worth as a person, she has considerable difficulty accepting the affirmation of worth. In that way, she is closed to aspects of her experience in the world. For example, when others comment on her progress and growth, she often feels irritated with them and refuses to accept the affirmation, insisting that they do not understand how much she continues to struggle. (This process may be tied directly to her not tightly grasping self–other permanence. If others see her as not desperately needing them, they may disappear.) In other words, she can be too closed in some instances and too open in others. In a similar vein, Carrie struggles with not being able to end her commitment to her parents, despite the experience of abuse and abandonment, while being unwilling to commit to others in her current life (e.g., potential close friends).

There are many ways Carrie shows great interpersonal courage. Despite her history, she has courageously risked relationships with others, including her therapist. She has relationships with members of her current church, despite the ways her father used religion in his sexual abuse of her. Her courage in her present life circumstances is one of her greatest strengths. However, being able to reconstrue her abuse such that the horrors no longer prevent her from entering into loving, reciprocal, sexual, romantic relationships is something yet to be accomplished. In fact, although this may seem to be a reasonable therapeutic goal for a woman her age, it may be an inappropriate focus for Carrie's therapy when her areas of developmental arrest are considered. Loving, romantic relationships are based on constructions of another's permanence and constancy. Until she develops greater meanings of the permanence and constancy of the other, any attempts to develop a romantic relationship may be chaotic, stormy, and destructive. Finally, Carrie does not have much experience of reverence; most of her current relationships are centered on meeting her needs. It may be possible to use the here-and-now of the therapy relationship to help her grow in this area; however, this work awaits her growth reaching a point where her basic needs are met in a healthier way.

Although all of these experiential conceptualizations offer therapeutic options, we discuss only some of the implications for discrimination. After Carrie's therapist has an experiential grasp of the horrors Carrie has experienced at the hands of men in her life, particularly her father, the therapist can wonder, with Carrie, about how Carrie determines which men can and cannot be trusted. The therapist also can help Carrie look at the subtle violence (Leitner & Faidley, 1995) of her mother's invalidations. Perhaps Carrie's underdiscrimination with women is tied to her inability to see the invalidations from her mother, the "good" parent. Because she had to rely on her mother for her physical and psychological survival, seeing her mother as invalidating could have precipitated overwhelming terror. Just as her mother cannot be an integration of good and bad qualities, other women cannot either. If the therapist prematurely attempts to force more discrimination with women, Carrie may have to reconstrue the only parent she could rely on during her early life, with potentially devastating consequences.

CONCLUSION

Overall, this system of diagnosis directs the therapist to many aspects of Carrie's life struggles. We can see the ways in which her injuries have left her without a solid foundation of self–other permanence. Her needs to retreat from the terrors of ROLE relating and the ways in which she makes that retreat can be seen in her interpersonal style and her experience of life in the present. Carrie and her therapist can engage all of these issues either directly and verbally or less directly in the moment-to-moment relationship that is therapy itself. Good therapy tactfully integrates both approaches into the needs of the moment. Not only does the conceptualization point to specific ways in which Carrie reveals her injuries, but it also aids her therapist in construing her injuries in ways that can help Carrie conquer the fears and terrors that haunt her existence.

In general, we presented a way of diagnosing the process of meaning making that simultaneously accounts for client distress, respects the lived experience of the person, and makes psychotherapeutic interventions understandable and plausible. In so doing, we believe we sketched a system that meets Kelly's (1955/1991a, 1955/1991b) criteria of transitive diagnosis, diagnosing in ways that truly make a difference in the lives of the human beings therapists attempt to serve. Future work could empirically explore the implications of the system. We hope that this system will continue to evolve as therapists attempt to reverently understand the horrific traumas and great courage of those special people who privilege therapists by opening their inner lives to them in psychotherapy.

REFERENCES

American Psychiatric Association. (1994). *Diagnostic and statistical manual of mental disorders* (4th ed.). Washington, DC: Author.

Bannister, D., & Agnew, J. (1977). The child's construction of self. In A. W. Landfield & J. K. Cole (Eds.), *Nebraska Symposium on Motivation: Vol. 24. Personal construct psychology* (pp. 99–125). Lincoln: University of Nebraska Press.

Barratt, B. B. (1977). The development of peer perception systems in childhood and early adolescence. *Social Behavior and Personality, 5,* 351–360.

Bowen, M. (1976). Theory in the practice of psychotherapy. In P. J. Guerin, Jr. (Ed.), *Family therapy: Theory and practice* (pp. 42–90). New York: Gardner Press.

Bowlby, J. (1969). *Attachment and loss.* New York: Basic Books.

Epting, F. R., & Leitner, L. M. (1994). Humanistic psychology and personal construct theory. In F. Wertz (Ed.), *The humanistic movement: Recovering the person in psychology* (pp. 129–145). Lake Worth, FL: Gardner Press.

Faidley, A. J., & Leitner, L. M. (1993). *Assessing experience in psychotherapy: Personal construct alternatives.* Westport, CT: Praeger.

Friedman, M. (1985). *The healing dialogue in psychotherapy.* New York: Aronson.

Horney, K. (1945). *Our inner conflicts: A constructive theory of neuroses.* New York: Norton.

Kegan, R. (1982) *The evolving self*. Cambridge, MA: Harvard University Press.

Kelly, G. A. (1991a). *The psychology of personal constructs: Vol. 1. A theory of personality*. London: Routledge. (Original work published 1955)

Kelly, G. A. (1991b). *The psychology of personal constructs: Vol. 2. Clinical diagnosis and psychotherapy*. London: Routledge. (Original work published 1955)

Klion, R. E., & Leitner, L. M. (1985). Construct elicitation techniques and the production of interpersonal concepts in children. *Social Behavior and Personality, 13,* 137–142.

Landfield, A. W. (1980). The person as perspectivist, literalist, and chaotic fragmentalist. In A. W. Landfield & L. M. Leitner (Eds.), *Personal construct psychology: Psychotherapy and personality* (pp. 289–320). New York: Wiley Interscience.

Landfield, A. W. (1988). Personal science and the concept of validation. *International Journal of Personal Construct Psychology, 1,* 237–250.

Leitner, L. M. (1985). The terrors of cognition: On the experiential validity of personal construct theory. In D. Bannister (Ed.), *Issues and approaches in personal construct theory* (pp. 83–103). London: Academic.

Leitner, L. M. (1988). Terror, risk, and reverence: Experiential personal construct psychotherapy. *International Journal of Personal Construct Psychology, 1,* 261–272.

Leitner, L. M. (1995). Optimal therapeutic distance: A therapist's experience of personal construct psychotherapy. In R. A. Neimeyer & M. J. Mahoney (Eds.), *Constructivism in psychotherapy* (pp. 357–370). Washington, DC: American Psychological Association.

Leitner, L. M. (1997, July). Cutting-edge issues in experiential personal construct psychotherapy. In T. Anderson (Chair), *Disruptions in the therapeutic relationship: Influences of mortality, ecology, diagnosis, and other cutting-edge issues*. Symposium conducted at the 12th International Congress on Personal Construct Psychology, Seattle, WA.

Leitner, L. M. (1999). Levels of awareness in experiential personal construct psychotherapy. *Journal of Constructivist Psychology, 12,* 239–252.

Leitner, L. M. (in press). Terror, numbness, panic, and awe: Experiential personal constructivism and panic. *The Psychotherapy Patient*.

Leitner, L. M., & Faidley, A. J. (1995). The awful, aweful nature of ROLE relationships. In R. A. Neimeyer & G. J. Neimeyer (Eds.), *Advances in personal construct psychology* (Vol. 3), pp. 291–314. Greenwich, CT: JAI Press.

Leitner, L. M., & Pfenninger, D. T. (1994). Sociality and optimal functioning. *Journal of Constructivist Psychology, 7,* 119–135.

Luborsky, L., & Crits-Christoph, P. (1990). *Understanding transference: The core conflictual relationship method*. New York: Basic Books.

Pfenninger, D. T., & Klion, R. E. (1995). Re-thinking hostility: Is it ever better to fight than switch? In R. A. Neimeyer & G. J. Neimeyer (Eds.), *Advances in personal construct psychology* (Vol. 3, pp. 271–289). Greenwich, CT: JAI Press.

Raskin, J. D., & Epting, F. R. (1993). Personal construct theory and the argument against mental illness. *International Journal of Personal Construct Psychology*, 6, 351–369.

Walker, B. M. (1990). Construing George Kelly's construing of the person-in-relation. *International Journal of Personal Construct Psychology*, 3, 41–50.

Walker, B. M. (1993). Looking for a whole "mama": Personal construct psychotherapy and dependency. In L. M. Leitner & N. G. M. Dunnett (Eds.), *Critical issues in personal construct psychotherapy* (pp. 61–81). Malabar, FL: Krieger.

IV

DISORDER AS NARRATIVE CONSTRUCTION

9

NARRATIVE DISRUPTIONS IN THE CONSTRUCTION OF THE SELF

ROBERT A. NEIMEYER

Countless lives inhabit us.
I don't know, when I think or feel,
Who it is that thinks or feels.
I am merely the place
Where things are thought or felt.

I have more than one soul.
There are more I's than I myself.
I exist, nevertheless,
Indifferent to them all.
I silence them: I speak.

The crossing urges of what
I feel or do not feel
Struggle in who I am, but I
Ignore them. They dictate nothing
To the I I know: I write.
　　　　—Ricardo Reis/Fernando Pessoa (1935/1998),[1] p. 137

---

[1]Ricardo Reis was one of several "literary heteronyms" of Fernando Pessoa, the early 20th century Portuguese poet, novelist, and literary critic. More than a series of conventional pen names, these semiautonomous personalities actually published under separate names, wrote in dramatically different forms and styles, and even critiqued each other's work in print. Pessoa (whose family name ironically translates as "person"), therefore, seemed to literally embody the postmodern predicament of a distributed self, as foreshadowed in the poem. From "Countless Lives Inhabit Us," by F. Pessoa, in *Fernando Pessoa & Company* (R. Zenith, Ed. & Trans.), 1998, New York: Grove Press. Original work published 1935. Copyright 1998 by Richard Zenith. Used with permission of Grove/Atlantic, Inc.

How can we as human beings understand the self as a narrative construction, an ordering of inchoate experience into a durable sense of identity? What functions does narration serve at both intrapersonal levels and interpersonal levels as we seek to construct accounts of our lives that not only prove viable for us but that also find support in the responses of relevant others? More particularly, how can a closer analysis of the features of narratives advance our understanding of human distress and provide a heuristic framework for psychotherapy? In seeking some preliminary answers to these questions, I touch briefly on the debate among postmodern theorists concerning the personal versus social origins of the self-as-story to lay the groundwork for a conception of narration that accredits its inherently relational character and makes room for our therapeutic participation as psychologists in the (re)authorship of lives.

A RECONSTRUCTION OF THE SELF

For most of the history of psychotherapy, the *self* has served both as an orienting concept for clinical diagnosis and as a target for clinical interventions. From Sigmund Freud's (1940/1964) classic structural formulation of ego functioning to its elaboration by object relations (Kernberg, 1976) and self-theorists (Kohut, 1971) and from early conceptions of the "proprium" (Allport, 1961) to humanistic theories of self-development (Rogers, 1961), various models of personality have provided a foundation for theories of psychotherapy. Even more "parsimonious" and contemporary cognitive–behavioral therapies (Beck, 1993) implicitly presume a foundational role for the self in their focus on training clients in self-monitoring, recording of self-talk, and similar procedures. Viewed in a critical sociohistorical perspective, such models can be seen as expressing a modern, post-Enlightenment discourse in which the self is viewed as individualistic, singular, essential, stable, and knowable, at least in principle (Neimeyer, 1998c). It follows that psychotherapy, as a series of authoritative technical procedures to bring about self-change, would focus chiefly on intrapsychic disorders that impair adaptation and then treat them in such a way as to enhance the client's self-awareness, self-actualization, self-control, self-efficacy, and the like.

In a sense, constructivist approaches to psychotherapy both extend and problematize this conception of selfhood. On the one hand, the self retains its role as an organizing concept in many constructivist theories, which focus on the "core ordering processes" (Mahoney, 1991) by which individuals construct a sense of personal identity in an intersubjective field (Guidano, 1991). Moreover, in keeping with humanistic personality theories, constructivists typically emphasize the role of personal meanings in shaping people's responses to life events and regard human beings as capable of at least a bounded agency in determining the course of their lives (Kelly, 1955). On the other hand, constructivists construe the self more as a process than a product, stressing the dialectical dynamics of ongoing self-development in response both to sensed discrepancies within the self-system (Greenberg & Pascual-Leone, 1995) and to perturbations of personal structure arising in the (social) medium in which humans exist (Maturana & Varela, 1987). Likewise, the recognition that constructivists accord to abstract or tacit features of personal knowledge (Hayek, 1952; Polanyi, 1958) and their conception of identity as comprising many "possible selves" (Markus & Nurius, 1986) temper their assumption of the ultimate knowability of the self and, with it, their enthusiasm for rationalistic self-control procedures (Neimeyer, 1993a, 1995b). Viewed in sociohistorical terms, such theories can be seen as edging toward a postmodern conception of the self as inherently social, multiplistic, contingent, evolving, and, in principle, unspecifiable (Neimeyer & Stewart, 1998a). It follows that psychotherapeutic procedures for fostering change would need to tack between the self and social system, helping clients to articulate, elaborate, and negotiate those (inter)-personal meanings by which they organize their experience and action (Neimeyer, 1995c).

Although this reconstruction of the self as permeable, pluralistic, and process oriented represents a genuine departure from more traditional conceptions of personality, some critics believe that it subtly reproduces the discourse of essential individuality in the attempt to transcend it. Thus, social constructionists argue that constructivists give insufficient attention to the extent to which the self is constituted in language, understood as a situated and shifting symbolic order that structures our relationship as people to "reality" and ourselves (Gergen, 1994). Because the very terms in which we construe ourselves are cultural artifacts, our selves are deeply penetrated by the vocabularies of our place and time, expressing dominant modes of discourse as much as any unique personality. Indeed, "like a foetus floating in an amnion of culturally available signs, symbols, practices and conversations, the 'self' symbiotically depends for its existence upon a living system that precedes and supports it" (Neimeyer, 1998b, p. 140). In more radical forms, this view of the "saturated self" as populated by the contradictory discourses in which one is immersed threatens the very conception of the individual as a coherent entity with identifiable boundaries and properties (Gergen, 1991). The extreme postmodern vision of the "death of the self" (Lather, 1992) heralds the demise of personal subjectivity and its replacement by the cacophonous echoes of incoherent conversations, anonymous media images, and fragmented communication networks that colonize our mental life. Passing fully through this postmodern mirror, "we enter into a universe devoid of both objects and selves: where there is only a swarming of 'selfobjects,' images and simulacra filling us without resistance" (Sass, 1992, p. 176).

In the next section of this chapter, I draw on the insights of both constructivist and social constructionist scholars to conceptualize various disruptions in the construction of personal identity, illustrating these with brief literary examples. Although I recognize at the outset that an effort to integrate the dichotomy of self versus society is likely to be less than fully successful (Gergen, 1999), I believe that progress can be made by situating the discussion in the lived world of our interactions and negotiations with other people. I hope that a focus on this dyadic-relational level of analysis can help bridge the seemingly distinct levels of personal–agentic functioning emphasized by constructivists and cultural–linguistic discourse emphasized by social constructionists, without doing injustice to either.[2] To shed further light on these challenges to self-construction, I draw extensively on narrative concepts and procedures, which offer an integrative metaphor for therapists in both the constructivist and social constructionist traditions. Throughout the remaining two thirds of the chapter, I focus on the clinical implications of a narrative perspective and illustrate each with actual case material derived from my practice as a psychotherapist.

NARRATIVE AS AN INTEGRATIVE METAPHOR FOR THE CONSTRUCTION OF THE SELF

Writing over 40 years ago, George Kelly, one of the founding figures of clinical constructivism (Neimeyer & Jackson, 1997), drew attention to the structural organization of experience by noting that life

> presents itself from the beginning as an unending and undifferentiated process. Only when man tunes his ear to recurrent themes in the monotonous flow does the universe begin to make sense to him. . . . [H]e must phrase his experience in order to make sense of it. The phrases are distinguished events. . . . Within these limited segments, which are based on recurrent themes, man begins to discover the bases for likenesses and differences. (Kelly, 1955, p. 52)

---

[2] This effort accords with the *epigenetic systems* perspective of human development, which views structures as emerging through coactions among multiple levels within an organism–environment system [Mascolo, Craig-Bray, & Neimeyer, 1997]. In the present context, self-structures are viewed as neither innate and preformed by individual genetics nor simply inscribed on the person by supraindividual social systems. Instead, the self as a locus of meaning and action is viewed as developing from transactions between and among at least four hierarchically organized levels, corresponding to biogenetic, personal–agentic, dyadic–relational, and cultural–linguistic systems. My main focus here is on the role of narrative at these latter three levels in helping to configure a viable sense of self-in-social-context. However, I occasionally allude to suggestive evidence that narrative processes may be instantiated at the level of basic neurological and memory processes as well.

Thus, for Kelly, as for many contemporary constructivists, people are viewed as proactively punctuating, phrasing, and segmenting events, carving the flow of experience into discrete episodes that attain significance when thematically related to or distinguished from others. Moreover, Kelly's essential optimism about human resilience derived from his conviction that "there are always some alternative constructions available to choose among in dealing with the world. No one needs to paint himself into a corner; no one needs to be completely hemmed in by circumstances; no one needs to be the victim of his biography" (Kelly, 1955, p. 15). In keeping with this philosophy of constructive alternativism, Kelly devised such therapeutic techniques as the *self-characterization procedure* to help clients articulate the thematic substructure of their life stories and therapist-drafted *enactment sketches* to promote experimentation with new roles that could prompt liberating readings of the past and future. Viewed in contemporary perspective, these pioneering contributions can be seen as early harbingers of narrative therapy (Neimeyer, 1993b), which has been elaborated in different directions by cognitive constructivists, on the one hand, and social constructionists, on the other.

Cognitive Constructivism and Quest for Coherence

In the past 15 years, a narrative conceptualization of human behavior has gained broad currency both within and beyond the bounds of psychotherapy (Howard, 1991; Polkinghorne, 1988; Terrell & Lyddon, 1995). As developed by more cognitively oriented constructivists, the metaphor of self-as-story casts the individual as both the author and principal character in his or her autobiography, binding experiences and ongoing life events into meaningful units across time, themes, and people (Mancuso & Sarbin, 1983).[3] By rendering an account of experience in personally significant terms, people construct a meaningful story of not only the events that constitute their lives but also themselves as protagonists. To invert Piaget's famous dictum, "intelligence organizes itself by organizing the world."

What functions does narration serve at this intrapersonal level? In a sense, this question is difficult to answer in the abstract, in view of the uniqueness of each individual's storied experience and how (or whether) it is conveyed to a particular listener. Even in the restricted context of

---

[3]Gonçalves, Korman, and Angus (chap. 11, this volume) argue persuasively that this narrative impulse is intrinsic to the human quest to create order out of the chaotic multiplicity of experience, and they discuss more thoroughly the experimental evidence that buttresses this conclusion. I refer the reader to their articulate presentation of the cognitive constructivist perspective for a more detailed presentation of this argument and a consideration of its implications for clinical practice and research. For a detailed review of empirical memory research and its relation to the self-concept, see Nurius (1998).

psychotherapy, written or spoken narratives may be shared to lighten a client's burden of secrecy, to buttress a tentative construction of important events, to place a set of confusing experiences on the table of therapeutic discussion, or to give form to a dialogue between one's sensed or possible selves. But at an overarching level, many of these specific intents serve a more general function: *to establish continuity of meaning in the client's lived experience* (Neimeyer, 1995a, p. 233, emphasis in original).

Mining the implications of this view for psychotherapy, several constructivist clinicians have offered narrative conceptualizations of problems in living that focus on the incoherence or incompleteness of the client's life story and, by extension, his or her sense of self (Neimeyer & Stewart, 1998b). For example, Gustafson (1995) noted that problematic periods in life are characterized by gaps in a person's story, and Polkinghorne (1991) drew attention to the way in which narratives "decompose" or "disintegrate" when they become unable to unify new or forgotten phenomena. Likewise, Wigren (1994) contended that problems ensue when an individual is unable to develop a narrative to subsume traumatic experiences, such as violent assault or incest. In each of these instances, the person is left with only a fragmented sense of his or her own continuity, which in extreme cases can be experienced with dissociative intensity. It follows from this view that the goal of therapy is to help the client to integrate problematic experiences more adequately within the self-narrative and to promote its ongoing revision and extension (Neimeyer & Stewart, 1998b).

A literary illustration of this process of narrative fragmentation is offered by Roy (1998). In her novel *The God of Small Things*, a young mother, Ammu, and her children become caught up in a tale of accidental death, betrayal, and ultimately the brutal murder of the man who is Ammu's lover and her children's friend. The emotional drama for the small family reaches its denouement when a grief-crazed uncle crashes into the locked room where Ammu sits nervously knitting, the children huddled fearfully around her, and in his rage changes their lives forever, ultimately destroying them. As Roy (1998) wrote,

> at the time, there would be only incoherence. As though meaning had slunk out of things and left them fragmented. Disconnected. The glint of Ammu's needle. The color of a ribbon. The weave of the cross-stitch counterpane. A door slowly breaking. Isolated things that didn't *mean* anything. As though the intelligence that decodes life's hidden pattern—that connects reflections to images, glints to light, weaves to fabrics, needles to thread, walls to rooms, love to fear to anger to remorse—was suddenly lost. (p. 215, emphasis in original)

In addition to possessing literary power, such an account of narrative disintegration receives support from scientific studies of autobiographical memory and the psychobiology of trauma. Thus, research in memory demonstrates that people ordinarily integrate thematically related events in declarative memory using large-scale "event structures" (Barsalou, 1988; Linton, 1986) or "story schemas" (Mandler, 1984). However, other studies indicate that these normal processes of encoding, consolidation, and retrieval are severely compromised by the heightened autonomic arousal associated with traumatic experiences (Siegel, 1995; van der Kolk & van der Hart, 1991). Such evidence suggests that a fundamental narrative structure underpins basic memory processes themselves, beyond the level of the conscious packaging of a story for oneself or others (Barclay, 1996; Howe & Courage, 1997).

Social Constructionism and Deconstruction of Discourse

As compelling as this intrapersonal formulation of narrative may be on its own terms, it is seriously deficient from the standpoint of a social constructionist analysis of "languaging" as a communal rather than individual process. Where more cognitive constructivists posit the somewhat romantic image of a heroic or embattled self striving to integrate and narrate a "welter" of complex and conflicting experiences, social constructionists see merely a local manifestation of a discursive dynamic whose origins are more cultural than personal. In this view, language and the culture tales to which it gives rise are always already there, providing a symbolic context that precedes any given individual (Gergen, 1994). This is not to say that language provides an unproblematic common frame of reference through which people coordinate their relations to one another, however. Indeed, the meanings of things remain open and contested, sites for significant conflict between members of the same language community. In narrating experiences, then, people implicitly or explicitly draw on different discourses or systems of statements (stories, images, metaphors, or ideologies) that together produce a particular version of events (Burr, 1995).

What functions does narration serve at this more interpersonal level? Again, the plethora of local contexts in which stories are told suggests the impossibility of providing any definitive taxonomy of answers to this question. But at an abstract level, narration can be seen not so much as a way of representing a personal reality as a way of constituting a social reality. This more performative view of language-in-use sensitizes us to what people are doing or attempting to do in their discourse in terms of the positions they are subtly assigning to themselves and others (Edwards & Potter, 1992). For example, the divergent stories of an episode of physical aggression between two spouses can hardly be viewed as neutral accounts, but instead they represent competing versions that cast the self and partner in different lights. Moreover, each account draws on a partially shared and partially distinctive set of cultural discourses about the respective roles of men and women, the nature of the marital relationship, and even the phenomenon of domestic violence itself. Although neither of these accounts has recourse to a transcendentally valid conception of appropriate gender relations, the legitimacy of force in human affairs, and so on, it is not a matter of indifference which of the partner's stories "wins out" in their eyes or those of relevant others. Stated differently, socially constructed discourses have "real effects" for those living within them (Foucault, 1970).

Working within this conception of narration as a form of social action, a number of theorists have begun to formulate concepts and procedures for deconstructing the text of dominant discourses by revealing their internal tensions, hidden contradictions, and concealed assumptions (Derrida, 1978). For example, Hoffman (1990) conceptualized clinical problems as stories that clients tell themselves, stories that inevitably change with the retelling. Efran and Fauber likewise see problems as constituted in language, resonating with "themes that are afoot in the broader community, and reflect[ing] the progress that the community has made in figuring out how people ought to live together" (Efran & Fauber, 1995, p. 280). From this perspective, the therapist's task is not to offer clients pat reinterpretations of their concerns but to help them "clear up the ambiguities of living and the conflicting role demands that derive from multiple community memberships" (p. 302). Finally, White and Epston work to reveal the hidden cultural discourses that sustain oppression, and confer dysfunctional identities (of anorexia, alcoholism, or self-hatred) on people (e.g., White & Epston, 1990). Therapy, in this view, becomes a form of resistance against such discourse and a search for "sparkling moments" that contradict the dominant narratives of clients' lives (Monk, Winslade, Crocket, & Epston, 1996). Each of these approaches involves elucidating and deconstructing the problem-saturated narratives of self that constrain what clients view as possible for themselves and others.

Whereas cognitive narrative accounts find support in research on basic memory processes, theorists concerned with the social construction of narratives are more likely to draw inspiration from contemporary literary theory. Postmodern critics have exposed all literary genres—even those such as poetry that traditionally have been regarded as most subjective—as "political acts," productions relying on an expressive repertoire, which is itself local and situated.

> Enmeshed within the fabric of social relations, emerging at this point in time, in this particular place, the poem is neither a mirror of nature nor the upsurge of a solitary mind but a constellation of meanings whose very intelligibility testifies to the irrevocably local conditions within which it assumed form. (Freeman, 1999, p. 100)

Likewise with the construction of self, "life narratives are thoroughly enmeshed within the fabric of culture: in language, in interpretive communities, in a sociohistorically delimited range of genres, tropes, and storylines" (pp. 105–106). By analogy, it follows that when the form or content of a life story becomes restrictive or oppressive, the application of deconstructive strategies deriving from literary criticism can help free the text and open up new possibilities (Neimeyer, 1998a).

A Relational Alternative

Literary theory also hints at a possible way of steering between the Scylla of a substantial and integral self envisioned by some cognitive constructivists and the Charybdis of its absorption into a sea of discourse celebrated by some social constructionists. This middle passage might focus more centrally on the phenomenological context in which narration actually takes place: in the nexus of conversations with real or imagined others. As Tappan (1999) argued, the "self is situated neither psychologically or socially, but dialogically—as a function of the linguistically mediated exchanges between persons and the social world that are the hallmark of lived human experience" (p. 118). Citing Bakhtin (1981), Tappan further contended that the authorship of the stories one tells about one's life is always a function of both the self and another; every utterance is always a response, to a greater or lesser degree, to the prior utterances of others. Moreover, even "inner speech" involves appropriating the language of others and adapting it to one's own purposes. Before this effortful (and incomplete) attempt at semantic assimilation,

> the word . . . exists in other people's mouths, in other people's contexts, serving other people's intentions. . . . Language is not a medium that passes freely and easily into the private property of the speaker's intentions; it is populated—overpopulated—with the intentions of others. (Bakhtin, 1981, pp. 293–294)

This "polyphonic" conception of selfhood provides a counterpoint to the alienation of the ontologically isolated *cogito*, but it introduces its own challenges to the narrative construction of selfhood, as "a variety of alien voices enter into the struggle for influence within an individual's consciousness" (p. 348).

Although a view of self as tenuously anchored in a shifting sea of relationships suggests that full personality integration is a chimerical goal, it also implies that whatever sense of coherence and continuity we achieve is in the context of such relationships. Kundera (1997) explored this theme in his novel *Identity* as he recounted a dialogue between a middle-aged man and his female lover following his visit to a dying high school friend. Reflecting on the deathbed scene, the protagonist remarks,

> at the end of my hospital visit, he began to reminisce. He reminded me what I must have said when I was sixteen. When he did that, I understood the sole meaning of friendship as it's practiced today. Friendship is indispensable to man for the proper functioning of his memory. Remembering our past, carrying it with us always, may be the necessary requirement for maintaining, as they say, the wholeness of the self. To ensure that the self doesn't shrink, to see that it holds on to its volume, memories have to be watered like potted flowers, and the watering calls for regular contact with the witnesses of the past, that is to say, with friends. They are our mirror; our memory; we ask nothing of them but that they polish the mirror from time to time so we can look at ourselves in it. (Kundera, 1997, pp. 45–46)

What complicates this process of reflection and validation of identity is that the relational webs in which we are immersed are themselves tangled, even contradictory. The self is thus heterogeneously distributed across a variety of distinguishable discourses, emerging from the intersection of various relational networks, familial patterns, linguistic categories, and meaningful objects (Wortham, 1999). In this regard, the first-person narration of experience serves a third vital function. In addition to the integration of disparate experiences emphasized by cognitive constructivists and the positioning of self in relation to others featured by social constructionists, narration (temporarily) asserts the primacy of a particular version of the self of the storyteller; it constructs an "as if" frame within which not only one's life but also one's identity achieves fictional coherence. As Bonnefoy (1989) observed, although speech represents "a maze without beginning or end of transitory representations, of fictions without any authority. . . When we speak, we [nonetheless] say 'I' and thanks first of all to this word, we give direction to our existence, and sometimes to that of others, we decide upon values [and even] die for the latter" (pp. 159–160). This expanded conception of a relational self, struggling to achieve a center of autobiographical plausibility in the face of the centrifugal pulls of historical heterogeneity, personal polyphony, and interpersonal inconsistency, provides a starting point for a closer consideration of narrative structure and the implications it carries for possible disruptions in the construction of self.[4]

---

[4] Although I am reluctant to add another "ism" to the sea of distinctions in which postmodern theory is awash, this dialogic alternative to the idiocentric discourse of cognitive constructivism and the sociocentric discourse of social constructionism might appropriately be labeled "relational constructivism." For me, this term emphasizes the primacy of interpersonal relationships and conversational exchanges in human life, in comparison with which both the intrapersonal world of cognitions and the suprapersonal world of culture represent (occasionally useful) linguistic abstractions. The phenomenologically primary place of narration in a person-to-person context could help bridge the cognitive and social domains without reifying a sense of self beyond the

NARRATIVE FORMS AND FEATURES

Although the discussions above of narrative in the construction of self are suggestive, on close inspection they provide practicing psychotherapists with more of a metaphor than a method. What seems required to enhance the practical import of a storied model of the self is an expansion of this metaphor along several dimensions, considering (a) narrative form and features, (b) points of view and voice, and (c) issues of authorship and audience. Each of these, I contend, offers prospects for conceptualizing the affordances and constraints of any particular account of experience, and each suggests possible ways of "intervening in meaning" in a way that prompts new narrative possibilities for the author–protagonist. I begin by focusing on the first of these dimensions: narrative forms and features.

As Russell and Lucariello (1992) observed, "most definitions of narrative require a protagonist inspirited with intentionality, undertaking some action, physical or mental, real or imagined, within the story itself" (p. 671). Moreover, if narratives are viewed as intentional pursuits whose goal is to construct meaning (Gonçalves, 1994), then they must establish implicit or explicit endpoints and marshal events that are relevant to these projected conclusions (Gergen & Gergen, 1986). Thus, narratives typically have both an historical horizon (of events that are recruited by the author as relevant to the plot) and an anticipatory thrust (in the sense of a sought-after conclusion that is stated or implied). The (attempted) integration of material in light of the author's intentionality imparts a narrative form to human experience (Neimeyer, 1995a).

Narrative form can be explicated further by considering several structural features that typify autobiographical accounts: setting, characterization, plot, theme, and fictional goal. Alternative taxonomies of narrative features have been provided by Mandler (1984) and McAdams (1993).

Setting

The setting of a narrative refers to the *where* and *when* of the story, its context (that which goes with the text), and provides the frame of intelligibility for the story as a whole. At a minimum, the setting situates the action in the stream of the storyteller's experience, and establishes its relevance for the listener, even if this listener is also the teller. Typically, this "stage setting" is done through articulation of concrete details that

---

development of a self-presentation that articulates with the history and requirements of a particular relationship. However, further developing this position would carry me too far afield from the narrative disruptions theme of this chapter. For steps in this direction, see Mascolo, Craig-Bray, and Neimeyer (1997).

provide a thick description of the scene and actors within it. As Gardner (1983) observed about good fiction,

> it's physical detail that pulls us into the story, makes us believe or forget not to believe . . . or accept the lie even as we laugh at it. If we carefully inspect our experience as we read, we discover that the importance of physical detail is that it creates for us a kind of dream, a rich and vivid play in the mind. (p. 30)

The accentuation of the setting conjures up a "possible world" that can be accepted as if it were a true account of the actions and intentions of the protagonist and other principal characters in the narrative or, alternatively, can be further interrogated for meaning. Thus, the rich embellishment of setting serves at least two psychologically relevant functions: enhancing the plausibility of the self-as-portrayed and opening the texture of the account to deepened or alternative readings.

Constructivist therapists have developed a variety of strategies for helping clients to overcome the sense of "stuckness" or stagnation associated with hackneyed, barren, and matter-of-fact accounts of a problem experience. For example, Guidano (1991, 1995) made use of a "moviola" technique, whereby the therapist slowly "pans the camera" of therapeutic attention across the details of an emotionally significant episode in the client's report, replaying in slow motion each relevant movement, expression, remark, and action. This careful sifting of experience often allows clients to articulate for the first time overlooked details that subsequently transform their explicit understanding of the event. Likewise, Gonçalves (1995) described several in-session and between-session procedures for helping clients "objectify" the details of their stories that are prototypical of their struggle in engaging the world, by identifying each sensorial dimension (visual, auditory, gustatory, olfactory, tactile–kinesthetic). Although this articulation of setting can lay the groundwork for attention to other potentially problematic features of autobiographical narratives discussed below, it may also be therapeutic in and of itself. For example, Pennebaker's (1997) extensive series of studies on therapeutic journaling of painful life experiences suggests that the recurrent telling of a tale, in all of its vivid immediacy, has profoundly positive consequences for both the author's emotional and physical well-being, even outside the context of psychotherapy.

The importance of "setting work" can be illustrated by my recent therapy with Barry and Matt, a father and son who sought help following the horrendous deaths of two other family members. Coming home from work early one day, Barry heard his wife, Lisa, call their 4-year-old daughter, Carrie, back to the bedroom. Two gunshots then exploded the relative tranquility of the house, the crack being clearly distinguishable from the musical background of the videogame that 15-year-old Matt was playing in a room down the hall. Running frantically into the bedroom, Barry saw Lisa standing over Carrie's broken and bleeding body. As he shouted, "What have you done?" Lisa leveled the gun at Barry's own torso and pulled the trigger. The impact of the shot to his chest slammed him against the wall, but he remained standing and lunged at her to remove the gun from her grip. Matt then ran into the room and assisted in tearing the gun from his mother's hand, as both men turned and knelt to render help to Carrie. Lisa then fell face forward onto the floor and died, apparently from the previously undiscovered second shot to her own chest.

Seeing them only 1 month after this tragedy, I confronted several urgent therapeutic tasks, among which was helping both Barry and Matt develop a coherent account of the traumatic event and struggle with the apparently unanswerable question of why Lisa took such desperate action. A turning point came in our fourth session, as I guided them through a step-by-step accounting of the scene of violence, with special attention to the vivid details that had captured their attention at the time. As each emotionally recounted his own perceptions, one image in particular—absent from previous more synoptic tellings—emerged. On first entering the murder–suicide scene, Barry vividly recalled his wife's impassive expression as she looked him in the eyes and shot him. In strong contrast, he described her "enraged and contorted" visage on seeing Matt enter the room, an expression he said he had never before seen on any human face. Matt confirmed the latter image, and the two worked together with only occasional prompting by me to formulate a rendering of Lisa's emotions, intent, and motives adequate to account for this powerful discrepancy. What emerged was a story of sexual betrayal anchored in abusive experiences in Lisa's own childhood and reenacted in subsequent relationships prior to the reactivation of similar themes in her marriage to Barry. With this much more complex narrative in view for the first time, Lisa's possible motivation to coldly punish Barry by killing those he loved, and her rage at the children for not supporting her story of abuse, was opened for the mutual consideration of both survivors. Both left the session feeling that their grieving, although complicated by this interpretation, had somehow been moved forward through active exploration of the details of the episode and the alternative, if disturbing "readings" of family relationships it suggested.

Characterization

Characterization refers to the *who* of the story: the multiple agents—protagonists, antagonists, and supporting characters—who engage in actions (Sarbin, 1986) as well as the attribution of intentionality to these characters. Although the personalities, motives, and emotions of each of the characters (including the self) may be directly described by the narrator, they may also emerge implicitly through a variety of more subtle literary devices, such as their dialogic relations with one another, inferences based on their behaviors, and soliloquies. One particularly interesting device of this kind is *double voicing,* in which the narrator positions the self with respect to other voices in the social world through quoting snippets of dialogue that cast the self and other in certain lights (Wortham, 1999). This form of "altercasting" is familiar to any therapist whose clients have replayed exchanges with significant others in a way that highlights the client's moral superiority, heroism, or victimization and the other's inferiority, villainy, or culpability.

Narrative therapists concerned with clients' lack of insight into others' intentions or their own have developed a number of methods for adding psychological depth to the conflicted stories that clients tell. Gonçalves (1995), for instance, devised various therapeutic exercises for subjectifying narratives by cueing clients to attend to the inner experiences, both cognitive and emotional, of each of the characters in their story. Constructivist contributors have been especially significant in exploring the multiple characterizations of the self, by providing metaphors and methods for articulating one's own internal complexity. These range from emotionally evocative two-chair dialogues for exploring sensed discrepancies within one's own position (Greenberg & Pascual-Leone, 1995) to narrative enactments of one's internal cast of characters in relation to the "subselves" of other group therapy members (Sewell, Baldwin, & Moes, 1998). Still other narrative strategies have been devised to help clients trace the delicate reciprocal relationships between constructions of self and other, as when one's own identity is eroded by the loss of a loved one (Neimeyer, 1998b).

A particularly powerful method for elucidating a client's deeper nonconscious intentions and purposes is provided by depth-oriented brief therapy (DOBT) devised by Ecker and Hulley (1996). This form of characterization work is illustrated by my current therapy with Bill, a divorced man whose subsequent marriage to Delanie exacerbated existing tensions in his relationship with his 17-year-old daughter, Cassie, by his previous marriage. Over the course of a dozen intermittent consultations during a 3-year period, we had dealt with a series of issues: the disabling flight phobia that restricted his work as an executive in a large company; his guilt about the affair (with Delanie) that had triggered his divorce; his indecision about committing to a second marriage, despite Delanie's growing impatience; and finally their mutual frustration over the merger of their families, as Bill became a "wonderful father" to Delanie's 16-year-old daughter but maintained only a fleeting and private correspondence with his own daughter, Cassie. In each case except the last, Bill made significant progress, ultimately flying on business for the first time in 20 years, becoming public about his relationship with Delanie, and even embracing the prospect of a married life together. Now, however, Delanie became increasingly insistent that she be included in Bill's "secret" (although infrequent) contact with Cassie, whose apparent "rejection" of Delanie left Bill feeling that he was being stretched in a "tug of war" between the two. Bill's external response to this dilemma was to avoid his daughter, now living in another state with her mother, having had no face-to-face contact with her for more than 3 years. Internally, he grieved the lapse in their relationship and feared for the viability of his new marriage unless the situation were resolved.

In DOBT terms, Bill's genuine motivation to transcend this pattern of anxious avoidance represented the anti-symptom position that motivated his return to therapy. The pain this "standoff" caused him was very real, and my first tasks as a therapist were to help him articulate it and to respond to it with genuine empathy. But a hallmark principle of DOBT is that a given symptom is actually coherent with a higher order, hidden purpose, a system of meanings and intentions that constitutes an unconscious pro-symptom position. Therapy therefore consists of a process of radical inquiry (Ecker & Hulley, 1996; also see chap. 4 in this volume), which has the goal to quickly lead the client to "bump into" these deeply embedded constructs in an experientially vivid way, without in any way attempting to interpret, invalidate, or challenge them. Once both the anti-symptom and pro-symptom stances are in clear view, the client's story makes a new kind of sense, setting the stage for the conscious affirmation of one position or the other or the possible integration of both into a more comprehensive self-narrative.

Using the technique of "symptom deprivation," I began by asking Bill to close his eyes and "get a clear visual picture of Delanie and Cassie together, engaged in an ordinary, day-to-day activity," to prompt his awareness of how he would experience reality deprived of their customary distance. After a moment of silence, Bill visibly winced, and said, "I wanted to say it would be wonderful, but my first reaction was to break out into a cold sweat. I immediately flashed to a big confrontation between two stubborn people." Intrigued, I instructed him to simply sit with this scene for a few more moments and to "let me know if anything else came up." This triggered a process of serial accessing of felt meanings, in which he first noted with a trembling jaw that the emotion that washed over him "felt exactly like the internal panic over getting on board a plane." He then swallowed hard, opened his eyes, and said, "It may not even be Delanie and Cassie together; it may be *me* and Cassie together that's the problem." He fell silent for a moment more, then added, "I've got something I can't break through here."

Rather than shifting to an abstract discussion of this impasse, I used the technique of sentence completion to keep Bill in contact with the further implications of this pro-symptom position. This involved my inviting him, without prereflection, to complete the stem, "If Cassie were to come here, then . . . ." His first response was predictable and safe: "we'd be happy to see her." His second went deeper: "I'd be nervous about losing one or both of them." As his eyes moistened, I prompted him with a third, more personal stem, to which he replied, "If Cassie were to come here, then *I* . . . might see her walk out of my life." Wiping away tears, Bill then flashed to an image of Cassie at age 9, as he sat snuggled up with her, telling her she would soon be a teenager and "all grown up." Putting her arms around his neck, she had lovingly reassured him, "I'll always be your little girl." Tears welled in Bill's eyes, and he removed his glasses to wipe them away, sobbing silently.

With all of the elements of his pro-symptom position now in view, Bill's deeper purpose in maintaining the distance with Cassie became clear, despite its great costs in their relationship and his marriage. Bringing the session to a close, I formulated this stance in sharply etched words on an index card, which I handed to Bill and asked him to read slowly aloud: "As painful as this present standoff is, I would rather suffer this terrible distance from Cassie than to have her walk away and never feel her arms around my neck, never hear her say, 'I'm still your little girl.' " Choking on the word *arms*, Bill stammered out the sentence and, drying his tears, quietly noted that inhabiting this position consciously "made me understand the things I've been doing in a whole different light." My request that he simply read the card a few times a day, with no attempt to change his behavior, set the stage for a deeper appreciation of his intentions and experimentation with new responses in the weeks to come.

Plot

The plot of a narrative refers to *what* transpired, to the "landscape of action," in Bruner's (1990) terms, rather than the "landscape of intentionality" associated with characterization. Emplotting events requires first carving them up as distinguishable episodes from the flux of experience and then relating them in a meaningful sequence that coheres over time. In the case of autobiographical narratives, there is the further requirement that the events thus plotted cohere with a sustainable sense of self as well.

Difficulties can arise when experiences seem radically discontinuous, dissociated, and divorced from the master narrative that imparts structure to one's identity (Neimeyer & Stewart, 1996). In such cases, "emplotment work" can take the form of helping clients re-story their experience in more adequate ways, finding ways to structure and construe events that were previously edited out of their accounts or suspended from their meaning systems (Kelly, 1955). For example, my therapy with a client who had been traumatically assaulted involved helping him reconstruct his "jigsaw memories" of the violent event by writing his fragmentary recollections on separate notecards and then attempting to devise a story structure that accommodated them (Neimeyer & Stewart, 1998b). As he recovered a plot structure for subsuming the assault, he discovered that previously forgotten or suspended aspects of the experience came back to him, and he could begin to reconstruct a more adequate account that answered some of his own questions about the traumatic event. More comprehensive approaches to narrative repair of the self include Mahoney's (1991) life review exercise and Stewart's (1995) imaginal writing procedures for survivors of combat trauma.[5]

Although inadequate emplotment of life events and a resulting incoherence in identity has been the predominant concern of cognitively oriented narrative therapists, those with social constructionist leanings have focused on instances in which the self is in a sense too coherent. For instance, White and Epston (1990) attempted to distinguish the story of the problem from the person who is recruited into accepting it as the dominant narrative of her or his life. From this perspective, it is the very hegemony of the problem-saturated story that requires deconstruction by first revealing its destructive "real effects" on the person whose life it invades and then seeking those "sparkling moments" of resistance against it (Monk et al., 1996). As these exceptional episodes are historicized, shared, and witnessed by relevant others, a counternarrative begins to take shape that undermines the apparent authority of the problem (e.g., bulimia, aggression), not only in the life of the client but also in the culture as a whole. Viewed from this perspective, incoherent subplots in personal narrative actually may serve as sources of liberation by subverting a dominant storyline that has become suffocating, stagnant, or stripped of future possibility.

Theme

The themes of a self-narrative refer to its *why*: the explanatory underpinnings that thread episodes through with significance. A biographical sense of identity becomes consolidated as one tacks back and forth between tacit participation in the plot structure of one's life (the experiencing *me*) and the explicit attribution of thematic meaning to these episodes (the

---

[5] As this summary implies, most constructivists have sought the means to help clients devise personally significant plot structures to impart continuity to events. However, others have argued that more superordinate mythic structures in any of the classic literary forms (comic, romantic, tragic, or ironic) can also shape the contours of a meaningful account (Atkinson, 1995; McAdams, 1993). For example, a client's struggle with progressive alienation, drug dependence, and eventual return to human society might be configured as a mythic hero tale, in which the protagonist (e.g., Odysseus) leaves his homeland, overcomes fearsome monsters, and eventually returns triumphant to his people. Narrative "classicists," in this sense, practice a version of therapy that is a hybrid of cognitive constructivist models (with their emphasis on personal meaning making) and social constructionist approaches (which stress the cultural origins of modes of thought that shape the experience of self).

explaining *I*; Guidano, 1991). Circumstances that preclude this braiding together of events and explanations threaten the strands of significance that give meaning to our lives.

The experience of psychological trauma represents one such circumstance. Not only do such traumatic experiences as physical and sexual assault, tragic bereavement, and natural catastrophe disrupt the presumed plot structure of our lives, but they also radically challenge its assumptive foundations (Janoff-Bulman & Berg, 1998; Neimeyer, 1998b). Faced with the invalidation of taken-for-granted beliefs in a just universe, a predictable future, a benign social world, and a beneficent God, the traumatized individual faces the unsustainability of those themes that had once given form and direction to his or her life. With the breakdown of thematic structure comes a disintegration of identity, as the person finds it impossible to assimilate the "traumatic self" (as, e.g., combat veteran, bereaved parent, rape victim) into the system of constructs that had previously organized his or her biography.

Constructivists have developed a number of techniques for assessing the thematic structure of self-narratives, ranging from systems for analyzing the constructs underlying autobiographical texts (Feixas & Villegas, 1991) to biographical grids that examine how the author integrates and differentiates important life events (Neimeyer & Stewart, 1996; Sewell, 1997). Hermans's (1995) self-confrontation method is especially useful in this respect, prompting respondents to recall significant episodes from their lives and then rate them in ways that ultimately yield scores on superordinate themes of self-enhancement, union with others, positivity, and negativity. Any of these relatively structured methods could be used not only for the purposes of assessment but also for prompting therapeutic discussion of the central themes around which a client's life script is organized.

"Theme work" in therapy can take other forms as well. Gonçalves (1995), for example, directly coached clients to formulate structural, orientational, and physical metaphors to symbolize elusive meanings in their self-narratives. Gendlin (1996) helped clients articulate their "felt sense" of a problem in imagistically rich language that conveys important themes more adequately than conventional speech. An example of the narrative structuring of a profoundly disruptive event is provided by the account of a bereaved father, who wrote the following metaphoric account of his life in the aftermath of the death of his 2-year-old son (Neimeyer, 1998b).

> I am building a three sided house.
>
> It is not a good design. With one side open to the weather, it will never offer complete shelter from life's cold winds. Four sides would be much better, but there is no foundation on one side, and so three walls are all I have to work with.
>
> I am building this place from the rubble of the house I used to own.
> . . . It had four good walls and would, I thought, survive the most violent

storm. It did not. A storm beyond my understanding tore my house apart and left the fragments lying on the ground around me. . . . And so I must rebuild. Not, as so many onlookers would suggest, because I need shelter once again. The storm now travels within me, and there is no shelter from that tempest behind doors or walls.

Who can show me how to build here now? There are no architects, no experts in designing three sided houses. Why is it then that so many people seem to have advice for me? "Move on," they say, quite convinced that another house can replace the one I lost. . . . I grow weary of consultations based on murky insight, delivered with such confidence. . . . [And yet] among those who wish to see my house rise again[,] there are real heroes too. People who are not daunted by the wreckage. It is not a pleasant role for them to play because the dust clings to those who come to see me and it will not wash off when they go home. . . . Above all they know how difficult this task is, and no suggestion comes from them about how far along I ought to be. (pp. 176–178)[6]

Such accounts serve multiple functions, constructing an emotionally vivid setting for the self-narrative, exploring the positions of self and others through skillful double voicing, emplotting a tragic life event, and rendering its thematic significance for one's changed identity in metaphoric terms.[7]

Fictional Goal

I use the term *fictional goal* to refer to the *wherefore* of the narrative, its overarching *telos* or projected endpoint. Like Vaihinger (1924) and Adler (1956), I presume that such goals are creative "as if" constructions, human inventions that posit certain possibilities as real (or realizable), whatever their actual truth status. As such, they are superordinate to the day-to-day themes threaded through a person's construction of events, and they bear more directly on the person's sense of identity. In cognitive constructivist theories, these central organizing themes are referred to as "core role con-

---

[6]From *Lessons of Loss: A Guide to Coping*, by R. A. Neimeyer, 1998b, New York: McGraw-Hill. Copyright 1998 by R. A. Neimeyer. Reprinted with permission.

[7]Although most constructivists adopt an essentially individualistic perspective in helping clients articulate personal themes that underpin their narration of life episodes, the dividing line between cognitive and social perspectives to theme work is often an (appropriately) indeterminate one. For example, Kelly (1955), who is often regarded as the prototypical cognitive constructivist, consistently went to great lengths to anchor the self in a social context. In connection with the clinical analysis of personal themes, he wrote that the therapist can "also look for thema in the social world which surrounds the subject. What are the family stories? What is the community folklore? What epic tales are told? What are the life-span patterns that are most clearly represented to the client as he looks about him? It is against these that he must somehow make his own story plots appear to be plausible. If the play is written by his culture group, how can he interpret his own part in order to fit into the plot?" (p. 770). Viewed from this angle, culture (at all levels from the macro to the micro) offers a repertory of life themes from which the person can draw, and a context against which individual innovations on these themes can be validated.

structs" (Kelly, 1955), the "metaphysical hard core" of a person's model of self and world (Guidano & Liotti, 1983), or "core ordering processes," expressing a person's sense of empowerment, reciprocity, and so on (Mahoney, 1995). In more explicitly narrative accounts, the superordinate fictional theme of a life story is termed its "generativity script" (McAdams, 1993) or the "macronarrative" that weaves together the "micronarratives" of everyday life (Angus, Levitt, & Hardtke, in press). At this level, any given narrative can be judged by its author (or its audience) as being progressive, regressive, or stable in the sense of moving toward or away from a desired end state (Gergen & Gergen, 1986).

Constructivists encountering nonprogressive narratives in their clients' lives have devised a number of procedures for helping them restore movement. Villegas (1992) designed therapeutically useful linguistic procedures for extracting the central organizing theme of an autobiographical text and for assessing its level of redundancy and coherence. Kelly's (1955) early experimentation with fixed role therapy, in which clients were coached to enact the script of a fictional identity for a designated period in daily life, had as its goal experiential immersion in a novel but temporary story of self and social relations. Similarly, Gonçalves (1995) devised techniques for prompting clients to "project" narratives, preconfiguring new "possible selves" toward which they might evolve. Finally, narrative therapists inspired by White and Epston (1990) have invented an ingenious set of future-oriented possibility questions and as if rituals that can help clients re-vision the fictional goals of their autobiographies and, in so doing, move them in more positive directions (Freedman & Combs, 1996; Parry & Doan, 1994).

Fictional goal work figured prominently in my therapy with Marcia, a 33-year-old woman who felt she had "lost her way" in life, repeating an endless series of unsatisfying relationships, against the backdrop of career stagnation. As her story emerged, the plot structure was remarkably predictable across variations in person and circumstance: She found herself attracting men easily through sexually provocative overtures, only to "cut them off" when they began to show anything more than physical interest in her. As a result, her biography was littered with the wreckage of scores of relationships, each of which she would dramatically reject by flaunting her next conquest. Her work life was equally unstable and showed a similar pattern: Just at the point when her entry-level job began to show promise of developing into a more substantial career direction, she would find ways to sabotage her own advancement. Marcia was keenly aware of this pattern but felt powerless to envision any future that departed from this ingrained narrative structure.

As Marcia and I discussed this pattern, she came to a dramatic insight. "Maybe," she suggested, "all of this has to do with when I was 11, and *my father killed myself.*" Struck by this linguistic turn, I asked her if she could repeat what she had just said. She complied by stating, "Maybe this has to do with when I was 11, and *my father killed himself.*" "No," I interjected, "you said 'killed *myself.*'" At this she moaned, "oh my God," buried her face in her hands, and began to sob uncontrollably.

As we "unpacked" the emotional truth of her slip, it became clearer to both of us that Marcia's father's suicide—at age 33, the very age at which she had sought therapy—had indeed "killed" (a part of) her as well. In response, Marcia had established an unconscious "revenge script" in which she repeatedly drew out men only to abandon them. Although this thematic reenactment of her own abandonment by her "first love" at least cast her in the protagonist rather than victim role, its painful repetitiousness had begun to outweigh any retributive satisfaction it offered. Moreover, Marcia's inability to project a future beyond that point in life when her father had abdicated his own suggested the complicated way in which she had internalized his life story to make it hers. Gradually, Marcia was able to consolidate these narrative insights and began to construct and realize a fictional goal more in keeping with the person she wanted to become.

POINTS OF VIEW AND VOICE

As stylistic characteristics of narratives, the kindred concepts of points of view and voice have been given less attention, at least in the constructivist psychotherapy literature, than the formal features of setting, characterization, plot, theme, and fictional goal described above. Ironically, attention to them even in "true" literature is a relatively recent phenomenon, where for the most part they are discussed more unsystematically than systematically. An exception to this general neglect is the comprehensive taxonomy of points of view offered by Moffett and McElheny (1995), who distinguished among (a) interior monologue, (b) dramatic monologue, (c) letter narration, (d) diary narration, (e) subjective narration, (f) detached autobiography, (g) memoir, and (h) anonymous narration. Each of these, in turn, can be expressed from the standpoint of single, dual, or multiple characters within the story or from the vantage point of none at all.

Overall, these styles are arranged on a continuum from the private to the public and from the specific to the general. In an ultimate sense, every narration can be considered a first-person account, insofar as it is the work of a given author. However, the first five styles are first person in the literal sense: They "keep alive the drama of the narrating act: they put the speakers on display so that we cannot ignore or forget the way they talk, the kind of logic they use, and the organization they impose on experience" (Moffett & McElheny, 1995, p. 558). In contrast, with later third-person accounts, it is easy to forget that there is a teller behind the telling, as the author adopts the more generalized position of multiple participants or even a posture of godlike omniscience. Corresponding to this shift in perspective is a shift in subject, moving "from relative, individual realities to a single, consensual reality" (p. 593). Thus, narrative therapists could attend to the form in which their clients narrate their experience because this carries subtle implications for the way they position themselves as authors and the knowledge claims they make about the world. Although it is infeasible in the current context to tease out the contribution of each of these styles to an understanding of self-narratives and their disruption, consideration of a few distinct styles can suggest their potential relevance to narrative therapy.

Interior monologue, whether spoken or written, represents the author's stream of consciousness. Like a theatrical soliloquy, it allows the audience to hear the individual's inner voice in a minimally edited form. In its psychotherapeutic application, it can take the form of the client "streaming" aloud, eyes closed and reclining, in the presence of a therapist who encourages but does not interpret the shifting flow of the client's awareness, thoughts, and feelings (Mahoney, 1991). Alternatively, it can take the form of a "free write," in which the client as author free associates on paper, without imposing conscious structure on his or her spontaneous self-exploration (Rainer, 1978). In either case, interior monologue aims to facilitate the client's self-exploration, minimizing the constraints of more objective discourse or more dialogical communication patterns.

Letter narration retains this first-person point of view but moves in the direction of a "tighter" organization. Whereas interior monologue can change courses abruptly, tracking whatever associative stream predominates in a given moment, letter narration is typically more deliberate. This is in part because the writer is not usually face-to-face with the reader, necessitating a more coherent exposition, and because the letter at least presumes a reader's response in a way that interior monologue does not. In psychotherapeutic use, this style might take the form of an "unsent letter" to a lost loved one, as a means of "continuing the conversation" that was interrupted by death (Neimeyer, 1998b). Not only can such an exercise be used to prompt further therapeutic processing of the unresolved relationship, but it can also initiate an "exchange" of letters with the deceased, as the client alternately "indwells" and writes from the other's perspective and his or her own.

Detached autobiography moves toward greater apparent objectivity, but by accomplishing an interesting epistemological shift, splitting the "I-now" from the "I-then." This corresponds to a shift in the author's mode of processing experience, from the relatively raw immediacy of interior monologue and letter narration to the more reflective evaluation made possible in retrospect. As such, it can represent a valuable means of consolidating changes that have occurred across a course of psychotherapy, perhaps taking the form of written "declarations of independence" from a presenting problem or audiotaped accounts of a history of resistance against a dominant narrative (White & Epston, 1990).

Anonymous narration can issue from the standpoint of a single or multiple characters in the story, yet it remains anonymous insofar as the character need not account for how she or he came to know what she or he does about the person described. When two or more viewpoints are played out in a given narrative, the tension between them can *be* the story and reveal the clearly perspectival nature of all perception. Kelly's (1955) instructions for his self-characterization technique, in which he encouraged the client to write a character sketch of himself or herself from the standpoint of "someone who knows you intimately and sympathetically, perhaps better than anyone actually could know you" (p. 323), represents one therapeutic application of this style. Kelly assumed that the adoption of a sympathetic third-person perspective gave the client permission to relinquish a confessional or self-incriminating stance and adopt a hypothetical, reflective position in relation to the larger themes of his or her life. A narration of the client's life story from multiple standpoints (as it would be written by, e.g., the client's mother, first love, spouse, children, or therapist) could also underscore the social construction of identity while subtly deconstructing the assumption that there is a single true perspective on who he or she really is.

Closely related to the concept of points of view is that of *voice*, by which I refer to the mode of expression in the narrative, irrespective of its form or the perspective from which it is written. For example, in some narratives one can discern a clear note of protest, a bid for understanding, an attempt at problem solving, or a quest for objectivity. To some extent, the vocal tenor of the narrative may be related to its unique structural features (e.g., stories with central themes that center on victimization are likely to be authored in a protesting voice), but the correlation between the two is approximate rather than predictable. Likewise, although narration from an internal monologic view is more likely to be written in a cathartic voice than a problem-solving one, the relationship between the two remains indeterminate. Thus, voice can be considered a distinguishable dimension of narrative in which description—or even prescription—by the therapist can advance the client's exploration of an authorial self.

Perhaps the most frequent discussion of voice by psychotherapists occurs in the feminist literature, where it is often contrasted to the "silencing" of women's experiences and values by androcentric cultures (Goldberger, 1996). In this sense, "finding one's voice" implies the affirmation of one's unique selfhood, the achievement of a measure of empowerment. Although not opposed to this reading,[8] I use the concept of voice to describe how a story is told rather than to connote a quality of personal agency that is either absent or present. Rainer (1978) seemed to have a similar usage in mind when she wrote about the cathartic, descriptive, intuitive, and reflective modes in which one can write in a personal journal or diary, seeing each as a potentially valuable way of processing experience.

The therapeutic use of point of view and voice can be illustrated by the narrative of Kerry, a woman in her late 30s, whose 2-year old son, Jacob, had died 3 years before from the complications of a congenital heart defect. Because his death seemed to represent a critical turning point in her life and identity, I invited her to compose a "loss characterization," modeled on Kelly's (1955) self-characterization, to emplot the experience and articulate its central themes. The instructional set, printed at the top of a single blank sheet of paper, read as follows:

> In the space that follows, please write a character sketch of Kerry, in light of her loss. Write it just as if she were the principal character in a book, movie, or play. Write it as it might be written by a friend who knew her very intimately and sympathetically, perhaps better than anyone really could know her. Be sure to write it in the third person. For example, start out by saying, "Kerry is . . ." (p. 154)[9]

Kerry's response spanned several pages, portions of which are excerpted below, interspersed with brief interpretive commentary.

> Kerry is a woman who feels and experiences her life deeply inside herself. Prior to the loss of her son, Kerry led what appeared to be a "charmed" life. From all outside appearances, everything in her life was easy and beautiful. Inside, however, deep inside, she knew that something was inferior about her life and the manner in which she was living it. Even though the external rewards of financial security and social belongingness (and the coinciding pressures to maintain them) were abundant in her exis-

---

[8] That is, I do not oppose this use of voice as an apt and liberating metaphor for the experience of many women, or for that matter, for many men, children, or even entire cultural groups. Indeed, the image of seeking and finding one's own narrative voice has frequently been useful to my own clients and students. But neither do I endorse the essentialist implications of this usage—the idea that one has a true voice or a single one for that matter. Instead, I find it more useful to speak of the polyphony of voices in each person, no one of which can shout down the others without marginalizing potentially valuable possible selves seeking their turn to be heard. Again, I trust that the reader understands, too, that I use this locution as a metaphor and am not espousing the view that the self represents a real coalition of homunculi responsible for human action. Rather, I see these voices as representing the reverberations of conversations with a heterogeneously distributed network of other people and symbolic resources, in keeping with the social constructionist thesis enunciated earlier in this chapter.
[9] The entire transcript of Kerry's loss characterization, along with a different deconstructive analysis of its form and content, can be found in Neimeyer (1998b). From *Lessons of Loss: A Guide to Coping*, by R. A. Neimeyer, 1998b. New York: McGraw-Hill. Copyright 1998 by R. A. Neimeyer. Reprinted with permission.

tence, she still didn't feel at one with herself or others. There was always that little part of her that felt something was wrong. She was doing something wrong. She could see others who appeared to have a depth and intelligence about themselves that she was somehow lacking, and there was a negative moral attachment to that. Something about her was wrong and inferior, and she knew it. But she couldn't get to it. (p. 155)[10]

In this opening paragraph, Kerry begins the narration of her loss by establishing its relevant setting—a "charmed" life, easy and beautiful—and engages in extensive characterization of herself at a psychological level. Moreover, she begins to introduce thematic dimensions that can be expected to underpin later passages (e.g., inside vs. outside; easy and beautiful vs. wrong and inferior). Finally, she hints at a fictional goal for the narrative and the life it depicts: the quest for a moral depth that would allow her to feel more at one with herself and others. All of this is framed from the standpoint of an anonymous single narrator, in a voice that is both reflective and compassionate. At a meta-analytic level, the listener or reader senses that this voice has become Kerry's, foreshadowing the resolution to the drama she is beginning to configure.

Kerry then shifts settings, carrying the reader back to her high school years, when the mother of her best friend died. Although this tragedy left her friend "troubled," she nevertheless remained popular with others, perhaps even more so. Kerry continues her third-person account,

> For Kerry, this was a puzzling juxtaposition in life: People with trouble and tragedy in their lives who weren't very happy were very loved by others. Those like herself, however, who were living what appeared to be quintessentially "normal" (often boring) lives, did not have the depth of feeling and magnetism of experience these other people seemed to embody. For years, she naively wished that she too could have that special something in her life. (She didn't realize what a price the others had paid.) Finally, at age 34 her wish came true. She had the chance to experience and develop that depth and inner intelligence that she had seen for so long in others. Her second child, Jacob, was born.
>
> Throughout his life, Kerry lived in a mode of survival. But she didn't know it. It was just life to her, and after a while, it seemed altogether normal. On some level, retrospectively, Kerry had to give up her own life for those years for Jacob to live and for the experience to ripen into vintage possibility for her soul's education. (pp. 155–156)[11]

In this passage of the loss characterization, Kerry positions herself as narrator not only as someone who knows herself as protagonist "intimately

---

[10] From *Lessons of Loss: A Guide to Coping,* by R. A. Neimeyer, 1998b. New York: McGraw-Hill. Copyright 1998 by R. A. Neimeyer. Reprinted with permission.
[11] *Ibid.*

and sympathetically," in keeping with the instructional set, but also as someone who has known Kerry as a lifelong friend, interpreting subsequent developments against the backdrop of her earlier intentions. This permits her not only to embellish the earlier themes contrasting superficial normality with a wished for "depth and inner intelligence" but also to approximate the voice of wisdom for which she had so long yearned. In rich detail, she then further sets the stage for narrating her son's final hospitalization and her devoted caretaking of him to the point of neglecting not only her own needs but also those of her young daughter, Sarah. Kerry's characterization work is especially poignant in a portion of her narrative when she describes Sarah's plaintive questioning of "where Mommy had gone and when she'd be back" and Kerry's own "screaming and thrashing inside at her inability to take this pain away from her daughter." Of interest is that Kerry "fast forwards" over those elements of plot that have to do with Jacob's actual death and burial, raising the question of how fully these tragic episodes have been integrated into her life narrative. Instead, she focuses on the thematic substructure of the story, as suggested in this closing passage:

> Once the death occurred, Kerry began to desperately search for reasons why this had happened to her (and her family). Twenty-nine years before, when her own mother was 29 years old, Kerry lost a sibling, who died just after birth. Kerry was almost exactly the same age as Sarah when they each lost siblings. As Kerry began to reexamine and reevaluate her own "normal" life in light of this loss, she could not ignore the synchronicity of events that was becoming apparent to her. She began to envision God as a "great karmic cashier in the sky." He (and make no mistake, it was a "He" at that time) would say to her, "There's a debt due here and someone is going to pay. You can pay me now, or you can pay me later, but someone is going to pay. And there's interest due!" Kerry began to recognize that it was time to "ante up." She knew that if she did not pay for the sin of unconsciousness bequeathed to her by her mother and her mother's mother, that sweet, darling, innocent Sarah would be forced to pay the debt of feminine unconsciousness in this matrilineal line. . . . She became determined to live her life and parent her children as consciously as she possibly could.
>
> There was a great price of suffering to pay for the consciousness which Kerry now possesses. She paid it in the loss of Jacob, in the loss of friends who couldn't stand the pain, and in the loss of a way of life that had previously been fairly comfortable. . . . At times, even those closest to her do not understand the rage she has felt these last years nor the changes that have occurred in the interior alchemical fire of her soul. (p. 157)[12]

---

[12] From *Lessons of Loss: A Guide to Coping*, by R. A. Neimeyer, 1998b. New York: McGraw-Hill. Copyright 1998 by R. A. Neimeyer. Reprinted with permission.

Ultimately, Kerry enlists elements of setting, characterization, plot, and theme in the service of a broader fictional goal: the quest for an inner depth and wisdom that could only be purchased through (noble) suffering. In terms of a social constructionist thesis, this personal goal draws on a cultural and gendered discourse: Kerry confronted "karmic" retribution by a male deity, who demanded atonement for transgenerational maternal unconsciousness by the attainment of a higher self-awareness forged in the "alchemical fire" ignited by her son's death. Thus, the third-person point of view from which the story is narrated, in the voice of someone who could almost have been a spiritual guide, permitted Kerry to weave an artful account of her loss that placed it in a broader frame of intelligibility. In so doing, she also sought (and perhaps helped establish) a changed identity for herself, one that was coherent with a fictional goal foreshadowed in her youth and perhaps even in previous generations. Kerry's account further illustrates the way in which various elements of narration converge not only to give a life narrative its dramatic intensity but also to reinforce a viable sense of self for its author.[13]

AUTHOR AND AUDIENCE

Although there are strong interpersonal and cultural overtones to the foregoing treatment of narrative form and function, as well as points of view and voice, for the most part the social domain recedes into the background when the focus is on narrative structure. In contrast, a focus on author and audience foregrounds the social, shifting attention from a monological perspective on story composition to an explicitly dialogical perspective on story telling. Such telling, which views narration as a social performance rather than a cognitive accomplishment, inevitably positions the author in relation to an intended audience and, at least implicitly, calls for an audience response.

This is nowhere clearer than in the interpersonal context of psychotherapy, where "client stories can be told to instruct, entertain, impress, implore,

---

[13] This is not to say that Kerry's account of her loss and its significance is fully coherent, true, or even represents the last word for her as an author. Indeed, I assume that her account could be further deconstructed through critical attention to its cosmological assumptions (e.g., karmic retribution), sensitive interrogation of thinly plotted elements (e.g., her son's death), or deeper characterization (e.g., in terms of the respective positions of different figures, including her son, daughter, and husband). In the context of ongoing therapy, Kerry herself might even initiate this deconstruction, perhaps even to the point of rewriting her fictional goal of pursuing her "soul's education" through the painful cultivation of her consciousness. But the inevitably open texture of any life narrative does not diminish its status as a provisional fictional frame for living, any more than the subtle contradictions or limiting assumptions of Thoreau's *Walden* diminish its status as a work of great literature.

test, admonish, invite, or distance the therapist; occasionally, several of these intents may be compressed into a single storytelling" (Neimeyer, 1995a, p. 233). Thus, in addition to listening closely to what is being told (at the level of narrative plot, theme, characterization, etc.) and how it is being expressed (in terms of point of view and voice), the therapist needs to attend to why the client is telling this story to him or her at this moment. Such an emphasis on the social function of narration accords clients the status of *discourse users*, manipulators of "interpretive repertoires" for constructing preferred versions of their motives and actions in relation to others (Potter & Wetherell, 1987). To serve their purpose, such narratives must receive at least tacit, and preferably explicit, support from relevant "validating agents" (Landfield, 1988), including the therapist.

Although most constructivist psychotherapists focus on the intra- rather than interpersonal functions of client narration, some recognize that any story being told is being told to somebody and for some reason. Hermans (in press) acknowledged that the dialogical reciprocity between listener and teller makes storytelling a highly dynamic interactive phenomenon, one that ultimately cannot be attributed to the work of an isolated subjectivity. Through his or her response (whether confirming, rebutting, interrogating, extending, analyzing, or reflecting), the listener inevitably helps shape the account that emerges and the corresponding sense of self that the client seeks to consolidate in the telling. Following a similar logic, Angus et al. (in press) developed a narrative processes coding system for psychotherapeutic transcripts, one that views any given narrative sequence as an emergent product of the therapeutic dialogue. Accordingly, these investigators made no attempt to distinguish between client and therapist contributions to clinically relevant narratives, coding stories that evolve across several conversational turns as *external* (focused on specific events or issues), *internal* (elaborating on subjective feelings and reactions), or *reflexive* (exploring one's own behavior or interpretations). Like Hermans, Angus et al. found a dialogical conception of narration to provide a useful heuristic frame for researching both meaning reconstruction and its impediments across the course of therapy.

Perhaps the most explicit attempt to orchestrate the relation between author and audience for therapeutic ends is found in the work of White and Epston (1990) and their associates. As clients gradually succeed in freeing themselves from the dominance of oppressive, problem-saturated life stories, therapists in this narrative tradition assist them in identifying and recruiting appropriate audiences for the "performance" of emerging more constructive stories of their lives and relationships. Initially, the therapist may be the first to notice a client's departures from a dominant narrative (e.g., moments when a guilt-ridden man treats himself in a self-nurturing way), encouraging the client to begin to consolidate such exceptional moments into a more hopeful life story (Monk et al., 1996). Ultimately, however, narrative therapists assume that the client's preferred identity claims are best authenticated in relation to broader audiences, including family, friends, and perhaps other people struggling with similar problems. The recruitment of such audiences might be prompted by such questions as the following: "Now that you have reached this point in life, who else do you think should know about it? What difference do you think it would make to their attitude toward you if they had the news? I guess there are a number of people who have an outdated view of who you are as a person. What ideas do you have for updating these views? What would be most newsworthy? If other people seek therapy for the same reasons you did, can I share with them any of the important discoveries you have made? If so, to what extent can I do this and under what circumstances?" The documentation of these "alternative knowledges" can take numerous forms, from straightforward conversations with relevant others within or outside therapy sessions to more formal written or taped histories of therapeutic accomplishments constructed principally by the client. A focus on the documentation and circulation of the new narrative is especially important toward the end of therapy, when it can serve as a rite of passage that permits the client to be reincorporated into the social world in a transformed status (Epston & White, 1995).

An example of this process is provided by my therapy with Carol, whose own tendency toward self-abuse and self-isolation cohered with a long history of sexual victimization and interpersonal rejection. Disheveled and almost mute in her early sessions, Carol's earliest "communications" to me took the form of subtle self-abuse in therapy (e.g., bruising her arms on the arms of her chair) and more flagrant self-injury (e.g., cutting her arms and breasts) between sessions. As Carol and I focused on the meanings of these actions, she came to describe them as "carving messages to me in her flesh," suggesting the dominance of a destructive, if inarticulate, narrative that was seeking an audience. My response was to suggest that she substitute a pen for a knife and a piece of paper for her flesh and to bring in the resulting communications for discussion in her therapy sessions.

What ensued was a remarkable narrative, whose form and structure mirrored Carol's own sense of incoherence. Early offerings took the form of fragmentary notes on random scraps of paper, often written in immediate anticipation of an act of self-injury. One such entry in what eventually grew to be a therapeutic "logbook" began with the following in large block letters:

> I feel very scattered now. Pills—I have lots of pills now. I'm very close to doing something. I don't know if you will help or not. Carol looks through a shadowy, dark fog—nothing is clear to her. She hurts. I can't stop the pain, and I don't know if you can either . . . she wants to cut herself now . . .

Then, in a small, uncertain cursive hand, she continued.

She wants to live. She cries. . . . What can you do? What can anyone do? Cut herself. See the blood flow, feel the pain. Take the pills and stop her breathing, stop her heartbeat. Then no longer a problem to you or anyone. Please help me. Please help me be happy again.

Carol concluded her entry with larger and more uneven words: "I didn't do it. Death."

These and similar entries—with their shifting points of view (from first to third person and back again) and fluctuating voice (from expository to commanding to plaintive)—sometimes set the stage for self-injury (as in the cutting that preceded the last five words above) and sometimes substituted for it. By listening carefully for the themes that ran through Carol's writing and by inviting deeper self-characterization of herself as a protagonist in a painful and repetitive script, I gradually helped her discuss and emplot, rather than impulsively enact, her inner drama. Of equal importance, I tried to attend to the responses that she implicitly sought from me as an initial audience to her narration. Her positioning of me evolved as the narrative itself evolved. Beginning with early bids for me to enact a protective role when she felt compelled to cut or burn herself, it progressed to later attempts to have me "walk alongside her" as she explored her history of abuse and conflicted sense of multiplicity. Months later, she positioned me principally as a witness to her remarkable growth, sharing with me her first fragile attempts to author a new sense of self. She wrote a simple poem excerpted from this phase of her therapy.

> As the sun rises
> The birds awaken.
> In the silence and stillness of the moment
> You can hear their songs.
>
> As the sun rises on my life
> I begin to sing.
> In the stillness of the moment
> My song can be heard. (Neimeyer, 1995a, p. 237)

Eventually, Carol broadened the audience for her diverse narrative productions (including a penetrating personal journal and an oral history of her family of origin, to which numerous people contributed) to include selected other people in her life. As her story transformed from one of self-abuse to one of self-discovery and self-acceptance, she found a still wider audience for public displays of her poetically annotated and psychologically poignant photographs and her humane and practical self-help columns in local mental health newsletters. The warm reception of these by many people who had silently shared her struggle ultimately reconnected her with the social world in a new way and helped consolidate a more coherent sense of self as author of a profoundly rewritten life narrative.[14]

CONCLUSIONS

Although various visions of the self have long served as orienting concepts in psychotherapy, postmodern constructions of identity have posed challenges to a conceptualization of therapy as a straightforward process of self-correction or self-actualization. In particular, viewing the self through the lens of narrative both problematizes a view of personality as a relatively stable identity to be repaired or discovered and offers fresh perspectives on how to deal with difficulties in self-construction in the clinical context.

My goal in this chapter was to develop this metaphor of self-as-story in ways that extend both a cognitive constructivist emphasis on narrative coherence and a social constructionist emphasis on the dynamics of discourse. Drawing on developments in fields as diverse as cognitive psychology and literary criticism, I argued that narration serves vital functions at both intra- and interpersonal levels and that these carry clear implications for an understanding of self-construction and its impediments. Thus, in constructing a narrative account of our experience and seeking an audience for it, we attempt not only to impart continuity to the story of our lives, but also to position ourselves with reference to others. In general, the act of narration can be viewed as a social performance, which if successful confers on its author a provisional fictional identity that meets with social validation.

A closer inspection of the structural and stylistic dimensions of narrative activity holds promise for integrating existing therapeutic strategies and suggesting new ones. This is especially the case among cognitive constructivists, who have devised a number of concepts and procedures to help clients extend, deepen, and sometimes deconstruct the problematic settings, characterizations, plots, themes, and fictional goals of their autobiographies. But promising contributions to narrative repair have also been made by social constructionists, who have begun to envision new ways to work with the points of view and voice embodied in any given account and to prompt the author of a revised life narrative to authenticate it in the presence of relevant audiences.

At one level, the goal of any social theory is to construct a story of human activity that is adequate to our emerging knowledge of who we are. I believe that a narrative perspective is well positioned to advance our

---

[14]Carol's narrative transformation is recounted more fully elsewhere (Neimeyer, 1995a). Her own writings provide a more eloquent testimony to the power of a narrative approach to therapy than any academic treatise on the subject.

contemporary self-understanding and that its more consistent application to the conceptualization of the self can contribute both depth and novelty to the evolving story of psychotherapy.

REFERENCES

Adler, A. (1956). *The individual psychology of Alfred Adler*. New York: Basic Books.

Allport, G. W. (1961). *Pattern and growth in personality*. New York: Holt.

Angus, L., Levitt, H., & Hardke, K. (in press). The narrative process and therapeutic change. *Journal of Clinical Psychology*.

Atkinson, R. (1995). *The gift of stories*. Westport, CT: Bergin & Garvey.

Bakhtin, M. (1981). *The dialogic imagination*. Austin: University of Texas Press.

Barclay, C. R. (1996). Autobiographical remembering: Narrative constraints on objectified selves. In D. C. Rubin (Ed.), *Remembering our past* (pp. 94–125). Cambridge, UK: Cambridge University Press.

Barsalou, L. W. (1988). The content and organization of autobiographical memories. In U. Neisser & E. Winograd (Eds.), *Remembering reconsidered* (pp. 193–243). Cambridge, UK: Cambridge University Press.

Beck, A. T. (1993). Cognitive therapy: Past, present, and future. *Journal of Consulting and Clinical Psychology, 61*, 194–198.

Bonnefoy, Y. (1989). *The act and the place of poetry*. Chicago: University of Chicago Press.

Bruner, J. (1990). *Acts of meaning*. Cambridge, MA: Harvard University Press.

Burr, V. (1995). *An introduction to social constructionism*. London: Routledge.

Derrida, J. (1978). *Writing and difference*. Chicago: University of Chicago Press.

Ecker, B., & Hulley, L. (1996). *Depth oriented brief therapy*. San Francisco: Jossey Bass.

Edwards, D., & Potter, J. (1992). *Discursive psychology*. Newbury Park, CA: Sage.

Efran, J. S., & Fauber, R. L. (1995). Radical constructivism: Questions and answers. In R. A. Neimeyer & M. J. Mahoney (Eds.), *Constructivism in psychotherapy* (pp. 275–302). Washington, DC: American Psychological Association.

Epston, D., & White, M. (1995). Termination as a rite of passage: Questioning strategies for a therapy of inclusion. In R. A. Neimeyer & M. J. Mahoney (Eds.), *Constructivism in psychotherapy* (pp. 339–356). Washington, DC: American Psychological Association.

Feixas, G., & Villegas, M. (1991). Personal construct analysis of autobiographical texts. *International Journal of Personal Construct Psychology, 4*, 51–83.

Foucault, M. (1970). *The order of things: An archaeology of the human sciences*. New York: Pantheon.

Freedman, J., & Combs, G. (1996). *Narrative therapy*. New York: Norton.

Freeman, M. (1999). Culture, narrative, and the poetic construction of selfhood. *Journal of Constructivist Psychology, 12*, 99–116.

Freud, S. (1964). *An outline of psycho-analysis* (Standard ed., Vol. 23). London: Hogarth. (Original work published 1940)

Gardner, J. (1983). *The art of fiction*. New York: Vintage.

Gendlin, E. T. (1996). *Focusing-oriented psychotherapy*. New York: Guilford Press.

Gergen, K. J. (1991). *The saturated self*. New York: Basic Books.

Gergen, K. J. (1994). *Realities and relationships*. Cambridge, MA: Harvard University Press.

Gergen, K. J. (1999). Beyond the self–society antimony. *Journal of Constructivist Psychology, 12*, 173–178.

Gergen, K. J., & Gergen, M. M. (1986). Narrative form and the construction of psychological science. In T. R. Sarbin (Ed.), *Narrative psychology* (pp. 22–44). New York: Praeger.

Goldberger, N. R. (1996). Women's constructions of truth, self, authority, and power. In H. Rosen & K. T. Kuehlwein (Eds.), *Constructing realities* (pp. 167–193). San Francisco: Jossey-Bass.

Gonçalves, O. F. (1994). From epistemological truth to existential meaning in cognitive narrative psychotherapy. *Journal of Constructivist Psychology, 7*, 107–118.

Gonçalves, O. F. (1995). Cognitive narrative psychotherapy: The hermeneutic construction of alternative meanings. In M. J. Mahoney (Ed.), *Cognitive and constructivist psychotherapies* (pp. 139–162). New York: Springer.

Greenberg, L., & Pascual-Leone, J. (1995). A dialectical constructivist approach to experiential change. In R. A. Neimeyer & M. J. Mahoney (Eds.), *Constructivism in psychotherapy* (pp. 169–191). Washington, DC: American Psychological Association.

Guidano, V. F. (1991). *The self in process*. New York: Guilford Press.

Guidano, V. F. (1995). Self-observation in constructivist psychotherapy. In R. A. Neimeyer & M. J. Mahoney (Ed.), *Constructivism in psychotherapy* (pp. 155–168). Washington, DC: American Psychological Association.

Guidano, V. F., & Liotti, G. (1983). *Cognitive processes and emotional disorders*. New York: Guilford Press.

Gustafson, J. P. (1995). *Dilemmas of brief therapy*. New York: Plenum Press.

Hayek, F. A. (1952). *The sensory order*. Chicago: University of Chicago Press.

Hermans, H. (1995). *Self-narratives: The construction of meaning in psychotherapy*. New York: Guilford Press.

Hermans, H. J. M. (in press). The person as a motivated storyteller. In R. A. Neimeyer & G. J. Neimeyer (Eds.), *Advances in personal construct psychology* (Vol. 5). Greenwich, CT: JAI Press.

Hoffman, L. (1990). Constructing realities: An art of lenses. *Family Process, 29*, 1–12.

Howard, G. S. (1991). Culture tales: A narrative approach to thinking, cross-cultural psychology, and psychotherapy. *American Psychologist, 46*, 187–197.

Howe, M. L., & Courage, M. (1997). The emergence and early development of autobiographical memory. *Psychological Review, 104,* 499–523.

Janoff-Bulman, R., & Berg, M. (1998). Disillusionment and the creation of values. In J. H. Harvey (Ed.), *Perspectives on loss: A sourcebook* (pp. 35–47). Philadelphia: Brunner/Mazel.

Kelly, G. A. (1955). *The psychology of personal constructs.* New York: Norton.

Kernberg, O. F. (1976). *Object relations theory and psychoanalysis.* Northvale, NJ: Aronson.

Kohut, H. (1971). *The analysis of the self.* New York: International Universities Press.

Kundera, M. (1997). *Identity.* New York: Harper.

Landfield, A. W. (1988). Personal science and the concept of validation. *International Journal of Personal Construct Psychology, 1,* 237–250.

Lather, P. (1992). Postmodernism and the human sciences. In S. Kvale (Ed.), *Psychology and postmodernism* (pp. 88–109). Newbury Park, CA: Sage.

Linton, M. (1986). Ways of searching and the contents of memory. In D. C. Rubin (Ed.), *Autobiographical memory* (pp. 50–67). Cambridge, UK: Cambridge University Press.

Mahoney, M. J. (1991). *Human change processes.* New York: Basic Books.

Mahoney, M. J. (1995). The continuing evolution of the cognitive sciences and psychotherapies. In R. A. Neimeyer & M. J. Mahoney (Eds.), *Constructivism in psychotherapy* (pp. 39–65). Washington, DC: American Psychological Association.

Mancuso, J. C., & Sarbin, T. R. (1983). The self-narrative in the enactment of roles. In T. R. Sarbin & K. Scheibe (Eds.), *Studies in social identity* (pp. 233–253). New York: Praeger.

Mandler, J. (1984). *Scripts, stories, and scenes: Aspects of schema theory.* Hillsdale, NJ: Erlbaum.

Markus, H., & Nurius, P. (1986). Possible selves. *American Psychologist, 41,* 954–969.

Mascolo, M. F., Craig-Bray, L., & Neimeyer, R. A. (1997). The construction of meaning and action in development and psychotherapy: An epigenetic systems approach. In G. J. Neimeyer & R. A. Neimeyer (Eds.), *Advances in personal construct psychology* (Vol. 4, pp. 3–38). Greenwich, CT: JAI Press.

Maturana, H., & Varela, F. (1987). *The tree of knowledge.* Boston: New Science Library.

McAdams, D. (1993). *The stories we live by.* New York: Morrow.

Moffett, J., & McElheny, K. R. (Eds.). (1995). *Points of view.* New York: Mentor.

Monk, G., Winslade, J., Crocket, K., & Epston, D. (1996). *Narrative therapy in practice.* San Francisco: Jossey-Bass.

Neimeyer, R. A. (1993a). Constructivism and the cognitive therapies: Some conceptual and strategic contrasts. *Journal of Cognitive Psychotherapy, 7,* 159–171.

Neimeyer, R. A. (1993b). Constructivist approaches to the measurement of meaning. In G. J. Neimeyer (Ed.), *Constructivist assessment: A casebook* (pp. 58–103). Newbury Park, CA: Sage.

Neimeyer, R. A. (1995a). Client-generated narratives in psychotherapy. In R. A. Neimeyer & J. Mahoney (Ed.), *Constructivism in psychotherapy* (pp. 231–246). Washington, DC: American Psychological Association.

Neimeyer, R. A. (1995b). Constructivist psychotherapies: Features, foundations, and future directions. In R. A. Neimeyer & M. J. Mahoney (Eds.), *Constructivism in psychotherapy* (pp. 11–38). Washington, DC: American Psychological Association.

Neimeyer, R. A. (1995c). An invitation to constructivist psychotherapies. In R. A. Neimeyer & M. J. Mahoney (Eds.), *Constructivism in psychotherapy* (pp. 1–8). Washington, DC: American Psychological Association.

Neimeyer, R. A. (1998a). Cognitive therapy and the narrative trend: A bridge too far? *Journal of Cognitive Psychotherapy, 12,* 57–66.

Neimeyer, R. A. (1998b). *Lessons of loss: A guide to coping.* New York: McGraw-Hill.

Neimeyer, R. A. (1998c). Social constructionism in the counselling context. *Counselling Psychology Quarterly, 11,* 135–149.

Neimeyer, R. A., & Jackson, T. T. (1997). George A. Kelly and the development of personal construct theory. In W. G. Bringmann, H. E. Lueck, R. Miller, & C. E. Early (Eds.), *A pictorial history of psychology* (pp. 364–372). Carol Stream, IL: Quintessence.

Neimeyer, R. A., & Stewart, A. E. (1996). Trauma, healing, and the narrative emplotment of loss. *Families in Society, 77,* 360–375.

Neimeyer, R. A., & Stewart, A. E. (1998a). Constructivist psychotherapies. In H. S. Friedman (Ed.), *Encyclopedia of mental health* (pp. 547–559). San Diego, CA: Academic Press.

Neimeyer, R. A., & Stewart, A. E. (1998b). Trauma, healing, and the narrative emplotment of loss. In C. Franklin & P. S. Nurius (Eds.), *Constructivism in practice* (pp. 165–184). Milwaukee, WI: Families International.

Nurius, P. (1998). Memory and constructivism. In C. Franklin & P. Nurius (Eds.), *Constructivism in practice* (pp. 25–56). Milwaukee, WI: Families International.

Parry, A., & Doan, R. (1994). *Story re-visions.* New York: Guilford Press.

Pennebaker, J. (1997). *Opening up.* New York: Guilford Press.

Polanyi, M. (1958). *Personal knowledge.* New York: Harper.

Polkinghorne, D. E. (1988). *Narrative knowing and human sciences.* Albany: State University of New York.

Polkinghorne, D. E. (1991). Narrative and self-concept. *Journal of Narrative and Life History, 1,* 135–153.

Potter, J., & Wetherell, M. (1987). *Discourse and social psychology.* Beverly Hills, CA: Sage.

Rainer, T. (1978). *The new diary.* Los Angeles, CA: Tarcher.

Reis, R. (1998). *Fernando Pessoa & Company* (R. Zenith, Ed. & Trans.). New York: Grove Press. (Original work published 1935)

Rogers, C. R. (1961). *On becoming a person*. Boston: Houghton Mifflin.

Roy, A. (1998). *The god of small things*. New York: Harper.

Russell, R. L., & Lucariello, J. (1992). Narrative, yes: Narrative ad infinitum, no! *American Psychologist, 47*, 671–673.

Sarbin, T. R. (Ed.). (1986). *Narrative psychology: The storied nature of human conduct*. New York: Praeger.

Sass, L. A. (1992). The epic of disbelief: The postmodern turn in contemporary psychoanalysis. In S. Kvale (Ed.), *Psychology and postmodernism* (pp. 166–182). Newbury Park, CA: Sage.

Sewell, K. W. (1997). Posttraumatic stress: Towards a constructivist model of psychotherapy. In G. J. Neimeyer & R. A. Neimeyer (Eds.), *Advances in personal construct psychology* (Vol. 4, pp. 207–235). Greenwich, CT: JAI Press.

Sewell, K. W., Baldwin, C. L., & Moes, A. J. (1998). The multiple self awareness group. *Journal of Constructivist Psychology, 11*, 59–78.

Siegel, D. J. (1995). Memory, trauma, and psychotherapy: A cognitive science view. *Journal of Psychotherapy Practice and Research, 4*, 93–122.

Stewart, J. (1995). Reconstruction of the self: Life-span oriented group psychotherapy. *Journal of Constructivist Psychology, 8*, 129–148.

Tappan, M. B. (1999). Authoring a moral self: A dialogical perspective. *Journal of Constructivist Psychology, 12*, 117–131.

Terrell, C. J., & Lyddon, W. J. (1995). Narrative and psychotherapy. *Journal of Constructivist Psychology, 9*, 27–44.

Vaihinger, H. (1924). *The philosophy of "as if."* Berlin, Germany: Reuther & Reichard.

van der Kolk, B. A., & van der Hart, O. (1991). The intrusive past: The flexibility of memory and the engraving of trauma. *American Imago, 48*, 425–454.

Villegas, M. (1992). Analysis del discurso terapeutico [Analysis of therapeutic discourse]. *Revista de Psycoterapia, 10–11*, 23–66.

White, M., & Epston, D. (1990). *Narrative means to therapeutic ends*. New York: Norton.

Wigren, J. (1994). Narrative completion in the treatment of trauma. *Psychotherapy, 31*, 415–423.

Wortham, S. (1999). The heterogeneously distributed self. *Journal of Constructivist Psychology, 12*, 153–171.

10

RESISTING THE DOMINATING STORY: TOWARD A DEEPER UNDERSTANDING OF NARRATIVE THERAPY

WENDY DREWERY, JOHN WINSLADE, AND GERALD MONK

The use of psychological explanation as a basis for interventions in mental health is inextricably linked with the historical context of research and science. In the Western world at least, researchers tend to be rather committed to the idea that they can find answers to the problems of mental disorder and that these answers will be found through what they know as scientific methods. This is a well-known tale that we do not elaborate in too much detail here. However, a revolution is occurring that is challenging not just the nature of empirical methodology but the very nature of explanation. Constructionism is recasting the way "physical" existence is understood and thus, by implication, it challenges the status of phenomena that researchers might regard as "mental."[1] Thus, a matter of epistemology has potentially profound implications for mental health practice.

---

[1] We distinguish constructivism from constructionism. *Constructivism* refers to the tendency for people to create structures for understanding phenomena mentally, whereas *constructionism* refers to an epistemological position that enables people to theorize the production of meaning within webs of power relations (Monk & Drewery, 1994).

Epistemology relates closely to the problem that is central to this book (and that is central to critiques of constructionism), namely, what is the ontological status of disorder, or does disorder exist? Is mental disorder real? Indeed, is anything real? This issue about reality seems to be one of the main sticking points in the elaboration of postmodern therapies (Held, 1995). Many postmodern theorists appear to deny the existence of a single reality, or at least they assert that researchers cannot know reality directly (Harré, 1986). Central features of postmodern therapies include an emphasis on language, a concern about the politics of therapy, and a rejection of reliance on psychological "laws." Narrative therapy is distinguished by an emphasis on the ways problems are constituted within speech and texts of all kinds. In this chapter, we offer a theoretical discussion of the process of narrative therapy that we hope provides answers to some of the critiques of this popular approach. To do this, we outline our theoretical origins and carefully define some concepts. We argue that to use words is to create frameworks for understanding that have tangible consequences for the people whose lives are so inscribed. We argue therefore that care is needed in the use of psychological concepts in therapeutic situations. To illustrate, we briefly draw on some anecdotal but real (yes!) case studies.

PHILOSOPHICAL ROOTS

The constructionist revolution is the product of a variety of converging disciplinary projects in the social and human sciences, in particular from philosophy, anthropology, sociology, and literary theory (Bakhtin, 1986; Foucault, 1970, 1980; Rorty, 1980; Wittgenstein, 1958). This turn in the history of human ideas focuses on how it is that there can be different forms of interpretation and competing versions of truth. Rather than assuming that language mirrors the world and words represent things in a one–one correspondence (an empiricist position), these philosophers of truth–science–knowledge have moved on from the phenomenological idea that it is possible that the same world looks different through the eyes of others. They have focused attention on meanings and interpretations rather than behavior. From this perspective, which is well understood by counselors, the same words can mean many things. Different people may describe the same phenomenon differently. The same words may be used differently by different people. This description of the revolution leaves reality as it is, only the description changes. But constructionism is more far reaching than a simple claim that different people see the same things differently. The difficult part of constructionism is the idea that what people experience in the world changes depending on how they understand it. That is, they seem to say that reality, which most people feel ought to be fixed and unchanging (i.e., what reality means to most people), actually changes.

This perspective is a drastic departure from the dominating empiricist epistemology and offers a new philosophy of explanation because it does not begin with assumptions, such as what exists is fixed and empirical explanations are the best kind. Instead, constructionists have noticed that what counts as explanation in one context may not count in another. For example, feminists may account for certain behavior by recourse to a theory of patriarchy, whereas a behavioral psychologist may give a very different analysis of the same behavior. Which explanation is accepted depends to a large extent on the context within which it is offered. This kind of approach helps one understand how it can be that different ideas have currency at different times in history. Even scientific accounts come and go with historical time, as any physicist or astronomer will testify. This is particularly clear when one thinks about how medical knowledge changes over time. It is perhaps more so in psychology, which by its very nature must postulate the existence of mental "conditions," states of mind, even mind itself, because it cannot point to them. It is interesting to note that therapists working in different counseling modalities tend to "find" conditions in the image of their preferred modality (Hubble & O'Hanlon, 1992). For example, unresolved grief, posttraumatic stress, unfinished business, and irrational thinking could all be labels for the same "condition," depending on the stance of the therapist. Of course, the really interesting issue concerns the kind of therapy prescribed on the basis of such diagnoses and its effectiveness. That is, such descriptions become, in the therapeutic interaction, not just tools for interpreting reality but stage directions for the production of real events. Evaluating the effectiveness of therapeutic interventions is difficult enough at any time, and this perspective challenges the standards by which such evaluations might be made.

Social constructionism (Burr, 1995; Gergen, 1985; Parker, 1998) enables one to consider different registers of talk and the possibility that different kinds of talk have different credibility and different relevance in different contexts. This is a complex idea. Where most work in the philosophy of science and in research methods focuses on establishing which explanations, using which methodologies, are more acceptable as reliable and true, we prefer to focus on such issues as how such questions come to be asked. Narrative counseling (Freedman & Combs, 1996; Monk, Winslade, Crocket, & Epston, 1997; Zimmerman & Dickerson, 1996) focuses on how different interpretations are produced, the circumstances of their production, and the consequences for the client of accepting certain interpretations and not others. Both in and outside the therapy room, we are interested in why some statements seem to carry more weight than do others.

TALK AS ACTION

After struggling for many years with the problem of how people can assert that they know things, the philosopher Wittgenstein (1958) suggested that people reach certainty on the basis of agreement about the rules for making meaning. He suggested that language can only have meaning in its use and in social contexts. Thus, he recommended careful consideration of how people come to know how to use particular words and sentence structures. He argued that "knowing how to go on" is constructed knowledge; it belongs in the social sphere rather than being the private knowledge of individuals (Wittgenstein, 1958). From this perspective, words (sentences, names, and propositions) are not representations, nor do they refer to any preexisting meanings or objects. Certainty is not a product of a correspondence between words and reality. Wittgenstein's crucial contribution focused on the constructive nature of language: on what is being brought into existence in talk. Talk is thus seen as primarily producing rather than reflecting meaning. From a social constructionist perspective, language is thought of as gaining meaning in its use, as opposed to meanings of words, for example, being treated as given prior to their use. The impact of this theory of knowledge is nowhere more powerful than in the language of mental health. Even such words as *memory, feeling,* and *cognition* can be explained by reference to ways of speaking rather than by pointing to something (Edwards, 1997). These ideas have huge significance for psychologists, many of whom work in an empirical tradition, and for counselors, many of whom work in a phenomenological tradition.

The phenomenological tradition in counseling (Rogers, 1951) teaches that it is important to try to see the world from the point of view of the client, and in this respect, it appears to be concerned with how people interpret the world. Certainly, counselors are often witnesses to struggles over meaning within a person's most intimate experience. The narrative approach differs significantly from phenomenological approaches: The basis of this approach is that all language is performative. Speech acts are one of the ways in which constructionists create their worlds (Austin, 1962). To speak is to participate in communities of meaning, but above all, to speak is to participate in performing an act in and on the world. This notion of talk as action, as producing common understandings about who one is and what is possible for one to do, is the theoretical fulcrum of narrative therapy. It is a notable departure from most of the earlier counseling traditions. Where phenomenology asserts that how people experience the world differs from person to person (although the world does not change), constructionism focuses on the creative and interactive use of language to define experience and the world and, furthermore, on how the language that forms what people personally inhabit shapes their lives. People's past, present, and even their futures are constrained by the language they use to understand them. Some ways of speaking open possibilities, and some ways of speaking close them down. Different forms of expression have different impacts. In everyday life, people are often torn by different ways of understanding the same events, and they spend much time agonizing over their descriptions. From an everyday perspective, it is almost a truism that people are able to say different things in different contexts. Often it is the context within which statements are made that enables those statements to be acknowledged as sensible and understood. A narrative approach enables focus on the context of the production of speech acts. Counseling in this mode is about being sensitive to what is actually happening in an interaction, about managing talk to produce preferred impacts.

But empiricism, not constructionism, is the dominating epistemology of the scientific world. From an empiricist perspective, facts are universal truths about the world. That facts are truths seems tautologically self-evident. However, the revolution people are participating in is challenging the dominance of such truths. Constructionist ideas give people new ways of talking about talk, which can be applied to counseling, but can just as easily be applied to ways of speaking in general. This is a major shift from the focus on expert language characteristic of debates about scientific reliability. Constructionism is first and foremost an epistemology. It offers a different set of questions about what exists and what does not, and it invites one to change the way one thinks about the distinction between subject and object. It does this by emphasizing the constructive nature of language. Constructionism is built on the notion of talk as action rather than as representation.

POSTSTRUCTURALISM AND POWER

In contrast with an empiricist philosophy of science, the revolution to which this book is a contribution has been called a "turn to language" (Rorty, 1980). Where empirical science focuses on method, the hermeneutic tradition is preoccupied with problems of interpretation (Bernstein, 1993; Packer, 1985). Hermeneutic philosophy is closely related to poststructuralism, which in turn takes its name from its contrast with structuralism. Structuralist thinking seeks to explain people's problematic experiences with reference to features of character or personality structure (e.g., individual disorders of various kinds) or to the structural essences of human development (e.g., developmental stages of grief, family life-cycle stages). By contrast, central features of poststructuralist work include exposition of the relation between power and knowledge (Foucault, 1980), blurring category boundaries and rendering clear distinctions unclear (Weedon, 1987). Poststructuralist work often takes the form of questioning the historical status of meanings and the interruption or deconstruction of taken-for-granted assumptions (Parker, 1999; Parker, Georgaca, Harper, McLaughlin, & Stowell-Smith, 1995). To espouse a poststructuralist philosophy does not prevent one from using structuralist ideas. But it invites one into a different, perhaps less trusting, relationship with such frames of understanding. If one does not regard conventional diagnostic categories as stable, acultural truths, then one is freer to use them when they serve a function for people and not use them when they hold people back.

Poststructuralism also implies a very different approach to the generation of knowledge: Knowledge is not given or to be discovered but is constructed in locally situated contexts. This does not mean that such knowledge is not valuable nevertheless: It only suggests that no claim to know is the final truth. This stance recommends such texts as the *Diagnostic and Statistical Manual of Mental Disorders* (DSM; American Psychiatric Association, 1994) in a different way: They are cultural products, historical documents that have specific uses in specific contexts, rather than authoritative advances in the inexorable progress of human knowledge toward some inevitably better understanding. We see such frameworks of knowledge as having an historical yet powerful position among the different accounts that can be given about the same phenomena. One effect of this idea about "alternative knowledges" is that it makes the authority of particular scientific accounts open to challenge. Counselors who take this perspective seriously may welcome the fact that clients want to resist the truths that are spoken about them in scientific diagnoses.

Poststructuralist theory is preoccupied with process rather than product, with how people come to make claims to know rather than with the objects of their knowledge. Thus, counselors who hear clients describe themselves as suffering from a defined condition are curious about how they came to know themselves in this way. Such curiosity does not spring from a desire to compete with or secretly undermine others' ways of knowing but rather out of a desire to open space for new knowledge, new descriptions, and new language. How, for example, does a person come to think of himself as "depressed"? Is this description relevant to all aspects of his or her life, or are there particular contexts where it seems more apt?

Because most diagnostic categories focus their gaze on the individual, it is rare for the analysis of people's problems to take power relations into account. Certainly the DSM reads as if power does not exist in the world. From a poststructuralist perspective, we would expect power to feature frequently in counselors' understandings of the problems their clients face. Many problems that people experience can be understood as effects of the operation of power. Thus, for example, a man's depression might beg to be understood in the context of cultural injunctions that shape the relations between his working life and his personal relationships. Discourses of paid work easily dominate over discourses of love, home, and family, particularly in discussions of career and life planning. So it is not surprising if there is often conflict between these two areas of living. It is especially not surprising because there are gender differences in the positions men and women are expected to take up within these different discourses. Of course, the dominance of usual positioning in discourse does not mean that each person will necessarily take up that position, but the existence of such discursive expectations can be a source of difficulty. So a man may find he has no agentic position in the way his family is run or a woman may find she is not recognized for her salaried contributions to the household. Such contestations can be understood in terms of power relations.

DISCOURSE AND SOCIAL CHANGE

Discourses are linguistic and social contexts within which certain statements make sense or not. The discursive context of a statement is the set of background assumptions, often hidden or taken for granted, that enable a statement to make sense. Political struggle occurs in and over discourse, and changing discursive practices are important elements of social change. In the mental health field, for example, it is well documented that different "conditions" come into and go out of prominence: Hysteria was once a central issue of concern; now depression is a major focus for research and treatment. Masturbation and homosexuality used to be described in terms of sexual dysfunction but are no longer. Posttraumatic stress was produced out of the need to describe soldiers' responses to the Vietnam War. Attention deficit disorders and conduct disorders have successfully contested much of the territory once occupied by juvenile delinquency. Also significant to our argument, voting is the preferred procedure for deciding which of the less clear labels will be included in the next edition of the DSM (Kirk & Kutchins, 1992). At any particular time and in any particular place, some discourses dominate and some are less dominant. Discourses of depression currently dominate psychological debates in the Western world, so it is easier at present to get medication for depression and there is less stigma attached to the diagnosis than there once was, for example, for women who experienced unhappiness in their lives and looked for alternatives (Russell, 1995). A poststructuralist response to this observation would be to ask how this state of affairs came about, at *this* time, in *these* places. These questions point to the contextual and historical nature of attitudes to and treatments of depression and could be useful in terms of finding causes for the "epidemic."

Different discourses or ways of speaking offer different positions to people. People can be positioned advantageously in some discourses and not in others. In a constructionist framework, people can take up a variety of positions, some of which may be contradictory. The authority of the self is always partial and relative to context. The power to interpret meaning is primarily located in socially derived (usually tacit) agreement rather than in the personal power of individuals. From this perspective, following Foucault, power is not a quantity but a productive process, vested (always temporarily) in various authorities, whose dominance is discursively produced. We understand discourse as a mode of action, one of the ways in which people act on the world (Fairclough, 1992). Such acting is less like being the cue that moves the first billiard ball and more like throwing your 2¢'s worth into a conversation among several people. Conversations can influence what one thinks about things and hence the possibilities for acting that appear open, in both momentous and unremarkable ways. Some discourses or ways of speaking can call people into impossible positions in their own lives, often leaving them without any agency to make changes for themselves. Counselors and psychologists can be understood to take up positions of power in relation to their clients when they speak with professional authority in description of their clients. In so doing, they are actively producing their own position of authority, a relation that may have the effect of subjugating a client to a particular interpretation of themselves (Hoffman, 1990).

OBJECTIFICATION AND REIFICATION

Some forms of language have the effect of turning the people spoken about into objects of the conversation rather than participants in it. Those who are familiar with critiques of positivism may not be surprised when we suggest that this effect seems to be a feature of scientific language. Indeed, it is not at all surprising when we point out that objectivity and erasure of the knowing subject are highly prized values of scientific language. Looking closely at texts from within medicine, education, and psychology, we realized how often the language of these disciplines objectifies the people they purport to serve and how unproblematic such practices appear to be to practitioners within those disciplines (although this effect is less in education). Objectifying practices have the effect of distancing people. They are, in Foucault's words, dividing practices, designed indeed, to invoke an expert position by creating new categories of analysis and diagnosis.

Authoritative diagnosis maintains expert power and thereby adds authority to the intervention that follows on the diagnosis. Recipients of medical care are traditionally thought of as patients, and it is no accident that the word *patient* derives from a term that invokes both suffering and passivity or that the role of doctor invokes so much power. In medicine, doctors help sufferers of sickness, and there is an implicit assumption that the sufferer cannot help her- or himself. Thus, taking on a sick role can involve becoming an object of interest (however humanitarian), requiring that one prostrate oneself to some degree before the powerful discourses of medical knowledge (Gergen, 1990). Thus, the call to a sick role can be a call to set aside one's agentic power. We are aware of current debates in this contested area and regret that it is beyond the scope of this essay to develop this specific point further.

We use the term *objectification* to refer to a process that denies an active role to the person whose life is in question. This is an effect achieved through particular forms of language, and it is related to the grammatical form of sentences. Related to this is the process of reification, which is also a grammatical effect by which words come to "stand for" a thing and eventually seem to refer to a thing. For example, posttraumatic stress disorder (PTSD) stands for a set of behavioral and biological manifestations or symptoms. It is not an object as such. Nevertheless, the linguistic process of referring to "it" tends to produce the impression that this condition "exists," and so it does, of course. The error that many people fall into is to proceed as if PTSD has a discrete biological basis that can be isolated and pointed to. This latter move is called "essentializing" by poststructuralists. Constructionists insist that essentializing is an unnecessary move. A lot of what is called deconstruction in both poststructuralist literature (Lather, 1991) and narrative therapy (White, 1991) is aimed at reversing this process.

AGENCY, SUBJECT POSITIONS, AND POSITION CALLS

Central to the practice of narrative therapy—the goal of talk management, if you like—is the notion of agency (Davies, 1991). The effects of not having agency are easily recognized in everyday lives, even if not so named. Contrast the following stories, which actually happened. A school principal told one of our student counselors in desperation about a young person (let us call him "Jimmy") who had created a great deal of trouble in his classroom. When confronted with his behavior, he said, "I'm ADHD, so I can't help it." Another school counselor, from a different school, reported a very different interaction: A 13-year-old student, Johnny, told him, "I'm ADHD . . . but I don't believe it." In the first incident, attention deficit hyperactivity disorder (ADHD) gave Jimmy permission to take a passive attitude toward his behavior. He positioned himself as a nonagent in his statement. As far as he was concerned, ADHD caused him to behave in this way; it "held all the cards." Johnny, by contrast, refused this move by positioning himself as an active agent in his sentence; ADHD was a description he was clearly contesting.

In their own terms, the different ways each of these boys spoke about ADHD opened very different possibilities for how they could go on in their lives. The boy who "didn't believe it" was taking some agency, and the other was taking none. The boy with no agency had nowhere to move; he was powerless before his diagnosis. Johnny, apparently, was able to stand back from the process by which he came to the label. He kept for himself the right to believe, or not believe, the description. In so doing, he also kept alive a different option for describing himself. It may be tempting to hear, "but I don't believe it," as an example of denial. Conventional psychological discourse often uses this move, which can be seen as a ploy to disqualify protest and maintain the power of the expert. But the school counselor heard Johnny wanting to be a subject in the process of describing, not just an object with a label. She heard him wanting to describe himself in his own terms, not just in someone else's. It is not that one way of speaking is wrong and the other is right; it is simply that there are more options for Johnny in the agentic version.

The notion of the position call is useful in teasing out a significant difference between therapeutic and not-so-therapeutic talk. We derived the concept of the position call, which might also be seen as a conversational move, from the notion of the subject position, which is central to much poststructuralist writing. The notion of a subject position derives directly from Foucault's work, and the concept has been used in many subsequent writings. In the writings of postmodern theorists, subject position is often used as a synonym for identity, similar to the way the term *role* is used (Wetherell, 1998), but we want to distinguish our usage from that. We do not want simply to draw attention to the possibility that one person may occupy several different subject positions or identities (although this is a useful observation). Instead, we use the term to describe a grammatical positioning that is either active or passive in a sentence or discourse. A subject position is the space a person may take up in different kinds of talk. Davies and Harré (1990) used positioning to theorize the effect of different ways of speaking on the options people may or may not take up in conversation. This is not simply a matter of grammar. We believe that it is possible to show that it is more politically advantageous and more personally healthy to be positioned as an agentic subject—as a speaker in, and therefore a producer of, the conversation that produces one's life—than as an object of a conversation about oneself. To date, we can offer largely anecdotal evidence in support of this claim, but we believe there is sufficient interest in our analysis to warrant further research.

In everyday life, as in therapy, how one speaks makes a difference in what one thinks one can do. Different ways of speaking offer different subject positions in many socially defined ways. People show that they "know how to go on," as they respond to these position calls. The concept of position call enables a focus on how language is a vehicle for power relations. We are especially interested in the ways that speech (and written texts) function to invite speakers into or exclude speakers from a conversation. A position call invites the person being spoken to into a particular subject position that the respondent may or may not take up. At the same time, a position call creates a kind of platform on which the speaker proposes to stand—a kind of scaffold, if you like. Position calls may be unproblematic, but they may just as readily reduce possibilities.

When I spoke about my daughter who had died some 10 years earlier and was slightly overcome by the emotions that returned along with her memory, I (Winslade) was once asked by a counselor, "Are you still grieving for her?" In this moment, I experienced being called into a position as a patient with some pathological condition. The word *still* implied some normal length of time for which it might be appropriate to grieve and, by inference, that I should think about myself as needing treatment if I was abnormally prolonging my grieving. The invitation was into a particular relation with the counselor's authority to assess and prescribe treatment (e.g., the corrective expression of "repressed" emotion). It was also an invitation to interpret my expression of such spontaneous emotion as symptomatic of unhealthiness and, by extension, interpret the ceasing of such a reaction as a "cure." What made the position call particularly potent was the impossibility of answering the question without taking up this pathological view of myself. If I had said *yes*, I would have entered into the position I was being offered. If I had said *no*, I would clearly have denied the evidence of my emotional response within the counselor's discursive framework, thereby proving her repression hypothesis. Such moments abound in counseling discourse.

COEXISTING FRAMEWORKS FOR TREATMENT

Objectifying people, reifying mental concepts, transforming the person into a subject, and inviting to take up more or less passive positions are all actions that are achieved through linguistic forms. They are achieved in the context of a dominating logic of predication (the subject–predicate form) in Western thought. These forms of language draw on the familiar modernist stance that is characterized by an understanding that all human scientific actions on the world have control or mastery as their objective. This modernistic attitude has been enormously successful in producing technological advances, such as medicines and motor cars, from which most Westerners have benefitted. The stunning success of this attitude of mastery underpins the concept of *diagnosis*, and with this kind of tradition behind it, it is no surprise that the expert language of psychological conditions carries great weight. It is important to reiterate that we do not offer a postmodern approach in exchange for modernistic clinical psychology. The notion of discourses and the acceptance of different ways of speaking allow us to offer different descriptions of the same phenomenon. Unlike Jimmy in our earlier story, perhaps not all people are happy when they become wholly identified by their problem description, particularly if that description leaves them without agency. It is important for therapists to be aware of the position calls they make and the discourses and power relations they invoke in so doing.

It would be naive and foolhardy to deny the contributions of modernist therapeutic practices. Modernist mental health practices have contributed to improving the well-being of large numbers of highly troubled people in the world's communities. Major reductions in distressing symptoms can occur when people gain access to the enormous range of antipsychotic and antidepressant medications that are themselves products of the success of modernistic science. The classification and naming of symptoms that accompany anxiety attacks, bipolar mood swings, depressive episodes, phobic responses, and a variety of learning and behavioral difficulties can provide assistance to a distressed family. Where previously they may have blamed themselves, the diagnosis may appear to offer a biological source of their difficulties, thus absolving them from blame. Furthermore, such labels gain power because of the treatment indicated, and thus a label may offer hope where previously there was incomprehension.

However, the liberation initially felt in having a set of private experiences authoritatively named may be replaced by a different kind of entrapment if the recipients allow themselves to become fully inscribed by the pathology or dysfunction implied by the naming of the symptom cluster (Gergen, 1990). We regard this as a form of colonizing, where the terms of the more powerful discourse are allowed to encompass completely the person's problematic experience, eliminating other possible options and requiring the client to speak in the terms of psychiatry. Although not eschewing the value of clinical diagnoses, we think it is important to accept that the choice of metaphorical framing also has importance in managing talk for therapeutic purposes. Even in cases where medication seems to be indicated, we caution against suggesting that management of a person's condition can be left entirely to a drug regime and the expertise of the psychiatrist. Narrative therapists tend to look for metaphors that have powerful connotations in a person's life and that accordingly offer strong invitations to an active positioning in relation to the problem (Monk et al., 1997).

The kind of assessment of people's problems that we advance includes a process of developing understanding about the subject positions they are called into in their lives in various dominating discourses and the sometimes troubling nature of these. It also takes into account the person's ability and opportunity to take an agentic stance toward these subject positions. This kind of assessment

- is an ongoing process rather than a reified product
- must be a collaborative process if it is not to be colonizing; the voice of the client must be heard
- is likely to emphasize the vernacular and idiosyncratic at times over the conventional, generalized scientific categories
- does not seek stability and official validation, so much as it thrives on the increased possibility for change that derives from more unstable descriptions.

WATCHING LANGUAGE

In a well-known videotape of a narrative counseling session, Michael White (1992) talked with Chris, who some might call manic depressive. White worked to cement Chris's position as an agent of his own life or, as Chris himself put it, to help him stay "in the driver's seat." Together, they worked on describing how Chris was able to maintain himself when he felt an attack of overenthusiasm coming on. It is a story of what Chris can rather than cannot do, of ability rather than disability and deficit. The language of psychiatric disorders has no place in this encounter: overenthusiasm can take over, but Chris is finding that he can deal with it:

White: And you talked about how you're walking around the block and if you think that overenthusiasm is going to get the better of you . . . and so . . . . You went away thinking more about some of the skills that you have available to you.

Chris: Yeah.

W: . . . that would help you . . . um . . . stay in the executive position.

C: Yeah.

W: . . . that would oppose overenthusiasm.

C: Mmm.

W: So . . . I'm just wondering if you have any more thoughts about those skills

C: Well . . .

W: . . . since we last met.

C: Well now I've been . . . instead of running away from it . . . say I'm talking to a person . . .

W: Yeah.

C: . . . and I'm getting overenthusiastic . . . Now I say "calm down, calm down, you know what's going to happen if this is . . . if you go much more over this. . ."

As we understand it, Chris remained on medication, but he was better able to control his "attacks" through this counseling. The interaction demonstrates a therapist working with the power of language in a life: The language one uses can put one in the driver's seat of one's life, but different language can take that possibility away. Chris was invited to talk about the skills he used to control his overenthusiasm. This is clearly an invitation to an agentic position in relation to his problem of overenthusiasm, a description that invokes the vernacular. At no time is there space to suggest that his condition is monolithic and unmanageable. The emphasis is on Chris's successes in managing it and on elaborating and supporting these successes. Chris is not powerless before his diagnosis.

The language of disorder may not always be most effective in engaging with people for therapeutic purposes. We contend that although the language of mental ill health may sometimes be helpful to experts in the field, it is very often productive of passivity and thus incapacity in the person of whom they speak. Or worse, a diagnosis may become a self-fulfilling prophecy, as in the case of Jimmy, particularly if psychological diagnoses are treated like disease and become analogous with physical conditions. We argue that it is possible to choose different ways of speaking that open more healthful possibilities. Health, in our view, has much to do with the capacity for agency and less to do with the absence of disease. In respect to mental health, these distinctions become even more sensitive and even more productive of nuances of meaning and activity in people's daily lives.

In the excerpt above, White (1992) worked with a central philosophical insight: Different ways of speaking create different options for the participants in the conversation. Thus, he avoided using the language of psychiatry and transformed the problem into one whose description was more manageable by Chris. This does not mean that the psychiatric description is not relevant; it was just not helpful to Chris's understanding and hence his management of his problem. There is nothing magical about the narrative therapy approach. It does not rely on any "special" capacity for empathy or some other mysterious charisma. Rather it should be seen as a deliberate use of the insight that language is performative. In a sense, the performance of lives is played out through the stories people tell, but it is much more than just telling different stories. The ways people speak produce very different linkages and have very different metaphoric powers. Some ways of speaking about disorder invoke helplessness. Some ways of speaking about it can reduce its power as disorder.

The secret of this kind of therapy is to find a way of speaking that does not close down but rather opens agentic options for other participants in the conversation at a time when that matters. Such a respectful way of speaking offers space for the people being spoken of to contribute to the conversation and the openness to expect that they may also make a difference in the direction of the conversation. Many experts are not used to this kind of conversation in their area of expertise. In particular, scientific speech depends on an unchallenged authority. Such authority in turn depends on unexamined respect for technological interventions. We are not advocating against technology or psychological concepts. But we do want to caution against some damaging ways in which technical language can be used.

We do not believe that anyone is helped by becoming identified with a syndrome: Although a diagnosis can be an opportunity for treatment, it can also be an experience that erases the sufferers, totalizing their existence as the diagnosis. What counts is not whether there is such a thing as ADHD but how it is treated (and what is expected) in the person to whom this description is applied. It is possible to use diagnoses in ways that erase the person from moral existence, as seen with Jimmy. We do not think this is helpful. When we put it this way, the reader may be able to see why we also believe it is not ethical. This is because it denies the power to act to the person whose life is in question. Of course, there are times when this must be done; for example, parents may take moral responsibility for children until they are old enough to take it for themselves. Some psychiatric patients may be in a similarly morally weakened state. But as it is for parents with children, so it is the responsibility of the mental health professional to work toward self-monitoring and independent judgment by the person they want to help. We recognize that this is a tenuous distinction requiring further work, but the point remains. Help should never be of a kind that actively produces moral helplessness.

ROSS'S STORY

The line between what is helpful and builds agency and what is not helpful and denies agency is sometimes a fine one. Recently, during a training workshop, a participant volunteered to be a client for me (Monk) to demonstrate the narrative approach. The whole group was transfixed by the story he told. Only a few months earlier, he had been in a very serious accident that had left him paralyzed in his right leg. He had spent several weeks in a hospital, some of them in intensive care. The entire incident had been extremely traumatic for him. At the end of the counseling demonstration, he was invited to reflect on how he had experienced the approach.

In response, he compared his present experience with several experiences of psychological counseling in the hospital.

Ross noted that his psychologist was primarily interested in helping him identify psychological responses that related to symptoms of PTSD. He was asked questions about the presence of dramatic swings in mood, reoccurring flashbacks, and troublesome nightmares. When Ross indeed confirmed that he was experiencing some of these symptoms, his psychologist suggested that it was likely that these symptoms would intensify. Ross felt reassured that the distress he would experience might be normal, given the seriousness of the injury. Yet he felt quite disheartened by the tortuous journey that seemed to lie ahead. Apart from the drugs he received to help him sleep, he felt burdened by the seeming inevitability of ongoing psychological disturbance. Not only was he now anticipating a possible deterioration in his mental health, he was also beginning to distrust the toughness in the face of challenge for which he was admired by his family and friends.

The weight of expert knowledge delivered by a person appointed by the community to assist those who are vulnerable and in distress is often quickly received and believed. Few people are prepared to challenge the authority of a helping professional, especially when the information is presented as a known and tested truth. In addition, when psychological knowledge is applied to people in the form of esoteric descriptions about the nature of their experience, there is often little space left for vulnerable individuals to generate alternative accounts of their lives. Ross felt appreciative of the efforts the psychologist had made to assist him to come to terms with his permanent loss of large motor functioning. However, he felt further burdened by the PTSD diagnosis. He was told that he would experience a period of shock for a time and certainly have episodes of denial about the extent of his injuries. Indeed, he was told that he would probably experience strong angry outbursts. He was not looking forward to this state of affairs because he had prided himself on being in charge of himself amidst turbulent and difficult times. Ross was told that he should not return to his graduate studies for at least 6 months. He needed time to get himself strong and work through some of the psychological reactions that would confront him.

Yet Ross was now back in class after 3 months. I met Ross on his first day back. He remarked that our conversation had taken a very different shape to the interactions he had had with his hospital psychologist. He was interested in talking about how he had prepared himself to come back to school earlier than advised. He was ready to talk about the competencies he had demonstrated in adjusting to the serious loss of functioning in his leg. He was happy to talk about the intense struggles he had experienced over recent months but was also delighted to talk about his own private thoughts that had given him hope in the darkest times. He enjoyed remembering the conversations he had had with himself about how he was not going to be beaten by this serious disability. He told himself at times that he was going to have a good life, despite this huge upheaval. Here he was, already being an active member in the class. Through our conversations, I tracked the preferred descriptions Ross offered about who he was as a person. Most of the conversation focused on the strategies, ideas, and knowledge he drew on to defy many of the predictions about how his life would unfold. He reported that he would often suddenly wake up at night in a cold sweat remembering the ugly scene of the accident.

The point is that, yes, maybe Ross suffers from PTSD, and maybe it is useful to know about that, but Ross wanted to get on with his life; he did not want to take on a passive or dependent sick role. This is not to deny that he may well have flashbacks, feel disturbed, and need medication and all the support of a medicalized psychological paradigm. But this is not all there is to say about his mental health. He has not taken on, first and foremost, the identity of a paralyzed, traumatized man. He continues to be a man who likes to be an agent of his own life, who now has a partly paralyzed leg, with all that that entails. He does not have to deny his disability to retain his agency. The difference is in the structure of his understanding: In his struggle to save for himself an agentic positioning, he did not reject but certainly withstood the totalizing force of the psychologist's ministrations.

SO WHAT IS REALITY AGAIN?

We spent some time in this chapter laying the philosophical foundations of our approach because we want to avoid some of the confusions that seem to be endemic in the narrative counseling literature. Good examples of questions that require answers from constructionists can be found in Barbara Held's (1995) carefully argued book on narrative therapies. Held argued that postmodern therapies are founded on two things: what she called the "problem of individuality" and the need for systematic and replicable therapeutic approaches. She argued that therapists are constantly faced with the uniqueness of clients and, therefore, that therapeutic tools should not be too rigid. However, if the practice of therapy is to mean anything, it must be more than a serendipitous response to whim; it must be systematic and generalizable (and thus—important from our point of view—teachable). In particular, she was concerned about the reputed denial of the real that she said is characteristic of postmodern therapies.

Although we share Held's (1995) general concerns, we do not feel well represented by her description of postmodernist therapies nor of narrative therapy. Her description of a narrative perspective as relativistic, cast adrift from reality, does not square with our experience. If anything, we would critique the conventional scientific approaches for their unacknowledged relativism. Scientific diagnoses of people's problems regularly fudge their relativity to cultural and historical context, even in their very focus on the individual as the prime site of psychological understanding. We would argue that a constructionist perspective is in fact more realistic because it brings cultural realities and power relations into focus. If this focus causes discomfort because it loosens the grip of some certainties that researchers have come to accept as universal truths, then we would argue that this discomfort is worthwhile. It enables clients to get a more realistic purchase on the vicissitudes of their problems and on their own agentic possibilities for change.

We are concerned when arguments about reality fail to acknowledge that the real takes many forms and that the language to describe it is complex and evolving both in its use and in the way it refers to the world. This is the condition of everyday life: People work on achieving better understandings of themselves and their worlds, and they discard those accounts that do not serve them well. This is as true of the performance of a leader of a country as it is of one's physical well-being. Furthermore, most people accept that this is their situation as communicating beings; constructionism has a huge intuitive acceptance among ordinary people because it taps into this "lay" understanding.

CONCLUSION

In this chapter, we offered a theoretical account of how different ways of speaking are productive of agency and capability and some are not. To some extent, the craft of the narrative therapist can be seen as the reverse of the craft of the author: Rather than creating texts, the narrative therapist is supremely sensitive to the constructive moments in speech interactions. The notion of deconstruction has a central place in this therapy, among other things, because so much of how people speak is destructive of possibilities, often closing down options without noticing the unnecessary damaging effects of doing so. When the possibility for subjective positioning has been erased from a life by a totalizing description, narrative therapy shows how it is possible to interrogate the linguistic processes that have brought this about and to reinstall the person as an agent. Different forms of speech are steps in the active creation of one's life. How one speaks matters because one's understanding at any moment says much about how one can go on in the next moment. This is not just a matter of choosing the "right" words but of how those words reflect one's relation to the world. These are grounds to suggest that invitations to agentic positioning are more therapeutically advantageous than invitations to objectified passivity. To be an agent of one's life is to have moral being. To cast any diagnosis, whether mental, such as schizophrenic, or physical, such as cancer, as if it were a complete description of the person, is to erase that person's possibilities for active involvement in the production of his or her health, and therefore his or her life.

Our purpose here was not to denigrate modernist technologies. But it is interesting to note how empirical psychology demands that human functioning be understood exclusively in empirical terms. Unnecessary implications of this stance include the misrepresentation of constructionism as a less rigorous competitor with empirical approaches. We are not interested in competition. We are interested in collaborative efforts to draw on the insights outlined here to create more sensitivity to the impacts of forms of language. We think sufficient evidence exists in the narrative work presented here and elsewhere to warrant further research. However, if this work is to proceed collaboratively, it will require that empiricists—even those sympathetic to constructionist ideas such as Held—understand that the terms of their orientation have particular effects beyond the therapeutic interventions they indicate and that these terms are themselves objects for remark and study. In our view, constructionist theory enables researchers to analyze and take into account the significance of both culture and context in psychological functioning. It is just what psychology has been looking for.

REFERENCES

Austin, J. L. (1962). *How to do things with words*. Oxford, England: Clarendon Press.

American Psychiatric Association. (1994). *Diagnostic and statistical manual of mental disorders* (4th ed.). Washington, DC: Author.

Bakhtin, M. (1986). *Speech genres and other late essays*. Austin: University of Texas Press.

Bernstein, R. J. (1993). *Beyond objectivism and relativism*. Oxford, England: Basil Blackwell.

Burr, V. (1995). *An introduction to social constructionism*. London: Routledge.

Davies, B. (1991). The concept of agency: A feminist poststructuralist analysis. *Postmodern Critical Theorising, 30*, 42–53.

Davies, B., & Harré, R. (1990). Positioning: The discursive production of selves. *Journal for the Theory of Social Behaviour, 20*(1), 43–63.

Edwards, D. (1997). *Discourse and cognition*. London: Sage.

Fairclough, N. (1992). *Discourse and social change*. Cambridge, UK: Polity Press.

Foucault, M. (1970). *The order of things*. London: Tavistock.

Foucault, M. (1980). *Power/knowledge: Selected interviews and other writings*. New York: Pantheon Books.

Freedman, J., & Combs, G. (1996). *Narrative therapy: The social construction of preferred realities.* New York: Norton.

Gergen, K. J. (1985). The social constructionist movement in modern psychology. *American Psychologist, 40,* 266–275.

Gergen, K. J. (1990). Therapeutic professions and the diffusion of deficit. *Journal of Mind and Behavior, 11*(3–4), 353–368.

Harré, R. (1986). *Varieties of realism: A rationale for the social sciences.* Oxford, England: Blackwell.

Held, B. (1995). *Back to reality: A critique of postmodern theory in psychotherapy.* New York: Norton.

Hoffman, L. (1990). Constructing realities: An art of lenses. *Family Process, 29,* 1–12.

Hubble, M. A., & O'Hanlon, W. H. (1992). Theory countertransference. *Dulwich Centre Newsletter, 1,* 25–30.

Kirk, S. A., & Kutchins, H. (1992). *The selling of DSM: The rhetoric of science in psychiatry.* New York: de Gruyter.

Lather, P. (1991). *Getting smart: Feminist research and pedagogy within the postmodern.* New York: Routledge.

Monk, G., & Drewery, W. J. (1994). The impact of social thought. *New Zealand Counselling Journal, 16*(1), 5–14.

Monk, G., Winslade, J., Crocket, K., & Epston, D. (1997). *Narrative therapy in practice: The archaeology of hope.* San Francisco: Jossey-Bass.

Packer, M. J. (1985). Hermeneutic inquiry in the study of human conduct. *American Psychologist, 40,* 1081–1093.

Parker, I. (Ed.). (1998). *Social constructionism, discourse and realism.* London: Sage.

Parker, I. (Ed.). (1999). *Deconstructing psychotherapy.* London: Sage.

Parker, I., Georgaca, E., Harper, D., McLaughlin, T., & Stowell-Smith, M. (1995). *Deconstructing psychopathology.* London: Sage.

Rogers, C. (1951). *Client-centered therapy.* Boston: Houghton-Mifflin.

Rorty, R. (1980). *Philosophy and the mirror of nature.* Oxford, England: Blackwell.

Russell, D. (1995). *Women, madness and medicine.* Cambridge, UK: Polity Press.

Weedon, C. (1987). *Feminist practice and poststructuralist theory.* Oxford, England: Basil Blackwell.

Wetherell, M. (1998). Positioning and interpretive repertoires: Conversation analysis and post-structuralism in dialogue. *Discourse and Society, 9*(3), 387–412.

White, M. (1991). Deconstruction and therapy. *Dulwich Centre Newsletter, 3,* 21–67.

White, M. (1992, October). *Recent developments in narrative therapy* [Videotape]. (D. Sollee, producer). Workshop presentation at the 50th Anniversary Conference of the American Association of Marriage and Family Therapy, Miami Beach, FL. Washington, DC: AAMFT.

Wittgenstein, L. (1958). *Philosophical investigations*. Oxford, England: Blackwell.

Zimmerman, J., & Dickerson, V. (1996). *If problems talked: Narrative therapy in action*. New York: Guilford Press.

11

CONSTRUCTING PSYCHOPATHOLOGY FROM A COGNITIVE NARRATIVE PERSPECTIVE

ÓSCAR F. GONÇALVES, YIFAHT KORMAN, AND LYNNE ANGUS

More than a decade ago, Seligman and Yellen (1987) described a demonstration carried out by Bernard Karmel in a colloquium at the University of Pennsylvania. They reported that in that demonstration Karmel crumpled a string of light bulbs that had been wired to blink sequentially. The lights appeared to blink in a random or chaotic order; Karmel then played a Beatles' song. With amazement and surprise, the audience appeared to discover and believe that the lights were then blinking with the rhythm of the music. Other researchers have also substantiated this finding that human beings tend to assume events they witness are related, even if the events are completely random (Trabasso, Suh, & Payton, 1995).

These findings illustrate some issues we believe to be central for a cognitive narrative understanding of psychopathology:

1. The world (both internal and external) is composed of a random and chaotic sequence of phenomena. At every moment, an individual experiences a multitude of sensory stimulation, emotional states, and cognitive processes. Some of these phenomena result from events taking place externally (i.e.,

sensory stimulation), whereas others are self-generated by the individual (i.e., thoughts, emotions).

2. In the face of this external and self-generated stimulation, the individual is confronted with the task of turning this random and chaotic experience into a meaningful process. In other words, all the diversity of sensorial, emotional, and cognitive stimulation constitutes only a potential experienced reality, until the individual can make it cohere in a meaningful system.

3. Finally, to construct a meaning out of this diversity of stimulation, the individual needs to actively impose a pattern, rhythm, or order on the experience, as exemplified by the illustration with the lightbulbs. We contend that this pattern or rhythm is, in the realm of human experience, a narrative order. That is, to construct a coherent meaningful experience out of the chaos, the individual is faced with the task of introducing a narrative order.

In this sense, from a cognitive-narrative perspective, *adaptive human functioning* can be defined as the capacity to absorb proactively and creatively the diverse sensorial, emotional, and cognitive experiences one encounters. Simultaneously, an adaptive system is also capable of constructing a sense of order and coherence in relation to this experiential process. That is, both the diversity of the experiences processed and the degree to which these experiences are processed in a coherent manner represent central concepts of a narrative conception of psychopathology.

Seligman and Yellen (1987) interpreted the demonstration with the lightbulbs in a way that is consistent with our arguments. These authors claimed that people have a tendency to actively impose a pattern on everything they experience. In the foregoing example, the audience filtered out those lights that were not blinking with the beat and perhaps focused on the lights that were blinking with the beat. We believe that the final outcome of this process was a pattern that integrated the diversity of sensory stimulation into a coherent experience. It is precisely this integration of the diversity of experience into a kind of temporal or spatial pattern that we refer to as "narrative order."

The introduction of a narrative order is probably the most fundamental aspect of human knowing. People understand, store, and relate separate experiences in their lives by representing them in a narrative form. The narrative ordering processes impose a specific pattern of temporal coherence in what otherwise would be a random and chaotic experience. This narrative ordering enables individuals to represent seemingly distinct experiences as meaningful wholes.

Russell (1991) argued that the narrative is a consequence of natural selection, proven to be superior to other forms of meaning making. Furthermore, current thinking suggests that the ability to narrate, like language itself, is an emergent property of the mind. Accordingly, Stern (1989) argued that the capacity to objectively view and narrate self-experiences emerges around the 3rd or 4th year of life, without explicit training or instruction, and appears later than the sense of self, which is the main figure of one's life story.

Some psychologists believe that self-identity can be construed as a function of having a coherent, acceptable, and mutable life story (Linde, 1993). According to Spence (1983), one's identity can be construed as "a narrative thread that gives meaning to life, provided—and this is a big if—that it is never broken" (p. 458). If it is broken, individuals will begin to construct stories that are incoherent or unacceptable to their society or culture (Howard, 1991; White & Epston, 1990). Therefore, when examining the specific and idiosyncratic processes of meaning organization in psychopathology, one must evaluate the key components of the individual's narrative.

In this chapter, we argue that there are three central dimensions in a narrative that are related to a coherent, diverse, and complex way of "narrative being":

- *narrative structure* refers to the way in which the different aspects of the experience connect with each other to provide a coherent sense of authorship.
- *narrative process* refers to the degree of openness to experience as revealed by the quality, variety, and complexity of the stylistic production of the narrative.
- *narrative content* refers to the level of multiplicity and diversity in the descriptive contents of the individual narratives or stories told.

The structural, processing, and content aspects of the narrative create a sense of narrative coherence, complexity, and multiplicity, respectively. It is our assumption that full narrative functioning includes the capacity to (a) construct a sense of connectedness within and across the different narratives (narrative coherence); (b) explore multiple narratives of the past, present, and future (narrative multiplicity); and (c) have these narratives enriched by the diversity of narrative experiential processes, such as sensorial experiences, emotions, cognitions, and meanings (narrative complexity).

Psychopathology can be understood as a function of problems in any of the above three dimensions: the narrative's structure, process, or content. Thus, a disruption in one's ability to create a structured coherent narrative, qualitatively enriched narrative, or a narrative with multiple plots would likely result in an unhealthy narrative. Each of these dimensions of the narrative and the manner in which they are related to psychopathology is described below.

NARRATIVE STRUCTURE: COHERENCE OF THE NARRATIVE

It is our assumption that humans have an ontological attitude that is characterized by a continuous need for meaning construction. The construction of a meaningful organization of experience is achieved by the imposition of a narrative order. To create meaning out of their experiences, individuals attempt to establish a sense of coherence and connectedness in their narratives. This applies to discrete individual events as well as to lifelong experiences.

Drawing on the work of Baumeister and Newman (1994), Angus, Levitt, and Hardtke (in press) suggested that it is important to distinguish between microlevel and macrolevel narratives when discussing issues of narrative and self-identity in the context of the evaluation of oral discourse. According to Angus et al., the term *micronarrative* refers to the specific stories or event descriptions told by individuals that have characteristics similar to those of written narratives (i.e., a clear beginning, middle, and end as well as a protagonist and a plot). In contrast, the term *macronarrative* describes the "thematic story-lines which weave together many different stories or micronarratives" (p. 191). In essence, each chapter in a person's life story, or macronarrative, can be conceptualized as being composed of several micronarratives. Accordingly, it is argued that the ontological quest for narrative coherence applies to both micro- and macronarrative productions.

Numerous researchers have discussed the basic human need to make sense of one's experiences and achieve coherence through storytelling (e.g., Irwin, 1996; Neimeyer, 1995; Rennie, 1994; Robinson & Hawpe, 1986; van den Broek & Thurlow, 1991). More specifically, according to Keen (1986), "the experience of being human is a coherent experience and an experience of coherence" (p. 188). He asserted that if an individual's stories are unclear or ambiguous, the individual will likely be misunderstood; if an individual *is* understood, it is because his or her stories make sense to others. Guidano (1991) recalled that "bringing forth a coherent world is the first and last condition for having a consistent self-identity" (p. 15).

In the face of the diversity of experience, the individual intentionally searches for a kind of connectedness and coherence, so that the different elements of the macronarrative can be thematically related to each other in a meaningful way. Additionally, different micronarratives across the life span need to be brought together to provide a sense of continuity. Without this gestalt organization in daily and life narratives, the individual lacks a sense of coherent identity and authorship. Life, then, becomes a compound of nonsensical, seemingly unrelated, discrete experiences that cannot be adequately understood.

Making meaning of one's own experience entails first and foremost the ability to construct some form of coherence. The meaning of a discrete experience is provided by a coherent organization of events within a specific micronarrative, whereas life span meaning is rendered possible by the existence of coherence across different life narratives or in the macronarrative. The sense of identity and personal authorship is, therefore, accomplished through a double search for structural coherence: (a) Micronarrative coherence (or coherence within each narrative) refers to the degree of causal, temporal–spatial, or semantic connectedness between different elements of the narrative; and (b) macronarrative coherence (or coherence across micronarratives) refers to the degree of connectedness between the different life experiences encountered by an individual over one's life span. Establishing connections between a diverse array of life experiences creates a sense of wholeness and allows individuals to view themselves as both subjects and objects of their self-authorship. Of central importance here is that diversity of experience is not sacrificed for a sense of coherence. That is, diverse experiences can be integrated into complex micro- and macronarrative themes and frameworks in a meaningful coherent manner.

According to Guidano (1991) this process of constructing coherence and creating a sense of personal authorship originates in children's ability to structure their immediate experiences in terms of early prototypical emotional schemata called *nuclear scenes*. The continuous activation of nuclear scenes creates an idiosyncratic sense of self-boundaries and continuity called a personal *nuclear script*. In fact, the concept of *script*, which is defined as "a set of expectations and predictions of how the self and other have and will continue to interact" (Leahy, 1991, p. 291), allows for the creation of macronarrative coherence (coherence across micronarratives). This is because scripts both allow for the generation of a self-consistent pattern and help the individual to identify and recognize patterns in the scripts of other individuals (Leahy, 1991).

Having shown the centrality of coherence in the development of a meaningful authorship, we now explain the structural elements of the narrative, which contribute to this coherence. What are the elements of a given narrative that need to be brought together to establish a coherent personal story? To answer this question, some researchers (e.g., Stein & Policastro, 1984) have examined the evolution of coherence in children's stories as a function of children's development. They found that the early stories told by children typically are composed of unrelated, descriptive states. Over time, children start to report actions that are connected temporally but not otherwise. As they develop, children start to tell stories that are also causally related. Still later, children describe actions with reference to purposes and goals. Finally, children learn to produce themes in which the protagonist's goals are blocked, and therefore subgoals are required. According to Trabasso (1991), as children's stories become more complex, they are also regarded as more coherent because they correspond more to adult definitions of a well-formed story.

Theoretically speaking, there are two ways in which coherence can be established in an individual's micronarrative. First, the establishment of connectedness or cohesiveness between events in a narrative contributes to its overall level of coherence. Russell and van den Broek (1992) identified the following set of relations: temporal, causal, coreferential (e.g., that "Evan" and "he" refer to the same person), and propositional; all of these relations function to connect one event category to another. Furthermore, van den Broek and Thurlow (1991) cited findings that indicate that people judge events that have many causal connections as more important and more coherent. Such events are also summarized more often, recalled more often, and retrieved more quickly than events with few causal connections.

Second, having a narrative structure that corresponds to a given order of sequential events is considered critical for a narrative to be regarded as coherent. Research into the structure of written narratives shows that narratives universally follow a set of predefined rules, despite gross differences in contents (Mandler, 1984). The structure of a coherent narrative adheres to a sequence of seven elements:

- The *setting* introduces the narrative and the background information about the characters and the scene of the narrative.
- The *initiating event* triggers the narrative's development.
- *Internal responses* reflect the subjective world of the characters and the circumstances that created them.
- The *goal* constitutes the desired objective of each character.
- *Actions* are the doings and behaviors of the different protagonists.
- The *outcome* is the result of the individual actions toward goals.
- The *ending* is simply the closing of the narrative.

Extensive research has been conducted on the structure of written stories, and the findings can be summarized as follows. Written stories that have a canonical form (i.e., have all the necessary event categories in the right order) are better recalled (Stein & Glenn, 1979), are read faster (Mandler & Goodman, 1982), and are rated as more acceptable examples of stories (Stein & Policastro, 1984) than those presented in a mixed-up order or that lack some of the constituents. Moreover, when participants are presented with a story in which a salient constituent is omitted, the participants, on recalling the story, tend to "fill in" the missing information in a way that preserves the canonical form of the story structure (Mandler & Johnson, 1977; Stein & Glenn, 1979).

On the basis of these findings, cognitive researchers (e.g., Mandler & Johnson, 1977) have asserted that people have a built-in "story schema" or "mental structure consisting of sets of expectations about the way in which stories proceed" (Mandler, 1984, p. 18). The story schema is believed to be a heuristic template that helps people in storing, retrieving, recalling, processing, and understanding new and old information. Because memory reconstruction is typically consistent with story schema structure and people reconstruct their memories in an effort to achieve coherence, it follows that narratives adhering to story schema sequences are more coherent than narratives with a different, mixed-up ordering. According to Mancuso (1986), this narrative grammar structure has two main characteristics. First, it develops epigenetically; that is, at an early age, the child acquires the capacity to bring coherence to his or her experience by imposing a narrative structure. Second, this epigenetic development is guided by an intrinsic motivational system: the need to make life coherent and escape the ambiguity and potential disconnectness of everyday chaotic experience.

Research on story schema, however, relies heavily on the analysis of written narratives, such as myths, folktales, and children's stories, that typically have a similar and rigid story structure. It is unclear whether the story-schema order of constituents that applies to simple written narratives also applies to oral narratives of personal experiences (Gee, 1985). Such an investigation into the structures of oral narratives is currently underway (Korman, 1998).

Narrative coherence can also be established within the macronarrative. According to van den Broek and Thurlow (1991), the mental representation of a macronarrative can be described as a network of related events, persons, objects, and other elements. These authors argued that understanding experiences in a network model can allow one to identify chains of related events, differentiate between different types of events, and recognize causal relations between groups of events or episodes. Pennebaker and colleagues' research on trauma survivors corroborates some of these assertions (Harber & Pennebaker, 1992; Pennebaker, 1995). The authors found that narratives written by trauma survivors that were not richly connected (i.e., were restricted to factual information without reference to emotions) did not produce psychological or physiological benefits. The authors asserted that describing a trauma using emotionally related concepts and language substantiates the connection between the traumatic event and other less aversive experiences, which in turn may buffer the impact of the traumatic recall. Without such a connection, the traumatic memory elicits only traumatic emotions and the associated distress. The researchers found that people who repress traumatic memories have fewer associative links to other memories; therefore, when fear is evoked, they have fewer channels that can dissipate the distress. In contrast, they suggested that people who have intricate and richly woven memories tend to have more flexible beliefs and are, therefore, more resilient in the face of negative events (Harber & Pennebaker, 1992).

In summary, narrative coherence, or the lack thereof, can be found in individuals' micro- or macronarratives. It is our belief that in the absence of such narrative coherence, psychopathology may arise. Difficulties at the structural level of narrative coherence are common in psychopathology. Frankl (1985) called this effort to find coherence in one's daily and life experiences the "universal search for meaning." Individuals avoid, ignore, or dissociate from certain life experiences because they are unable to find any coherence in what they are experiencing or in the connection between what they are now experiencing and other past experiences. Meaningless days, blanks in the past, depersonalization, lack of a sense of direction, and different forms of dissociation are common complaints that arise from the difficulties people may experience in establishing coherence at the structural level of the narrative. These symptoms, particularly exacerbated in dissociation and eating disorders, are common to individuals who experience difficulties in demarcation from others and in the authoring of their own narrative. Often in this situation, these individuals complain of a sense of emptiness. We find that their narratives are superficial, disconnected, and incoherent. The patient with anorexia, however, is often very skillful at abstracting and theorizing about his or her experiences as way of avoiding the personal impact or confronting the problem.

Hermans and Hermans-Jansen (1995) pointed out that dissociation is a common strategy to avoid experiencing events that do not cohere with the individual's self-narrative. Dissociative disorders, such as amnesia, fugue, and dissociative identity disorder, can be understood as resulting from difficulties in micro- and macronarrative coherence.

Rasmussen and Angus (1997) qualitatively examined the therapy sessions of borderline and nonborderline clients and found that borderline clients reported experiencing a lack of narrative coherence in their sessions and tended to shift the discussion into seemingly unrelated topics. This was in contrast to nonborderline clients, whose topic shifts were thematically related and who reported experiencing narrative coherence in their sessions.

Other psychopathologies may also be understood in terms of structural narrative coherence. According to Agar and Hobbs (1982), the speech of people with schizophrenia lacks coherence because of the way they structure their micronarratives. Those authors noted that the speech of people with schizophrenia displays no temporal or causal relationship between one sentence and the next. Thus, it is difficult for the listener to comprehend the connection between successive statements. Moreover, people with schizophrenia may also appear to be going on a never-ending tangent because there is no apparent overall plan or goal to their stories. In contrast, people who suffer from obsessive–compulsive disorder tend to manifest a debilitating pursuit of connectedness in stretches of their speech. Thus, they overly identify the connections between successive statements.

In summary, many individuals impose coherence on their experiences by creating structured narratives about those experiences. The more complete and structured the narrative, the more coherent the meaning of the experience. It is through the process of narrative structuring that human beings find coherence and connectedness and come to the epigenetic construction of a sense of authorship.

Gergen and Gergen (1986) also recognized that a narrative sense of coherence and connectedness is dependent on the imposition of a structure. However, the authors added a second dimension: the movement and direction of the narrative through time. Here again, the structural elements are constituted by a goal, a set of events relevant to that goal, and a logical connection between these events. However, it is the time movement toward the goal that exemplifies three essential prototype narratives: (a) *progressive narratives*, in which progress toward goals is enhanced; (b) *regressive narratives*, in which protagonists move away from their goals; and (c) *stability narratives*, in which the characters remain unchanged, from beginning to end, in their movement toward their goals. These are the three narrative types through which personal narratives gain coherence and differentiation as tragic, comedic, or melodramatic experiences.

Briefly summarized, at the structural level, micro- and macronarratives may be governed by a set of implicit rules that connect different story elements and allow the construction of coherent narratives. The structural level has both a static component (i.e., a set of relations that connect events in the narrative to a story schema structure) and a dynamic component (i.e., movement in time). By combining these elements, one can establish a set of prototype structural narratives that form the basis for the development of coherence in both micro- and macronarratives. Narratives vary not only in their degree of coherence but also in their level of stylistic quality and diversity of production. We now address the qualitative, stylistic, or procedural aspects of narrative development.

NARRATIVE PROCESS: COMPLEXITY OF THE NARRATIVE

The stylistic and qualitative means by which stories are enriched in their complexity are the main source of what Gergen and Gergen (1986) defined as the "dramatic engagement" of the narrative. People can present coherent narratives that still lack qualitative complexity. For example, an obsessive client can present well-organized and structured narratives but nevertheless be unable to provide details about the diversity of sensorial experience, the complexity of subjective states, or the multiplicity of meanings the experience might have had. As a consequence, despite having narrative coherence, the micronarrative lacks the qualitative components that enrich one's experience.

In fact, one of the most interesting characteristics of a healthy narrative is that it always remains open and flexible. That is, within a given narrative, the individual can construct a multitude of sensorial, emotional, cognitive, and meaning experiences and thus gain awareness of the different potential meanings of any experience. Having an established coherent narrative does not preclude diversity. In fact, a narrative can offer an infinite set of possibilities and alternatives but also be coherent. Having a narrative attitude refers not only to the ability to structure narratives in a coherent way but also to the ability to explore the multiple possibilities of every experience.

It is this exploration of the multiple interpretations of an experience that seems absent in certain types of pathology. For example, the phobic client lacks the capacity to explore the sensorial diversity of experience; the avoidant client lacks the capacity to explore the complexities of subjective experience; and the depressed client frequently lacks the ability to construct a variety of meanings for a given narrative (cf. Guidano, 1991). By contrast, a healthy narrative implies the capacity to explore a variety of sensorial experiences related to the narrative, including the multiplicity of cognitive and emotional aspects of the narrative. In this way, the complexity of meanings provided by each experience can readily be examined. This is narrative being, a being that creatively constructs a multitude of possibilities for every life experience.

According to Angus, Hardtke, and Levitt (1996), there are three essential narrative process modes. They constructed the narrative process coding system, a process of analyzing narrative sequences through the identification of the three specific narrative modes: (a) The *external mode* consists of the description of real or imagined events in the past or present, (b) The *internal mode* corresponds to the elaboration of the subjective experience in terms of feeling states and affective reactions, and (c) The *reflexive mode* refers to interpretations, meaning constructions, and understandings of the specific, subjective aspects of the experience.

Angus et al. (1996) applied this system to therapy transcripts of poor-outcome and good client–therapist dyads. In several studies, it was found that poor-outcome dyads tended to have a greater overall percentage of external narrative process types compared with good-outcome dyads, which used higher degrees of reflexive and internal narrative processes in their discourse (Angus & Hardtke, 1994; Angus et al., in press). Angus's research on narrative processes that are related to more effective modes of functioning provides some initial support for the importance of establishing certain narrative modes in psychotherapy.

It is our belief that therapeutic change corresponds to the progressive acquisition of a narrative attitude that allows clients to introduce creatively and proactively more flexibility into their narratives. This narrative attitude is characterized by a variety of narrative processes or modes that include references to the external, internal, and reflexive dimensions of experience. Gonçalves (1995) argued that there are five central narrative processes and attitudes that are fundamental to an increase in the quality and diversity of each narrative: recalling, objectifying, subjectifying, metaphorizing, and projecting. In his cognitive narrative psychotherapy model, the therapeutic process is organized around the development of each of these attitudes as they apply to individuals' micro- and macronarratives. The following is a brief summary of the characteristics of these attitudes and their functions in the therapeutic process.

The *recalling* attitude refers to the ability to recollect concrete and episodic experiences. One of the necessary processes of narrative being is the close connection it maintains with an episodic recollection of an event rather than with the semantic understanding of it. The person needs to be acquainted with the process of recalling episodic narratives to develop new micro- and macronarratives.

The *objectifying* attitude involves exploring the multiplicity of the sensorial world as a tool to expand the limits of one's experience. What brings the reader or listener into the text is, to a certain extent, the capacity of the narrator to construct the scenario for the narrative. This is accomplished by specifying the sensorial dimensions of the event introduced. For example, a client suffering from panic attacks is encouraged to shift attention from physical sensations to an exploration of the unlimited possibilities of different sensorial experiences. The depressed client in this process is encouraged to explore the varieties of sensorial perceptions and to introduce multiplicity to what was previously seen as a single, colorless, bland, and absolute reality.

The development of a *subjectifying* attitude is characterized by an increased capacity to explore the multiplicity of internal experiences, both cognitive and emotional. The aim here is to gain awareness of the internal or subjective dimension of every experience. Clients are invited to go beyond the usual limits of their subjective experiences, through which the clients typically express only a limited range of feelings and thoughts. For example, a dichotomy of emotions (guilt and shame) and a recursive process of cognitions most often characterize the obsessive–compulsive client. Developing a subjectifying attitude helps the client experience a multiplicity of emotions and cognitions. This, in turn, promotes more creative ways of coping.

The *metaphorizing attitude* is characterized by the capacity to construct multiple meanings from a single narrative. Metaphors are the ideal means for condensing meanings and for developing reflexive attitudes about one's experience. The person is encouraged through metaphor production to explore the multiple meanings of every episode in their micro- and macronarratives. For example, the patient with posttraumatic stress disorder who uses the trauma metaphor to classify most daily episodes is progressively encouraged to open up to a variety of multiple meanings for each experience. The client learns that every experience has the potential for a kaleidoscopic exploration of meanings.

Finally, the development of a *projective* attitude parallels what Markus described as "experimenting with possible selves" (Markus & Nurius, 1986). Possible selves represent alternatives for "how one thinks about one's potential and one's future . . . images of the individual as he would like to be, and fantasizes about or dreads being" (Wurf & Markus, 1991, p. 40). A *projective* attitude invites the client to develop new alternative characters and narratives for his or her projected future. With the projective attitude, all previous work is put together to explore new metaphors and novel ways of subjectifying and objectifying one's experience. These alternative narratives, in turn, contribute to the emergence of a new author and provide the client with an alternative sense of identity and authorship (Lehrer, 1988).

In summary, the quality of a narrative and its dramatic engagement depends on mastering several narrative modes and attitudes. Narrative being depends on an elaboration of narrative attitudes that progresses from (a) differentiating sensorial experiences; to (b) experiencing multiplicity of emotions, cognitions, and meanings; and finally to (c) constructing future narratives. Because the objective of every narrative is not to make us better readers but to turn us into improved writers (Bruner, 1991), narrative being includes the ability to proactively and creatively project and create future narratives. Adopting the five narrative attitudes just described allows for the construction of a meaningful past, present, and future. We are reminded by Kierkegaard that although people understand backward, they live forward; narrative is always about creating a connection between understanding and living, past and future.

Pennebaker (1993, 1995) also studied narrative processes. He focused on the therapeutic effects writing and talking about core personal narratives have on personal well-being. In the typical paradigm followed by his studies, participants were asked to write about highly personal traumatic topics for periods of 15–20 minutes over the course of 3–5 consecutive days. The participants were then compared with controls (who were asked to write about factual superficial topics) on a number of physical and psychological outcome measures. Participants who wrote about deeply personal topics showed highly significant effects on several clinically relevant measures. For example, those who wrote about their personal experiences had significant decreases in health center visits for periods of up to 6 months, demonstrated improvements in their immune system, had fewer absences from work, and showed improved grade point averages.

To explore the positive therapeutic effects of the narratives, Pennebaker (1993) and his colleagues qualitatively examined the narratives' linguistic patterns. Several results are worth mentioning. First, the health-improved group presented significantly more negative-emotion words and fewer positive-emotion words, whereas the low-improvement group showed an increase in the use of positive emotional words across the 3–4 days of writing. Moreover, these researchers found that only narratives about a trauma that disclosed potent emotions (e.g., anger and depression) produced psychological or physiological benefit. Second, high-improvement and low-improvement participants did not differ globally on the use of *insight* and *causal* and other self-reflective cognitive words. They did differ, however, in their use of cognitive words, with the highly improved sample showing an increase in the use of cognitive words across the days of writing. These findings support Angus's (Angus et al., 1996) findings, which highlight the therapeutic effects of internal (emotionally focused) and reflexive modes of processing in psychotherapy. Third, highly improved participants showed an increase across sessions in both their level of narrative structural organization and their degree of optimism.

In summary, Pennebaker's studies suggest that personal disclosure of negative emotions and the progressive construction of a clear and meaningful cognitive narrative seem to be central components of therapeutic writing. As Pennebaker (1993) concluded,

> the recent social construction (e.g., Gergen & Gergen, 1988) and narrative (Meichenbaum & Fong, 1993) explanatory models are conditionally supported in our findings. However, holding a coherent narrative to explain a traumatic or upsetting experience may not always be healthy at the beginning of therapeutic writing sessions. Movement towards the development of a narrative is far more predictive of health than having a coherent story per se. The construction of a story rather than having a constructed story, then, may be the desired endpoint of writing and, by extension, some therapy. (p. 546)

NARRATIVE CONTENT: MULTIPLICITY OF THE NARRATIVE

Narratives vary not only in terms of structure and process but also in terms of content. The diversity of content is a central aspect for a narrative conception of psychopathology. A healthy narrative is characterized by a continuous diversity of topics, with multiple plots that allow for an adaptation to a world that is itself multifarious. That is, an individual with a healthy, multifaceted view of self and reality will likely narrate stories that have multiple contents and diverse themes.

In contrast, a poor narrative content is illustrated by a restricted diversity of topics that often operate within a single plot. These poor micro- and macronarratives tend to have a recurrence of single themes and limited patterns. They lack diversity, flexibility, and multiplicity. Regardless of the story the individual tells, it sounds like a compulsive repetition of old themes.

A psychopathological organization can be characterized by the strict and inflexible ruling of prototype narratives. Rather than presenting flexibility, the individual is stuck with invariant themes or prototypes. If we understand different psychopathological organizations to be idiosyncratic processes of meaning making, we can easily establish that the content of narratives in different types of pathologies can be subsumed under specific prototype narratives. The individual is stuck with a prototype narrative as an invariant aspect of meaning making where all the stories, current or past, are rendered meaningful within this same, inflexible plot.

It is important to understand how individuals become prisoners of these prototype narratives. Several clinicians have highlighted the importance of key personal narratives that are central to one's cognitive organization and self-development (e.g., Guidano, 1991; Mahoney, 1991). According to Guidano (1991), initial prototypical emotional schemata are formed from one's interpersonal attachment processes. Once certain key scenes are constructed as prototypes, these prototypes rule subsequent cognitive categorization of experiences.

Eleanor Rosh was perhaps the first author to discuss prototypes in the process of knowledge categorization. She asserted that "categories are built around a central member or prototype—a representative example of that class which shares the most features with other members of the category while showing few, if any, features with elements drawn outside the category" (cited in Gardner, 1985, p. 346). Certain narratives assume the role of best examples and become the essential prototypes for the categorizing and reordering of future experiences. Those narratives turn into scripts, which the individual continuously refers to in an effort to understand and coherently make meaning of experiences (Leahy, 1991).

Although key prototype scripts are an economic way of understanding experiences coherently, they may sometimes function as inflexible and strict interpretive templates. The objective of psychotherapy is to introduce greater flexibility into clients' micro- and macronarratives. Furthermore, the objective of narrative being is to avoid getting stuck in a certain script or prototype narrative and to open individuals to the diversity of their experiencing.

Note that narrative content is related to narrative coherence. The ability to link events and experiences is a necessary condition for a coherent representation of the self. Without such links, it is extremely difficult to understand one's experience. Clients' narratives might have considerable gaps in their capacity to recall significant events and thus provide an incomplete understanding of those events.

In therapy, the contents of a client's micronarrative can be altered by articulating what has been forgotten or perhaps never fully been understood. Moreover, by providing supplementary information or insights and creating more emotional, thematic, or motivational links, clients and therapists can thematically tie together different parts of the narrative in a way that enhances understanding and produces a more coherent and complete story (Angus et al., in press). The contents of a client's macronarrative achieve greater coherence if insight is gained about recurrent themes in the client's life story. Thus, tying different life experiences, or micronarratives, together through emotional or motivational themes can create a better understanding of the self and a more coherent life story.

To clarify how psychopathology can be conceptualized in terms of specific narrative contents, Gonçalves and his colleagues tried to identify prototype narratives of individuals with different psychological dysfunctions (Gonçalves, Alves, Soares, & Duarte, 1996; Gonçalves, Maia, et al., 1996). Micronarratives that described significant life events were collected from agoraphobic, opioid-dependent, alcoholic, anorexic, and depressed patients. All prototype narratives were constructed for each dysfunction using a grounded theory procedure. A diagnostic and control sample were then introduced to the prototype narratives and were asked to evaluate the degree to which that narrative could be understood as a personal life event. The diagnostic samples evaluated the prototype narrative as significantly more related to their personal lives than the control sample. These results illustrate how in psychopathological situations, individuals seem to rely on inflexible and foreclosed prototypes when generating narratives of their life experiences. Rather than exploring the multiple possible meanings for their life stories, these individuals seemed to experience their lives as a continuous and vicious repetition of a single script. By contrast, healthy psychological functioning involves the exploration of multiple narrative contents. In therapy, individuals are encouraged to develop a range of prototypes and to break out of their old interpretations, so that they can begin to explore life from other perspectives. The overall objective of therapy, in this regard, is to allow the possibility for a never-ending diversity of interpretations, liberating the individual from the recursive repetition of a single prototype.

CONCLUSION

We end by reiterating some of our core assumptions. We argued that narrative is the essential process through which individuals construct meaningful experiences. Thus, understanding individuals involves inspecting the characteristics of their narratives. Three central elements of the narrative need to be considered:

- *Narrative structure:* the level of coherence and connectedness between different elements in the narrative. Research indicates that narratives have a series of implicit rules that assure their structural coherence. Micro- and macronarrative coherence is fundamental for the development of an integrated and continuous sense of personal authorship or self-identity.
- *Narrative process:* the qualitative dimension of the narrative, that is, the different modes or attitudes (i.e., stylistic maneuvers) that allow the differentiation of the narrative into a multitude of sensorial, emotional, cognitive, and meaning experiences. Healthy living is dependent on the capacity to explore the complexities and possibilities available in every moment of one's experience.
- *Narrative content:* the multiplicity of narrative production. In psychopathological situations, narrative production is characterized by low content complexity. That is, rather than presenting multiple life narratives, individuals seem to get stuck within a single narrative prototype from which all their narratives seem to derive. In contrast, a highly complex and healthy narrative is characterized by the differentiation of contents; the individual can provide multiple narratives about his or her own personal experiences.

In summary, if we assume that narrative is the essential process for meaning making, then a healthy adaptation to life can be seen as synonymous with a coherent, differentiated, and complex process of narrative production. In a narrative being, life is portrayed by multiple narratives (i.e., contents), which are differentiated on a variety of elements of experience (i.e., processes) and have a sense of coherence and connectedness within both the micro- and macronarratives (i.e., structures). In contrast, a psychopathological narrative may by portrayed by (a) a single invariable plot (i.e., content), (b) a constricted experiential quality (i.e., process), or (c) a fragmented story structure.

The objective of cognitive narrative psychotherapy (Gonçalves, 1995) is to assure the conversational conditions for the development of such narrative being. In the words of Gergen and Kaye (1992), a narrative being is prepared for the

> reconception of the relativity of meaning, an acceptance of indeterminacy, the generative exploration of a multiplicity of meanings, and the understanding that there is no necessity either to adhere to an invariant story or to search for a definitive story. (p. 181)

REFERENCES

Agar, M., & Hobbs, J. R. (1982). Interpreting discourse: Coherence and the analysis of ethnographic interviews. *Discourse Processes, 5,* 1–32.

Angus, L. E., & Hardtke, K. (1994). Narrative processes in psychotherapy. *Canadian Psychology, 35,* 190–203.

Angus, L., Hardtke, K., & Levitt, H. (1996). *The narrative processes coding system manual: Revised edition.* Unpublished manuscript, York University, North York, Ontario, Canada.

Angus, L., Levitt, H., & Hardtke, K. (in press). The narrative processes coding system: Implications for psychotherapy research and practice. In C. Matens (Ed.), *Psychotherapy process research measures: A guidebook.* Valencia, Spain: Universidade.

Baumeister, R. F., & Newman, L. S. (1994). How stories make sense of personal experiences: Motives that shape autobiographical narratives. *Personality and Social Psychology Bulletin, 20*(6), 676–690.

Bruner, J. (1991). *Acts of meaning.* Cambridge, MA: Harvard University Press.

Frankl, V. E. (1985). Logos, paradox, and the search for meaning. In M. J. Mahoney (Ed.), *Cognition and psychotherapy* (pp. 259–276). New York: Plenum Press.

Gardner, H. (1985). *The mind's new science.* New York: Basic Books.

Gee, J. P. (1985). The narrativization of experience in the oral style. *Journal of Education, 167*(1), 9–35.

Gergen, K. J., & Gergen, M. M. (1986). Narrative form and the construction of psychological science. In T. R. Sarbin (Ed.), *Narrative psychology* (pp. 22–44). New York: Praeger.

Gergen, K. J., & Kaye, J. (1992). Beyond narrative in the negotiation of therapeutic meaning. In S. McNamee & K. J. Gergen (Eds), *Therapy as social construction* (pp. 166–185). London: Sage.

Gonçalves, O. F. (1995). Cognitive narrative psychotherapy. In M. J. Mahoney (Ed.), *Cognitive and constructive psychotherapies* (pp. 139–162). Elmsford, NY: Pergamon Press.

Gonçalves, O. F., Alves, A. R., Soares, I., & Duarte, Z. (1996). Narrativas prototipo y psicopatologia: Um estudio con pacientes alcoholicos, anoréxicos y opiáceodependientes [Protype narratives and psychopathology: A study with alcoholic, anorexic and opioid-dependent patients]. *Revista de Psicopatología y Psicología Clínica* (Spain), *1*, 105–114.

Gonçalves, O. F., Maia, A., Alves, A. R., Soares, I., Duarte, Z., & Henriques, M. (1996). Narrativas protótipo e psicopatologia [Prototype narratives and psychopathology]. *Psicologia: Teoria, Investigação e Prática* (Portugal), *1*, 307–318.

Guidano, V. F. (1991). *The self in process*. New York: Guilford Press.

Harber, K. D., & Pennebaker, J. W. (1992). Overcoming traumatic memories. In S. Christianson (Ed.), *The handbook of emotion and memory: Research and theory* (pp. 359–387). Hillsdale, NJ: Erlbaum.

Hermans, H. J. M., & Hermans-Jansen, E. (1995). *Self-narratives: The construction of meaning in psychotherapy*. New York: Guilford Press.

Howard, G. (1991). Cultural tales: A narrative approach to thinking, cross-cultural psychology, and psychotherapy. *American Psychologist, 46*, 187–197.

Irwin, R. R. (1996). Narrative competence and constructive developmental theory: A proposal for rewriting the *Bildungsroman* in postmodern world. *Journal of Adult Development, 3*(2), 109–125.

Keen, E. (1986). Paranoia and cataclysmic narratives. In T. R. Sarbin (Ed.), *Narrative psychology: The storied nature of human conduct* (pp. 174–190). New York: Praeger.

Korman, Y. (1998). *Narrative coherence in brief good outcome client-centered psychotherapy*. Unpublished master thesis, York University, North York, Ontario, Canada.

Leahy, R. L. (1991). Scripts in cognitive therapy: The systemic perspective. *Journal of Cognitive Psychotherapy, 5*, 291–304.

Lehrer, R. (1988). Characters in search of an author: The self as a narrative structure. In J. C. Mancuso & M. L. Shaw (Eds.), *Cognition and personal structure: Computer access and analysis* (pp. 195–228). New York: Praeger.

Linde, C. (1993). *Life stories: The creation of coherence*. New York: Oxford University Press.

Mahoney, M. J. (1991). *Human change processes: The scientific foundations of psychotherapy*. New York: Basic Books.

Mancuso, J. C. (1986). The acquisition and use of narrative grammar structure. In T. R. Sarbin (Ed.), *Narrative psychology* (pp. 91–110). New York: Praeger.

Mandler, J. M. (1984). *Stories, scripts, and scenes: Aspects of schema theory*. Hillsdale, NJ: Erlbaum.

Mandler, J. M., & Goodman, M. S. (1982). On the psychological validity of story structure. *Journal of Verbal Learning and Verbal Behavior, 21*, 507–523.

Mandler, J. M., & Johnson, N. S. (1977). Remembrance of things parsed: Story structure and recall. *Cognitive Psychology, 9*, 111–151.

Markus, H., & Nurius, P. (1986). Possible selves. *American Psychologist, 41*, 954–969.

Neimeyer, R. A. (1995). Client-generated narratives in psychotherapy. In R. A. Neimeyer & M. J. Mahoney (Eds.), *Constructivism in psychotherapy* (pp. 231–245). Washington, DC: American Psychological Association.

Pennebaker, J. W. (1993). Putting stress into words: Health, linguistic, and therapeutic implications. *Behaviour Research & Therapy, 31*, 539–548.

Pennebaker, J. W. (Ed.). (1995). *Emotion, disclosure, and health.* Washington, DC: American Psychological Association.

Rasmussen, B., & Angus, L. (1997). Modes of interaction in psychotherapy with borderline and nonborderline clients: A qualitative analysis. *Journal of Analytic Social Work, 4*, 53–73.

Rennie, D. L. (1994). Human science and counseling psychology: Closing the gap between research and practice. *Counseling Psychology Quarterly, 7*, 235–250.

Robinson, J. A., & Hawpe, L. (1986). Narrative thinking as a heuristic process. In T. R. Sarbin (Ed.), *Narrative psychology: The storied nature of human conduct* (pp. 111–125). New York: Praeger.

Russell, R. L. (1991). Narrative, cognitive representations, and change: New directions in cognitive theory and therapy. *Journal of Cognitive Psychotherapy, 5*, 241–256.

Russell, R. L., & van den Broek, P. (1992). Changing narrative schemas in psychotherapy. *Psychotherapy, 29*, 344–353.

Seligman, M., & Yellen, A . (1987). What is a dream? *Behaviour Research & Therapy, 25*, 1–24.

Spence, D. (1983). Narrative persuasion. *Psychoanalysis and Contemporary Thought, 6*(3), 457–481.

Stein, N. L., & Glenn, C. G. (1979). An analysis of story comprehension in elementary school children. In R. O. Freedle (Ed.), *New directions in discourse processing* (Vol. 2, pp. 53–120). Norwood, NJ: Ablex.

Stein, N. L., & Policastro, M. (1984). The concept of story: A comparison between children's and teacher's viewpoints. In H. Mandl, N. L. Stein, & T. Trabasso (Eds.), *Learning and comprehension of text* (pp. 113–155). Hillsdale, NJ: Erlbaum.

Stern, D. N. (1989). Developmental prerequisites for the sense of narrated self. In A. Cooper, O. F. Kernberg, & P. E. Spector (Eds.), *Psychoanalysis: Towards the second century* (pp. 168–178). New Haven, CT: Yale University Press.

Trabasso, T. (1991). The development of coherence in narratives by understanding internal action. In G. Denhière & J. P. Rossi (Eds.), *Text and text processing* (pp. 297–314). Amsterdam, The Netherlands: Elsevier Science.

Trabasso, T., Suh, S., & Payton, P. (1995). Explanatory coherence in understanding and talking about events. In M. A. Gernsbacher & T. Givón (Eds.), *Coherence in spontaneous text* (pp. 189–214). Philadelphia: John Benjamins.

van den Broek, P., & Thurlow, R. (1991). The role and structure of personal narratives. *Journal of Cognitive Psychotherapy, 5,* 257–274.

White, M., & Epston, D. (1990). *Narrative means to therapeutic ends.* New York: Norton.

Wurf, E., & Markus, H. (1991). Possible selves and the psychology of personal growth. *Perspectives in Personality, 3,* 39–62.

V

CONTEXTUAL CONSTRAINTS AND DISCOURSES OF DISORDER

12

DISCOMFORTS OF THE POWERLESS: FEMINIST CONSTRUCTIONS OF DISTRESS

LAURA S. BROWN

Feminist psychology has a long and ambivalent relationship with the construction of psychological distress as evidence of disorder or pathology. Because it is rooted in political analysis rather than in mental health epistemic traditions, the paradigm for disorder in feminist psychology diverges from that of the rest of psychology. From feminist psychology's inception, the field has framed the oppressive forces of patriarchal cultures—racism, sexism, classism, and heterosexism, to name but a few—as the actual pathologies and disorders with which clinicians ought to concern themselves (Chesler 1972). Feminist psychologists have long argued that psychologists "construct the female," to paraphrase from the title of an early feminist critique of psychology's views of women (Weisstein, 1970).

Simultaneously, however, practicing feminist-informed psychotherapists have been confronted with the reality of suffering human beings seeking care to ameliorate their distress. These individuals frequently must be given a formal diagnosis of a disorder to gain access to or payment for services. Additionally, although this is not true for all people who suffer emotionally, many people with emotional distress do report that they find it helpful to know that their variety of trouble has a name, that they are not randomly crazy but experiencing something reified, and thus apparently "real."

The practical result of this collision of theory with reality has been the current feminist vision of psychological "disorder," one in which various writers have attempted to accommodate the divergence between theory and people's experiences. In this chapter, I briefly introduce feminist theory of practice as a foundation to understanding feminist constructions of disorder. I then visit feminist critiques of dominant views of disorder. Next, I discuss the present state of feminist constructions of emotional pain and distress. Feminists in psychology have attempted to find a place in between the pathologizing of oppressive cultures and the recognition of clinical realities by constructing most psychological distress not as forms of disorder but as understandable, possibly inevitable, and therefore not per se disordered responses to a dangerous and painful social context (Brown & Ballou, 1992; Lerman, 1986, 1996).

Simultaneous with the critique and deconstruction of common diagnostic nosologies, attempts have been made by some feminist authors on psychological disorder to intentionally define as forms of disorder and pathology certain worldviews and patterns of behavior that are currently considered common and somewhat acceptable among the dominant classes of a culture (Caplan, 1995). This strategy of constructing as a disorder those behaviors that are ignored or celebrated by the cultural mainstream, while building a theory that has otherwise avoided locating disorders in a person, has created an interesting dynamic tension in feminist thought on this topic.

Feminist psychologists have also found difficulties in responding to purely or primarily biogenetic models of disorder—a problem that is addressed here. Although the feminist model of behavior, and thus of distress, is a biopsychosocial one, feminist theory problematizes essentialist explanations and consequently biological theories of distress. Although feminist psychology is not purely social constructivist in its orientation, there is a strong strain of constructivist thinking in the field that is particularly visible at the point where psychopathology is discussed. Yet another source of complexity and ambivalence found in feminist constructions of disorder arises from the problem of practicing clinicians who are required to use formal diagnostic labels to be paid. In this chapter, I touch on attempts to merge feminist analysis with the apparently unavoidable use of formal diagnostic labels for disorder and distress as found in the fourth edition of the *Diagnostic and Statistical Manual of Mental Disorders* (*DSM-IV*; American Psychiatric Association, 1994).

Feminist psychology is not a unified approach; it has emerged from the work of a number of feminist-informed researchers and practitioners. There is no single identified founding parent of this perspective (Brown & Brodsky, 1992), leading to some diversity of viewpoints within feminist psychology. I defined feminist practice as "practice defined by feminist political philosophy and analysis, grounded in multicultural feminist scholarship on the psychology of women and gender" (Brown, 1994, p. 22). Currently, several trends and groupings within feminist practice have emerged, some more intrapsychic (Jordan, Kaplan, Miller, Stiver, & Surrey, 1992) and others more oriented to social constructivist models (Brown, 1994; Hare-Mustin & Marecek, 1990). All of the feminist frameworks for psychotherapy practice have generated discussion on questions of distress or disorder. Most of these discussions of the question of disorder assume that ascriptions of pathology derive heavily from social context and from stereotypic assumptions about women and men (Brown, 1994; Brown & Ballou, 1992; Caplan, 1995; Kaplan, 1983; Lerman, 1986, 1996; Weisstein, 1970). What draws these diverse thinkers, researchers, scholars, and practitioners together are certain core concepts about what constitute feminist theories of behavior and behavior change.

GUIDING PRINCIPLES IN FEMINIST PRACTICE

Hannah Lerman (1986) was the first author to synthesize work in the field of feminist practice and to propose core principles of a feminist conceptual model. Her eight meta-assumptions are that to be feminist, a model of behavior (which implicitly subsumes a model of disorder or distress) would (a) be clinically useful; (b) encompass human diversity and complexity; (c) view women—the "other" in a positive and central manner rather than in comparison to a dominant "norm" group; (d) arise from the experiences of women—the other; (e) be closely bound to the data of experience, that of both client and clinician; (f) recognize the inextricable feedback loop between internal realities and external real-world experiences; (g) avoid obscure and particularistic terminologies to be accessible and comprehensible to client and professional alike; and (h) support feminist (e.g., egalitarian and liberatory) modes of practice.

I proposed six additional components that expand on Lerman's principles, arguing that a feminist conceptual model should, additionally (a) embody an understanding of the relationship between feminist political analysis and concepts of behavior change; (b) critique and analyze dominant cultural models of gender, power, and authority in mainstream approaches to behavior and behavior change; (c) view psychotherapy (and, by implication, the construction of disorder) as it obtains meaning from the larger social context; (d) ground concepts of normal growth and development, and thus distress and the diagnosis of distress, from the standpoint of feminist political analysis; (e) reflect an ethics of practice (and, by implication, the conceptualization of disorder) tied to feminist politics of social change; and

(f) be informed by a multiculturally and conceptually diverse knowledge base (Brown, 1994).

A theme running through these feminist frameworks for understanding behavior is that all behavior has meaning only as it is constructed within the politics of the culture in which it is viewed. Even a behavior that is grounded in a biological reality has meaning and value ascribed to it by the social and political milieu. Thus, any diagnosis of psychopathology reflects not only the subjective experience of distress but also the construction of the meaning of that distress within the culture. To create a "norm," whether moral or statistical, and then to construct the cultural vision of goodness as being equivalent to normalcy is a political dynamic with which mental health diagnosis is saturated. The designation of behaviors as "abnormal" is highly culturally determined; psychological diagnosis does not represent a description of that which is clearly present but a mutual decision by professionals to classify certain ways of being as outside the dominant norms. In the history of American psychiatry and psychology, behaviors as diverse as being a runaway slave and a protesting student have been consigned to the category of mental illness (Lerman, 1996).

Consequently, to comprehend distress and its constructions and to eschew normative assumptions, feminists argue that the culture itself must be subjected to analysis and critique and that underlying oppressive normative assumptions be exposed. To assign a behavior to a category of disorder involves a complex process of sorting *distress* (the phenomenological experience of pain and misery) from *pathology* (something wrong, disordered, abnormal), even in those circumstances where the distress may lead to an impairment in function. Feminists do not view distress as isomorphic with pathology. Distress may represent resistance and necessary noncompliance with social norms (Brown, 1994; Rivera, 1996); impairment in function may punctuate problems in assumptions about how humans "should" function in a particular setting, such as a family or marital relationship (Caplan, 1995; Luepnitz, 1988). Feminist political analysts in psychology are particularly concerned with constructions of gender and interpersonal power dynamics as factors shaping relationships and the culture (Bem, 1993; Hare-Mustin & Marecek, 1990), which in turn define the parameters of what is seen by the mental health professions as being disordered or abnormal behavior. Feminists have interrogated the interstices of those phenomena both in daily personal life and on the broader cultural scale, and they do so at the location of psychodiagnosis.

Because feminism has its roots in struggles for the liberation of women, gender became a central organizing theme for feminist thinkers attempting to describe the ways in which hierarchies of difference are socially constructed. This has led to the mistaken notion in the general public that feminist theories describe only women's behaviors. However, as feminist historian Gerda Lerner (1993) observed, in most cultures, gender serves as a placemarker for other forms of human difference: skin color, social class, physical or mental ability, religion, and so on. She noted that in *patriarchal societies*—a term that can accurately describe most cultures currently extant—the position of cultural dominance is assigned characteristics that are considered inherent in the male sex and imbued with social desirability, whereas all nondominant groups, women or men of a "wrong" class or color, are socially constructed as female and as less socially desirable.

Thus, in North American cultures—characterized by the dominance of Caucasian, middle-class, heterosexual, young, Christian, able-bodied men—both White women and people of Color (and members of various other nondominant groups) are socially constructed as less rational, more physical or "close to nature," weaker, and less mentally fit than are members of the dominant group (Hacker, 1976; Lerner, 1993). In patriarchies, the naive or lay theories of human behaviors ascribe any apparent differences to inherent, biological traits that are inescapable or essential to the nature of the individual and, thus, natural or normal. Biological explanations of behavior tend to be privileged over other, multifactored, and psychosocial ones that would presume the mutability of human behavior rather than its inherence. Such cultural assumptions pervade diagnostic models of disorder and abnormalcy.

In patriarchal cultures, the presumed inherent nature of human difference is frequently used as a rationale supporting unequal differential treatment of various nondominant groups. The notion that certain groups like being treated unequally is commonly found in this sort of reasoning. In psychology, the characteristics that are socially constructed into the identity of nondominant groups are frequently construed as problematic or pathological; not only in musical comedy does one find the insistent question of why a woman cannot be more like a man (e.g., "reasonable"). Diagnoses exist to describe the excesses of femininity but not those of masculinity. Conversely, whatever characteristics are currently associated with the dominant group tend to be those associated with mental health and are more likely to be socially desirable (Broverman, Broverman, Clarkson, Rosencrantz, & Vogel, 1970; Landrine, 1988).

Feminist theories also interrogate power relationships, with *power* broadly defined not only in terms of a control over resources but also as a capacity for interpersonal influence and impact. In feminist thought, the existence of hierarchies of power or value, such as found in patriarchy, is considered inherently problematic, and the leveling of power between and among people is viewed as an inherent good, to be pursued through the variety of means available. Thus, in feminist psychological practice, a central idea is that of the egalitarian therapy relationship, in which the power and value of the client are explicitly attended to and enhanced and the power and value of the role of therapist are intentionally shared in various ways (Brown, 1994). One of the ways in which power can be shared is by including clients in the process of defining what constitutes "disordered" or "abnormal" for them and by assisting clients in challenging ascriptions of abnormalcy or disorderedness that they have previously internalized.

POWER OF NAMING

Feminist theorists have long identified the right to name as a form of power (Lakoff, 1975). For example, if Sharon can tell Elaine who Elaine is, then Sharon takes over the authorship of Elaine's life narrative. When the dominant group names the behaviors of the nondominant group, the naming process can be used to ascribe pathology and to make the ascription have the ring of truth and rightness. Rivera (1996) quoted a person who grew up in a highly abusive environment on the issue of being called a "disorder":

> Words are powerful symbols. . . . Our language does not enlighten my struggle; it increases it. I am aware that what was once adaptive is now rather messy, to put it mildly. But I am not crazy. I am not ill. I am not a disorder. (p. 4)

One of the strategies of feminism is to give names to the experiences of oppressed people (e.g., sexual harassment, marital rape) that were previously rendered invisible or illegitimate in society because there was no name for those phenomena. This reclaiming of the power to name from the hands of the dominant group is seen by feminists, both within and outside of psychology, as an important aspect of the feminist project of social and personal change (Brabeck & Brown, 1997; Brown, 1994).

The naming power of the mental health professions defines the terms of what constitutes normal and abnormal, the "manufacture of madness," to use Szasz's (1970) term. The naming of certain human experiences as disordered or pathological and the naming of an individual as being possessed of or being a particular disorder represents a form of therapist power that is inconsistent with a feminist stance. To diagnose, to name the distress for the person, is to hold the power to define another, to determine how that person may be treated both in- and outside of therapy. Standard models of diagnosis have come under extensive critique by feminists, not only for taking the power to name distress away from those experiencing it and placing it into the hands of professionals but also for the manner in which certain categories or classes of behavior have been assigned to or left out of the parameters of disorder (Caplan, 1995; Lerman, 1996). Feminist theory asks why some ways of being are defined as abnormal or disordered, even when it is common for certain groups of people to behave or feel in those ways, whereas other ways of being are defined as normal, nonpathological distress, and still other ways of being are defined as so acceptable in the culture that they are not worthy of diagnostic scrutiny.

An example of the power of the naming process can be seen in the case of "Ruth," a woman who had served as a nurse in Vietnam and developed nightmares, flashbacks, and frightening intrusive images in response to this experience (Brown, 1986). Before entering feminist therapy, Ruth had thought of herself as a crazy woman who had overreacted to her experiences because, as she put it, she had not been in a formal combat zone but rather stationed in the hospital to which battlefield casualties were evacuated by helicopter. She had not named her experiences as traumatic. For Ruth, naming her experiences as traumatic—allowing herself to remember that in Vietnam, the lines between combat and noncombat experiences were thin indeed and that she had been under mortar fire on more than one occasion—assisted her in coming to see her strong distress as a reasonable, rather than crazy, response.

Because of the political analysis at the core of feminist visions, the location of disorder is moved from its usual position within the individual who experiences distress. The culture that permits or encourages oppression and inequality is construed as abnormal rather than the person who suffers distress due to these cultural disorders. Constructions of disorder, such as those represented in the *DSM-IV* or other commonly used models of psychopathology, locate disorder primarily in the distressed person, not in the social milieu. Disorder discomforts or challenges dominant behavioral norms or exposes unpleasant facts about the social context.

Implicit in some diagnostic labels, particularly those that confer the status of severe and enduring psychopathology (e.g., personality disorders), is that the individual might not be distressed her- or himself but others will find the individual's behaviors distressing (as is true, e.g., with the diagnosis of histrionic personality disorder). The *DSM* model of distress-as-pathology, although claiming to be atheoretical, in fact promulgates the theory of the dominant culture, in which there are implicit behavioral norms, significant deviance from which in certain directions is then defined as a form of mental illness. Some models of disorder, such as family systems theory, may go beyond an individualistic analysis and position disorder in the system or among some of its members while acknowledging that there is inevitably an identified patient in these systems.

Feminist theory, however, largely locates disorder (vs. the phenomenological experience of distress) in the culture rather than in the person or the interpersonal system (except when the latter represents an institutional variant of the culture, such as is frequently true for families constituted on patriarchal authoritarian lines). Were there to exist an explicitly feminist diagnostic manual, it would likely describe variations on oppressive cultures and behaviors reflecting oppressive norms as the disorders to be diagnosed. This notion that psychological abnormality is an entirely or primarily socially constructed entity that has taken on the false face of reality constitutes a loud voice in the feminist discourse and is discussed at greater length later in this chapter.

This viewpoint, in which distress and impaired function are not constructed as necessarily disordered, presents certain practical challenges to clinicians, however. Dominant culture constructs the presence of distress as evidence that something must be wrong. What is to be made of recent advances in the biology of distress that argue for primarily biological roots to disorder? How does one theorize the pain of a person who is highly privileged from dominant group memberships and appears to suffer no oppression if the model of distress-equals-oppression is the prevailing conceptual framework? Is it possible, or even allowable in a feminist model, to propose anything resembling a norm or to define what constitutes health or good function and to then create a category of abnormal or pathological? What difference does this theoretical analysis make to the person overwhelmed by feelings of anxiety or paralyzed by sadness when told that her or his problems are reasonable responses to unreasonable events in her or his larger society, when the prospects for anything changing in that social context seem distant if not utterly bleak? After all, as Lerman (1986) noted, if a model is not clinically useful, it may not be feminist. To answer those questions, feminists interested in diagnosis and the construction of disorder have turned to criticisms of standard diagnostic models as a strategy for unpacking the problematic in those models and attempting to find useful concepts for clinical practice. I next review those critiques.

Feminist Critiques of Mainstream Constructions of Disorder

Millennium-era Americans live in a "feel-good" society. Simply to be unhappy has little or no cultural room, as shown in Peter Kramer's (1993) discussion of giving a powerful antidepressant to people, not because they suffered depression but because the drug took away moodiness, surliness, and sharp edges. The specter of Huxley's *Brave New World*, in which all are medicated into a constant state of goodwill, is not as fictional as it seemed when his book was published because legally prescribed mood-altering drugs have increasingly become part of the cultural landscape. Substitute Prozac for Huxley's fictional Soma and the reality becomes chillingly clear.

At the same time, however, American culture seems to facilely define a plethora of behaviors as psychopathological. As noted by Kaminer (1992) and Kutchins and Kirk (1997), almost every behavior conducted to what some would consider excess is now ripe for inclusion in the *DSM*. Clinics for the treatment of reading addiction can be found, and the devotee of coffee now suffers from "caffeinism." In the midst of this culture of forced cheer, oddly coupled with a willingness to assign pathology to a plethora of behaviors, comes the feminist practitioner, who questions the very notion of disorder and pathology yet honors the experience of distress as evidence of cultural disorder.

Early in the development of feminist models of practice, the assignment of disorderedness and formal diagnosis to the behavior or feelings of an individual and the diagnosis of an individual's distress as pathological were considered incompatible with a feminist analysis. Diagnosis as used by the mainstream of the mental health professions was seen as only, or primarily, a strategy for grabbing power and creating mystification for the client. Many diagnostic categories came under fire as examples of the uses of psychology and psychiatry to maintain the patriarchal status quo (Chesler, 1972; Greenspan, 1983).

There are solid kernels of truth in these criticisms that have persisted over time. I discussed earlier the notion that by taking the power to name distress, mainstream mental health professionals enshrine an aspect of power imbalance in therapy relationships that fundamentally undermines any attempts at the empowerment of the client. The clinician decides what the name and nature of the problem are and, by so doing, defines the person with the problem. Lerman (1996), researching the roots of psychodiagnosis, found that the original rationale for developing the *DSM* taxonomy was to improve the quality of communication between professionals and to make it easier for one therapist to understand precisely what the other was observing in a patient. Although there is nothing inherently problematic in this function, Lerman noted that formal nosology grew to become a sort of secret code, knowledge of which was evidence of admission to the guild of mental health professionals and use of which was forbidden to the patient. Self-diagnosis is often constructed in dominant models of pathology as a sign of illness itself and of resistance to change. The patient or client who dares to take the power to name her or his own distress is punished by being further defined as pathological, a move that reasserts the power of the professional.

It has also become more clear over time, with mounting empirical research evidence, that much of standard diagnostic nosology did indeed contain sexist, racist, classist, and heterosexist bias (Brown, 1994; Brown & Ballou, 1992; Caplan, 1995; Kaplan, 1983; Landrine, 1988, 1992; Lerman, 1996). Beginning with the research of Broverman, Broverman, Clarkson, Rosenkrantz, and Vogel (1970), the general sexist as well as racist, classist, and other oppressive biases in mental health professionals' assessment of women and the specific biases present in particular diagnoses were exposed (Becker & Lamb, 1994; Brown & Ballou, 1992; Landrine, 1988, 1992). The "diagnostic wars" of the late 1980s, in which organized psychiatry attempted to create a diagnosis of self-defeating personality disorder that seemed tailored for the stigmatization of women with a history of interpersonal victimization, resulted in feminists in psychology and psychiatry waging a sort of guerrilla struggle to "sink" the diagnosis. This process of resisting misdiagnosis also served to lay bare to feminist critique the methodological problems inherent in many aspects of the *DSM* system (Brown, 1994; Caplan, 1995).

Rosewater (1985) commented on how battered women could be misdiagnosed as suffering from psychosis or borderline personality disorder. For "Ilene," who had been battered for many years by the husband she was now divorcing, this kind of misdiagnosis became apparent during the battle for custody of their 10-year-old daughter. Although the original evaluator noted that Ilene seemed to be an excellent parent with a clear bond to her daughter and able to be empathic with the child's needs, the evaluator noted his concern that Ilene scored high on psychological test scales that indicated the presence of a thought disorder. He raised questions in court about Ilene's fitness to parent on the basis of these test findings. Only when Ilene's attorney was able to offer a rebuttal witness who was able to document that many battered women score high on such dimensions and that these scores were indicative of the impact of battering rather than of underlying psychopathology was Ilene's access to her child secured. In this and many similar cases, the effects of being subjected to physical and emotional abuse may superficially resemble the signs of disordered thinking; but only when they are placed in their proper context and constructed as postabuse phenomena are they adequately comprehended. Mainstream diagnostic formulations, which routinely fail to account for these social and contextual variables, risk pathologizing that which is distress and risk mislabeling a range of behaviors.

Are There Useful Constructions of Disorder?

Even diagnoses that initially appear benign or helpful from a feminist perspective are potentially problematic when subject to closer analysis because of assumptions woven into the diagnosis. These are the assumptions that any form of distress must be evidence of the abnormality and disorderedness of the distress itself. The *DSM* is very explicit about this. For instance, the diagnosis of an adjustment disorder defines the problem as an abnormal response to nontraumatic psychosocial stressors, although the nature of a normal response to those same stressors is left undefined. Thus, the question is left in the hands of the professional to determine what constitutes abnormality and which diagnostic judgment can proceed without awareness of context or culture.

Nowhere does this conflict between feminist theory and pathologizing constructions of distress appear more sharply than at the location of the diagnosis of posttraumatic stress disorder (PTSD). This diagnosis was welcomed by many feminist practitioners when it was included for the first time in *DSM-III* (American Psychiatric Association, 1980). Here, finally, was a diagnosis that acknowledged the effects of context and experience on distress and that was explicitly tied to a person's exposure to trauma. For feminist practitioners working with battered and raped women and sexually abused children, there appeared to finally be a name that recognized survivors' realities (Walker, 1989).

But the initial version of this diagnosis was flawed in an expectable way by what I described as a false assumption of an invariant and detectable human norm for response to events. A trauma could be identified and diagnosed as causing PTSD only if an experience was "outside the range of usual human experience" and "frightening or threatening to almost anyone" (APA, 1980). At around the same time this diagnosis was taken into the canon, data began to emerge about the frequency and usualness of violence against children, abuse of women, hate crimes, and other forms of trauma that were embedded in the framework of patriarchal cultures worldwide. How, then, could one diagnose PTSD in the presence of something well within the common range of human experience? This question began to be asked frequently in legal settings, where attorneys would challenge a diagnosis of PTSD following sexual assault because of the statistical frequency with which such assaults happened.

Additionally, what constituted an event that would frighten or threaten almost anyone? This statement again assumed a generic, normative human rather than allowing for individual variability. Feminist researchers were finding that certain interpersonal experiences took their meaning primarily from context; however if they were decontextualized, an event might appear benign or neutral, whereas in the context of race, class, gender, sexual orientation, disability, or other demographic markers it would seem very frightening indeed. The field of sexual harassment litigation provides a fertile ground for this sort of debate over the meaning of events. When some feminists described the psychological consequences of sexual harassment as being PTSD, nonfeminist thinkers challenged this on the grounds that the typical scenarios of sexual harassment could not possibly be frightening or threatening to almost anyone (read as "any man"). This challenge extended itself to the point where one set of authors opined that any woman who did feel upset by being sexually harassed (rather than finding it amusing) must suffer from severe personality pathology (Feldman-Shorrig, 1995). Although occurring largely in the forensic arena, this debate served to highlight problems of normative assumption as applied to diagnosis. Whose usual experiences and reasonably scared responses were being used as the comparison group? If the event would indeed be frightening to almost anyone, why was the response to that event being defined as pathological rather than simply miserable and difficult to live with?

Thus, another question is raised for feminist analysis by the definition in *DSM* of the posttrauma response as a disorder and pathology. Empirical evidence demonstrates that not all people exposed to a traumatic stressor—no matter how that is defined—will develop the pattern of symptoms called PTSD. Some may experience other combinations of distress. Others may report an absence of distress or even exhilaration. This last category seems especially true for potential traumata not of human design; those who chase tornadoes, swim with sharks, and engage in so-called "ultimate" sports find joy in the exposure to circumstances that terrify others. But does this mean that the person who does experience PTSD after trauma exposure is manifesting a disordered response and a form of psychopathology?

A common feminist frame for describing PTSD is that it represents a reasonable response to unreasonable events (Walker, 1989); this, however, begs the following question: Reasonable to whom? Even that phraseology implies that there are unreasonable (and disordered?) responses to the events in question. Perhaps the better term is *meaningful*; is the event emotionally meaningful to the person experiencing it? Rivera (1996) wrote that to define these responses as a disorder would be to "collude in the on-going process of . . . objectification" (p. 4); thus, even if one framed PTSD as a normal response, allowing the *disorder* term to stand continues to assign pathology to the behaviors and to invite denigration of people experiencing this response pattern. Root (1992) suggested that for individuals subjected to lifelong oppression such as cultural racism, classism, sexism, and so on, there is an experience of "insidious traumatization" that over time can render certain apparently neutral stimuli life threatening, thus moving the location of reasonable to within the context of the person experiencing the distress. Feminist constructions thus question any nomothetic models. A person's distress can be evaluated and defined only in relation to her or his own baseline and her or his own cultural and social context.

These arguments for the normalcy of a posttraumatic stress response to trauma, particularly interpersonal violence, waver in the face of some findings suggesting that the difference between the trauma-exposed person with PTSD and the one without it is inherent and biological, consisting of differences in the production and metabolism of neurohormones and corticosteriods (Yehuda & McFarlane, 1995) as well as other research on the brains of people with PTSD indicating a decreased volume of the hippocampus—a brain structure implicated in memory for events (Bremner et al., 1995). Are these biological differences evidence of a response to trauma or a predisposition or sensitivity to develop distress when exposed to it? Do these biological differences indicate that the posttraumatic stress response as defined by the diagnosis of PTSD is truly evidence of a disorder, albeit biological? Is the normal response to trauma exposure one of transient or no distress over the long term?

Biological explanations are seductive. When a biological "fact" is observed, it is given much weight in a scientific and popular discourse that leans heavily in the direction of essentialism. Indeed, as Rothblum, Solomon, and Albee (1986) noted, it is difficult to get research funded that does not privilege a biological hypothesis, which, in turn, leads to more evidence supporting biological hypotheses and, by implication, undermining more psychosocially focused theories of distress. But even if biology were to be strongly implicated, feminist analysis would question the manner in which these findings are interpreted. Is it possible that current discussions are locating the norm in the wrong place? That is, are those who do not develop a posttraumatic stress response responding in an abnormal or disordered manner that is obscured by cultural demands for calm and cheer? Could the biological markers found by these studies be those of normal function or structure? Or is PTSD worthy of being labeled a "disorder" simply because it is so disruptive to life and functioning, regardless of its origins or cultural meanings or the normalcy of its underlying biology?

It is possible to argue that a construction of the posttraumatic stress responses of dissociation, numbing, hyperarousal, and intrusion in the aftermath of trauma as normal would serve to relocate the abnormality in the events that traumatize people (Rivera, 1996; Root, 1992). That is, if a culture took the response of a traumatized person as a marker of the horrendousness of a traumatizing event, perhaps more collective energy would be directed toward the prevention of such events rather than the diagnosis and treatment of those whose postevent behaviors are alarming. In an era when some authors have argued that much sexual abuse of children may be "neutral or even pleasurable" to the abused child (Ceci, Huffman, Smith, & Loftus, 1994) and more energy is put into ensuring that no adult comes under the scrutiny of the criminal justice system because of possibly imperfect allegations of such abuse (Ceci & Bruck, 1995; Ernsdorff & Loftus, 1993), it becomes more difficult to muster collective indignation about this and similar interpersonal traumata. People who experience a posttraumatic stress response to sexual abuse can be doubly stigmatized as having an abnormal response simply for having found the experience traumatic. As Armstrong (1994) noted, the pathologizing of the response of interpersonal violence survivors under the rubric of PTSD and other disorders reinforces an inattention to the pathology of cultures of violence or those who enact such violence. If the distress were seen as a norm, rather than as a pathology or disorder, how might that shift cultural vision, social policy, and collective action?

The direction that feminist constructions could go in an attempt to reconcile the biological data with a political critique is that of a biopsychosocial model of distress. Such a conceptual framework defines distress as complex in its origins, striving to avoid pathologizing individual differences in biological sensitivities and responsiveness to psychosocial events and processes, while acknowledging the contribution of those sensitivities to the manner in which a given person responds to life experiences (Brown, 1994). Thus, human differences in the capacity to respond to particular life events, variations in temperament, and degrees of in-born abilities to function in certain modalities would be taken into account without being made primary categories of analysis. This model also argues that such sensitivities to a particular form of posttraumatic stress response (vs. the more pathologizing concept of predisposition) be scrutinized as potential evidence of ancestral enhanced responsiveness to certain types of danger rather than as, in the dominant view, the manifestations of biological deficit. Consider the analogy to the sickle-cell factor. This blood factor appears in people of African and Mediterranean ancestry and originally was related to the capacity to effectively resist or survive malarial illness. Because the deficit model for biological sensitivities to certain expressions of distress is as yet unproven, existing largely as a dominant taken-for-granted notion that has received little challenge, feminist constructionists would argue that it is equally possible that as with the sickle-cell factor, the biological differences observed in trauma survivors with PTSD may represent a once-functional or even protective substrate that has lost some function in the immediate psychosocial milieu but is not disordered by and of itself.

Feminist Constructions of Distress

As can be inferred from the discussion of feminist critiques, the feminist construction of distress strains to keep away from the notion of disorder in the individual. How does a feminist model construct distress? The feminist construction begins with a framework that first describes the strengths, skills, and resiliencies of the individual and then defines the nature of the social, interpersonal, and political milieu in which that individual functions. As noted by Landrine (1988), simply placing diagnosis into its epidemiological context begins to illuminate the relationship among certain forms of distress and particular social milieus. If poor people are more likely defined as schizophrenic, women as depressed, youths of color as oppositional–defiant, it is just as likely that the cultural context is being manifested in these designations rather than any disorder of the diagnosed people. As Landrine, Klonoff, Gibbs, Mannings, and Lund (1995) demonstrated empirically, sexism per se accounts for a significant amount of the variance in women's experiences of distress, with all other life stress factors held constant. Although difficult to find because such research is rarely funded, and thus infrequently published, this sort of data underscores the feminist call to diagnose cultures, rather than people, as pathological.

Strengths and coping strategies available to individuals through their relation to their culture of origin, and stressors on that culture, are also analyzed and taken into account in a feminist model. The person–situation and person–culture matrix are the units of analysis, even when only the individual her- or himself is the focus of assessment or treatment. *Normal* as a construct that would cross persons and situations specifically is not defined, aside from a recognition of purely statistical norms that are themselves lacking in inherent value or meaning about pathology. Rather, the feminist construction of distress asks what would be usual for a given person–situation and person–culture encounter and then whether the forms taken by the individual's distress are indeed disordered or within the usual continuum of functional responses to that person–situation encounter. Distress might be quantified in terms of the potential interpersonal costs attendant on a particular behavioral pattern and in terms of the subjective experience of the person. In addition, distress is conceived of as a potential outcome of behaviors that are empowering and affirming to the person, their social network, or both rather than as evidence of the presence of disorder.

Feminist constructions of distress also attend to the functional values and practical usefulness of behavior to individuals in their milieus, with even distressing or impaired behaviors framed as possible strategies for meeting certain valued interpersonal or intrapsychic goals. If, for instance, a person can only achieve attachment and care by means of self-abasement or dependent behaviors, then the agency and function of these behaviors and their goal directedness would be highlighted rather than any pathology. The immense diversity of possible interpersonal matrices leads to a variability in the development of such strategies; no one strategy is defined as disordered per se because each might be highly functional under certain circumstances.

For example, as Freyd (1996) noted, in some circumstances, it is extremely functional to fully experience one's pain and in other circumstances, potentially dangerous to do so. Thus, full emotional and bodily awareness may be useful at times, whereas numbness and dissociation equally helpful at others. Freyd offered the example of the skier who breaks her leg. When done in the company of others, it is a more functional coping strategy for the injured skier to attend to the pain, to not move, and to allow others to seek help so she avoids further injury to her leg. However, when done in isolation, it is most functional for the wounded skier to be able to dissociate from the pain to move and get help. Freyd extrapolated from this concrete model to questions of how posttraumatic amnesia for abuse might be a functional coping strategy for small children rather than evidence of a disorder, even though both the amnesia and its cessation are likely to occasion distress and impairment.

Disorders of Power: DDPD

I argued that a hallmark of mainstream diagnosis is that it pathologizes the manner in which the powerless discomfort the powerful. Nowhere is this more evident than in Cluster B of the personality disorders, which includes histrionic, borderline, and dependent personality disorders. Aside from questions of the ultimate reliability or validity of these diagnoses (see Brown, 1994; Caplan, 1995; Kutchins & Kirk, 1997; or Lerman, 1996, for a detailed discussion of this issue), it does not require a close look at these diagnoses—either in the *DSM* itself or as they are described in the treatment literature—to observe that these disorders, although occasionally subjectively distressing to those diagnosed, are more frequently, particularly in the case of the histrionic and dependent varieties, very distressing to others, especially psychotherapists. These are the disorders of powerless people, the diagnoses often assigned to the people who create discomfort for the powerful.

The presence of distress in individuals discomforts the powerful of a dominant culture, and it could be said to discomfort the culture itself because that distress potentially exposes the ills of the society and its deficiencies as a civil entity. As in the relationship between a highly narcissistic parent and her or his children, where the child must pretend her or his well-being so as not to insult the fragile self-worth of the caregiver and engender that parent's rage and blame (Miller, 1981), so too is the relationship between oppressed or marginalized people and the institutions and agents of cultural dominance. The rage of the culture is translated into the diagnosis of the oppressed person's distress as a form of pathological deviance. Under slavery, the "happy darky" was normal and the runaway slave was diagnosed with "drapetomania." When organized psychiatry attempted in the mid 1980s to insert the diagnosis of self-defeating personality disorder into the *DSM*, arguments were made that the self-defeating pathology of these patients (largely women) was evident in their continual thwarting of psychiatrists' attempts to help; in other words, these patients made their doctors feel powerless and crazy (Brown, 1994; Caplan, 1995).

Feminist thinkers have made the occasional attempt at turning the tables on this conceptual framework. In 1991, during the revisions of the diagnostic manual aimed at the creation of the *DSM-IV*, Pantony and Caplan (1991) proposed a diagnosis that would pathologize the manner in which members of the dominant group, or those imitating dominant norms and attitudes, treated nondominant groups and people. Caplan (1995) wrote that the formal diagnosis emerged from a series of discussions with other feminists, suggesting that such a diagnosis would be a useful addition to the canon. Starting with the concept of a "macho" personality disorder, they titled their proposed diagnosis delusional dominating personality disorder (DDPD), some of whose diagnostic criteria include the following:

> Inability to establish and maintain meaningful interpersonal relationships. . . . Inability to identify and express a range of feelings in oneself (typically accompanied by an inability to identify accurately the feelings of other people). . . . Inability to respond appropriately and empathically to the feelings and needs of close associates and intimates (often leading to the misinterpretation of signals from others). . . . Tendency to use power, silence, withdrawal and/or avoidance rather than negotiation in the personal or interpersonal conflict or difficulty. . . . The presence of any one of the following delusions: a. the delusion of personal entitlement to the services of i. any woman with whom one is personally associated, ii. females in general or males in general, iii. both of the above; b. the delusion that women like to suffer and be ordered around; c. the delusion that physical force is the best method of solving interpersonal problems; d. the delusion that sexual and aggressive impulses are uncontrollable in i. oneself, ii. males in general, or iii. both; e. the delusion that pornography and erotica are identical; f. the delusion that women control most of the world's wealth and/or power but do little of the world's work; g. the delusion that existing inequality in the distribution of power and wealth are a product of the survival of the fittest and therefore allocation of greater social and economic rewards to the already privileged are merited. (Note: The simultaneous presence of several of these delusions in one individual is common and frequently constitutes a profoundly distorted belief system.) (Caplan, 1995, pp. 170–171; see also Pantony & Caplan, 1991)

The additional diagnostic criteria continue in a similar vein, including such things as "an infantile tendency to equate large breasts on women with their sexual attractiveness" (p. 171) and "a tendency to feel inordinately threatened by women who fail to disguise their intelligence."

Caplan (1995) wrote that her proposal of this diagnosis was serious; however, as she described it, this effort at balancing the vision of formal diagnosis was taken in anything but a serious manner by the revision committee for the *DSM-IV*. The empirical basis of the diagnosis was stringently questioned (in sharp contrast to the acceptance, entirely without empirical basis, of the proposal for self-defeating personality disorder only a few years earlier). When Caplan responded with information on the empirical basis, her scholarship was dismissed as not pertinent. Ultimately, Caplan's proposal was shut out of further considerations. One cannot diagnose this set of behaviors as pathology equivalent to that of the Axis II disorders. As she noted, in the formal construction of disorder using the *DSM* process, feminist visions, feminist scholarship, and feminist analysis are kept out by "consensus," whether visions critical of extant diagnoses or of those, such as Caplan and her proposed DDPD, who see oppressive behaviors and attitudes not as a social norm but as social pathology. Caplan's experience with the proposal of DDPD underscores the feminist analysis of psychodiagnosis as a strategy for the maintenance of the social status quo through the assignment of pathology or normalcy to certain sets of behavior.

However, this diagnostic proposal raises again the question of whether feminist models *ever* should assign pathology to the individual. Arguably, the behaviors described by DDPD are as much evidence of how dominant-group members are oppressed and deformed in their humanity by patriarchy as histrionic personality or PTSD might be similar evidence of the oppression and deformation of nondominant-group people. I believe that it would be inherently problematic in a feminist frame to create a model for distress in which it would be acceptable to assign pathology to individuals, regardless of the manner in which oppression manifested itself in their behaviors. Thus, although serving the useful function of exposing the imbalances and normative assumptions embedded in the current models of distress and psychopathology, DDPD is not a solution to the problem of oppressive norms.

CONCLUSION: ARE THERE FEMINIST CONSTRUCTIONS OF DISORDER?

The answer in one word is maybe. But they are not disorders of the person. A closely applied feminist model could never assign disorder or pathology to a distressed individual. Feminist theories view the concept of pathology as so profoundly socially constructed and politically driven that it lacks the use for understanding or transforming behavior. This sort of radical egalitarianism, in which no person would be defined as pathological, combines with a pragmatism that acknowledges that certain patterns of distress create life difficulties for people. Additionally, as did Caplan (1995), the feminist model would explicitly define as distress certain normative modes of functioning that might not be subjectively distressing to a person but that did create distress in that person's interpersonal and social networks.

The name of the problem (e.g., the precise formal diagnosis) would be much less important than a description of the phenomenology of the experience for individuals and those to whom they relate. As Rivera noted, "precise diagnostic nomenclature tends to reify what is actually a large and fluid category. I think it is, paradoxically, more scientific to be a bit more casual or even eclectic with our use of language" (1996, p. 4). This apparent imprecision is borne out by empirical evidence that many of the current formal diagnostic categories are not statistically orthogonal but overlap greatly. This overlap is acknowledged formally for the clusters of Axis II disorders in *DSM-IV* and can be informally observed by, for example, the similarity of symptoms found in PTSD and some of the depressive diagnoses.

Adherents of the "brain disorder" models of certain forms of distress (e.g., schizophrenia and manic depression) would argue at this point that individuals with these diagnoses are physically ill, not experiencing oppression or socially constructed problems. No one would argue with the extreme degree of distress experienced by many individuals who are currently so named, least of all feminists who attempt to respect people's definitions of their own experiences.

However, as activists from the Psychiatric Inmates Movement have argued (Chamberlin, 1978, 1994), much of the distress experienced by these individuals may not be due to their internal disordered states per se but by the manner in which the culture responds to people with those states. If the result of saying that one has seen a vision of the Virgin Mary is that one is canonized, one is unlikely to be as distressed as the same person whose vision leads to being involuntarily incarcerated in an unpleasant setting and given drugs with potentially dangerous side effects. The degree to which the problems of schizophrenic or manic-depressive people are iatrogenic, caused by the "treatments" provided, is entirely unclear. Perkins (1991) wrote compellingly of how she came through a period of severe depression with the loving support of many friends, without the interventions of mental health professionals or hospitals. Her narrative undermines the conventional wisdom about the pathology of this experience versus its simply distressing nature.

Disorders continue to be described and defined as social phenomena. Sexism, racism, institutionalized violence and discrimination, inattention to social problems by governments, unequal distribution of necessary resources—all are defined as social pathologies that could, in turn, lead to distress in individuals. Various biological sensitivities to social pathology may be construed as useful early warning signals in individuals or even in sensitive social groups. Attention is paid to iatrogenesis arising from oppressive treatment and intervention strategies and to the distinguishing of those behaviors or experiences from the phenomenology of the distressed person, so that greater care could be taken to devise interventions that are not themselves pathological (e.g., antiegalitarian or oppressive).

Feminist constructions of human behavior sit uneasily in the mental health canon. The striking difference between feminist and other constructions of disorder highlights this. Yet it also, ultimately, raises important questions that have yet to be answered adequately by nonfeminist models of distress. By subverting cherished normative assumptions about human behavior and the problems that people experience, a feminist framework may lead to greater precision and care in the assignment of disorders.

REFERENCES

American Psychiatric Association. (1980). *Diagnostic and statistical manual of mental disorders* (3rd ed.). Washington, DC: Author.

American Psychiatric Association. (1994). *Diagnostic and statistical manual of mental disorders* (4th ed.). Washington, DC: Author.

Armstrong, L. (1994). *Rocking the cradle of sexual politics: What happened when women said incest.* Reading, MA: Addison Wesley.

Becker, D., & Lamb, S. (1994). Sex bias in the diagnosis of borderline personality disorder and posttraumatic stress disorder. *Professional Psychology: Research and Practice, 25,* 55–61.

Bem, S. L. (1993). *The lenses of gender: Transforming the debate on sexual inequality.* New Haven, CT: Yale University Press.

Brabeck, M., & Brown, L. S. (1997). Feminist theory and psychological practice. In J. Worell & N. Johnson (Eds.), *Shaping the future of feminist psychology: Education, research, and practice* (pp. 15–36). Washington, DC: American Psychological Association.

Bremner, J. D., Randall, P., Scott, T. M., Bronen, R. A., Seibyl, J. P., Southwick, S. M., Delaney, R. C., McCarthy, G., Charney, D. S., & Innis, R. B. (1995). MRI-based measurement of hippocampal volume in patients with combat-related posttraumatic stress disorder. *American Journal of Psychiatry, 152,* 973–981.

Broverman, I. K., Broverman, D., Clarkson, F. E., Rosencrantz, P., & Vogel, S. (1970). Sex-role stereotypes and clinical judgments of mental health. *Journal of Consulting and Clinical Psychology, 34,* 1–7.

Brown, L. S. (1986). From alienation to connection: Feminist therapy with posttraumatic stress disorder. *Women and Therapy, 5,* 13–26.

Brown, L. S. (1994). *Subversive dialogues: Theory in feminist therapy.* New York: Basic Books.

Brown, L. S., & Ballou, M. (Eds.). (1992). *Personality and psychopathology: Feminist reappraisals.* New York: Guilford Press.

Brown, L. S., & Brodsky, A. M. (1992). The future of feminist therapy. *Psychotherapy: Theory, Research, Practice, Training, 29,* 51–57.

Caplan, P. J. (1995). *They say you're crazy: How the world's most powerful psychiatrists decide who's normal.* Reading, MA: Addison-Wesley.

Ceci, S. J., & Bruck, M. (1995). *Jeopardy in the courtroom: A scientific analysis of children's testimony.* Washington, DC: American Psychological Association.

Ceci, S. J., Huffman, M. L. C., Smith, E., & Loftus, E. F. (1994). Repeatedly thinking about a non-event; Source misattributions among preschoolers. *Consciousness and Cognition, 3,* 388–407.

Chamberlin, J. (1978). *On our own: Patient-controlled alternatives to the mental health system.* New York: McGraw-Hill.

Chamberlin, J. (1994). A psychiatric survivor speaks. *Feminism and Psychology, 4,* 284–287.

Chesler, P. (1972). *Women and madness.* Garden City, NY: Doubleday.

Ernsdorff, G. M., & Loftus, E. F. (1993). Let sleeping memories lie? Words of caution about tolling the statute of limitations in cases of memory repression. *Journal of Criminal Law and Criminology, 84,* 129–174.

Feldman-Shorrig, S. (1995). Sexual harassment. *American Journal of Psychiatry, 152,* 478.

Freyd, J. J. (1996). *Betrayal trauma: The logic of forgetting abuse.* Cambridge, MA: Harvard University Press.

Greenspan, M. (1983). *A new approach to women and therapy.* New York: McGraw-Hill.

Hacker, H. M. (1976). Women as a minority group. In S. Cox (Ed.), *Female psychology: The emerging self* (pp. 156–170). Chicago: SRA.

Hare-Mustin, R., & Marecek, J. (Eds.). (1990). *Making a difference: Psychology and the construction of gender.* New Haven, CT: Yale University Press.

Jordan, J. V., Kaplan, A. G., Miller, J. B., Stiver, I. P., & Surrey, J. L. (1992). *Women's growth in connection: Writings from the Stone Center.* New York: Guilford Press.

Kaminer, W. (1992). *I'm dysfunctional, you're dysfunctional.* Reading, MA: Addison-Wesley.

Kaplan, M. (1983). A woman's view of the *DSM-III. American Psychologist, 38,* 786–792.

Kramer, P. (1993). *Listening to Prozac: A psychiatrist explores mood-altering drugs and the new meaning of self.* New York: Viking Penguin.

Kutchins, H., & Kirk, S. A. (1997). *Making us crazy: DSM: The psychiatric bible and the creation of mental disorders.* New York: Free Press.

Lakoff, R. (1975). *Language and woman's place.* New York: HarperColophon.

Landrine, H. (1988). Revising the framework of abnormal psychology. In P. Bronstein & K. Quina (Eds.), *Teaching a psychology of people: Resources for gender and sociocultural awareness* (pp. 37–44). Washington, DC: American Psychological Association.

Landrine, H. (1992). Clinical implications of cultural differences: The referential versus indexical self. *Clinical Psychology Review, 12,* 401–416.

Landrine, H., Klonoff, E., Gibbs, J., Mannings, V., & Lund, M. (1995). Physical and psychiatric correlates of gender discrimination: An application of the Schedule of Sexist Events. *Psychology of Women Quarterly, 19,* 473–492.

Lerman, H. (1986). *A mote in Freud's eye: From psychoanalysis to the psychology of women.* New York: Springer.

Lerman, H. (1996). *Pigeonholing women's misery: A history and critical analysis of the psychodiagnosis of women in the twentieth century.* New York: Basic Books.

Lerner, G. (1993). *The creation of feminist consciousness.* New York: Oxford University Press.

Luepnitz, D. A. (1988). *The family interpreted: Feminist theory in clinical practice.* New York: Basic Books.

Miller, A. (1981). *The drama of the gifted child.* New York: Basic Books.

Pantony, K. L., & Caplan, P. J. (1991). Delusional dominating personality disorder: A modest proposal for identifying some consequences of rigid masculine socialization. *Psychologie Canadienne, 32,* 120–133.

Perkins, R. (1991). Therapy for lesbians? The case against. *Feminism and Psychology, 1,* 325–338.

Rivera, M. (1996). *More alike than different: Treating severely dissociative trauma survivors.* Toronto, Ontario, Canada: University of Toronto Press.

Root, M. P. P. (1992). Reconstructing the impact of trauma on personality. In L. S. Brown & M. Ballou (Eds.), *Personality and psychopathology: Feminist reappraisals* (pp. 229–266). New York: Guilford Press.

Rosewater, L. B. (1985). Schizophrenic, borderline, or battered? In L. B. Rosewater & L. E. A. Walker (Eds.), *Handbook of feminist therapy: Women's issues in psychotherapy* (pp. 215–225). New York: Springer.

Rothblum, E. D., Solomon, L., & Albee, G. (1986). A sociopolitical perspective of the *DSM-III*. In T. Millon & G. Klerman (Eds.), *Contemporary directions in psychopathology: Toward the DSM-IV* (pp. 167–192). New York: Guilford Press.

Szasz, T. S. (1970). *The manufacture of madness.* New York: Harper & Row.

Walker, L. E. A. (1989). Psychology and violence against women. *American Psychologist, 44,* 695–702.

Weisstein, N. (1970). *Kinder kuche kirche* as scientific law: Psychology constructs the female. In R. Morgan (Ed.), *Sisterhood is powerful* (pp. 205–219). New York: Vintage.

Yehuda, R., & McFarlane, A. (1995). The conflict between current knowledge about PTSD and its original conceptual basis. *American Journal of Psychiatry, 152,* 1705–1713.

13

RECONSTRUCTING PSYCHOLOGICAL DISTRESS AND DISORDER FROM A RELATIONAL PERSPECTIVE: A SYSTEMIC COCONSTRUCTIVE–DEVELOPMENTAL FRAMEWORK

SANDRA A. RIGAZIO-DiGILIO

Constructivist ideas question the epistemological ground of psychological practice and challenge therapists to step beyond the dichotomy of traditionally defined notions of health, distress, and disorder and to see clients as unique, competent, and capable of constructing their own meanings within a cultural setting. Although these challenges provide the potential for new treatment options, the majority of constructivist models do not adequately address relational methodologies.

This chapter presents the theoretical and clinical aspects of systemic cognitive–developmental therapy (SCDT), a postmodern therapy that emphasizes the systemic and relational dimensions of illness narratives (Rigazio-DiGilio, 1993, 1997; Rigazio-DiGilio & Ivey, 1991, 1993). Starting with the family unit and working internally with its members and externally with the wider social environment, SCDT operationalizes developmental constructs that can be systematically applied and studied in therapeutic and consultative contexts. The central thesis of my chapter is that all manifestations of psychological distress have a relational component and that only by understanding how the relational systems construct their interpretations and reactions to this distress can therapists hope to understand how individuals and wider communities construe their situations. This thesis is illustrated through a case study involving a newly formed family.

THE HANSON FAMILY

Toni Hanson, age 23, requested services because her husband, Ben, age 26, had been physically and psychologically abusive for the last 12 months of their 2-year marriage. She reported an increase in the duration, frequency, and intensity of abuse, with psychological exchanges occurring regularly and physical violence occurring approximately twice per month, involving shoving, slapping, and throwing things. She stated a desire to "go back to how it was before the birth of Celia." She "loved Celia and Ben but could not handle the constant fighting" that had started after her daughter's birth, 1 year earlier. "We were very happy before Celia was born, but her special problems are making things difficult for Ben and me. I need to know what to do to make things easier on us."

As a child, Ben had lived in a single-parent household in an economically depressed inner-city community. He had dropped out of school at age 15 and had held many manual jobs over the next 8 years. Before meeting Toni 3 years ago, he had secured a more stable laborer position at a local construction firm. Toni, a daughter of Caribbean immigrants, was working on her associates degree in business when she met Ben. As their relationship grew, she decided to quit school and to move in with and eventually marry Ben. After the marriage, she gained employment at a local bank. Her business and social skills were noticed by the district manager, who had just notified her that she was in line for managerial training when she discovered she was pregnant.

The pregnancy was hard on the couple. Toni had to leave work in her 5th month because of medical complications that resulted in the premature birth of Celia. The couple had assumed that Toni would be able to return to work soon after Celia's birth. However, this was not the case because Celia was born 2 months premature with a congenital heart defect and severe meningitis. Both complications required extensive neonatal inpatient and outpatient intervention, and the prognosis for later atypical development had not yet been determined. In effect, Celia's birth and the severity of her special needs brought on more demands than Toni and Ben had prepared for. Medical interventions, such as pharmacological treatment, surgeries, inpatient recuperation periods, and at-home care required Toni to remain at home and required Ben to request time off during the more critical aspects of treatment. The amount of release time Ben was requesting put his job in jeopardy and required the couple to reconsider how he would be involved in Celia's care.

As the tension of realigning roles and responsibilities and medical interventions increased, a spiral of psychological and physical abuse began, leading to actual physical violence over the last 9 months. Toni had already filed several police reports, charging Ben with domestic violence. However, the physical violence did not abate. Distress increased when the couple was forced to leave their residence and move in with Toni's mother, Alicia, age 48.

FAMILY AS A MEDIATING FORCE IN THE COCONSTRUCTION OF DISORDER

All families serve two basic functions: to provide for the psychosocial needs of their members and to balance the demands of the broader culture with their own needs and cultural mores (Minuchin, 1974). The Hanson family was having difficulties in both preserving the safety and care of its members and managing interactions with components of the wider sociocultural context. All the members were experiencing distress in relation to the intra- and extrafamilial changes required by the addition of a physically challenged child.

The family is the smallest societal system that can change in relation to internal and external demands yet maintain enough continuity to support its members. Families provide a primal socialization matrix for individuals to develop, and as individuals develop, the family's boundaries extend to include wider contexts that influence different aspects of each individual's possibilities. How much multiplicity is tolerated and supported within the family depends on the family's capacity to mediate information from within and outside itself.

Simultaneously, families are subsystems of larger units. Families rely on their developmental and contextual histories to give meaning to and operate within these larger contexts. In addition, these contexts elicit or constrain certain family resources. This recursive interplay influences how families change to meet the developmental and contextual demands of members and of their multiple ethnic, racial, religious, class, political, institutional, and cultural affiliations. Families must use resources and challenge constraints to maintain a balance of continuity and change. To do so requires a flexible worldview, a viable information-processing style (Anderson,

Goolishian, & Winderman, 1986; Hoffman, 1990), and power and influence (Goldner, 1993; Pedersen, 1991).

External medical and financial demands and internal requirements for realignment and support were inhibiting the Hanson family's ability to meet the psychosocial needs of its members and to interact effectively with wider participating institutions. Helping the family understand the degree of power and influence each of these stressors exercised as well as identifying options that might lead toward effective management were important treatment goals.

SYSTEMIC COGNITIVE DEVELOPMENTAL THEORY AND THERAPY

SCDT provides a perspective for how individuals, families, and wider networks (i.e., the three key domains of the *interactive triad*) participate in defining psychological distress and disorder. SCDT offers an easily learned, practiced, and researched approach (Borders, 1994) for working within these three domains. The model provides a developmentally sensitive and culturally responsive approach (Arciniega & Newlon, 1994) to identify resources that promote the cogeneration of multiple perspectives and options toward resolving psychological distress and disorder.

As an alternative treatment model, SCDT offers a postmodern holistic, nonpathological approach to family therapy. SCDT considers family distress to be a natural and logical consequence of developmental and contextual history, and it reframes disorder as the consequence of limiting dialogues that occur among current participating members of the triad. SCDT also recasts clinicians as mutual partners engaged in cocreating therapeutic and consultative environments and illness narratives that are solution focused rather than problem saturated.

Construed and illustrated in this way, the importance of families as mediators in transactions that define narratives about distress and disorder can be examined. The Hanson case illustrates how the family's mediating role can be activated in therapy and consultation using SCDT methods. By reviewing how meaning making might occur within families, therapy, and consultation (Andersen, 1993; Cecchin, 1992; Pinsof, 1994; White & Epston, 1990), key relational constructs are operationalized that help differentiate health from distress and disorder and link theoretical conceptualizations to practice.

As a metatheoretical framework, SCDT provides a classification matrix that integrates SCDT questioning strategies and interventions from traditional and contemporary family therapy approaches. Clinicians can organize familiar perspectives and strategies, so that they can tailor treatment to their clients' unique developmental and cultural needs.

ILLNESS NARRATIVES AND PSYCHOLOGICAL DISTRESS AND DISORDER

According to SCDT, illness narratives can be classified along a continuum representing varying levels of disorder. At the "ordered" pole, narratives elicit a sense of shared responsibility for defining and managing, toward a useful end, perceived or real illness behavior and associated experience. At the "disordered" pole, triadic discourse does not result in the coconstruction of a unifying narrative that lends itself to mutual understanding and problem solving. Members of the triad are either vying for who holds the "truth" or placing blame and responsibility in one direction without recognizing that change may need to occur in each domain. For example, when a family is labeled "dysfunctional" and the family introjects this notion, then the interactive triad need not implicate communities, institutions, or sociopolitical and economic frameworks that reflect devaluing or dehumanizing elements of a society.

Concerning the family's role as mediator, families have the capability to construe illness narratives in ways that can promote or inhibit healthy responses. Families can mediate the context by (a) integrating multiple perspectives generated within and across the interactive triad, (b) providing or requesting environments that reframe or ease illness experience and behavior, and (c) coordinating key players to coconstruct congruent themes aimed at defining and managing perceived or real illness. In terms of the Hansons, an illness narrative was developing that centered on Ben and Toni's reaction to Celia's needs. All participating members of the immediate family and outside agencies were unintentionally colluding to maintain a disordered narrative, implicating Ben and Toni as dysfunctional.

INTEGRATING SCDT THEORY AND THERAPY IN RELATION TO PSYCHOLOGICAL DISTRESS AND DISORDER

SCDT offers a linguistically based assessment strategy (see Exhibit 13.1) that can be used at the beginning and throughout therapy and consultation to generate discourse about three essential clinical variables: (a) the multiple interpretations of illness appearance and behavior that promote or hinder psychological distress, (b) available collective cognitive–developmental resources, and (c) the recursive dimensions of the interactive triad that support or inhibit psychological disorder.

Exhibit 13.1.
Sample Systemic Cognitive–Developmental Assessment Interview

Part 1: Open-Ended Questions for Preliminary Assessment
(Assessing the primary collective cognitive–developmental orientation)

1. Can you talk together and reach consensus regarding the issues that have brought your family to treatment?
2. Can you talk together and reach consensus about what your family envisions will come out of therapy?

Part 2: Cognitive–Developmental Questioning Sequence
(Assessing the family's ability to collectively access resources in each orientation)

Sensorimotor–Elemental Explorations

1. Choose an image that the family can generate when members focus on the issues that promoted treatment. Describe the image that you are generating. How does it look? What are the sounds? How do you feel as you generate this image?
2. Summation question: What does this image and the feelings it generates say about your family?

Concrete–Situational Explorations

1. Choose an example that highlights what occurs in the family in relation to the issues that brought you here. Once an example is chosen, ask a variety of behavioral tracking questions such as, Who is involved? What happened next? What did he or she do then? How did your parents react? Who steps in at that point? What happens afterward?
2. Summation question: Given how facts emerged, what are you learning about how you influence one another?

Formal–Reflective Explorations

1. Can you describe other situations that require members to take on roles similar to the ones you just described?
2. Can you describe other situations that generate the same behaviors even when you wish it would be different?
3. Summation question: What are you learning about the similar ways you act in seemingly different situations?

Dialectic–Systemic Explorations

1. Integration: From what you have been discussing thus far, as a family, how would you organize the central themes?
2. Coconstruction
   (a) How would you define some of the rules that seem to operate in your family, those that influence how each of you thinks, feels, and acts in relation to these themes?
   (b) Where did these rules come from? Where did you learn these rules? Who taught you these rules?
   (c) What role did or does your wider context play in the development and maintenance of these rules?
3. Multiple Perspectives
   (a) Are there other ways to look at these rules that have come to influence your family so much?
   (b) How might another family see things differently?
4. Deconstruction
   (a) Can you identify ways that these rules may not be working so effectively for you and your family now?
   (b) Do you notice any flaws or constraints in these rules, ways that these rules do not get you or your family what you need?
   (c) How do these rules help or hinder your current way of understanding and acting?
5. Reconstruction and Action
   (a) If you could add to or change these rules, how would you do it?
   (b) Based on these possibilities of change, is there anything you could do differently right now to see the issues that brought you here from a different perspective?
   (c) Based on these possibilities of change, is there anything you could do differently right now to work on the issues that brought you to treatment?
   (d) Summation question: Based on all this, is there anything your family might try a little differently—right here in this room—to work on the issues that have brought you here?

SCDT Assessment Phase

Assessing how Ben and Toni were constructing both individual and collective worldviews in relation to the issues promoting treatment was an initial and essential task. SCDT uses the term "cognitive–developmental orientations" to distinguish the types of individual and family worldviews that might be operating in a particular context. Using a metaphorical reinterpretation of neo-Piagetian constructs (i.e., sensorimotor–elemental, concrete–situational, formal–reflective, dialectic–systemic), Rigazio-DiGilio and Ivey (1991) developed and validated a classification scheme to identify which types of worldviews individuals and families rely on to formulate their experiences. In general, it is assumed that each of the four orientations offers individuals and families particular reference points from which to experience, understand, and act on their life tasks. The more orientations available, the greater potential for effective adaptation.

Assessment questions cover two distinct phases. The first consists of open-ended questions that elicit family dialogue about multiple views of the problem and attempts at resolution, with minimal therapist interference. The second consists of questions derived from the unique reference points of each of the four cognitive–developmental orientations. During this phase, the therapist becomes more involved in focusing the family dialogue within the parameters of each orientation (see Exhibit 13.1).

The assessment interview was used as a therapeutic strategy to access both the signs and interpretations of illness appearance and the behavior and nature of the Hansons' cognitive–developmental resources. Additionally, it was used as a consultative strategy to access the recursive dimensions of interactions across the individual, family, and wider contextual environment, providing a comprehensive conceptualization of the Hansons in context. Accessing these three variables set the stage for designing a developmentally tailored and culturally responsive treatment plan.

Although types of psychological distress are diverse, these can be characterized within common dimensions. The first deals with chronicity and severity; the stage of distress (e.g., onset, life threatening), its virulence (e.g., insidious, aggressive), and type (e.g., stable, recurrent) affect each person, family, and community differently. What roles are the person or relationship demonstrating distress excused or prohibited from or in need of modifying? For how long has this been occurring? What people are directly and indirectly affected by the illness?

Another dimension concerns the antecedents considered to have contributed to the distress. Is distress self-imposed, such as alcoholism and smoking; family imposed, such as abuse and incest; environmentally imposed, such as in lead poisoning and posttraumatic stress; or community imposed, such as racism and sexism? The clarity of the diagnoses is another factor in how distress is interpreted. Particularly significant is if the distress is physical or psychological and whether it is considered real or fabricated. Prognosis and treatment regimes also affect the level of distress. Illness appearance and behavior may imply a diagnosis, but it is the actual interpretations that stem from these characteristics that hold the most weight in labeling the distress. Interviews with the family and consultative meetings with agents in the community can offer holistic impressions of the illness narrative.

SCDT provides questioning strategies that free families to discuss illness history and impact, using their own language and preferred antecedents and consequences. Families focus on real or perceived stressors of most concern. SCDT questions promote robust conceptualizations of how individuals and families organize the illness narrative. Furthermore, important family dynamics emerge involving structural arrangements and patterns of interaction as well as cultural and contextual issues that significantly influence a family's sense of self and psychological distress.

Initially, identifying data were cogenerated about the Hansons from SCDT assessment interviews with Ben, Toni, and Alicia. The couple was feeling overwhelmed by the birth of their child, the concomitant intrusion of outside services, financial burdens, changes in the divisions of labor and living arrangements, and family-of-origin issues. Toni's narrative about the antecedent events leading to the arrests for domestic violence was that after Celia's birth, Ben had to work harder to make ends meet and could not be there for her or Celia; this made him feel incompetent, and he took his frustrations out on her. Ben's narrative was that since Celia's birth, he had not felt control over his life or his ability to care for his family; this made him overwhelmed and confused. Alicia expressed concern for Toni and Celia because Ben could not be an adequate provider, father, or husband. The family presented a chaotic dialogue, illustrating an inability to navigate the maze of social services or to find predictable routines for living with Alicia and caring for Celia.

Using an *ecosystemic* lens, the SCDT therapist turns into a consultant and asks members of the wider domains to provide their understanding of the distress and their position regarding the success of the partnerships among the interactive triad. This lens allows therapists to determine where they can most flexibly intervene to relieve unproductive stress and disorder.

Consultation with representatives of the medical system revealed that they considered the Hansons' situation sad but the inevitable dysfunction to be a result of their limited cognitive and instrumental resources and the severity of Celia's disability. The representatives saw their role as assisting to limit stress on the family, especially Ben, by helping Alicia and Toni to take care of Celia. They did not see the long-term consequences of perpetuating a gendered division of labor, providing services versus imparting knowledge, or marginalizing Ben in Celia's caretaking. Given Ben's violent behavior, the representatives did not think they should work around his schedule and encourage his involvement. Their fear of his abusive behavior in fact made this an unacceptable solution because they believed this would heighten his stress, making abuse more probable. The story for this institution was short term and crisis oriented: to assist in the management of crisis in the moment but not in the training of those adults who would later be solely involved in the long-term care of Celia.

Members of the police system stated it was their job to decrease the probability of life-threatening behaviors at times of distress. They had no educational or rehabilitative role. More subtly, they envisioned violence as an inevitable consequence of the Hansons' unfortunate situation. Because the abuse was minimal compared with other cases, they did not think this case should be referred to the town's crisis intervention team because this team was financially reserved for more difficult, life-threatening cases. They did assure the consultant, however, that should the abuse become more frequent or severe, the services of this team could be retained. In effect, the message to the Hanson family was that they would have to be labeled more dysfunctional to receive this service, which might lead to a jail sentence.

Synthesizing the stories of all involved, including the family, established an illness narrative that identified a situation where the psychological distress—as labeled by the court psychologist using nomenclature from the *Diagnostic and Statistical Manual of Mental Disorders* (4th ed., American Psychiatric Association, 1994) for Axis I: intermittent explosive disorder, physical abuse of adult—was seen as an inescapable consequence of an overstressed, angry, and peripheral African American man faced with adult responsibilities beyond his capabilities. The family was seen as overwhelmed and without resources, the protective matriarch as essential, and the wife as doing the best she could. The thrust of this narrative was to prematurely foreclose the search for any alternative perspectives that might better explain the violent behavior and lead to different possibilities for resolving the psychological distress.

Identifying Family Resources

Relational systems require a repertoire of options to adapt effectively to or challenge demands for change. Three SCDT constructs are used to identify the resources families access to coconstruct viable options for change.

Collective Cognitive–Developmental Orientations

SCDT defines *troubled families* as having particular ways of being disempowered during interactive discourse. These can be related to both issues of instrumental power and the power inherent in the family's collective meaning-making process.

SCDT classifies frames of reference families rely on to coconstruct perspectives of themselves and to experience, interpret, and act in their world and on their life tasks. These worldviews are called "collective cognitive–developmental orientations" and are divided into the same four categories used to classify individual worldviews: sensorimotor–elemental, concrete–situational, formal–reflective, and dialectic–systemic (Rigazio-DiGilio & Ivey, 1991). Unlike the hierarchical notions of Piaget (1954), SCDT does not ascribe to a "higher-is-better" view of development. Rather, each orientation is viewed as useful in its own right, providing resources the family can draw on to deal with specific life tasks.

Understanding the resources within each orientation assists clinicians to assess the capacities families can access at any given time. In the same vein, understanding their representative constraints clarifies the types of disordered discourse families may encounter when coconstructing illness narratives. Each of these orientations is described in Exhibit 13.2.

The first phase of the SCDT assessment interview helps determine individual and family predominant orientations in relation to the illness experience. Although individuals and families can access various orientations across situations, they tend to operate from a predominant orientation to work through life tasks. SCDT posits that when individuals and families can access

Exhibit 13.2.
Collective Cognitive–Developmental Orientations

Using a *sensorimotor–elemental orientation,* families count on sensory experience to understand and relate to the illness narrative. If constrained here, families can be easily overwhelmed by slight variations in illness discourse, tending toward chaotic narratives that lack any semblance of a gestalt.

Drawing on a *concrete–situational orientation,* families sequentially describe illness narratives that allow for predictable action. Constrained families develop narrow visions, tending toward linear, contingent if–then perspectives. Using minimal affect or reflection, they develop predictable ways of labeling and operating in the triad and attempt to ensure that their views will be embraced by all involved.

Reflective illness narratives evolve within the *formal–reflective orientation.* Families rely on pattern recognition, abstract thinking, and understanding of self and situations to comprehend distress. Reified families overemphasize the analysis of illness within the triad but cannot act on or challenge these analyses.

Using the *dialectic–systemic orientation,* relational systems coconstruct narratives about the connectedness of multiple contexts. Constrained families become overwhelmed by the transactional complexities of their stories. This makes challenge likely but action less likely.

resources in several orientations, in addition to their predominant one, they will be more capable of working through any intrafamilial or extrafamilial difficulties. However, families who cannot access a range of resources or who overuse one orientation at the sacrifice of others are constrained.

In terms of individual orientations, Ben was viewed as operating at a predominantly sensorimotor level. He could not coherently relay abusive events; instead, he showed visible signs of nervousness. He could respond to directives that would facilitate a more relaxed posture and discuss the things he did to try to maintain control. He expressed remorse and embarrassment and asked for help to control his temper and to be a better father and husband. He feared his inability to control his violent outbursts without assistance. He viewed himself as ineffective in creating a protective environment for his family, which he saw as his responsibility. He feared failure; he knew he was disappointing his wife and her family.

Toni was considered to be operating at a concrete level. She could detail abusive events and make if–then linear conclusions regarding these events. For example, she "knew" it was her overreactions to situations that led to Ben's violence and wished she would remain calm when Ben was under stress. She wanted help to learn how to provide a calm atmosphere and to deal with issues regarding Celia on her own, so she could be a better wife and mother.

Alicia was also assessed as functioning at a concrete level. She described Toni and Ben as being in over their heads, even before Celia's birth. Although overburdened with her own hardships, she saw it as her responsibility to step in and help in any way she could to ease the stress on Ben and, therefore, save her daughter and grandchild from harm.

In terms of their collective worldview, the family was viewed as functioning within a sensorimotor orientation. Ben, Toni, and Alicia saw themselves as working as hard as they could to make it, relying on their church for spiritual support. They could not agree on how things had gotten out of control or escalated to violence. Rather, they accepted their situation as inevitable and looked to God's guidance for direction. They did not identify rules, roles, or lines of authority as these pertained to their new living arrangements or their taking care of Celia. They did not understand how to stop intrusions from outside systems. Each one expressed a sense of responsibility and blame for the family's state of affairs. Alicia and Ben would fight about how things could be better, but this would not move toward problem-solving negotiations. The conflict would stop at Toni's request or if Celia cried. When asked, as a family, what they wanted from therapy, they looked at one another, became tearful, and stated that they did not know.

In Phase 2 of the Hanson family interview, the therapist determined the degree to which presenting issues could be explored within other orientations. Toni used the dialogic encounter of the *formal* questioning sequence to review how her family had marginalized and disregarded male figures over generations; she could link this to Ben's current role in the family. From this vantage point, she could view his violence as affected by his lack of position and sense of control; she remembered her father's similar position and behaviors. Ben used the *concrete* therapeutic dialogue to describe how his work schedule precluded his involvement with medical personnel who helped Toni and Alicia with Celia; he could name other situations where he did not know how to be more involved in the family. Collectively, the family used the *dialectic* exchange to wonder aloud about their financial future if both women did not work and about how services could be better coordinated to help them get back on their feet rather than just to manage stress. This latter exchange was one of the first that brought the family outside of the pathogenic view of itself and closer to the idea of an interdependent system.

Collective Cognitive–Developmental Structures

Structures represent the degrees of organization families develop across all orientations. The collective structure is composed of those orientations a family accesses when participating with the triad to cogenerate multiple perspectives and solutions.

Analogous to Kelly's (1955) construct theory, SCDT categorizes four collective structures. *Flexible* structures characterize families with collective access to multiple orientations, giving them several resources when defining and managing the illness narrative. *Rigid* structures typify families who tightly hold to one orientation, regardless of the illness narrative construed. They adhere to previously successful meaning-making processes and attempt to impose their sense of self and worldview into the triadic narrative. Underdeveloped structures characterize families who marshal resources in an orientation, even though full use of those resources has not been developed. They do not have a collective sense of self. Under stress, they are easily influenced by narratives constructed by outside systems or try to engage in the triad without the skills to maintain an equal voice. Families who randomly shift between orientations without fully developing resources in any one orientation evidence *haphazard* structures. They overrely on external definitions, are easily confused by variations in illness narratives, and show little ability to hold a clear sense of self or a clear way of navigating in the triad.

Phase 2 of the assessment interview also is used to determine what flexibility families have access to. The second phase of SCDT assessment helps determine which members and submembers are able to initiate and maintain conversations within each of the four orientations. As noted above, it also assesses the family's collective capacity to access alternative frames of reference available within alternative orientations.

In terms of cognitive–developmental structures, both Toni and Ben had *diffuse* structures. Each had formal memories of family-of-origin abuse but did not link this to their current situation. Each wanted concrete services but did not know what type or how to access help. Instead, they were overwhelmed and paralyzed with emotions and sensations. Alicia had a rigid structure. She said her job, like that of mothers before her, was to protect Toni and Celia from hardship. Although she spoke of her family's challenges with oppression and racism, she did not connect these with the current stuation.

The family had an underdeveloped structure. Toni and Ben did not fully experience, individually or together, the severity of Celia's disability within their sensorimotor orientations or their need to return to Alicia's home. Alicia had not taken all this in yet at a sensorimotor level either. The new family constellation had not yet organized formal ways of collectively interpreting their situation or built a concrete routine around Celia's caretaking.

Phases of Systemic Development

Families continually recycle through phases of development represented by internal arrangements, meaning-making processes, and degrees of internal and external permeability. These phases are system exploration, consolidation, enhancement, and transformation. Each is described briefly in Exhibit 13.3.

SCDT defines adaptive families as those that continually recycle through these phases in response to demands for change. Less adaptive families may become arrested in any phase, limiting their ability to respond to life's demands at the level of the members, submembers, or the entire unit. They have difficulty partnering with other members of the triad and tend to impose narrow beliefs or be overpowered by the beliefs of others.

The complete SCDT assessment interview can be used to ascertain the developmental phase of the family. In terms of developmental phases, for the Hansons the couple system, family-of-procreation, and intergenerational family were family constellations that had not had the opportunity to move through systems exploration. Although the couple had a brief period to begin negotiating whose values would emerge as central to couple formation, they had no time to determine how these would be revised in light of Celia's birth or living with Alicia. The intergenerational family unit and the critical juncture experienced made the system susceptible to a unidirectional, diffuse external boundary, wherein outside influences were given a great deal of

Exhibit 13.3.
Phases of Systemic Development

Phase 1: System Exploration
As individuals form systems, boundaries protecting their collective integrity are not yet established and internally generated. Shared images do not yet exist. Instead, the emerging system constructs itself within two primary domains of influence, encompassing (a) each individual's developmental history and preexisting worldview and (b) wider contextual influences that govern mores and norms and define health, distress, and disorder. At this phase, the evolving relationship reflects a diffuse interpersonal environment (Gray, 1981).

Phase 2: System Consolidation
When system precursors merge to form organizing images and themes, relationships are established that exist over time. A strong boundary-making process represents this phase, wherein a less permeable boundary surrounds the system to consolidate and protect the integrity of internally supported images and themes. Families use their energy to reinforce shared ways of experiencing, interpreting, and acting in the world, so that thoughts, feelings, and behaviors become somewhat predictable.

Phase 3: System Enhancement
Families operate with clear boundaries concerning their sense of self. Information can be accepted from any domain and used to enhance the family's collective image. Although influence comes from multiple sources, the family weighs its importance and uses it to enhance its current functioning. During this phase, members and families reflect on and modify unique views without threatening mutuality or individuality. They expand the influence and centrality of mutual goals, values, and views by elaborating their ideas to cover a range of issues.

Phase 4: System Transformation
New input from various sources challenges the existing image of the family and leads to new narratives. The viability of the existing image is questioned in light of internal or external demands for change that challenge the parameters of existing themes. In an attempt to adapt to these ever-changing circumstances, families deconstruct less useful options and reconstruct alternative options that provide continuity for the family while encouraging new perspectives. Basically, the resolution of this phase leads to a return to systems exploration as members seek to discover new ways of making sense of and operating in their world.

weight in the coconstruction of the family's identity and position in the wider context.

Recursive Dimensions of the Interactive Triad

Contextual issues operating in wider environments influence discourse regarding illness narratives as much as do a family's cognitive resources. The interactions among individuals, families, and wider environments provide the context in which worldviews are tested, reinforced, and modified. Two constructs are defined and illustrated to explore a family's developmental and situational contexts. Each construct is discussed in terms of its impact on clinical conceptualizations of the Hanson case.

Embeddedness

Embeddedness represents the degree of power and influence any triadic domain exerts during dialectic transactions that define illness narratives. Embeddedness has two components: (a) the extent to which each triadic domain is related to the others when defining and managing psychological distress and (b) the significance of the real or perceived power differentials governed by this connectedness.

For example, if a family's primary sense of consensual validation and identity has more basis in societal norms than its own family ideology, then the family and its embedded members will be guided by societal definitions and responses over their own values and experiences. However, families who participate in multiple environments, such as neighborhood and church groups, to coconstruct their worldview will be less embedded and, therefore, less likely to unwittingly accept the labels of communities or institutions participating in the naming or management of distress. In effect, their unwillingness to abide by the conceptualizations of significant others may effectively challenge reified notions of psychological distress, responsibility, blame, and management.

Embeddedness also represents the degree and type of power differentials operating within triadic domains. Power and influence can be defined in many ways. Throughout this chapter, I focus on the power of multiple perspectives and options. Beyond this, however, are issues related to who has the instrumental means to wield the most power and influence in arenas such as status and legitimacy. These issues of social reality determine whether multiple options for challenging reified definitions of illness and treatment actually exist. Legitimized power sources include socioeconomic status, educational attainment, professional status, community standing, and political and legal power.

The Hanson family had not yet developed a collective sense of self in relation to its new constellation or to the care of Celia. In terms of their degree of embeddedness, they were not yet depending on their new family constellation for their sense of consensual validation. Rather, they depended on societal norms more than on their own unique family ideology, such as the traditionalization of families after the birth of children, especially disabled children, and the mythical ideal of nuclear-family self-sufficiency. The family also was embedded in the predominant belief system that suggests lower socioeconomic populations and cultures, which are different from the predominant one, are more apt to use violence under stress. As such, they saw themselves as dependent on services offered by the wider context, and they agreed with others that the amount of stress they faced made psychological distress inevitable.

Collective Cognitive Balancing Styles

Families are information-processing systems that govern the amount and type of data exchanged to support, modify, or transform preexisting worldviews. The Piagetian (1954) construct of equilibration encompasses two opposing forces. *Accommodation* refers to when families integrate new information to refine or modify existing worldviews. *Assimilation* refers to when families modify or deny incoming information to fit with their existing worldviews. Both processes are necessary for adaptive change, one promoting necessary change and the other promoting necessary continuity. The various ways families attempt to balance accommodative and assimilative processes as they encounter new or incongruent information within the interactive triad result in six resolutions, called "collective cognitive balancing styles," which are described in Exhibit 13.4.

When asked to explore other ways society could assist, the Hansons focused on self-blame and responsibility, basic to their intergenerational history of dealing with stress through violence. They could see that their assimilation into the American ideal of self-sufficiency had brought them to be oppressed by mainstream American ideals, underusing resources inherent in a dialectic–systemic orientation that is actually more in tune with the African American cultural belief that "It takes a village to raise a child." However, although they recognized the limits of their excessive self-reliance, they did not put together the idea that a more interlocked network of services, with them as equal partners in determining appropriate services, could be of assistance to a family with a disabled child—which represents a more mature alpha solution.

When asked about what they hoped would happen in therapy, they were governed by past assimilations regarding their own inadequacies and found it difficult to incorporate new ideas about interdependence, signaling a negative alpha solution. However, when asked concrete questions about how therapy could help the family become self-sufficient, Ben to become a better husband and father, and Toni to be a better wife and mother (using their language), they were able to begin to piece together ways that Alicia and the medical system might be of better service to them—although they were not yet able to determine ways to influence these contexts. This indicated that they had achieved a beta solution.

SCDT Treatment Phase

SCDT emphasizes the use of therapeutic environments that correspond with the orientations explored at different times during therapeutic or con-

Exhibit 13.4.
Collective Cognitive Balancing Styles

Negative Alpha Solutions

There are two cognitive balancing styles contained within the negative alpha solution. Families governed by past assimilations who find it difficult to incorporate unfamiliar information use an *overassimilative* style. An *overaccommodative* style is used when families completely incorporate new or incongruent information, without questioning the validity or use of the data.

Mature Alpha Solution

Families who access the more mature alpha solution recognize that some of their ideas distort or overgeneralize situations they are participating in within the triad. However, they cannot see that a large part of their worldview is discrepant with individual or contextual perceptions or situations.

Beta Solution

Families relying on the beta solution are able to accurately describe their context and other contexts they or their family members work within to understand and manage the illness narrative. However, they are not yet able to collectively determine ways to influence or alter triadic experiences.

Early Gamma Solution

Families who access the early gamma solution can construct a partial synthesis, accommodating to new or incongruent information within the triad. These families appraise different situations, do not react with intensity or insecurity, and make decisions to use an assimilative or accommodative response.

Transcendent Gamma Solution

Integrating new information using the transcendent gamma solution represents a complete synthesis of incoming information from multiple domains of the interactive triad. A transforming solution provides families with new ways of looking at their situation and opens up alternative possibilities for change. By assuming an assimilative, accommodative, or combinatory stance, families are more able to generate multiple perspectives and to question the validity and use of both incoming and preexistent information.

sultative encounters. There are four therapeutic environments: environmental structuring, coaching, consulting, and collaborating. These environments are coconstructed using SCDT questions and other approaches—organized in the SCDT classification matrix—to extend, challenge, and expand the parameters of the cognitive structures influencing key domains of the interactive triad (see Table 13.1).

The objectives are, first, to build on and enhance familiar resources and, later, to challenge and extend the use of underused or never-used resources. Although it is essential to work from several intervention points within the interactive triad, it is important that the family become an active and equal participant in constructing and acting on illness narratives.

Table 13.1.
SCDT Classification Matrix

Therapeutic environments	Corresponding SCDT questioning strategies	Approaches of the associated family therapy		
		Structural	Transgenerational	Experiential
Environmental structuring: Used to assist families to explore issues within the sensorimotor orientation; a highly directive stance by the therapist provides structure for the clients to directly experience emotional and physical sensations in a safe holding environment	How do the two of you feel right now as you see your son and wife act this way? Tell your daughter what happens inside you when she talks about her pain. What is happening for you now, at this moment?	Heightening intensity Crisis intervention	Directing core affective exchanges Creating contextual holding environments	Fantasy alternatives Separating interpersonal from intrapersonal stress
Coaching: Helps families understand their thoughts, feelings, and behaviors from a concrete, if–then, linear perspective; the therapist adopts a coaching stance and encourages families to act on and identify concrete aspects of their situation	Would you two discuss what happens just before your daughter has a temper tantrum? Who stepped in afterwards? Given the way these facts emerged, what do you think causes or triggers what?	Enactment and boundary making Punctuation to extend linear sequence of events	Constructing therapeutic triangles, facilitating direct communication, and teaching about emotional systems	Teaching stories Role replacement Sculpting
Consulting: Promotes reflections about actions, thinking, and emotions; the therapist adopts a consultative stance; the family takes the lead in surfacing formal meanings and searches for patterns and cycles of interactions across time and contexts	Has anything like this ever happened before? What else in the family seems related to or influenced by this problem? Can you describe other things that happen that seem to require each of you to take similar positions?	Reframes that extend the story Punctuation that highlights strength	Genogram-pattern analysis Enlargement of the field of participation Externalize and separate feelings, fantasy, and cognition	Relational symptom expansion Family maps and metaphors
Collaborating: Challenges the family to examine the constraining and oppressive rules, beliefs, and assumptions undergirding their thoughts, feelings, and actions; the therapist assumes a collaborative stance to assist the family in identifying new constructs of self and reality and to introduce a dialectic interaction between the family and other members of the wider interactive triad	How would you define the rule(s) that influence how your family thinks, feels, and acts? What role does your religion, ethnicity, family background, and wider context play in the way you developed and hold to these rules? Could you describe your family from another point of view?	Reframe that transforms and challenges worldview Structural and developmental assessment techniques	Community genogram: exploration of culture, gender, and intergenerational interpretations Contextual transference and countertransference	Transgenerational symptom expansion Family reconstruction Spontaneous self-disclosure

Note. SCDT = systemic cognitive–developmental therapy.

The initial intervention phase represents the ongoing development, exchange, and integration of a cogenerated narrative that synthesizes data received from significant members of the triad. The purpose is to introduce change in ways that are accepted, hopeful, somewhat unfamiliar, and yet nonthreatening and to validate that each member is being heard and has legitimate concerns.

The coconstruction of an alternative illness narrative becomes the foundation that influences (a) each individual's and each collective's sense of self and self in relation to others and in relation to psychological distress, (b) the selective historical sequences of events and experiences that are shared by key members of the triad to reinforce the alternative narrative, (c) the ongoing selection of events and experiences that reinforce or challenge the alternative narrative, and (d) the actions to take to deal with psychological distress under the new meaning structure.

In terms of the Hanson family, the alternative illness narrative was drawn on multiple perspectives, and different action plans were legitimized. A few key themes cogenerated in the triad focused on the wider context. One theme was how premature foreclosure on action plans identified the family as a chronic-care-maintenance and acute-crisis-intervention case. This identity would result in the use of immense financial resources over Celia's life, which may not be required if a more intensified, future-oriented plan were initiated instead. This plan required a new look at the family as one responding to stress overload in a chaotic (sensorimotor) fashion because of its underdeveloped versus pathogenic nature. This new perspective and the potential for long-term financial relief prompted outside systems to think about providing both stress reduction and educational services to help the family become more self-sufficient.

Some cogenerated themes focused on the family. One examined multiple precursors to violence, seeing that current actions that focused on ameliorating Ben's stress levels had not shifted the violence behavior. If all members of the triad, especially Ben, addressed other precursors to violence, such as lack of involvement in the new family constellation, lack of knowledge regarding Celia, and a sense of disempowerment, then other actions could be entertained. Another theme challenged the traditional stereotype of marginalized and incompetent men in African American households. This challenge required Ben to find responsible ways to build a different position in the family and required the women and outside systems to make room for him. Regarding the couple, if both expected Ben to be a good father and husband and if Ben responsibly learned the skills to do so, the couple could determine how they wanted to manage their situation and prepare for the future. They could then guide Alicia, and later outside systems, to provide services thought necessary by the entire interactive triad.

For this case, the work was to have all members of the triad reconsider their basic assumptions as part of the system exploration phase and then consolidate shared understandings around less pathogenic, broader assumptions. The new narrative defining Ben's violence prompted retrospective searches that verified that instances other than stress overload were precursors to his violence and that demonstrated that protecting Ben from family stressors did not decrease his violent behavior. Other probable antecedents were found in events that represented his marginal status in the household and his acting out against female authority figures. These searches allowed for the cocreation of multiple perspectives and set in motion a different sequence of treatment events. One treatment event was to involve Ben in a group of male batterers in which violence was not seen as a means to signal disapproval and where group members discussed concrete action plans to take responsibility for their violence. Another was assisting Ben and Toni to clarify their desired internal arrangement by renegotiating roles, responsibilities, and division of labor and establishing a predictable routine around taking care of Celia. A third was to assist the family to reexamine the role of the matriarch in "sheltering the couple from" versus "guiding the couple to" obtaining adult status and responsibility. Another was to assist the family to coconstruct a more accurate sense of the knowledge and skills they needed to effectively manage Celia. This latter intervention would begin to reestablish the proverb above, "It takes a village to raise a child," but under the new condition, the family, and later the couple, should be equal partners in determining what services would best benefit them and their daughter. Many of these dialogic exchanges represented early gamma solutions.

In terms of medical and police services, examining the history of the Hanson family revealed no incidents of police involvement until after the birth of Celia and medical records indicated that the couple had competently dealt with Toni's pregnancy. In addition, clearly financial stress was not a result of mismanagement but rather Alicia's inability to work due to a physical impairment and Toni's need to take care of Celia. These easy-to-garner client data prompted a healthier perspective of the family and allowed for a future-oriented treatment plan, opening up alternative services, not simply for stress reduction but also for family education and long-term planning. These consultative explorations moved through early gamma and transcendent gamma solutions.

Style Mismatching and Rematching

Interventions aimed at alternative orientations move members toward multiple perspectives, increasing their flexibility. Individuals or systems with the ability to use resources in less central orientations begin to have a voice. This expands awareness for key members, who begin to consider new perspectives and options without threatening the integrity of any individual or group. In this phase of treatment, the triad moves toward systems enhancement, broadening the types of perspectives and actions made possible within the evolving therapeutic narrative.

The Hanson family had moved from a sensorimotor orientation with chaotic and confused functioning to a concrete orientation "bootstrapped" by the use of several services, such as group therapy for Ben, alternating couples and family therapy, and consultative sessions for the family and medical personnel. This prompted a new family narrative that built on and contributed to eliminating violent behaviors, realigning the new family constellation, taking care of Celia, and repositioning the family in the community. Drawing on this competency-based narrative, they could now work within the security of a new consolidated structure to explore underlying themes they had deemed important for the future.

Conversations moved to themes that encompassed formal and dialectical perspectives. The point of departure for these conversations was the family's ability and desire to continue to build Ben's more central and responsible role in the family and the couple's continued ability and desire to guide Alicia's role and to garner necessary services. Formal explorations included (a) Toni's desire to explore multiple alternatives to fulfill her caretaking role, prompting a therapeutic exchange that broadened this concept to include both emotional and financial caretaking, and (b) Alicia's exploration of the new freedoms and the more long-term effect her altered position would have on her family. In effect, she was able to continue to fulfill her predominant role of protective matriarch in other ways. Instead of sheltering Toni and Ben from adult responsibilities and stress, which felt burdensome and never ending, Alicia could guide them through the steps of maturity necessary to ensure the competent caretaking of Celia over the course of her life, which felt like a more delegating role and accessed her sense of generativity. Another theme for formal exploration was (c) how Ben's renewed confidence in mastering his environment and the collective belief in his gaining confidence assisted Toni to rely on this relationship more than on her female relationships, as was the preexisting pattern in her family-of-origin. Together, Ben and Toni focused on future goals that better assisted them to know what to ask for from Alicia, such as taking care of Celia while Toni was in school and until Ben got home, and from the community, such as requests for home health care assistance during crucial medical treatments for Celia.

Dialectic exploration included (a) the family's desire to reconstruct old rules that were no longer of assistance to them or were no longer operating in this new family constellation, such as a preexisting assumption that men were less competent and more peripheral, that women kept men in disempowered and peripheral positions, and that a matriarchy must hold excessive intrafamilial power for a family to survive, and (b) the family's sense that they had been engulfed by an American ideal of self-sufficiency and that this had immobilized the members while social service systems, with the best of intentions, tried to shelter them from unnecessary stress because of this immobilization, which was seen as unchangeable. They desired to return to an African American ideal, wherein they embraced a more interdependent, community worldview that included reliance on their community and their church as well as an interdependent partnership with appropriate professional services that Celia would require over the course of her life span. There was a return to the philosophy of the "village" proverb, with an enhanced understanding that such a village works only when roles are clearly defined, rules are consistent, and ultimate authority (i.e., the couple) is clearly established (Hines, Garcia-Preto, McGoldrick, Almeida, & Weltman, 1994). This work led to a strong family narrative that prompted members to rebalance their sense of consensual validation to include both family ideals and their position within institutions that would remain involved in the care of Celia.

This work moved the triadic system from a prematurely foreclosed, underdeveloped system to a flexible, better organized, and solution-focused one. By doing so, supportive, future-oriented, and educative care for Celia was put in place. As such, the agencies providing services needed to question their continued involvement and work with the family to determine the appropriate level of services required under the alternative narrative. In addition, they needed to make future-oriented arrangements with the family regarding ways they could be of referral assistance throughout Celia's development.

Monitoring Therapeutic and Consultative Movement

Four criteria are used to assess SCDT effectiveness. First, are families and key members able to access more competencies across orientations and to generate multiple perspectives and interpretations? Second, are relevant cognitive–developmental structures more developed, so families are able to make conscious use of competencies and an awareness of constraints that require problem-solving strategies? Third, are families and key members able to use higher order cognitive balancing solutions to integrate new information and synthesize enhanced worldviews? Finally, is the interactive narrative more ordered, so that key players minimize power differentials, dissonance, oppression, and stress as well as use dialogue that ensures multiple perspectives about illness behavior and experience and can generate multiple options for change? Using these indicators, clinicians, families, and wider networks can assess therapeutic and consultative progress and determine future directions for both.

CONCLUSION

This chapter introduces the SCDT model and metaframework as a coconstructive, nonpathological, and integrative treatment approach for working with and explaining relational issues. The central thesis that all individual disorders have a relational component was supported by the examination of the role of the family in mediating cultural and individual variables.

Constructivist therapists can use the SCDT assessment strategies to access and assess the primary collective cognitive–developmental orientation of relational systems and to determine their capacity to access other orientations. By using SCDT questioning strategies and the SCDT metaframework, clinicians can then use systemic intervention strategies to orchestrate a therapeutic process tailored to the developmental needs of families and other relational systems over the course of treatment.

As constructivistic perspectives continue to move toward the mainstream of psychological work, the need to operationally define constructs will be important to ensure that empirical work can be replicated and clinical work can be consistent. The constructs defined in this chapter provide the foundation for future study and dissemination of a cognitive–developmental framework aimed at promoting human and systemic growth.

REFERENCES

American Psychiatric Association. (1994). *Diagnostic and statistical manual of mental disorders* (4th ed.). Washington, DC: Author.

Andersen, T. (1993). See and hear: And be seen and heard. In S. Friedman (Ed.), *The new language of change* (pp. 54–68). New York: Guilford Press.

Anderson, H., Goolishian, H. A., & Winderman, L. (1986). Problem determined systems: Toward transformation in family therapy. *Journal of Strategic and Systemic Therapies, 5*, 1–14.

Arciniega, M. G., & Newlon, B. J. (1994). Counseling and psychotherapy: Multicultural considerations. In D. Capuzzi & D. Gross (Eds.), *Counseling and psychotherapy: Theories and interventions* (pp. 557–587). Englewood Cliffs, NJ: Merrill.

Borders, L. D. (1994). Potential of DCT/SCDT in addressing two elusive themes of mental health counseling. *Journal of Mental Health Counseling, 16*, 75–78.

Cecchin, G. (1992). Constructing therapeutic possibilities. In S. McNamee & K. J. Gergen (Eds.), *Therapy as social construction* (pp. 86–95). Newbury Park, CA: Sage.

Goldner, V. (1993). Power and hierarchy: Let's talk about it! *Family Process, 32*, 157–162.

Gray, W. (1981). System-forming aspects of general system theory, group forming and group functioning. In J. Durkin (Ed.), *Living groups: Group psychotherapy and general system theory* (pp. 199–215). New York: Brunner/Mazel.

Hines, P., Garcia-Preto, N., McGoldrick, M., Almeida, R., & Weltman, S. (1994). Intergenerational relationships across cultures. In A. Skolnick & J. Skolnick (Eds.), *Family in transition* (pp. 436–454). New York: HarperCollins.

Hoffman, L. (1990). Constructing realities: An art of lenses. *Family Process, 29*, 1–12.

Kelly, G. A. (1955). *The psychology of personal construct* (Vols. 1 and 2). New York: Norton.

Minuchin, S. (1974). *Families and family therapy.* Cambridge, MA: Harvard University Press.

Pedersen, P. B. (Ed.). (1991). Multiculturalism as a fourth force in counseling [Special issue]. *Journal of Counseling and Development, 70.*

Piaget, J. (1954). *The construction of reality in the child.* New York: Basic Books.

Pinsof, W. (1994). An overview of integrative problem-centered therapy: A synthesis of family and individual psychotherapies. *Journal of Family Therapy, 16*, 103–120.

Rigazio-DiGilio, S. A. (1993). Family counseling and therapy: Theoretical foundations and issues of practice. In A. Ivey, M. Ivey, & L. Simek-Morgan (Eds.), *Counseling and psychotherapy: A multicultural perspective* (3rd ed., pp. 333–358). Needham Heights, MA: Allyn & Bacon.

Rigazio-DiGilio, S. A. (1997). Systemic cognitive-developmental therapy: A counseling model and an integrative classification schema for working with partners and families. *International Journal for the Advancement of Counselling, 19*, 143–165.

Rigazio-DiGilio, S. A., & Ivey, A. E. (1991). Developmental counseling and therapy: A framework for individual and family treatment. *Counseling and Human Development, 24*, 1–20.

Rigazio-DiGilio, S., & Ivey, A. (1993). Systemic cognitive–developmental therapy: An integrative framework. *The Family Journal: Counseling and Therapy for Couples and Families, 1*, 208–219.

White, M., & Epston, D. (1990). *Narrative means to therapeutic ends.* New York: Norton.

14

FROM DISORDERING DISCOURSE TO TRANSFORMATIVE DIALOGUE

KENNETH J. GERGEN AND SHEILA McNAMEE

> Lovers and madmen have such seething brains,
> Such shaping fantasies, that apprehend
> More than cool reason ever comprehends.
> —William Shakespeare

In this chapter, we explore the discourse of mental disorder. Our attempt is to augment the already articulated "merits" of diagnosis by proposing some of the limitations of such discourse. Specifically, we discuss the ways in which diagnosis—or the discourse of mental disorders—invites therapists into patterns of stigmatizing and blaming clients, desecrating traditions, deteriorating relationships, and disempowering people. We offer, instead, the metaphors of dialogue and multiplicity as possible openings toward transformation.

We begin this chapter with a simple query: Of what therapeutic value are the diagnostic categories of mental disorder? Because such terms have been generated largely within the context of what is understood as a knowledge-generating process, this question is seldom voiced. Yet—momentarily putting aside the problems and prospects of a science of mental disorder—what therapeutic benefits or liabilities accrue from the standard practices of assigning terms of mental disorder to the actions of individuals seeking therapeutic treatment? For whatever the capacities of the science, it is ultimately the well-being of society's members that is at stake. If the diagnostic categories are problematic, or possibly injurious, in terms of a client's well-being, then serious reconsideration is required with respect to therapeutic practice, managed care requirements, and possibly the knowledge-generating process.

We raise this question from the standpoint commonly identified as "social constructionist" (Gergen, 1994; McNamee, 1996; McNamee & Gergen, 1992). Of central concern to constructionists are the processes by which human communities generate meaning. Particularly focal are the multiple possibilities for meaning that exist within a culture and indeed around the globe. As people coordinate their actions within a community, so do they typically generate a language that is functionally integrated into their practices. Perhaps the clearest illustration is furnished by the game. For example, the game of baseball not only requires a set of coordinated activities but also a functionally integral vocabulary. There are pitchers, fielders, and batters, just as there are innings, outs, and foul balls. The terms are an integral part of the game as traditionally played. To destroy the discourse (or its functional equivalent) would render the game impossible. Note, however, that the discourse of baseball, although essential to those engaged in the game, is of marginal relevance outside the domain. If this discourse were suddenly imported into another game—let us say, eliminating a tennis player from a match because "he missed the third strike"—the results would be chaotic.

So it is within the various professions. The discourse of law is not that of physics or chemistry, the language of botany is of little use when launching a rocket, and the discourse of literary theory would be counterproductive for a disaster relief agency. Here we must ask, then, Whose interests are being served by the discourse of mental disorder? How does this discourse function outside the mental health establishment? In particular, how does it function when transported into the lives of clients?

Let us increase the stakes: Social constructionist theory also calls attention to the close relationship between meaning and value. In particular, as communities of coordination emerge, so do they generate (and typically articulate) standards of conduct, or views of what constitutes "good" behavior within the community. Because the discourse of the community is thus inextricably wedded to its traditions, it also carries with it either implicitly or explicitly the values of the tradition. Failing to play by the rules of baseball, which includes calling events or people by their conventionally sanctioned names, is grounds for expulsion. Much the same holds true in physics, botany, and firefighting. To participate is to accede to the values of the community in question. To put it more broadly, a community's construction of the world sustains what Wittgenstein (1953) called its "form of life." Thus, when one credits people with the capacity for "independent thought," one acts to sustain a tradition of democracy; when one attributes to them a spiritual dimension, one favors the sustenance of religion. Every discourse invites a way of life while discouraging or repelling others. The discourse of mental disorders does not differ in this respect.

Again, to rephrase our initial query, What values are carried by the discourse of mental disorder? What traditions are sustained? What traditions are lost? If the language of mental disorder becomes the primary means of generating meaning, whose voices are suppressed?

One is left to wonder how such a strange set of odd and irrational, ever-changing diagnostic categories (the DSM) has come to be so widely used to extend all-powerful control over the field of psychopathology.
—George W. Albee

To properly set the stage for what follows, one must recognize a final constructionist concern: the social and material context of meaning generation. To the extent that any community functions within a cultural or geographic vacuum, it may comfortably rely on a single, strong tradition. Its traditional discourses may serve it well, and its values may go unchallenged. Coordination could approach perfection. For example, members of inner-city gangs coordinate their activities around particular beliefs and practices. In so doing, their day-to-day lives are somewhat seamless, and their collective understandings of themselves and their surroundings are not at risk. They know what it means to be a member of the community (gang) and what is expected of each participant. They listen carefully to each other's accounts of what they are doing, and their values rarely waver. However, as other communities whose realities and values are potentially antagonistic increasingly populate the environment, then their commitment to a singular tradition becomes problematic. Not only do "true believers" become insensitive to the needs and interests of those around them but also, with such insensitivity, potential for action is reduced. Each vocabulary offers a way of life, alternative possibilities for action and value. At worst, intense commitment sets the stage for open hostility and possible attempts to eradicate the other.

In this context, we are invited to consider the "mushrooming" of communication technologies, particularly during recent decades. With the rapid expansion and increased efficacy of telephone systems, jet transportation, television, and computers, the possibilities for communal coordination—from the very local to the global—become enormous. In effect, one of the chief hallmarks of what is variously called the "age of information," "culture of chaos," or "postmodern culture" is the multiplication and expansion of discursively coordinated communities (Gergen, 1991). The emergence of multiplicity is accompanied by increasing challenges to the established truths and values of any group.

Again we reframe our initial query: On what grounds, save those that are shared within their own community, can mental health professionals claim superiority in naming? On what grounds, save their own, do they function to eliminate alternative possibilities? Is resistance to the multiple possibilities of interpretation desirable? Is the "single calling" possibly injurious not only to the profession but also to those clients who live in alternative realities?

> Clinicians appear to ascribe violence, suspiciousness, and dangerousness to Black clients even though the case studies are the same as the case studies for the White clients.
>
> —M. Loring and B. Powell

In light of the challenges posed by these questions, we propose the following. First, we consider a range of problems deriving from the traditional discourse of mental disorder. Our intention here is to unsettle the tranquility of the conventional, the secure sense that the vocabulary of mental disorder is either neutral or harmless. We then open discussion on an alternative direction for mental health professionals. We attempt to replace the urge toward certainty—the closed community—with a telos of protean potential. More succinctly, we propose that in both therapy and diagnosis we may profitably move from disciplinary determination to dialogues of difference.

DISORDERING THE DISCOURSE OF DISORDER

> Psychiatrists are physicians, and physicians are supposed to help people. That is true. But it does not follow that the result is necessarily helpful for the so-called patient—as he, the patient, would define what constitutes help.
>
> —Thomas Szasz

For people working within the mental health professions, the value of diagnostic categorization is seldom questioned. Standardization of terms is essential to carrying out the practices that represent the goal of the profession. Yet much hangs in this case on what is considered to be the goal of the profession. If the goal is to cure the patient, then a diagnostic vocabulary seems reasonable enough. However, the discourse of "disease" and "cure" is itself optional. One person's "mental illness" may be another's "salvation." If the goal of the profession is to aid the client—which seems more supportable—

then the door is opened to the more pragmatic questions. In what senses is the client assisted and injured by the demand for classification? Although we touch on possible ways in which the client could be assisted, our aim here is more catalytic. To instigate dialogue, we focus on five particular ways—some now well documented—in which both the client and society may be harmed by constructing people within the discourse of mental disorder.

Stigmatization

Much has been said about the implicit value systems underlying the concept of mental health and the contrasting concepts of mental illness or disorder. Images of the "fully functioning," "well adjusted," or "normal" person are burdened with values and ideals, both in one's daily relations with peers and family and in the mental health professions (Laing, 1972; London, 1986; White & Hellerich, 1998). Kleinman (1988) offered many beautiful illustrations of the cultural variation in diagnosis. A form of schizophrenia deemed severe in Western culture is viewed as a minor oddity in Asian culture. These variations can be traced in large measure to different conceptions of value. Because of this valuational component, diagnosis does not function neutrally, to merely describe. It renders a moral judgment. It communicates a deficit in worth. "You are not active enough," or "you are too active." "You are not sexual enough," or "you are too sexual." "You don't eat enough," or "you eat too much." "You don't make rational sense," or "you are excessively rational." In effect, the diagnosis can function as a form of stigmatization, rendering one undesirably different. The repercussions of social stigmatization are well documented (see, e.g., Goffman, 1963; Rosenhan, 1973).

A diagnosis of schizophrenia is worse in some ways, than being told you have cancer. What would it be like if nobody who got cancer got better, and they were called by their illness? If people said, "What should we do with these cancers? Isn't it too bad. Let's send these cancers to the hospital since we can't cure them."

—Marcia (diagnosed with schizophrenia)

The problems owing to stigmatization are exacerbated by two factors. First, diagnostic procedures are unreflexive. The categories of disorder are treated as if neutral, as dispassionate assessments of "what is the case." This is not to deny that "something is the case." However, to treat these callings as if they were not value-loaded interpretations, representing the investments of particular subcultures in society, is to leave the client with little means of deliberating on the issues. There is no opening for debate on the values embedded in the diagnosis, nor on these values as compared with others.

Thus, for example, the diagnosis of attention deficit disorder, although treated as objectively neutral, reflects traditional investments in a quiet and well-ordered classroom. It is the diagnosed individual who is "disordered." In contrast, if parents, teachers, and children could talk over the assets and liabilities of "ordered education," rather than focusing on the child's "illness," the child would not be stigmatized and Ritalin would not be a million-dollar business.

Furthermore, there is little way for a client, once stigmatized, to escape. Labels for mental disorder are notoriously vague; they typically refer to mental tendencies, dispositions, and afflictions not available to public scrutiny (Kutchins & Kirk, 1997). As diagnostic procedures demonstrate to the clients, they are not in a position to judge for themselves. The result is that one can never be certain that he or she has ever been "cured." One remains with the sense that beneath the veneer, lurking in the unconscious, will always remain the obsessive, the anorexic, the multiple personality, or the schizoid tendency. In effect, to be diagnosed in terms of mental disorder is for many to embark on a lifetime of existence on the boundary of normalcy. It is to carry forever a sense of self-enfeeblement, self-doubt, incompetence, and general deficiency.

Individual Blame

It is not only that the discourse of mental disorder stigmatizes the client but also that the cause of the dysfunction is located within the person. The attribution signals a personal flaw or failing, an inability or incapacity. To be sure, preceding conditions (e.g., child-rearing practices, environmental tensions, molestation) may be initially responsible for the "disordered mind," but the result of these conditions is now a disability within the person (e.g., "my anxiety," "uncontrollable desire," "chronic depression"). With individuals now carrying with them the weight of "evil origins," the invitation is to withdraw from a relationship. If it is one's problem, then one must worry about inflicting it on others and about their justified blame. The logic invites one into privacy, "working it out for oneself" (or with one's private therapist and an appropriate regime of drugs). In effect, the tendency may often be toward disengagement from a relationship.

They would have labeled me an ego-dystonic homosexual. They pretend to be hip now, so they say it's normal to be homosexual. Of course they don't think it's normal at all, but that's what they're giving lip service to these days. But they think you're even more abnormal if you do not accept your abnormality.

—Ruby (a patient)

This tendency is often intensified by the way in which the same diagnosis invites others into a posture of blame: "She's at it again," "you never know what he will do," "she always does that." The diagnosis, then, places therapists in a position as righteous and all knowing, with the disordered individual subject to the therapist's judgment. This distancing of oneself from others is encouraged further by the very diagnostic that places the other in a different category: ill or infirmed. The diagnostic informs therapists that they are different, better, and correct. In the diagnostic laying of blame, the wall between the therapist and client grows higher.

Of equal importance, with individual blame established through diagnosis, the therapist may suspend inquiry into other contributions to the condition, including his or her own. Explorations of family conditions, peer relationships, the workplace, technology, and the like are bracketed. The "buck" has stopped. For example, in the case of sex offenses, there is good reason to inquire into the cultural conditions—the erosion of moral consensus, the reduction of religious influence, the influence of television and pornography—and the way in which many people contribute to these conditions. Yet once the individual is diagnosed as a sex offender, the need for such reflection is reduced. With individual blame in the vanguard, one closes off possibilities for relational responsibility (McNamee & Gergen, 1998).

Desecration of Tradition

Consider a person who becomes listless, loses enthusiasm and ambition, sleeps long hours, and begins to take little interest in food. These are all classic symptoms of the mental disorder called depression. There are numerous therapeutic treatments for depression, with psychopharmacological solutions increasingly favored. Yet there are other traditions in which these symptoms might be recognized, with far different outcomes. For example, there is a strong folk tradition in which one can "feel blue." To "have the blues" is not an illness; it is an honorific state; it signifies that one truly knows life and has experienced its depths and defeats. It is to elicit sympathy, not because one is ill but because people recognize the condition as a "poor lot." The afflicted one is not weakened by disease but is strong in his or her resistance. To have the blues enables one to serve as a witness, to inform others of one's journey. In a good blues club, one pays handsomely to hear others' experiences related.

Other traditions are capable of rendering intelligible what might otherwise be called depression. The "loss of meaning" in life has been of chief concern to traditions of the spirit; in response, not therapy but teachings from the Bible or the Koran, along with pastoral counseling services, are favored. There is also a longstanding folk tradition, stemming perhaps from the Germanic tradition of *bildung* (roughly translated as character development), that views life as a challenge to one's strength and simultaneously an invitation to grow stronger. To avoid the challenges of daily life, as in the case of what might be called depression, would be to abandon the "good fight." The proper reply in this case is not sympathy but remonstrance and encouragement: "Pull up your socks," "get a grip," or "you can do it."

A spiritualized society would treat in its sociology the individual, for the saint to the criminal, not as units of a social problem to be passed through some skillfully devised machinery and either flattened into the social mold or crushed out of it, but as souls suffering and entangled in a net and to be rescued, souls growing and to be encouraged to grow.
—Sri Aurobindo

In summary, in demanding terminologies of mental disorder, we imply or presume the inferiority or irrelevance of alternative traditions. Therapeutically speaking, the client is discouraged against reliance on many of the existing resources within the culture. By implication, there is only one resource, made available only by the mental health professional.

Deterioration of Relationship

We already discussed the way in which tendencies toward individual blame, invited by disordering discourse, can undermine relationships. The precarious state of such relationships is further underscored when one considers the way in which such discourse invites the client into a state of dependency on the mental health professions. To be diagnosed by the profession is to be informed that the professionals—not family, friends, community, spiritual advisors, and the like—are the proper source of guidance, support, and cure. In this way, as the disordered individual enters a treatment program, the problem may be removed from its normal context of operation; others are encouraged to "back off," "avoid interfering," and "let the professionals do their work." The mental health professions thus disrupt the processes of relational realignment that might otherwise take place within the community. Relations organic to the community are undermined, communication is attenuated, and common patterns of interdependency thwarted. In effect, the deficit terminology functions within a process that removes the client from his or her ecological niche.

[Hysteria] is not a disease; rather, it is an alternative physical, verbal, and gestural language, an iconic social communication.
—Mark Micale

One may argue that processes of natural realignment are often slow, anguished, or brutal and that life is too short to endure the seemingly chronic deviant. However, the result is that problems otherwise generating significant "challenges to the community"—those that give strength and identity to a community—are largely "removed from the ledger." Marriage partners may carry out more intimate conversations with their therapists than with each other. Partners of "problem" people are invited away into codependency support groups, where they discuss the now-objectified partner with strangers. Parents may discuss their problems with a specialist or send problem children to treatment centers and thereby reduce the possibility for communication with their offspring. Organizations place alcoholic executives in treatment programs and thereby reduce the kind of self-reflexive discussions that might elucidate their own contribution to the problem. In each case, the ties of communal interdependency are injured or atrophy, and the client's resources for recovery are reduced.

Disempowerment of the Person

Although the therapeutic process is often justified on the grounds of its empowering the otherwise infirm and dependent, there is an important sense in which the reverse is true and in which diagnostics are a chief vehicle for disempowerment. In the works of Michel Foucault the logic of disempowerment becomes most clear. Foucault (1979) was particularly concerned with the way in which people unwittingly subjugate themselves to subtle forms of power. Language is a critical feature of such power relations, especially the discourse of knowledge. Foucault was centrally concerned with subjugation by various groups who claim "to know" or to be in possession of the "truth," about who people are as human selves (e.g., professionals in the disciplines of medicine, psychiatry, sociology, anthropology, and education). Professionals within these "disciplinary regimes," as Foucault called them, generate languages of description and explanation—classifications of selves as healthy or unhealthy, normal or abnormal, upper class or lower class, intelligent or unintelligent—along with explanations as to why they are so. Professionals also use various research procedures whereby individuals are scrutinized and classified in the terms of these regimes. In effect, when one offers oneself for examinations of various sorts, from medical examinations to college board assessments, one is giving oneself over to the disciplinary regimes to be labeled and explained in their terms. When one carries these terminologies into one's daily lives—for example, speaking to others of one's depression or anxiety—one engages in power relations, essentially extending the control of the disciplinary regimes. As these disciplines of study begin to influence public policy and practices, one becomes further ordered in their terms. As diagnostic terminology is increasingly sanctioned by managed care systems, so is it increasingly difficult to escape. As pharmaceutical companies increasingly profit from curing those labeled in these ways, so are these companies contributing to the disempowering of the individual. In the current condition, the client has virtually no freedom to reject psychodiagnostics.

For drug companies, the unlabeled masses are a vast untapped market, the virgin Alaskan oil fields of mental disorder.
—Herb Kutchins and Stuart Kirk

TOWARD TRANSFORMATIVE DIALOGUE

There are significant ways in which the discourse of mental disorder functions to the disadvantage of the client. This is surely not all there is to be said about such discourse, particularly in terms of its positive potentials. Countless individuals have been helped within the terms of this discourse and its attendant therapeutic practices. Many clients are both pleased and relieved to have their otherwise complicated and unintelligible problems identified with the following standard nomenclatures: "At last someone understands"; "I am like many others"; "they understand"; and "my problem can be solved." As Showalter (1997) argued, people often feel that problematic behavior is symptomatic of an underlying cause. Professional authority figures soon furnish a name for the illness. Support groups are formed, publications generated, and a sense of bonding may emerge. Furthermore, such terms function to coordinate teams of researchers seeking physiological or pharmacological means of reducing the intensity or consequences of reported problems. Regardless of the pervasive criticism of biological reductionism in such cases, countless individuals look to psychopharmacology with gratitude.

Clearly, we do not propose here an abandonment of the discourse of mental disorder. Rather through our critique, we are primarily attempting to set the stage for alternatives to the prevailing movement toward universal diagnostics. We seek means of replacing the automaticity of diagnosing clients, using these terms as a standard aspect of treatment, and requiring these diagnostic labels for purposes of insurance claims. We do not favor a "fight to the finish," where the mental health establishment finds itself increasingly placed on the defensive by various advocate groups. The image of psychiatry, in particular, suffered greatly when it succumbed to the persuasive arguments of gay men and lesbian activists that homosexuality is not a mental disorder. Feminist criticism of the pathologizing of women becomes increasingly sharp. Groups of former mental patients are more effectively organizing to do battle with the mental health establishment over the inhumanity and injustices they feel they suffered. It is only a matter of time before those handicapped by the diagnosis of attention deficit disorder organize against the established order. The battle lines are forming, and the ethos is turning increasingly hostile.

In this context, we turn to the potentials of dialogic processes, in general, and, in particular, to what may be called "transformative dialogue" (Gergen, McNamee, & Barrett, in press). Through dialogic means, the range of participatory voices (traditions) can be expanded and traditional forms of argumentation can be abandoned in favor of mutual exploration of options, assets, and limitations. The point of such dialogue is not to battle over the "correct" interpretation; all interpretations can be correct within a particular tradition. Rather, the hope would be to emerge with an expanded array of possibilities, an array that would sensitize professionals, clients, and the surrounding community to myriad factors possibly at play and a range of possible strategies, relational forms, or institutional arrangements that can serve as resources. Finally, with multiple options on the table, moment-to-moment adjustments to changing circumstances could replace lock-step regimens that result from confident labeling.

We do not view this invocation of dialogue as mere academic idealism at play. Rather, there are significant explorations already in motion, practices that may be interrogated and used to seed further variations. We consider here two domains of dialogic practice, the first relevant to the "diagnostic moment," and the second, to the ongoing process of therapy.

Diagnostics as Dialogue

Contemporary diagnostics typically take place within the professional compound, by professionals who largely share the same training and conventions of labeling. An outstanding exploration of alternatives is furnished by Jaakko Seikkula et al. (1995) in the western Lapland province of Finland. Their work is based largely on the dialogic orientations of Mikhail Bakhtin (1981), Valentin Volosvinov (1973), and Lev Vygotsky (1970). The corpus of writing on dialogism draws a distinction between dialogue and monologue. In a monologic interchange, the utterances of each participant are designed only to achieve his or her own ends—much like the traditional way of diagnosing and forming therapeutic treatment plans without involving patients, family members, or others invested in the conversation. In the traditional therapeutic conversation, the professional searches for answers that will support his or her hypothesis about the client's "problem." The professional "knows" how to put the pieces together, what to look for, and what counts as "normal." In contrast, Seikkula et al. proposed a dialogic approach to therapeutic conversation in which emphasis is placed on what people do together. In their work, they focus on expanding the voices that have knowledge of the problem by including patients, family members, and invested others in the conversation. As Sampson (1993) put it, "if we are dialogic, conversational beings, we cannot be understood by probing inside for personal and private processes taking place deep within each individual" (p. 98). To involve a multitude of voices in the conversation about the problem invites each member's truth about the situation into discussion. Each "utterance has an equal value in constructing a polyphonic truth; we must not aim at one truth or solution but at generating a dialogue between the different voices" (p. 69).

Seikkula et al. (1995) described diagnosis and the therapeutic process as "open dialogue," by which they mean that rather than draw boundaries around the treatment team, all interested and invested parties, including the patient, are invited into the discussion about diagnosis and treatment. Seikkula et al. (1995) felt that "by opening the boundaries of discussion, the joint process itself started to determine the treatment, rather than the team itself or the treatment plan of the team. . . . All participants are in a mutual co-evolving process so that the treatment team is also changing all the time" (p. 64). One of the most salient features, then, of the Finnish work is operating "on the boundary." By repositioning the therapeutic conversation away from the "experts" and into the polyphonic arena of all participants, each with an array of expertise (both local and professional), the potential resources of all involved are made available and are used. The open dialogue created includes "the risk of vulnerability, because one's own utterances are open to the other's comments" (p. 73). In such a conversation, "psychosis is no longer seen as some independent quality in the patient but as one voice of the therapeutic interaction taking place at the moment" (p. 74).

We see Seikkula et al.'s (1995) work as a form of transformative dialogue that largely avoids the stigmatizing, alienating, blame, and evaluation that accompanies the monologic attribution of mental disorder. In their guiding principles, they include (a) mobility and flexibility, a special team is organized to diagnose and treat each case; (b) network perspective, an attempt is made to include in the team those who are worried or involved in the case; (c) tolerance for uncertainty, the team does not give solutions too quickly or understand the situation too early; (d) dialogical orientation, the task of the team is to generate dialogue (rather than diagnose the problem) and, therefore, all opinions can be voiced and all voices can be heard; and (e) therapeutic orientation, the team leader takes care of the continuity of the therapeutic process and ensures that all topics, including difficult ones, are discussed. The major task of the team is to develop a treatment plan with the patient, family, and involved others. By so doing, the distinction among diagnosis, therapy, and management of everyday life is blurred. The therapeutic conversation is less "institutional" and more like human dialogue. Also the participatory process of the team seems to generate a participatory relationship among family and involved others. The skill of the team is in its ability to generate dialogue among different voices using all available resources. In so doing, all voices are seen as resources rather than obstacles. Consequently, the meaning is recognized as a by-product of the community of people in relation rather than the sole possession of one individual. Psychosis is not seen as an "obvious quality" of the client but as one way of understanding complex and ever-shifting patterns of action.

Significantly, this dialogic orientation effectively reduced the number of people diagnosed with schizophrenia, the number of psychopharmacological prescriptions, and the number of hospital beds occupied in this region of Finland from 320 to 63 (Seikkula et al., 1995). The open dialogue initiated by Seikkula et al. worked to establish new relational networks within the community. With these expanded webs of relations, community members now had a multitude of resources to draw on (collectively) in helping each other help "the mentally ill."

Therapeutic Movements Toward Multiplicity

Although the Finnish work fruitfully blurs the distinction between diagnosis and treatment, there are also advantages in focusing on therapeutic process itself. Dialogic process may be stimulated effectively within the ongoing process of therapy. In particular, any move within the therapeutic relationship that brings a new or alternative voice into the conversational arena increases the dialogic potential. As voices, opinions, interpretations, values, and the like are added to the conversational mix, opportunities for moving beyond the tyranny of the coherent monologue are increased.

The most simple openings to dialogue may result from such questions as the following: What do you think X would think about this? Would your husband agree with this interpretation? Another opening may result from the therapist's thoughts on how various others (employers, spouses, etc.) might consider the case. In a more sophisticated way, the Milan Associates (Boscolo, Cecchin, Hoffman, & Penn, 1987) introduced to the field of family therapy the idea of circular questioning. Here, family members are asked to comment on their situation from each other's position. This enables them to see the situation from another perspective and thereby reflect on their own. They are encouraged to see things differently, to understand as someone else might understand. In so doing, they are inspired to entertain the variation they also harbor.

One of the most dramatic ways of introducing other voices was developed by Tom Andersen (1991, 1995). He and his colleagues ask a team of individuals to observe family therapy proceedings. At a certain juncture, this reflecting team is admitted into the presence of the family and is asked to talk about what they have heard and seen. There is no attempt in this case to reach consensus or to apply a standard diagnosis. The team members simply give voice to their more pronounced sense of what is occurring. When the observing group finishes offering their reflections, the family is invited to talk about what they heard. This shifting from what Andersen calls the "listening position" to "reflecting position" invites the clients into a dialogue with the observers.

This practice not only brings fresh voices and otherwise absent perspectives to the therapeutic conversation. Of equal importance, it allows clients to understand the constructed character of the realities in which they live, to see them as contingent and negotiable. Furthermore, as the family engages in conversation with the reflecting team, it comes to see itself increasingly as forming an interdependent unit. As a further variation on the reflecting team, Andersen (1995) sometimes asks all participants (patients, family members, therapy team members, others involved) to shift between listening and reflecting stances. Those who listen are given a moment to offer their reflections on the conversation they heard. As the others adopt the listening position to hear these reflections, they are invited into a moment of self-reflexivity, encouraged to suspend their certainty of their own position and to entertain other possibilities. Then those listening are invited to reflect in turn. This constant movement back and forth between listening and reflecting stances among varying groups of participants in the therapeutic conversation contributes further to the transformative potential.

Also relevant here is the work of Penn and Frankfurt (1994) on therapeutic letter writing. Drawing from Bakhtin's (1981) work on dialogism, Penn and Frankfurt (1994) reasoned that the construction of self requires the "other": "Voice . . . is generative; it is unfinished and awaits a reply[,] . . . it invites the other into what one might call a dialogic space" (p. 222). Using these ideas, they found that different voices can be invited into the therapeutic conversation through letters written by the client to others. Because writing takes place at a different pace than talking, they found that it makes room for the "thickening" of "layering" of sensitivities and reactions and thereby stimulates the creation of multiple readings of the self, other, and relationship. Writing, they explained, "encourages us to develop many different readings of our experience" (p. 230). It also invites clients to consider otherwise silent voices as possible resources for relating or as voices that further contribute to understanding. As they work inside and outside of the therapeutic context, clients can also review their writing. They are invited to reexamine, edit, elaborate, and retain their prose. This work not only demonstrates a way of actively bringing others' voices into the situation but also adds a significant new element. It brings into focus the sense in which one's actions are always "for another," always directed to a particular audience. As one begins to recognize the particular audience to whom one is addressing in one's actions and realize that this is only one audience among many, one can see possibilities for expanding one's sensitivities to the multiple potentials within oneself. In addition, as the descriptions are realtered for these various audiences, the "hard reality" of the present becomes relativized.

Mony Elkaim (1990) also developed a therapeutic practice that helps to generate multiple realities. As the client describes him- or herself or the problem at hand, Elkaim suggested that the therapist should listen internally to his or her own voices of reply. The therapist listens by asking him- or herself a series of questions: What is this description inviting in the way of a response? Is this description asking me to speak as a father, a combatant, or an admirer? Elkaim theorized that if a longstanding pattern is to be broken, it is important that the therapist avoid responding in the invited way. Rather, the therapist explores alternative voices available to him or her that would also be intelligible as reactions but would not fortify or sustain the well-rehearsed patterns that contribute to the client's anguish. By drawing on these alternative voices, the client is invited to tap into alternative selves, to give expression to other capacities for being.

Finally, Harlene Anderson (1997) generated a significant means of aiding therapists to multiply the perspectives available to the therapeutic conversation. Participants are invited into what she calls an "as-if exercise." Whether they be therapists in training, family members, or other professionals, they are given a brief synopsis of a problem case with all relevant parties to the problem described. The participants are asked to listen to the story from the position of one of the parties involved. After the short summary is presented, all those who have listened from one member's point of view are invited into a conversation with each other. For example, there are three people listening from the position of the mother in a problem family and two people listening from the position of the father or an adolescent boy. After the presentation, those listening from a given position are invited into a conversation; they generate many different possibilities for understanding the individual's situation. These discussions are followed by an open meeting in which each group introduces its members' thoughts on the party whom they represent. This exercise has an enormous impact on expanding the voices of those involved, and it opens avenues for self-reflexivity and options for action. Anderson's practice effectively helps people move beyond one, unified voice—the voice of certainty—and enter further into transformative dialogue.

CONCLUSION

These various innovations demonstrate the possibilities for open and generative dialogue in our attempts to understand actions frequently serving as candidates for therapeutic treatment. In our view, transformative dialogue is vastly superior to the attempt of any one group to fix the domain of interpretation. The discourse of mental disorder, and the tradition in which it was spawned, may be enormously valuable as an entry into the dialogue of problems and prospects. However, as we proposed, to allow this discourse to dominate can be an enormous disservice to clients seeking help and injurious to society as a whole. In terms of implications, it seems essential to dismantle requirements demanding psychiatric diagnosis as an entry ritual for clients seeking insurance coverage. Whether a client receives a diagnosis in terms of current "conventions of pathology" should be optional, for both client and therapist alike. As we noted in this chapter, many constructionist therapists are experimenting with ways to broaden the psychotherapeutic dialogue. Now therapists are challenged to expand the dialogue beyond the therapist–client relationship to develop alternative means of determining whether a client deserves insurance coverage. Clearly, the broader issues at stake here are likely to depend on another site of transformative dialogue: one among the many communities concerned with mental health, such as clients, drug and insurance companies, religious leaders, and others concerned with society's future. Problematic behavior should not be placed in the hands of any single profession; instead, it should command sustained dialogue among all involved.

REFERENCES

Albee, G. W. (1998). Is the Bible the only source of truth? *Contemporary Psychology*, *43*, 551–552.

Andersen, T. (1991). *The reflecting team*. New York: Norton.

Andersen, T. (1995). Reflecting processes; acts of informing and forming: You can borrow my eyes, but you must not take them away from me! In S. Friedman (Ed.), *The reflecting team in action* (pp. 11–37). New York: Guilford Press.

Anderson, H. (1997). *Conversation, language, and possibilities*. New York: Basic Books.

Bakhtin, M. (1981). *The dialogic imagination*. Austin: University of Texas Press.

Boscolo, L., Cecchin, G., Hoffman, L., & Penn, P. (1987). *Milan systemic family therapy*. New York: Basic Books.

Elkaim, M. (1990). *If you love me, don't love me*. New York: Basic Books.

Foucault, M. (1979). *Discipline and punish*. New York: Vintage.

Gergen, K. J. (1991). *The saturated self*. New York: Basic Books.

Gergen, K. J. (1994). *Realities and relationships*. Cambridge, MA: Harvard University Press.

Gergen, K. J., McNamee, S., & Barrett, F. J. (in press). Toward transformative dialogue. *International Journal of Organization Theory and Behavior*.

Goffman, E. (1963). *Stigma*. Englewood Cliffs, NJ: Prentice-Hall.

Kleinman, A. (1988). *The illness narratives*. New York: Basic Books.

Kutchins, H., & Kirk, S. A. (1997). *Making us crazy*. New York: Free Press.

Laing, R. D. (1972). *The politics of the family*. New York: Vintage Books.

London, P. (1986). *The modes and morals of psychotherapy*. New York: Hemisphere.

McNamee, S. (1996). Psychotherapy as a social construction. In H. Rosen & K. T. Kuehlwein (Eds.), *Constructing realities* (pp. 115–137). San Francisco: Jossey-Bass.

McNamee, S., & Gergen, K. J. (1992). *Therapy as social construction*. London: Sage.

McNamee, S., & Gergen, K. J. (1998). *Relational responsibility: Resources for sustainable dialogue*. Thousand Oaks, CA: Sage.

Penn, P., & Frankfurt, M. (1994). Creating a participant text: Writing, multiple voices, narrative multiplicity. *Family Process, 33*, 217–232.

Rosenhan, D. L. (1973). On being sane in insane places. *Science, 179*, 250–258.

Sampson, E. E. (1993). *Celebrating the other*. Boulder, CO: Westview.

Seikkula, J., Aaltonen, J., Alakara, B., Haarakangas, K., Keranen, J., & Sutela, M. (1995). Treating psychosis by means of open dialogue. In S. Friedman (Ed.), *The reflecting team in action* (pp. 62–80). New York: Guilford Press.

Showalter, E. (1997). *Hystories: Hysterical epidemics and modern media*. New York: Columbia University Press.

Volosvinov, B. (1973). *Marxism and the philosophy of language*. New York: Seminar Press.

Vygotsky, L. (1970). *Thought and language*. Cambridge, MA: MIT Press.

White, D. R., & Hellerich, G. (1998). *Labyrinths of the mind*. Albany: State University of New York Press.

Wittgenstein, L. (1953). *Philosophical investigations* (G. Anscombe, Trans.). New York: Macmillan.

AUTHOR INDEX

Numbers in italics refer to listings in reference sections.

SUBJECT INDEX

Biological etiology, *continued*
  posttraumatic stress disorder,
    298–299
Blame, 338–339
Blues, 339
Body–mind dualism, 23
Borderline disorder, 302
  narrative coherence in, 272
Brief therapy, 7–8. *See also* Depth-
    oriented brief therapy

Change mechanisms and processes, 8
  accessing and assimilating feeling
    states, 98
  acquisition of narrative attitude in,
    275
  adaptive families, 321
  assimilative and accommodative,
    324
  change in narrative content, 279
  client expectations, 43, 57
  contextual conceptualization,
    138–139
  conversational psychotherapy, 27–31
  in core ordering processes, 48
  creating alternative illness narratives
    with families, 327–330
  depth-oriented brief therapy, 66, 69,
    84
  diagnosis and, 153
  experience of disorganization in, 45
  experimenting with possible selves,
    276
  exploring meaning of symptoms, 11
  externalization of problem, 29–30
  family as mediator of, 313
  goals of cognitive–narrative therapy,
    280–281
  integration of experience and mean-
    ing of life events, 11, 102–104
  models of cognitive processes,
    137–138
  monitoring therapy effectiveness,
    330–331
  narrative linguistic patterns, 277
  neuromuscular manifestations, 74
  as orthogonal interaction, 139–140
  outcome measurement, 8–9
  reordering of experience, 11
  resistance to, 45, 46, 102–103, 148
  as shift in worldview, 122–123

symptom coherence, 65, 67–69
  in systemic cognitive–developmental
    therapy, 309–310
  transitive diagnosis, 156
Children
  developmental capacity for narrative
    construction, 269–271
  sexual abuse, 299
Cognitive constructivism, 16
  narrative theory, 211–213, 237
  relational model of self, 215–216
Cognitive–developmental orientation,
    315
  collective orientation, 317–320
  collective structures, 320–321
Cognitive functioning
  in attention deficit hyperactivity dis-
    order, 165
  circumspection–preemption–control
    cycle, 157–158
  computational model, 91–92
  constructivist model, 92–93
  core ordering processes, 47–48
  family information processing, 324
  forms of self-deception, 127–128
  impulsivity, 157–158, 161
  logical-type confusion, 132
  models of rationality, 91, 137
  personal construct theory, 146–147,
    160
  reification processes, 132–136
  self-control beliefs, 136–137
  self-referencing, 136–138
  unconscious processes in, 83–84
Cognitive–narrative model of distress, 12,
    265–268
Complexity of narrative, 273–277
Complexity studies, 56
Confidentiality, 33
Confusions of logical type, 127–128
  adaptive change, 138–140
  meaning, 132
  reification, 132–136
  self-referencing cognitions, 132,
    136–138
Constructionism
  collaboration with empirical prac-
    tice, 261
  concept of language in, 244,
    246–247
  conceptual basis, 244–245

psychoanalytic theory, 153–154
rationale, 336
reified, 168–169, 250–251
role of, 145
social construction of, 10–11
sociopolitical context, 249, 293–294
stigmatizing, 337–338
therapeutic value, 333–334,
336–337
transitive diagnosis, 11–12, 166–167
Dialectical constructivism, 83, 164
Dialogism, 343
Dispositional assessment, 163
Dissociative disorders, 272
DOBT. *See* Depth-oriented brief therapy
DSM. See *Diagnostic and Statistical Manual of Mental Disorders*

Eating disorders
narrative coherence in, 272
symptom coherence in, 82
Ecosystemic assessment, 316
Empathic sociality, 188
Empirically validated treatments, 8–9
Enactment sketches, 211
Epidemiology, 151
Epistemology
adaptational landscapes, 51
constructionist, 243, 247
constructivist, 92–93
critical constructivist, 167
empiricist, 247
models of rationality, 91–92
postmodernist, 5, 243
poststructuralist, 248
Etiology
conceptual development, 150–151
constructionist reconceptualization,
243
constructivist psychotherapy, 6
narrative theory, 7
organic, 150
social constructionist theory, 6–7
trauma, 224
Evolutionary theory, 47
Expectations
anticipation, in personal construct
theory, 146–148, 155
disempowering effects of diagnostic
labeling, 258
of treatment, 43, 57

Externalization of problem, 29–30
Families
adaptive, 321
assessment, 315–317
cognitive–developmental orientations, 315
collective cognitive balancing styles,
324
collective cognitive–developmental
structures, 320–321
contextual assessment, 322–323
embeddedness of, 323–324
identifying resources, 317–322
in mediation of distress, 313
psychosocial function of, 311–312
socialization role, 311
in systemic cognitive–developmental
therapy, 309–310
systemic development, 321–322
systemic model of distress, 312, 313
Fear, courage and, 192–193
Feminist psychology, 12, 229–230
biopsychosocial model of distress,
300
conceptual basis, 288–292
construction of distress, 300–302,
304–306
constructivism in, 288
critiques of standard diagnostic models, 294–296
delusional dominating personality
diagnosis, 302–304
gender issues in, 290–291
naming rights in, 292
pathologizing of sociopolitical worldview, 288, 293–294
posttraumatic stress disorder diagnosis, 296–299
power relations issues, 290–292
psychopathology concepts, 287–288
Forgiveness, 193–194
Functional symptoms
anxiety, 78–82
panic attacks, 75–78

Games, 334
Generativity script, 226
Goal orientation, 273
Grief work, 230–233
Guilt, 157

Habit, 134

Health care system, 145. *See also* Managed care

Help seeking, fraudulent motivation for, 131–132

Hermeneutics, 247

Histrionic personality disorder, 302

Homosexuality, 18, 249
DSM classification, 22–24

Hostility
assessment, 163–164
as manifestation of insecure attachment, 183
personal construct theory, 157

Hypocritical behavior–thinking, 128–132

Hysteria, 249

Insurance, 348

Intentionality
elucidating nonconscious intentions, 220–221
in narrative construction, 217, 219–220

Interpersonal relations
assessment, case illustration, 108–111
capacity to love, 54
commitment in, 192
dependency relations, 184–186
developmental role of caregiver–child interactions, 96–97
diagnosis, 183–184
distancing, 186–187
empathic sociality, 188
experiential personal construct psychotherapy, 175–176
function of hypocrisy, 128
hypocrisies in, 129–131
insecure attachments, 182–183
language as social action, 124–126
mental health resources in, 340–341
personal construct model of psychopathology, 12
in psychological development, 46
psychotherapy as social influence, 122–124
reification effects, 135–136
role conflicts, 123
self-relationship and, 54
social construction of experience, 93–94, 215–216

validational feedback, 185
See also ROLE relationships

Labeling, 153, 155–156
client perception of diagnosis, 169
coopting of, 31–33
disempowering effects of diagnosis, 258–259
stigmatizing effects of diagnosis, 337–338

Language
affective processes and, 137
as change mechanism, 11
construction of meaning in discourse, 334
constructionist conceptualization, 244, 246–247
contextual determinants of meaning, 247
diagnostic and therapeutic significance, 121, 140–141
dialogic construction of narrative, 234
dialogic construction of self, 215–216
discourse as action, 249–250
of liars, 128–129
of mental health, 246
narrative linguistic patterns in outcomes, 277
nonpathologizng, 255–257
nonimmediacies, 129
objectification in, 251
as orthogonal interaction, 139–140
in pathogenesis, 127
pluralist perspective, 9–10
postmodern conceptualization, 5
power relations and naming rights, 292, 341–342
problem definition in therapy, 30
reification phenomenon, 132–136, 250
self-description, 125
self-referential property, 132
sentence completion therapy, 221–222
as social action, 124–126
social construction of experience, 93–94
social construction of meaning, 246
social construction of narrative, 213

Orthogonal interaction, 139–140
Outcome factors
    narrative processes, 276–277
    narrative quality, 274–275
Outcome measurement
    narrative linguistic patterns, 277
    postmodern psychotherapy, 8–9

Pain, experience of, 49
Paraphilic rapism, 24
Pathology, concepts of, 21
    accessibility and assimilation of feel-
      ing states, 98
    as behavior discomforting to society,
      302
    blame in, 338–339
    classification of homosexuality,
      22–24
    cognitive–narrative conceptualiza-
      tion, 12, 265–268, 280
    complexity of narrative in, 273–275
    as confusion of logical type,
      127–128, 132
    constructionist, 243, 245
    constructivist, 17–18
    continuity of self-narrative, 98–102,
      280
    core ordering processes in, 11
    as disordering process, 44, 46–47, 56
    distress vs., 290
    experiential personal construct psy-
      chotherapy, 12
    family assessment, 313, 315–317
    feminist construction of distress,
      300–302, 304–306
    in feminist psychology, 287–288,
      293–294
    functional–functionless symptoms,
      65
    historical development, 149–151,
      154–155
    as hypocritical behavior, 127,
      128–132
    as illness narrative, 313
    indications for psychotherapy, 121
    limitations of, 122
    linguistic processes in, 127
    as meaning construction, 21
    narrative content in, 277–279
    as narrative disintegration, 212–213
    personal construct theory, 147–149,
      156, 157–158, 160–161, 179
    in position call, 253
    power of naming in, 292–293
    power relations in, 248–249
    primary–secondary gain, 82
    pro-symptom construction, 67–68,
      70
    as problem of narrative coherence,
      267–268, 272–273
    as problems of living, 27
    psychosis, 101–102
    relational systems in, 309–310
    as response to threats to identity,
      156–157
    as role conflict, 123
    as self-deception, 121, 127–128, 141
    social power relations in, 291
    sociocultural context, 290, 300–301,
      335, 337
    sociopolitical discourse in, 249–250
    as structural arrest in development,
      179–180
    symptom coherence, 65, 82–83
    in systemic cognitive–developmental
      therapy, 312
    therapeutic value, 334
    transformative dialogue for recon-
      structing, 342–348
    trends within psychology, 342–343
    unconscious constructs of reality, 64,
      65–66, 85
Perception, reality and, 52
Personal construct theory, 11, 16, 17
    attachment processes, 182–183
    circumspection–preemption–control
      cycle, 157–158
    concept of pathology, 12, 148–150,
      160–161
    conceptual basis, 146–147
    conceptual development, 151–153
    conceptualization of symptoms,
      187–188
    construct system operations,
      147–149
    construction of disorders in, 18–19
    depth-oriented brief therapy and, 83
    developmental concepts, 177–179
    diagnostic concepts, 147, 152–153,
      155, 177. *See also* Transitive diag-
      nosis

as threat to personal construct, 148
 unconscious constructs in, 84
Role conflicts, 123
Role construct repertory test, 158–159
ROLE relationships
  adaptive change in, 189–190
  assessment, 177–178, 195–201
  commitment in, 192
  courage in, 192–193
  dependency allocations, 184–186
  developmental process, 177–180
  diagnosis, 184
  discrimination in, 188–189, 198–199
  distancing in, 186–187
  flexibility in, 189
  forgiveness in, 193–194
  meaning of, 176
  meaning of symptoms, 187–188
  openness to reconstrual, 191–192
  responsibility in, 190–191
  reverence in, 194–195
  self–other constancy, 182
  self–other construct, 180–181
  self–other permanence, 181
  significance of, 176, 184
  therapeutic implications, 176–177

Schizophrenia, 18, 337
  narrative coherence in, 272–273
  social context of pathology, 305
Scientific method, 243
Scripts
  in narrative construction of self, 269
  prototype narratives, 278–279
Second-order significances, 127
Self
  clinical conceptualizations, 208
  coherence of narrative structure, 269
  constructionist model, 249–250
  constructivist model, 208–209
  continuity of self-narrative, 98–100
  core ordering processes, 47–48
  disintegration in trauma, 224
  effects of therapeutic change in self-
   concept, 74–75
  emotional continuity and integration
   of experience, 95, 97
  emplotment of life narrative,
   222–223
  experimenting with possible selves,
   276

exploration of multiple-character
  self-narratives, 219–220
internalization of diagnosis, 31, 338
narrative construction, 12, 96, 237,
  267
ordering of experience in construction of, 94
personal construct theory, 12, 148
postmodern conceptualization, 5,
  209–210
regulation of inner coherence,
  96–98
reification of self-attributes, 133–136
relational model, 215–216
reverence of, 194
ROLE relationship constructions,
  180–183
in ROLE relationships, 176
self-continuity as identity, 53–54
self-control beliefs, 136–137
self-description, 125
sense of continuity, 94–95
social construction of, 93–94,
  209–210
theme of life narrative, 223–224
therapeutic reconstruction, 11,
  102–104, 106–108
threats to core structures, 156–157
unconscious processes, 65
Self-abuse, 235–236
Self-characterization procedure, 211
Self-characterization sketch, 159
Self-confrontation, 224
Self-defeating personality disorder, 24,
  295–296, 302
Self-diagnosis, 295
Self-efficacy, 133
Self-esteem, 133
Self psychology, 53–54
Sensory processes
  in narrative construction, 275
  in perception of reality, 52
Sentence completion, 221–222
Sexism, in *DSM*, 24–25
Social cognitive theory, 55
Social constructionist approach, 3, 16,
  245
  cognitive model, 92–93
  concept of self, 209, 210
  constructive alternativism and,
   33–34

About the Editors

Robert A. Neimeyer, PhD, is a professor in the Department of Psychology at the University of Memphis in Memphis, TN, where he also maintains an active private practice. Since completing his doctoral training in clinical psychology at the University of Nebraska in 1982, the majority of his research has centered on constructivist approaches to personality and psychotherapy. He has published 17 books, including *Personal Construct Therapy Casebook* (Springer, 1987), *Advances in Personal Construct Theory* (Vols. 1–4; JAI Press, 1990, 1992, 1995, 1997), and *Constructivism in Psychotherapy* (with Michael J. Mahoney; American Psychological Association [APA], 1995). The author of over 200 articles and book chapters, he is currently most interested in developing a narrative and constructivist framework for psychotherapy, with special relevance to the experience of loss and grief. Dr. Neimeyer is the coeditor of the *Journal of Constructivist Psychology* and serves on the editorial board of numerous other journals. In recognition of his scholarly contributions, he has been granted the Distinguished Research Award by the University of Memphis (1990), designated Psychologist of the Year by the Tennessee Psychological Association (1996), made a fellow of APA's Division 12 (Clinical Psychology, 1997), and received the Research Recognition Award of the Association for Death Education and Counseling (1999).

Jonathan D. Raskin, PhD, received his AB from Vassar College and his PhD in counseling psychology from the University of Florida. Presently, he is an assistant professor of psychology at the State University of New York at New Paltz. Dr. Raskin has authored or coauthored articles applying constructivism to psychotherapy, psychopathology, sexuality, and ethics. He is currently secretary of APA's Division 32 (Humanistic Psychology). He is also the book review editor of the *Journal of Constructivist Psychology* and a licensed psychologist in the state of New York.

373